Routledge
Taylor & Francis Group

LONDON AND NEW YORK

First edition published by Routledge in 1999
Reprinted 2000, 2004 Second edition published 2008
by Routledge 2 Park Square, Milton Park, Abingdon, Oxon OX14 4RN

Simultaneously published in the USA and Canada
by Routledge
270 Madison Avenue, New York, NY 10016

Routledge is an imprint of the Taylor & Francis Group, an informa business

© 1999 Editorial matter and selection Chris Brewster and Hilary Harris; individual chapters, the contributors; 2008 Editorial matter and selection, Michael Dickmann, Chris Brewster and Paul Sparrow; individual chapters, the contributors

Typeset in Perpetua and Bell Gothic by Keyword Group Ltd
Printed and bound by Antony Rowe Ltd, Chippenham, Wiltshire

British Library Cataloguing in Publication Data
A catalogue record for this book is available from the British Library

Library of Congress Cataloging in Publication Data
International human resource management: a European perspective / edited by Michael Dickmann, Chris Brewster & Paul Sparrow. – 2nd ed.
p. cm.
1. International business enterprises–Europe–Personnel management.
2. Personnel management–Europe. I. Dickmann, Michael. II. Brewster, Chris. III. Sparrow, Paul.
HF5549.5.E4I5774 2007
658.3–dc22   2007039889

ISBN10: 0–415–42392–9 (hbk)
ISBN10: 0–415–42393–7 (pbk)
ISBN10: 0–203–08902–2 (ebk)

ISBN13: 978–0–415–42393–9 (pbk)
ISBN13: 978–0–415–42392–2 (hbk)
ISBN13: 978–0–203–08902–6 (ebk)

To my father, whose unbounded optimism has always energized me, and
my mother, whose unfailing love and understanding has been a tremendous support.
Michael Dickmann

Thanks to Lynn – for everything.
Chris Brewster

As always to Sue who lets me be focused but keeps me balanced.
Paul Sparrow

Contents

CONTENTS

Figures

Tables

Text boxes

Case studies

Contributors

Jaime Bonache is Professor of International Human Resource Management at Cranfield University, School of Management, UK. He holds an MBA and a Ph.D. from the University of Madrid and an MA from Carleton University (Ottawa, Canada). Before joining Cranfield, he was Professor of Management at Carlos III University (Madrid, Spain). His current research and teaching interests are in the areas of International Assignments, Comparative HR Practices and Knowledge Management.

Werner Braun's research focuses on HR functional transformation in a global context. In particular he investigates companies' strategies and decision-making processes to outsource or to enter into internal shared service centre arrangements. His research also looks at the design and structure of high performance-retained HR functions. He is a member of PA Consulting Group.

Chris Brewster is Professor of IHRM at the University of Reading, UK. He had substantial experience as a practitioner before becoming an academic, and consults and teaches on management programmes throughout the world. He has conducted extensive research in the field of international and comparative HRM, and has written around 20 books and over 100 articles. He was awarded the Georges Petitpas Memorial Award by the world practitioner body, the WFPMA, in recognition of his outstanding contribution to IHRM.

Jean-Luc Cerdin is Professor of HRM at ESSEC Business School, Paris, France. He has recently been a visiting professor at Rutgers University and University of Missouri St-Louis. He has also been a visiting scholar at Wharton. His research interests include expatriate management, career management and international human resource management.

David G. Collings is a Lecturer in International Management at the J.E. Cairnes Graduate School of Business and Public Policy, National University of Ireland, Galway. Previously he was on the faculty at the University of Sheffield Management School. His research interests focus on management in multinational corporations with a particular emphasis on staffing and industrial relations issues. His work in these areas has been published in outlets such as the

Journal of World Business, International Journal of Human Resource Management and the *International Journal of Management Reviews*.

Michael Dickmann is a Senior Lecturer in HRM and Director of the Cranfield M.Sc. in IHRM. Much of his research focuses on cross-border human resource strategies, structures and processes of multinational organizations. He leads the International Mobility Initiative, a joint research activity with PricewaterhouseCoopers. He has several years of work experience for major consultancies and in industry, is a visiting scholar at half a dozen universities and consults a large range of supranational and multinational organizations.

Noeleen Doherty is a Research Fellow at Cranfield University, School of Management, UK. Her research interests are in the area of career management, both organizational and individual aspects, which cover the career implications of redundancy, talent development and the management of potential. Her current research agenda focuses on the field of global career management, including company-backed and self-initiated expatriation.

Ina Ehnert is at the University of Bremen, Germany. She is currently writing her Ph.D. on sustainability and HRM from a paradox/duality perspective. She has published several book chapters, conference papers and journal articles on this topic and in the areas of expatriate preparation, effectiveness of cross-cultural training, evaluation, and trust across cultures. She is a reviewer for the *European Journal of International Management*, a member of PHRESH (The Dutch Ph.D. network in HRM), EGOS (European Group for Organizational Studies), and FINT (The first international network of trust researchers).

Marion Festing is Professor of HRM and Intercultural Leadership at ESCP-EAP European School of Management, Berlin Campus, Germany. Her research interests include IHRM with special emphasis on transnational strategies, global performance. management, global careers and global compensation issues in differing institutional and cultural contexts. Together with Peter J. Dowling and Allen D. Engle she is author of the textbook *International Human Resource Management* (5th edn).

John Hailey is a visiting professor at Cass Business School in London and a consultant with a special interest in the management of international development agencies and NGOs. His research includes work on the leadership of such organizations and the challenges of localizing their governance and management capacity.

Wes Harry is Reader in International HRM at Lancashire Business School. Following an international senior management career in banks, airlines, oil industry and sovereign wealth management, mainly in Asia, he moved into academia to share knowledge and increase the capability of people to work well with people from other cultures. His current research interests include management in Asia, managing performance, international careers, localization, global corporate governance and ethics, human rights and resistance to globalization.

Arno Haslberger is a Senior Research Professor at Webster University, Vienna, Austria. His main focus of research is cross-cultural adjustment, expatriate assignments and international careers.

Iris Kollinger is Regional HR Manager at CEE and external Lecturer at the Department of HRM at the University of Economics and Business Administration, Vienna, Austria. Her research interests are foreign assignments, female expatriates, IHRM and cross-cultural issues.

Margaret Linehan is at Cork Institute of Technology, Cork, Ireland. Her main research interest is women in international management. She is author of the book *Senior Female International Managers: Why So Few?* She has authored and co-authored over 60 journal articles and conference papers in this field. She is also interested in mentoring, role modelling, networking and the repatriation of female international managers.

Wolfgang Mayrhofer is a Professor in the Interdisciplinary Unit of Management and Organizational Behaviour. He conducts research in the area of comparative international human resource management and leadership, work careers, and systems theory and management. He regularly consults to both private and public sector organizations, with an emphasis on leadership, team and self-development by outdoor training/sailing.

Stephen J. Perkins is Professor of HRM at London Metropolitan Business School. His research interests include comparative and international approaches to the employment relationship and people management, with a specific focus on employee reward issues and practice.

Hugh Scullion is Professor of International Management, National University of Ireland, Galway, Ireland. His research interests include IHRM in European multinational companies, developments in global staffing – alternative forms of international assignments, the role of the corporate HR function in the international firm, global talent management and leadership development, expatriate psychological contracts and new international working, social capital and international HRM and corporate governance at Celtic Football Club.

Paul Sparrow is Director, Centre for Performance-led HRM and Professor of IHRM at Lancaster University Management School. He has published over 100 books, journal articles and chapters and consulted with major multinationals, public sector organizations and intergovernmental agencies. His research covers cross-cultural and international HRM, HR strategy, cognition at work and changes in the employment relationship.

Vesa Suutari is Professor of International Management in the Department of Management, University of Vaasa, Finland. His research interests are in cross-cultural management, career management, expatriation, international knowledge transfers and IHRM in general. He has published various international journal articles and book chapters on issues such as European management cultures, expatriation, global leadership, global careers, international knowledge transfers and management development.

Estelle Toomey is currently progressing her Ph.D. at SAID Business School, Oxford University. Within the fields of organizational behaviour and IHRM, she is particularly interested in employee attitudes related to job satisfaction, performance, leadership and international mobility, as well as employee diversity (gender, generation, cultural values) and organizational differences (sector, location).

Angelika Zimmermann is Lecturer in International Business and Strategy at Loughborough University Business School. Her research is in the area of international management, in particular regarding international teams, IHRM and expatriate adjustment. She is currently studying mutual perceptions in international teams and HRM of foreign firms in China.

Acknowledgements

We would like to express our gratitude to the many people who have supported us in making this book a reality. These include the series editors, who gave us the opportunity to work on the theme and the excellent contributors who compiled insightful overviews of important international HRM topics, combined with compelling arguments for their points of view. We also appreciate Prof Susan Vinnicombe's help to create space in busy schedules. A special thanks goes to Lisa Hall who worked with professionalism and dedication on putting this book together. Lastly, we would like to acknowledge the help we received from the team at Routledge, Francesca Heslop, Simon Whitmore, Russell George and Jodie Tierney.

Context for internationalization

Chapter 1

A European perspective on IHRM

An introduction

Chris Brewster, Michael Dickmann and Paul Sparrow

CHAPTER OBJECTIVES

By the end of this chapter, readers will have:

- an appreciation of the growing internationalization of the world in which HRM is conducted
- an understanding of the additional complexity of HRM in an international context
- identified some of the key HR challenges facing organizations working internationally
- an overview of the format of the rest of the book

A EUROPEAN PERSPECTIVE ON INTERNATIONAL HUMAN RESOURCE MANAGEMENT

This book provides some of the latest thinking on the subject of international human resource management from a European perspective. Although one of the very earliest contributions to the study of the international transfer of employees was undertaken by a Swedish expert (Torbiörn 1982), most of the early research and writing on the topic of international human resource management (HRM) was undertaken in North America and even the work that was done outside that country tended to follow the US (and Canadian) lead. Each of the contributors to the book acknowledges a debt to that work and incorporates it in the chapter. However, by the 1990s it became clear not only that European multinational corporations (MNCs) tended to manage their international workforce rather differently than did MNCs from the USA (or from Japan or other countries for that matter) but that some European researchers in the area tended to be examining issues that were rather different from those being examined elsewhere. In some cases, as with the European MNCs, it could be argued that European researchers were taking the lead.

The first edition of this book (Brewster and Harris 1999) was one of the earliest non-US books to address this topic. Not surprisingly, perhaps (although it was a surprise to us at the time), it came to be widely used by not only the researchers it had been aimed at, but also by teachers as they began increasingly to include international HRM as a topic in their HRM and management programmes and by practitioners.

Since that first edition the world has become ever more international and the topic itself has developed considerably (see later discussion). The first edition of this book was followed by many others with very similar titles. There has been a growth in both the scope of the topic and in our knowledge about it. Some of the chapters here simply update the chapters in the previous edition, since they either covered a subject that has still not been addressed elsewhere in the literature or were sound summaries of the subject in the first place. Some have been radically amended to reflect the latest debates in the area and some are totally new. This new edition is more structured and more comprehensive than its predecessor and includes some features that will make it easier for tutors and students to use. It maintains, however, its ambition to bring a European perspective to the topic, with chapters written by experts from a range of European countries.

This first chapter provides the background by examining the growing internationalization of the world in which HRM is conducted, exploring the additional complexity of HRM in an international context and identifying some of the key HR challenges facing organizations working internationally and indicates the value of a European focus on these issues. It then outlines the rest of the chapters in the book.

GROWING INTERNATIONALIZATION OF WORLD BUSINESS

Trade across borders is an old phenomenon of human economic activity and multinational companies may be traced back to at least 1135 as international banking was conducted under the Knights Templar (*Economist* 2007a). While significant cross-border activity was conducted through major trade routes (the trade in spices) or between European nations and their colonies, it is well known that modern transport capabilities, the availability of (international) finance and the erosion of trade barriers (e.g. through the GATT mechanism) led to waves of a

4

different kind of globalization. These globalization patterns are different from purely natural resource-based trade in that manufacturing capacity was relocated.

In a first extensive wave of globalization beginning roughly after the Second World War and culminating approximately three decades ago, low-level manufacturing work began to transfer to low-cost locations. Going beyond manufacturing, simple services like credit-card processing began to relocate in a further wave. In the third wave higher skill white-collar work is being transferred. Engardio, Bernstein and Kripalani (2003) argue that from the USA alone more than 3 million white-collar jobs will shift to low-cost countries by 2015. A stark example is IBM in India. IBM returned to India in the early 1990s when the Indian government began to deregulate and move away from nationalistic policies. In 2007, 'Big Blue' had 53,000 employees in India and has now more employees in the subcontinent than in any other country except the USA. In 2006 the firm announced a tripling of its investments in India for the remainder of the decade (*Economist* 2007b). By now, it is clear that companies' rationale goes beyond costs to include the search for quality and innovation (Bartlett and Ghoshal 1995). In terms of European examples, Philips has shifted research and development on most TVs, cell phones and audio products to Shanghai and Nokia has research centres in Budapest and Bejing. New technology, intense time- and ideas-based competition and the search for global talent are key influencing factors for this global transfer of work. These patterns are affecting the nature of work and the organizational structure and processes that are viable in Europe and the rest of the world.

International expansion is not the exclusive domain of corporations from developed countries. Multinational companies from developing countries are acquiring foreign companies – in the first 3 months of 2007 large Indian companies acquired 34 corporations abroad for a combined $10.7 billion (*Economist* 2007a). The reasons often go beyond market seeking behaviour where foreign operating units are merely serving the head office. They are likely to include knowledge acquisition in order to enhance organizational capability and the establishment of centres of excellence. This is demonstrated by the takeover of Corus by Tata Steel which *The Economist* (2007a: 11) argues would have never happened had the Anglo-Dutch company not had its expertise in making 'fancy steel'. Many of these highly international corporations (still) use expatriation and other forms of international work intensively. For instance, Wipro, a technology, research and consulting firm from India employed 54,000 people in 2006 – 11,000 of these outside India. More than 90% of staff abroad are Indian, due to the explicit wish to transfer the Indian work culture and work intensity (*Economist* 2006). These unabated trends show that the internationalization of world business is continuing forcefully with all its resulting challenges for international HRM.

5

HRM IN AN INTERNATIONAL CONTEXT

In all these international organizations or MNCs, HRM is a key to success. There are a number of reasons for this. First, for the vast majority of organizations the cost of the people who do the work is the largest single item of operating costs that can be controlled and adapted to circumstances. Second, the capabilities and the knowledge incorporated in an organization's human resources are generally the key to success. HRM is becoming crucial to the survival, performance and success of domestic organizations. Third, when we consider international organizations, the additional complications of dealing with multicultural assumptions about the way people should be managed and work together becomes an important contributor to the chances of that success.

A large range of HR specialists have to adopt an increasingly international orientation in their activities. This is not just true for large MNCs, but also for many small to medium size enterprises (SMEs) that find themselves operating in globalizing labour markets. Recent times have witnessed a reduction of restrictions to labour movement in areas such as the European Union and, with the advent of new technology, many fledging enterprises can operate internationally almost as soon as they are established. The need for an international orientation does not just apply to the private sector. The UN family, the OECD, regional trade bodies all have employees working across national borders, as do many charities and religious groups. HR professionals working in a wide range of organizations now need to understand the developments outlined in this book.

It is not only HR professionals who have to understand these developments. Line managers working in an international environment are subject to the impact of multi-country, regional and global change and dynamism of the business environment. Business and operational choices in this new international context have become complex and ambiguous.

KEY CHALLENGES IN INTERNATIONAL HRM

The international context adds extra complexity to the management of people beyond that found in a purely national setting. International HRM (IHRM) therefore has to examine the way in which international organizations manage their human resources across these different national contexts.

When organizations manage people in different institutional, legal, and cultural circumstances, they have to not only be aware of what is allowed and not allowed in the different nations and regions of the world, but also of what makes their different management practices cost effective. An often quoted example is that of a performance appraisal system that depends on a US-style openness between manager and subordinate. In such a system, each party has to explain plainly how they feel the other has done in their work, be this well or badly. Such a system may work in some European countries but is unlikely to fit with the greater hierarchical assumptions and 'loss-of-face' fears of some of the Pacific countries. The literature provides many examples of how important home country practices may be allowed in other countries, but which might inadvertently have the effect of depressing rather than improving productivity and effectiveness because of the way they are perceived by local employees.

Therefore, when organizations address IHRM, they have not only to deal with a variety of practices, but, when considering how they wish to execute their strategy, they may also face a range of policy and strategy issues. As a subject, IHRM has to explore how MNCs manage the competing demands of ensuring that the organization has an international coherence in and cost-effective approach to the way it manages its people in all the countries it covers, while also ensuring that it can be responsive to the differences in assumptions about what works from one location to another. The management of those people who have to work internationally is a particular case in point.

WHY A EUROPEAN FOCUS?

So why do we need a European focus on IHRM? In all this complexity, it is important to be clear about the different kinds of analysis that can inform our understanding. These are not always obvious from the literature, partly, perhaps, because of a historical confusion in writing in the USA, where 'international' is sometimes applied to anything outside the USA. International HRM (and its more recent 'strategic' derivative, SIHRM) examine the way organizations manage their human resources across these different national contexts. It remains the case that most of the work on international HRM is done in North America and, despite the sterling work of some key players in Canada, specifically in the USA. This is important because the hegemony of the USA in the worlds of business and management and in their study in universities, business schools and consultancies means that the North American paradigm tends to dominate our thinking about these subjects, determine the content of academic publications (and hence, to a degree, of research), and impact on the way that leaders and managers conceive of the topic (Brewster and Harris 1999; Brewster 2007). This seems to be particularly true of HRM, which has been subject to what has been called the 'Gulf Stream' of ideas, 'drifting in from the USA and hitting the UK first, then crossing the Benelux countries ... and Germany and France and proceeding finally to southern Europe' (DeFidelto and Slater 2001:281).

Questions are being raised about this, however. Are these various countries just taking their time to 'catch up' or may it be that they have a different conception of HRM and see the need to address different elements of it in different ways?

Arguably, one of the effects of the North American hegemony is to create something of a straitjacket that researchers in the USA, and many of the Gulf Streamers in Europe, find it difficult to break out of. However, the different paradigm operating in large parts of Europe means that a lot of the more critical thinking and the more innovative research takes place in that continent.

Since the first edition, there has been an explosion of work on the topic of IHRM in particular, in English, from the Asia-Pacific region (Budhwar 2004), from Latin America (Elvira and Davila 2005), from Europe (Brewster and Larsen 2000; Larsen and Mayrhofer 2006), and from Central and Eastern Europe (Morley et al. 2007), as well as other parts of the world. European researchers, however, continue to make a significant contribution and, in many cases, have been at the forefront of developing the scope and concept of the subject.

REVIEW OF THE FIELD

Before we outline each chapter, we outline how the agenda for the subjects to cover and the perspective taken within this agenda has changed between the first and second edition. At the time of the publication of the first edition of this book in 1999 the key discussions within IHRM were mostly centred around the identification of practitioners' concerns, ultimately providing a mostly descriptive agenda that was often linked to a US view of the world. In the last decade, however, particularly in Europe, the field has moved on in a few key respects.

Perspectives

Arguably, discussions of HRM in Europe tend to be more 'critical' than discussions of the topic elsewhere (Brewster 2007) and that too is reflected here. Not only are the interests of the organization not necessarily assumed to be the only criterion for successful IHRM policies and practices, but some chapters in this book, such as the one on localization, challenge the very notion of the value and ethics of international assignments.

Interactions

The use of diverse theoretical underpinnings and the exploration of important contextual factors has enabled researchers in this book to better understand the wider picture of IHRM and some of the interactions across levels of analysis. For instance, in this book, many of the chapters see organizations as firmly embedded into society. Other contributions – such as those on career capital, repatriation or career expatriation – concentrate on the interaction between individual and organization.

8

Other chapters, for instance the one on expatriate adjustment, go beyond this to explore interactions between individuals, their work environments, the foreign culture and the role of the expatriate's family. While some of these dynamic relationships were looked at a decade ago, the scope of analysis has been broadened and the focus and discussions have become more refined. It also leads to more critical questioning of some established frameworks in the literature.

Foundations

Clearly, the other side of the coin of using broader theoretical approaches within IHRM is to critically (re-)assess the frameworks most commonly used and the base of empirical data that is available. Ideas of what constitutes international work, theoretical approaches as to the domains and measurement of expatriate adjustment, the concept of 'success' in international HRM or the strategic foundations of organizational rationale for using international mobility are critically evaluated and further developed in this book. For example, the chapter on adjustment shows that we need to consider a much wider range of domains than are suggested in the seminal work of Black and his co-writers on this topic.

Temporal vistas

Many of the contributions to this book extend the timeframe used to examine important phenomena in order to develop a better understanding. For example, much of the earlier writing on international mobility has concentrated on the time from appointment to an international assignment up to repatriation. Many authors in this volume are taking a more holistic approach in that they also explore the time before and after the foreign work experience. In terms of careers, this can include the lifetime of working after the return of the sojourn abroad.

Boundaries

At the end of the 20th century, the field of IHRM, albeit no longer perhaps in its infancy, still ran the danger of being subsumed under the broader fields of international management or HRM. In order to establish a separate field, academics working in the discipline worked hard to explore the differences to these larger neighbours and to establish a set of boundaries. While it is still open to discussion how demarcated these boundaries are, writers are increasingly working to dissolve fixed borders and draw lessons across boundaries. Similar to developments in the field of international business, academics have begun to use new perspectives as explored above. This has, in our persuasion, enriched the field. Examples include the integration of IHRM strategies, structures and processes from organizational theory (Dickmann and Müller-Camen 2006) or the knowledge management

9

chapter in this book. Another example is the integration of outsourcing and off-shoring activities from international business perspectives. An increasingly wide range of perspectives are being applied. This is leading to richer theoretical attempts to analyse and understand IHRM. Ideas and approaches from sociology, human geography (migration studies), psychology, economics, labour studies, comparative HRM and international business, to name but a few, are being applied to the IHRM field which, in turn, creates a more context-sensitive, varied and nuanced understanding.

What seems clear is that although once a 'core identity' was identified for IHRM, the field is currently experiencing a range of changes that serve to enrich its contribution to the understanding of international work and organization. Sometimes this leads to a lack of attention to traditional topics. It is interesting to note, for example, that although some attention has been given in the past to the issue of managing performance on international assignments, we could not find any significant recent attention to this topic. Perhaps reflecting the broader context surrounding the management of individuals as part of an internationalization process, questions surrounding assignment performance have either become too complex to analyse or are considered too narrow a topic.

We have tried to reflect a more context-sensitive, varied and nuanced understanding of IHRM in this text. To accommodate the developments inherent in the comments already made, following this introductory chapter, the book is divided into three parts: examining successively the context of internationalization; the management of international employees; and some of the strategic issues currently facing international HR managers. Part I provides some of the context for the rest of the book, exploring issues such as localization, HR and business process outsourcing and offshoring and the nature of knowledge transfer in international organizations. Part II covers the well-established areas of IHRM in which many practitioners work. The titles in this part, unlike in the others, are short and simple since most specialists in IHRM will recognize the topics and have some understanding of the field. The various elements of managing international assignments, working roughly through the expatriation cycle, are presented here with each chapter aiming to summarize our existing knowledge and, using the latest research, take us a step or two further forward. Part III of the book examines some of the key strategic issues that are coming to the fore in terms of both research and practice, although arguably each of these topics remains significantly under-researched. Thus there are chapters examining the recent attention to forms of international experience other than the 'standard' expatriation, the notion of career capital as applied to international assignments, the continuing shortage of women in international work and IHRM in the most international organizations of all: intergovernmental organizations such as the United Nations.

PART I: CONTEXT FOR INTERNATIONALIZATION

In Chapter 2, John Hailey and Wes Harry provide an updated examination of a key and – still – largely unexplored subject that was raised for perhaps the first time in the first edition of the book. Wes Harry is a new collaborator on this chapter bringing a wealth of experience and know-how to the topic. The authors explore the replacement of expatriates by local staff. Taking a fairly polemical viewpoint, the chapter explores the limited research that has been done on the topic to date and then concentrates on various drivers for localization: cost and performance; contacts and legitimacy; political and ethical; and staff tension drivers. The chapter offers strategies for localizing and a four-stage process for achieving it.

Chapter 3, by Paul Sparrow and Werner Braun, is a completely new chapter that explores the different strategies that are at play in terms of both sourcing and shoring of HR services. A brief review of theoretical perspectives is followed by a warning that theory tends not to align with the judgements made by the key actors in practice. The chapter identifies a range of variables that affect the success or not of such judgements. It also demonstrates the need to understand parallel developments in the strategic re-orientation of the HR function. It is noted that there remain continued and substantial international differences in the pursuit and preference for HR outsourcing. Despite the fact that outsourcing vendors are building impressive delivery centres and capabilities spanning the globe, their ability to truly optimize HR processes on a global scale remains to be proven. There are significant developments in these areas and the service offerings of vendors are evolving rapidly to address such concerns.

Chapter 4, by Jaime Bonache and Michael Dickmann, is also a new topic for this edition of the book. The chapter explores the creation and transfer of HR know-how as a key strategic goal in MNCs. In so doing, the authors view the organization as a network so that knowledge is flowing in various directions within the MNC. They identify four main types of subsidiary: globally integrated units, autonomous units, learning units and implementer units based on the degree to which they are involved in the transfer and creation of knowledge. The chapter then identifies constraints and challenges to knowledge management and explores mechanisms that favour the transfer of existing knowledge, while others favour the creation of new knowledge. One of the strengths of this chapter is that the authors concentrate on discussing HR knowledge management distinguishing between bureaucratic, social and personal mechanisms. There is discussion of the role of international HRM planning, reporting and information systems, cross-border communities of practice, globally distributed teams, HR centres of excellence and expatriation as well as HR reporting lines, head office visits and 'knowledge transferors'. Finally, the chapter identifies barriers to the efficient working of these knowledge management mechanisms and explores HR initiatives as a key element to overcome those barriers.

11

PART II: HR MANAGEMENT OF INTERNATIONAL EMPLOYEES

In Chapter 5, David Collings and Hugh Scullion develop one of the topics covered in the first edition. The chapter emphasizes that resourcing international assignees is a complex and multifaceted task that needs to be approached strategically. While multinational organizations pursue a range of objectives in their internationalization, the authors outline several constraints that international HR professionals face, including supply- and demand-side issues, cost, performance evaluation and instances of expatriate failure. Based on Dowling and Welch (2004) the authors attempt to dispel the myths that there is one universal approach to management, that all people can acquire multicultural adaptability and behaviours, that there are no impediments to mobility and that success of international managers is based on a set of common characteristics irrespective of other factors such as foreign location. Addressing practical issues of international resourcing, Collings and Scullion distinguish between individual factors – technical ability, cross-cultural suitability and family requirements – and situational factors – country/cultural requirements, multinational organization requirements and language – while acknowledging the challenges that multinational corporations face in implementing more sophisticated selection systems. The chapter ends by outlining a way forward that endorses alternative forms of international working.

Chapter 6, by Ina Ehnert and Chris Brewster, also updates a chapter in the earlier edition. Ehnert brings a new perspective to the topic based on extensive research in German organizations. The chapter discusses research to date on expatriate preparation and its links to expatriate success, performance and adjustment. Accepting that there is, of course, no substitute for the experience of actually living in another country, the chapter argues that nonetheless appropriate preparation can help the expatriate's time to proficiency and the likelihood of proper adjustment to the new environment. One implication of the research concerns the value of an integrative view on selection, training and preparation of expatriates. The chapter outlines expatriate training and evaluation, with particular emphasis on alternatives to training, the value of training and development in the host country and the need for pre-return preparation. It is argued that in order to identify the appropriate form of training for any expatriate, the population has to be disaggregated. Finally, the chapter indicates what can be done to improve preparation and training and proposes an integrative framework for understanding it.

In Chapter 7, Arno Haslberger distinguishes between macro- and micro-variables in the context of individuals and families that determine the overall adjustment challenge. The author stresses that individuals working/living abroad learn in different life domains such as in the work, social life or systems of public order contexts. He discusses the well-known Black et al. (1991) model of international adjustment rather critically and argues for moving beyond it to distinguish psychological,

12

socio-cultural and cognitive dimensions of adjustment (Ward et al. 2001). The chapter subsequently distinguishes between emotions, behavioural effectiveness and cognitive confidence of individuals and maps these different processes of adjustment. The lack of attention paid to adjustment efforts of family members means that we need to understand the spillover and crossover effects of different actors and diverse life domains. Building on this, the author explores expatriate adaptation and identity issues and concludes his discussion by depicting company support measures. Overall, the much travelled Austrian expert adds several new dimensions to the traditional US approach to expatriate adjustment.

Chapter 8, by Stephen Perkins and Marion Festing, examines a critical issue for IHRM specialists. The topic was covered in a chapter in the earlier edition, but Perkins and Festing draw on new research. The authors discuss rewards from a large variety of perspectives. They start by outlining a 'traditional' approach to expatriate remuneration, followed by a summary of HR considerations. The strength of this chapter lies in the presentation of accumulated theoretical and empirical insights on international rewards from the organizational and individual perspectives, including their interrelationship, drawing on psychological, socio-logical (neo-institutional), economics and managerial research approaches. Throughout, Perkins and Festing challenge the common approach to 'keep the expatriate whole' (Philips and Fox 2003) and to compensate individuals for their hardship, changes in lifestyle or the potentially negative family impact. Instead, they urge the reader to move to consider a principle of reward for contribution, acknowledging myriad difficulties in doing so — not least when they discuss proces-sual aspects of expatriate compensation and the tensions between the home and host context. Practitioners and consultants to multinational corporations, espe-cially, may find the 10 practical steps they develop for designing international reward systems useful.

Chapter 9, by Noeleen Doherty, Chris Brewster, Vesa Suutari and Michael Dickmann, also takes a topic covered in the earlier edition but again presents new analyses and original research that has been conducted in the years since that pub-lication. The authors make a spirited case for regarding repatriation not as an end but as part of the process of international careers, learning and the utilization of skills, knowledge and abilities that have been acquired abroad. The chapter initially describes the return of the expatriate as the end of the international assignment and outlines the organizational and individual challenges. The authors argue that, often, returning assignees do not experience a hero's return due to unmet expec-tations, a loss of status, family re-adjustment issues, uncertain work and career opportunities and possible repatriate attrition. Doherty et al. then proceed to out-line how individuals and their employers can tackle these challenges. The main argument is that both organizations and individuals could see repatriation as the middle of international careers. For the individual the development and use of career capital (Inkson and Arthur 2001), having realistic expectations and experiencing positive career outcomes become crucial. For the organization, repatriate retention, performance and promotion are the key in the long term. The authors argue that aligning both perspectives and linking them to the relevant organizational and individual context and core objectives are main steps to improve repatriation planning and practice. This may allow the actors to move beyond the notion of repatriation as 'the toughest assignment of all' (Hurn 1999).

In Chapter 10, Jean-Luc Cerdin explores the complex interrelationship of careers and international work. He argues that international assignments should be considered as a process that takes both organizational and individual activities during expatriation and repatriation into account. The chapter starts by outlining the development of managers through expatriation and presents both individual motivations to work abroad and different organizational rationales. This is followed by a discussion of individual career characteristics and expatriation, incorporating the career anchors work by Edgar Schein. The chapter moves beyond traditional notions in presenting modern forms of international work – such as self-initiated expatriation, frequent flying or eurocommuting – and by exploring both the dark and light sides of repatriation and career outcomes. In so doing, Cerdin puts forward a case for linking assignment success, repatriation and career success.

PART III: STRATEGIC CHALLENGE OR SITUATIONAL RESPONSE?

Chapter 11, by Wolfgang Mayrhofer, Paul Sparrow and Angelika Zimmermann, builds on this need to move beyond expatriation and the international assignment. It concentrates on the different forms of international work and experience that have been mentioned briefly several times in other chapters. They reflect on the individual, organizational and, at times, societal effects of these different forms. The authors concentrate on those forms where managers and experts move where the work is – such as international commuters; employees going on long-term business trips; traditional international assignees, inpatriate managers and permanent cadres of global managers – and on the instances where work moves to where expert staff are, for instance virtual international employees active in cross-border project teams or skilled individuals working in geographically remote centres of excellence serving global operations. Moreover, they include in their discussions self-initiated movers transferring abroad on their own initiative and immigrants attracted to a particular national labour market. Mayrhofer et al. argue that modern forms of international work are mostly fragmented in the organizational reality and represent a tactical response to globalization. They propose that organizations need to integrate their IHRM practices more coherently and to create a more strategic approach to the rationale and assessment of the costs and benefits of international work.

14

In Chapter 12, Noeleen Doherty and Michael Dickmann explore one of the liveliest new topics in IHRM. Doherty and Dickmann apply the concept of intelligent careers (Arthur et al. 1995) to expatriation, developing further the notion of an international assignment as the middle of a career. Using a mutual dependency perspective of individual and organizational agency and interaction, they develop a framework that goes beyond the traditional expatriate cycle (Harris et al. 2003) to explore critical activities and processes before, during and after an international assignment. The framework contrasts individual attitudes and behaviours with organizational policies and practices. For instance, it depicts the key motivations for persons to seek or accept international assignments with the organizational rationale to offer expatriation. The individual negotiates the terms and prepares for working abroad, goes through adjustment processes and accumulates career capital by living and working in the foreign location. In parallel, the organization – both the HR department and line manager – tackles issues of resourcing, preparation, international development, career and performance management. The proposed framework includes reintegration and career management efforts by the organization and re-adjustment processes by individuals who also attempt to use their acquired career capital in their next positions. The authors critically evaluate these processes and the interaction of individual and organizational agents and argue that in many cases a 'career wobble' ensures after return. Overall, the authors argue that positive career capital results of international assignments are far from certain for either the former expatriate or the organization and that the development of global career capital is multifaceted and merits further exploration.

Chapter 13, by Iris Kollinger and Margaret Linehan, develops the theme raised in the first edition of the book by Hilary Harris. They chart the development of interest in gender issues in IHRM from Adler's seminal studies of the 1980s through to the present day. The authors explain why there are so few women in international management and illustrate how organizations can benefit from having female international managers. They examine steps that might be taken to increase the representation of female international managers and develop a range of practical recommendations. These include human resource policies to encourage women to join and develop a variety of networks, suggestions that organizations gain better data on the career aspirations and individual requirements of women and factor these into their general career systems, a proposal for MNCs to develop and apply more formalized selection approaches and more sophisticated policies in relation to dual-career couples. Given the continued under-representation of women in international mobility, the authors suggest that one key step would also be for female managers to be more proactive and to ask for international assignments.

Finally, in Chapter 14, Estelle Toomey and Chris Brewster examine the largely unresearched topic of the way that international HRM is conducted in the most international of all organizations – intergovernmental bodies such as the United Nations. These bodies are 'stateless' in the true sense, in that they are based on international territory and are subject to no laws other than their own and where nearly every manager reports to someone from a different nationality and supervises people from other nationalities again. HRM in these international bodies is largely unresearched and their IHRM almost totally so. The chapter uses the example of the United Nations to explore the nature of international organizations, to examine some of the specific HRM issues that such organizations have in distinction to multinational for-profit organizations and, finally, to analyse in detail the unique circumstances of international assignments in international organizations (IOs). In these organizations, many professionals at headquarters are not from the country in which those headquarters are located in the first place and employees are far more likely to be 'internationalists'. While the IHRM challenges of MNCs and IOs are often in similar fields – employee turnover, performance and general international mobility policies, practices and employee motivation – the diverse political and societal contexts, monetary possibilities, staff characteristics, and assignment nature mean that the IHRM paths of IOs are likely to be quite distinct from the MNCs. The authors summarize some of the lessons learned and point to possible research avenues.

RESEARCH ISSUES IN IHRM

What messages can we draw from these contributions? We hope that this book equips those who teach, study or research the field of IHRM with new perspectives that will enable them to remain abreast of contemporary developments. The strategic context for IHRM can be seen to revolve around fundamental questions concerning the localization of capability, multiple options for sourcing and shoring HR activity and the need for multi-direction and multi-channel transfer of relevant knowledge. Moreover, the traditional IHRM functions of resourcing, departure preparation, managing adjustment, rewarding, repatriation and career management must all now be seen in broader context. Not only does recent examination of these IHRM functions suggest that we should dispel a number of myths and question a number of our taken-for-granted academic and practitioner frameworks, it demonstrates that there are multiple options that may be pursued within any one IHRM function and increasing dependency of each function on the total set of management practices. In order to make sense of these varied and complex choices and interdependencies between management practice, we must bring a richer range of theory to bear. Moreover, the historical fascination with international assignments and attention given to a single breed of international manager has been replaced by the need for much better disaggregation of employees as subjected to international management.

16

As a wider and more diverse range of employees become subject to international management, then we must consider the spillover and crossover effects of these different actors and the diverse life domains that influence the choices they make at work. It also requires much better targeting of policies and practice around the need to create increasingly specific and differentiated mindsets, actions and behaviours. The outcomes that are required from international employees need to be managed in a more refined way. Moreover, internationalization of employees (and of their careers, for example) is a two-way process. It becomes ever more important for organizations to align their requirements for more globalized forms of management and employee action with the fact that for employees this forms part of a life journey. This is not just about contained assignments and the need for organizations to make good decisions about the resourcing, tasking, rewarding and subsequent utilization of international employees. The question remains, then, whether the ways in which core IHRM functions are now being managed represent a coherent strategy or a series of tactics that are helping firms cope with globalization. There are a number of ways in which the activities, forms of work and management processes of international organizations might be judged in this regard. It is becoming ever more necessary to ensure that core IHRM processes contribute to both the strategic goals of the organization and the life goals of the individuals who make up the current and future generations of internationalists. This requires an understanding of how both these individuals and their employing organizations build respective forms of capital and how each gains a return on such investments throughout the employment relationship (and beyond).

It would be unfair and unwise to say that such learning has been driven solely by European writers. However, it would be safe to conclude that the context in which the organizations that they study operate, the academic disciplines that underwrite their professional and academic careers and the theoretical lenses that they prefer to use to make sense of the organizational world all serve to create rich territory through which contemporary developments in IHRM should now be understood.

REFERENCES

Arthur, M.B., Claman, P.H. and DeFillippi, J.R. (1995) 'Intelligent enterprise, intelligent careers', *Academy of Management Executive* 9,4:7–22.

Bartlett, C.A. and Ghoshal, S. (1995) *Transnational Management,* 2nd edn, Boston, MA: Irwin.

Black, J.S., Mendenhall, M. and Oddou, G. (1991) 'Toward a comprehensive model of international adjustment: an integration of multiple theoretical perspectives', *Academy of Management Review* 16,2:291–317.

Brewster, C. (2007) 'Comparative HRM: European views and perspectives', *International Journal of Human Resource Management* 18,5:769–787.

Brewster, C. and Harris, H. (eds) (1999) *International HRM: Contemporary Issues in Europe*, London: Routledge.

Brewster, C. and Larsen, H.H. (2000) *Human Resource Management in Northern Europe*, Oxford: Blackwell.

Budhwar, P. (ed.) (2004) *Managing Human Resources in Asia-Pacific*, London: Routledge.

DeFidelto, C. and Slater, I. (2001) 'Web-based HR in an international setting', in A. J. Walker (ed.) *Web-based Human Resources: The Technologies that are Transforming HR*, London: McGraw-Hill.

Dickmann, M. and Müller-Camen, M. (2006) 'A typology of international human resource management strategies and processes', *International Journal of Human Resource Management* 17,4:580–601.

Dowling, P.J. and Welch, D.E. (2004) *International Human Resource Management*, 4th edn, London: Thompson.

Economist (2006) 'Special report staffing globalisation: travelling more lightly', 379, 8483:99–101.

Economist (2007a) 'Globalisation's offspring', 383,8523: 11.

Economist (2007b) 'Hungry tiger, dancing elephant', 383,8523:69–71.

Elvira, M. and Davila, A. (2005) *Managing Human Resources in Latin America*, London: Routledge.

Engardio, P., Bernstein, A. and Kripalini, M. (2003) 'The new global job shift', *Business Week*, 3 February.

Harris, H., Brewster, C. and Sparrow, P. (2003), *International Human Resource Management*, London: CIPD.

Hurn, B.J. (1999). 'Repatriation: the toughest assignment of all', *Industrial and Commercial Training* 31,6:224–228.

Inkson, K. and Arthur, M. (2001) 'How to be a successful career capitalist', *Organisational Dynamics* 30, 1:48–60.

Larsen, H. and Mayrhofer, W. (2006) *Managing Human Resources in Europe*, London: Routledge.

Morley, M., Heraty, N. and Michailova, S. (2007) *Managing Human Resources in Central and Eastern Europe*, London: Routledge.

Philips, L. and Fox, M. (2003) 'Compensation strategy in transnational corporations', *Management Decision* 41,5:465–476.

Torbiörn, I. (1982). *Living Abroad*, New York: Wiley.

Ward, C., Bochner, S. and Furnham, A. (2001) *The Psychology of Culture Shock*, 2nd edn, London: Routledge.

Chapter 2

Localization

A strategic response to globalization

John Hailey and Wes Harry

CHAPTER OBJECTIVES

By the end of this chapter, readers will have:

- an understanding of the contemporary research into localization with the purpose of providing valuable insights and useful information on one of the most difficult issues in international HRM
- examined organizations that claim to be 'global' yet resist allowing host country nationals (local staff) to hold crucial and important jobs
- an appreciation of an analysis of some of the factors affecting the smooth transfer of jobs to local staff
- explored some of the ethical and business reasons for assisting or resisting this process

INTRODUCTION

Localization is an issue that affects managers around the world. It applies as much in Eastern Europe as in Eastern Asia and in a Japanese bank in London or a British bank in Tokyo. We concentrate here on management positions, often held by western expatriates, but are conscious that many of the issues apply to other less high-value jobs. We have also tended to look at the situation of the global firm or international organization with a head office in the developed world. We also recognize that many of the issues can apply to local firms that employ expatriates such as is common in the Middle East, or regional firms employing fellow nationals such as many Taiwanese or Hong Kong firms operating in the Peoples' Republic of China or to not-for-profit organizations. The situation of expatriates moving from low-cost locations to high-cost ones, for example, from Eastern Europe to London, adds other dimensions to the localization issue that have been discussed elsewhere (Hailey 1998; Harry 2007).

This chapter does not present easy answers to this complex and often controversial topic but it is hoped that the following discussion will enable the reader to develop informed opinions on this important aspect of globalization.

There is continued unease at the cost to multinational companies, international development agencies and non-governmental organizations of employing expatriates in management positions and there are ongoing tensions in the relations between those expatriates and local staff. This raises the question as to whether the extensive deployment of expatriate executives is an efficient as well as an ethical use of organizational resources. The degree of distrust and level of tension between expatriates and local staff is hard to measure, but evidence from different studies reflects the intensity of such tensions.

One of the most extreme examples was documented by Gamble (2000), who describes the situation in a German/Chinese joint venture. In this joint venture, which had gone completely sour, the finance director described how personnel matters were dealt with by the Chinese side: 'When young people come here to work, the first thing they learn is "do not talk with foreigners". It is a nightmare.' The situation was so bad that, at the conclusion of the interview, the manager apologized that he was unable to offer a plant tour. He felt it best not to show his face on the shop floor, because 'it might exacerbate the ill-feeling and tension between expatriates and the Chinese in the plant' (Gamble 2000: 887).

This example graphically reflects the intensity of bad relations in a failing joint venture where trust had been breached by both sides. In this case, the German management accused Chinese managers of fraud and technology theft and Chinese managers saw the German managers as interfering, untrustworthy and lacking respect. At worst, this would lead to loss of face, plant closure and loss of investment. However, experience tells us that there can be far more extreme consequences of the failure of expatriate management to engage effectively with local managers. In the case of the Union Carbide plant at Bhopal in India, the failure of expatriate management to ensure that local staff were adequately trained and managed led to the death of thousands and the continuing contamination of the local environment (Banai and Sema 2000).

Sadly, such tensions are not merely found in the private sector and evidence from the development sector suggests that similar levels of distrust exist. Thus local staff employed by major international development agencies commented on the lack of trust displayed by expatriates in their local counterparts. Typical of their comments was that in their regular reports to donors expatriate staff 'portray an image of local staff being incompetent' or that 'local staff are lazy and not committed'. Respondents felt that many expatriates had a fixed image of local staff being 'not reliable, lacking commitment, and not trustworthy', and as a result 'don't seem to trust local staff or involve them in decision making ... and only have faith in other expatriates' (Hailey 1998).

20

Such attitudes and tensions are unwanted and unnecessary in a rapidly globalizing world. They result in inappropriate behaviours, low morale, high staff turnover, loss of productivity and poor performance. Major investments are jeopardized, relations with key partners undermined, joint ventures put at risk, valuable contacts and market relations threatened and the flow of resources or aid support potentially curtailed. Consequently, there is pressure on both international development agencies and multinational companies to manage their international human resources in a way that such tensions are minimized and local management talent is developed and promoted. The development of effective localization strategies and the promotion of local executives to senior positions is a major human resource issue that such international organizations need to address.

This chapter explores the issues around the localization of executive and managerial positions by drawing on a cross-section of contemporary research. The drivers for continued localization of management positions are reviewed and some of the major human resource challenges analysed. We conclude by suggesting that effective localization depends on strategies that are aligned with wider corporate goals. In other words, that such strategies are fit for purpose, appropriate to local needs and not applied in isolation.

RESEARCH ON LOCALIZATION

By localization we are referring not merely to a local citizen filling a job, but to the situation 'when a local national is filling a required job sufficiently competently to fulfil organizational needs' (Potter 1989), or more recently 'the extent to which jobs originally filled by expatriates are filled by local employees who are competent to perform the job' (Selmer 2004). Evans et al. (2002) see localization as the systematic investment in the recruitment, development and retention of local employees and, as such, as an important element in the globalization strategy of multinationals.

The localization of key management positions is a challenge for multinational companies and international development agencies attempting to balance their global interests with the demands of rapidly changing local conditions. In light of this, it is surprising how little research there has been about how best to localize senior management positions or develop indigenous management talent. The bulk of research in this area, as indicated elsewhere in this book, has concentrated instead on the role and performance of international managers and expatriates generally, managing international transfers and the recruitment, training and development of expatriates.

The evidence (Joynt and Morton 1999) suggests that multinational companies continue to use expatriates to fill key positions in their overseas operations.

21

Multinational firms explain this trend in terms of their expanding role in the global marketplace, the need to transfer skills and expertise and the advantage of giving key staff overseas experience and the application of company systems internationally. Furthermore, expatriates are no longer merely employed by traditional large 'blue-chip' companies with well-established international interests. They are increasingly being used by companies who have little tradition of operating overseas and have little experience of working with expatriates and lack established systems to manage and support them (Brewster and Scullion 1997; Foster 1997; Forster 2000; Banai and Harry 2004).

While much of this research is rigorous and enlightening it is somewhat imbalanced because it is so dependent on the perspective of expatriate managers and is rooted in western attitudes and values (Nakajima and Harry 2006; Harry and Jackson forthcoming). There has been a longstanding concern that much of the research into international human resource issues is fundamentally flawed because it is so focused on the concerns of expatriates that it 'ignores the importance of local inputs and local personnel' (Leach 1993:316). Consequently, the analysis in much of the international HRM literature on expatriates is rather one-sided and, as a result, our understanding of the complex dynamics of the localization process is relatively undeveloped.

However, there is now a small, but growing body of research that focuses specifically on localization and its strategic implications. Despite a plea that localization should be incorporated into the wider context of international HRM strategic thinking (Jain et al. 1998), the reality is that most research in this area is concerned with the specifics of the localization process. For example, early studies focused on developing the skills and expertise of host-country managers (Potter 1989; Vance and Ring 1994). Other studies drew on evidence from particular country studies. Cohen (1992) drew on research in Kenya to analyse the issue of 'failed retention' or why it is that a disproportional number of local staff who have been trained to take over positions previously held by expatriates did not actually fill these posts. Leach (1993) reviewed the role and cost of expatriates in developing projects in Tanzania and Hailey (1994) examined the failure of localization strategies introduced in Nigeria. This research analysed the reasons why in many developing countries the post-independence pressure from politicians and trade unions to localize and remove expatriate managers from high-profile positions was not sustainable and how, in the resulting managerial vacuum, 'return expats', or consultants ('disguised expats') were employed at great expense.

Researchers have also drawn on experience in China and Southeast Asia. Lassere and Ching (1997) in a review of the role of local managers working for multinationals operating in China concluded that the case for localization was overwhelming. Hailey's research in Singapore and Malaysia highlighted the tensions between local staff and their expatriate colleagues and concluded that multinationals need to implement effective and transparent localization policies (Hailey 1996, 1998).

22

However, such conclusions were questioned by Gamble (2000) whose research examined the situation facing foreign investors in China. He argued that calls for wholesale localization of senior management positions were premature and that there was still a role for the skills, organizational networks and neutrality that expatriates provide. By the 1990s, studies analysed the practical aspects of localization in the Chinese context (Selmer and Luk 1995; Lee 1999; Wong and Law 1999). More recently, research has emphasized the complex dynamics of implementing localization strategies in China (Worm et al. 2001; Fryxell et al. 2004; Law et al. 2004; Selmer 2004). Some international companies, banks and oil companies, among others, have used host country nationals transferred to the head office or regional office to transfer knowledge from the 'field' to the 'headquarters' (and, in an instructive terminology, referred to not as expatriates but as 'inpatriates'). This is seen as a useful strategy to increase cross-cultural and cross-national understanding as well as giving opportunities for career development of such 'inpatriates'.

In a study of employment creation and localization in the Gulf States, Harry (2007) concluded that, despite governments' pressure to localize jobs, many employers prefer not to recruit local citizens and instead employ expatriates: who they consider cheaper, more easily controlled and more capable than most local staff. One explanation for this is that the supply of expatriates, in technical and managerial jobs, is much more elastic and competitive than that of host-country nationals; consequently, local managers may be more expensive than expatriates. Banai and Harry (2004) also pointed out that some expatriate managers (and many others in less senior positions) see themselves as 'international itinerants' moving from place to place pursuing an international career and not seeking to go 'home'.

A number of researchers have pointed out that all too often localization as a research issue has either been overlooked or treated as the flipside of the expatriation debate (Banai and Harry 2004; Rowley and Benson 2004; Sparrow et al. 2004). As such it is one of the Cinderella subjects in the field of international HRM. In reality, it is a human resource issue in its own right of considerable international consequence, as well as major commercial and ethical dimensions. In light of this, it is surprising how few researchers have analysed drivers of localization and its effectiveness and value; or examined how best to localize senior management positions and what strategies are needed to develop indigenous management talent.

DRIVERS FOR LOCALIZATION

There are a number of fundamental drivers behind the move to localize key management positions. These include issues around the cost effectiveness and performance of expatriates, concerns about the ability of expatriates to establish local contacts, political and ethical pressures to employ local citizens and the impact on the morale and performance of local staff of having foreigners in senior management posts.

Cost and performance as significant drivers for localization

The direct costs of employing expatriates are high. The typical expatriate management package covers a range of high-cost allowances and perks, including family relocation expenses, expensive accommodation, healthcare, educational and social benefits. Expatriate costs are usually a multiple of the national employee costs and expatriates are among the most expensive employees internationally (Banai and Harry 2004; Scullion and Brewster 2001). Even the cost of administering the expatriate employees' conditions of service can be high, compared with that of the administration of host-country nationals, with HR staff engaged in carrying out cost of living comparison studies, developing tax equalization formulae and managing international careers (Dowling and Welch 2004). It is estimated that an expatriate employed by an American multinational will cost two or three times an equivalent position in the USA (Black et al. 1999). The cost of expatriate labour is greater, over the long term, than most societies would willingly bear; for example, expatriates working in China can be paid five times more than local staff in comparative positions (Selmer 2004).

There are also the costs associated with expatriates who return early because of job dissatisfaction or difficulties in adjusting. While the evidence of expatriate failure is well documented, the exact proportion of employees who fail to complete an assignment is probably lower than previously thought, but the cost of each such failure can be enormous (Harzing 1995; Foster 1997). Furthermore, many of those who completed their contracts were not as effective or productive as projected. More than one-third of American expatriates performed below the expectation of their superiors (Stroh et al. 2000).

The lower costs of the host-country staff and their continuity of employment means that the return on investment in recruiting and training these staff may be higher than for expatriates. Organizations that encourage the development and promotion of local managers are likely to see improved morale and greater retention rates of their best staff (Harry and Collings 2006). Host-country managers are generally a more reliable resource than temporary expatriate managers, who may have divided loyalties and certainly see their ultimate destination as a different location from where they currently work (Black and Gregersen 1992).

Indirect costs arising from the poor performance of expatriates or mistakes because of their ignorance of the local business environment or culture must also be considered. These indirect costs are hard to quantify and there have been few attempts to assess them. Armstrong's (1987) highly critical analysis of expatriates in Tanzania and her assessment of the cost of their mistakes on limited local

24

resources and staff time is one of the rare attempts to measure such costs. Such analysis may well underestimate the costs involved because of the difficulty of factoring into such an analysis the opportunity costs of failing to develop local management talent.

There are also costs associated with the frustration felt by local managers at their perceived lack of responsibility and limited access to international training and promotion (Harry and Collings 2006). One consequence of this is that high-calibre local managers look for positions elsewhere. The real cost of not promoting talented local staff who understand the local market or have good contacts is high. Business is lost, performance suffers and market share is threatened. Furthermore, there are costs arising from poor personal relations between expatriates and local staff as we saw in Gamble's (2000) quote at the beginning of the chapter. Such personal misunderstandings and cross-cultural tensions can jeopardise decision making, inhibit flows of information and hinder effective teamworking. Two studies by Hailey (1996, 1998) highlighted the underlying resentment of local staff at the continued employment of expatriates, not just because of their perceived power, perks and salary, but also because of their poor performance and the way expatriates blocked the career ambitions of talented local staff.

One must see the high direct and indirect costs, including potential for decreased performance, associated with employing expatriates in key managerial positions as a significant driver to introduce localization strategies. While there is an obvious need for high-quality skills and expertise in complex international organizations, it is debatable whether the continued reliance on expatriate staff is an efficacious response to internationalization. There is sufficient evidence to suggest that the continued use of expatriates is an expensive and inefficient use of organizational resources. Consequently, multinationals and international development agencies need to invest more in developing the skills, confidence and capabilities of local staff. As one respondent in Singapore succinctly commented: 'If an organisation can afford expatriates then they can afford to train locals' (Hailey 1996).

Contacts and local legitimacy as significant drivers for localization

The economic and operational logic of promoting local staff and developing indigenous talent is obvious. It is based on their knowledge of, and contacts in, the local community; their experience and understanding of local markets; and ability to work successfully in the local socio-economic culture. Local managers have the ability to speak the vernacular language and be culturally assimilated. Possibly most important, they are more likely to take a long-term perspective on the organization's operations in the local community and make a career commitment to developing activities locally, rather than the limited perspective of expatriates on short-term contracts whose commitments may be elsewhere.

25

Evidence suggests that of the many operational problems facing expatriate managers their inability to adapt to the local business or develop an understanding of the local marketplace is crucial. This is partly because of the time-bound nature of their posting and associated issues around building mutual trust or networks of local contacts (Hailey 1998). It also reflects the inability of some expatriates to adjust to different business cultures and form effective relations (Banai and Harry 2004). This not only impacts on sales and profits, but also cuts across longstanding relationships between local staff and potential customers. Efforts to build a permanent niche in the local market are also threatened by the perception that expatriates are merely a 'temporary fixture' and, as such, not worth doing business with.

The importance of local contacts and legitimacy as a key driver of localization strategies should not be underestimated. The employment of talented local managers in positions traditionally held by expatriates may improve communication, performance and productivity. Local-to-local communication is usually more effective than when foreigners are involved. Local managers are in a better position to understand the needs of local customers who share the same language and tastes. They are also better placed to develop local contacts and even though expatriate managers may have greater access to higher level institutional or political contacts, local employees will, generally, be in a better position to develop business relationships with lower levels of organizational and government hierarchies (Selmer 2004).

Political and ethical pressures as significant drivers of localization

Governments actively promote localization policies because of fears of growing unemployment, as well as economic and demographic factors. And in countries with growing, youthful, populations, such as found in the Arab states of the Gulf, it is recognized that unless effective localization strategies are introduced, there could well be long-term economic and political consequences (Yamani 2000; Harry 2007). Thus there is a growing unwillingness among governments in many developing countries to allow key positions in foreign-owned operations to be occupied indefinitely by expatriates and such firms are having to pursue localization policies actively (Sparrow et al. 2004).

The promotion of local managers to senior executive positions may well also have indirect political benefits. Host-country governments may view the localization process as an indication of attachment or commitment to the host country and may assist the firm in gaining lucrative contracts or tenders with local public-sector organizations (Harry and Collings 2006). Localization of such senior positions will also facilitate relations between foreign investors and host-country governments. Selmer (2004) notes that in the case of China, the government favours the development of local employees and both central and provincial authorities view localization as an indication of foreign firms' commitment to the country. The long-term

26

relationship between the local operation and the host population often means that the company is no longer seen as foreign but local and, as Sparrow et al. (2004: 133) point out, 'regulators and governments look at the behaviour of a company against local legal, socio-cultural and environmental norms'. A further advantage of using local managers in key positions, for example, running a foreign subsidiary, is that overseas firms can adopt a lower profile in times of unstable or sensitive political conditions than would be the case if there was an expatriate in charge (Scullion 1995). Thus, from a multinational's point of view an effective localization strategy may help ensure that their foreign operations operate with minimum levels of conflict with the host authorities.

There are a number of longer term reputational and ethical benefits from employing local staff (Hailey 1999; Litvin 2003). There is a nascent debate as to whether it is ethical to continue to use expatriates, who can be seen as an 'alien' and expensive overhead, while not employing local staff in similar posts. It has been argued that the failure to promote and develop local managers is a reflection on unethical human resource practices (Hailey 1999). Based on this analysis, local staff can legitimately argue that they have a 'fundamental right' to be given the same opportunities as any expatriate staff. It is therefore unethical to deprive them of training opportunities, promotion or personal support that might be available to expatriate staff. Vance and Paderon (1993) also explored the concern that multi-nationals were not making effective, and therefore ethical, use of the host-country workforce. They argue, among other things, that multinational companies had a moral responsibility to train host-country workers because of the need to avoid any form of racial or ethnic discrimination, prejudice and their obligation to ensure local staff have the same opportunities as expatriate staff. Their analysis not merely emphasized the extent of the moral obligation that multinationals have to their local staff but also highlighted the ethical dimension of HRM policies.

Political and ethical considerations are also significant drivers of moves to localize key management positions. International firms and agencies need to recognize that they have a moral and ethical obligation, as well as a political imperative, to invest in developing the skills and competencies of local staff, establishing equal opportunities policies and, above all, learn to trust their overseas employees whatever their nationality or background (Bedi 1991; Selmer 2004).

Staff tensions as significant drivers of localization

Most commentators acknowledge that the issue of trust lies at the heart of the localization debate (Selmer et al. 1994; McAllister 1995; Banai and Reisel 1999). Unfortunately, the evidence from a number of different studies suggests that the level of distrust between local staff and their expatriate managers is both high and dysfunctional (Hailey 1996, 1998). All this supports the findings of an early study by Zeira et al. (1974), which found that local employees were dissatisfied and frustrated with ethnocentric staffing policies whereby senior management positions are filled by expatriates. The resulting tensions fuel resentment of expatriates – their power, perks and privileges – and act as a further driver for localization.

These tensions were outlined in some detail in Hailey's two studies of the perceptions of local staff working for both multinational corporations and international development agencies (1996, 1998). Both studies highlighted the potential tensions between local staff and expatriates and raised questions about the efficacy and ethics of continuing to employ expatriates. Most local managers interviewed commented adversely on the perks and privileges of expatriates, the difficulties arising from the failure of expatriates to adjust their management style and tensions arising from cultural misunderstandings and insensitive expatriate behaviour. Many felt that their careers had been inhibited by the continued employment of expatriates and that the relationship of trust between colleagues seems to have been broken.

In general, it appears that the previous respect for expatriate managers shown by local staff is waning. This shift has been fuelled by resentment at the disparity between their own pay and the 'lavish' packages of their expatriate colleagues, as well as their inherent insularity and insensitivity (Cohen 1977; Bedi 1991). Local staff appear neither to trust expatriates nor necessarily value their performance. There was also concern at what has been referred to by some locals as the 'two-faced' ethics of many expatriates and their willingness to breach procedures with impunity when it suited their own needs. The evidence suggests that many local managers saw expatriates as patronizing, colonial and racist. This was exemplified by such observations as they 'still perceive orientals as incapable' or the way expatriates use their own networks means that 'white men speak only to white men' (Hailey 1996). The growth in educational opportunities has given host-country nationals the chance to build their capabilities so that now many will be better qualified and more able than the expatriates sent by the international organization (Banai and Harry 2004).

These demotivating tensions and frustrations are clearly drivers for localization. If such problems are left unchecked then employers may face growing resistance from local staff that threatens not just productivity but corporate loyalty. It will result in low morale, increased staff turnover, growing criticism from local politicians and trade unions and increased difficulties in accessing local business networks, distribution channels and markets generally, let alone forming successful joint ventures or strategic alliances. It is against this background that the pressure to localize crucial management positions must be seen.

STRATEGIES FOR EFFECTIVE LOCALIZATION

Effective localization implies that an organization must develop strategies that both promote and support local staff while still maintaining quality and productivity.

However, the evidence outlined in this chapter suggests there are a number of obstacles to this process including: insufficient investment in developing the skills and competencies of local managers; inappropriate and biased recruitment and selection procedures; underestimation of the skills and experience required; limited and irrelevant training; poor terms and conditions; and attempts by existing expatriates and consultants to maintain their status and position and consequently undermine localization strategies (Harry and Collings 2006; Harry 2007).

BARRIERS TO EFFECTIVE LOCALIZATION

It is also clear that a major obstacle to developing a new generation of local managers is the lack of available managerial talent in rapidly developing economies, for example, in the Gulf States, China or Eastern Europe. The pace of development has been so rapid that there is great demand for the few graduates who have undertaken advanced management courses (Micklethwait 1996). In the Gulf States, for example, the emphasis in education is often on culture or nation building rather than on ensuring employability in the workplace (Harry 2007). There is also concern that many graduates are more likely to want to work in government or be entrepreneurs than to work for foreign firms or be under foreign managers. In this regard Gamble (2000) provides some useful illustrations of the reluctance of Chinese citizens to work under the supervision of Japanese expatriates in the retail sector in China.

It should also be noted that some international organizations are hesitant to employ local managers in key posts because they do not have the skills to take on the necessary responsibilities or handle the procedures and systems common in many multinational firms or international agencies. This, in turn, impacts on headquarters' operational control of the host operations (Child and Yan 1999). A further concern raised by some researchers is the fear of inappropriate use of corporate resources, embezzlement or even loss of intellectual property. Selmer (2004) describes this as an 'agency problem' and argues that an expatriate presence may help to guard against local managers pursuing their personal self-interest in managing the subsidiary or making decisions that are incongruent with the organization's global strategy. In a similar vein, Boisot and Child (1999) noted that due to concerns over embezzlement many foreign firms operating in China have reserved the right to appoint their chief financial officers from within the organization.

LOCALIZATION STRATEGIES: A FOUR-STAGE PROCESS

Despite the fears and concerns it is clear that if the localization of particular management posts is identified as a key human resource priority then localization

29

strategies can be successful. Experience suggests that such strategies must be aligned to the organization's wider strategic goals or corporate strategy. In other words, it must be driven by the search for strategic advantage and not as a compromise solution to short-term problems or merely as a cost-cutting exercise (Taylor 1999; Selmer 2004). The evidence also suggests that such strategies take time and can be complex to implement. As Gamble (2000: 883) commented: 'Localization is likely to proceed at a much slower pace than its main advocates may wish or anticipate, and … there are practical, cultural, and strategic factors which may, and perhaps should inhibit rapid localization.' Because of the link to wider strategy and the possibility of short-term problems it is essential that localization strategies have top management commitment and support. Localization cannot therefore be an HR initiative alone.

The localization process can be divided into four key stages. The first stage is ensuring there is a genuine commitment to localization. Second is the design of appropriate localization strategies – the strategizing stage. Third is the application of these strategies – the localizing stage; and fourth is a consolidation stage when the new incumbents are given ongoing developmental support and the success of the localization policy is reviewed. The first stage requires senior management in the parent organization and the host-country operation to commit their personal support, as well as sufficient resources (especially in terms of selection and training), to ensure efforts to localize succeed. Often expatriates and foreign managers have appeared to be supporting localization while actually undermining or under-resourcing the process. Without such commitment localization will be a troubled process that leads to resentment, and worse, within the organization (Nakajima and Harry 2006).

The second stage with its focus on strategizing is based on an initial clarification of goals and achievable objectives, as well as an assessment of the costs and benefits involved and the investment necessary. The evidence suggests that the development of effective strategies and appropriate objectives is crucial to ensuring the success of long-term localization (Wong and Law 1999; Law et al. 2004; Harry and Collings 2006).

The third stage is concerned with the direct application of specific HR policies that are appropriate to the local environment and culture and have the buy-in of both host and expatriate managers (Wong and Law 1999: Fryxell et al. 2004). This localizing stage includes the establishment of effective recruitment and selection procedures to identify appropriate candidates for specific jobs, the introduction of strategies for their ongoing development and must include incentives to encourage local staff to assume the new roles expected of them (Law et al. 2004). The selected HR practices must be appropriate for the host environment and not just be brought from 'home' or headquarters and applied without taking into account expectations and standards of the local citizens. Training, mentoring and coaching are an essential element and are central to the success of these strategies.

30

Braun and Warner (2002) highlighted the importance of in-house training, assignments abroad and mentoring programmes in the development of local Chinese managers taking over posts held by expatriates. Fryxell et al. (2004) emphasize that this implementation of localization strategies is not about applying generic solutions or simple recipes, but adapting them to specific needs and the particular cultural context. Indeed, they argue that successful localization is marked by the application of an appropriate combination of elements, rather than the imposition of a linear relationship between separate elements of the programme. Successful locals will often be role models for others and can be the best mentors and coaches for later generations.

The fourth, consolidation, stage occurs when locally employed staff have the necessary skills and competence to assume roles previously assumed by expatriates and the success of the localization process is evaluated and lessons learnt (Wong and Law 1999). This stage also involves ensuring expatriate support in the development of new local managers by actively involving them in the planning of the localization process and providing them with a suitable and attractive repatriation package (Law et al. 2004; Selmer 2004) or by opening up new career opportunities (Banai and Harry 2004). During the consolidation stage there will be feedback on the causes of successes or failures and in the localization process, aimed at improving the development of staff to replace other expatriates.

This staged approach to localization gives a structure to what is potentially a complex and divisive organizational and political issue. By taking a systematic approach with objectives and timelines, progress can be measured, obstacles recognized and dealt with. The evidence suggests that if there is a genuine commitment from senior management to effective and ethical localization then there is a high chance of success (Harry and Collings 2006). This is particularly true if time and resources are invested in the planning stage, appropriate HR policies and practices are applied in the localization stage, and these are followed up by appropriate and timely development support and ongoing monitoring (Hailey 1999; Fryxell et al. 2004; Law et al. 2004).

LOCALIZATION IN PRACTICE: SELECTION, TRAINING AND EXPATRIATE ATTITUDES

Case study 2.1
Localization issues in an Asian airline

Not so long ago several very successful East Asian airlines marketed themselves, not very subtly, as having reliable (Caucasian) pilots and glamorous (young, female, Asian) cabin crew. The high-paid jobs were reserved for expatriates and the low-paid service jobs for the locals. Behind the scenes and outside the marketing campaigns a similar division of labour between high-paid prestigious jobs and low-paid menial jobs was visible. Managers were Europeans and office staff Asian. Engineers were white, mechanics were brown. The airline in this case fitted this pattern.

During its early history the airline had no locals trained as pilots, although the country's armed forces had pilots and neighbouring states had trained pilots for their successful commercial airlines. Engineering and other highly technical and professional jobs were held by foreigners. There was no programme for training or developing the host-country nationals to take these roles. About 25 years ago modest programmes were started to train pilots and engineers but with little enthusiasm on the part of the expatriate managers or staff. Local staff were recruited in small numbers but the number of expatriates stayed the same and even increased as the firm expanded and more expertise was needed to support the training efforts.

Slowly the number and capability of local engineers increased until they started to take on highly skilled and managerial roles. These engineers showed they had at least as much ability and even more commitment to doing well as the expatriates. A critical mass of local and internationally qualified engineers developed. Management was no longer able to justify keeping high-cost expatriate engineers and most of the engineering function was 'localized'.

Among the pilots, expatriates continued to dominate. Few local pilots were appointed and their promotion was very slow. A range of excuses were given to explain this state of affairs, including that local staff do not like to be away from home overnight and are therefore not suitable for international flights or that they do not have the education or work ethics of the expatriates, even that their culture does not make them suitable for technical roles. As pilot jobs are governed by strict rules of seniority, the expatriates knew that if they left the Asian airline even as experienced flight crew they would have to start at the bottom of the seniority list in a new airline. So the expatriates resisted and slowed the recruitment and promotion of the local pilots. It probably took a decade longer than necessary to appoint local pilots in sufficient numbers. Now, more than 25 years after the airline started to localize pilot jobs, there are still expatriates employed as captains and first officers. But now over 70% of pilots are locals. There are even local female pilots – an inconceivable proposal when the idea of localization of these high-value, high-paying and high-status jobs was first suggested.

Questions

1 Would marketing campaigns that emphasize the use of western pilots and young female Asian cabin crew be successful nowadays? Why might this be the case (or not)?

2 Why might a commercial airline prefer not to train staff, but to 'buy' in ready-trained personnel?

3 Are people from some societies better at dealing with 'technical' tasks than those from other societies? Why might some observers think it is the situation?

4 How could developing a critical mass of employees lead to changing policies and ways of working?

5 Is promotion based on seniority a useful model for jobs that need a lot of experience?

As the case study shows, localization strategies have a number of implications in terms of HR practices. Human resource strategists must ensure that there are effective selection and promotion procedures in place to support localization. This is a matter of some concern because of the evidence that many multinationals use inappropriate methods to select employees or their systems are inappropriate to the cultural context in which they are applied (Sparrow 1999; Briscoe and Schuler 2004; Weir and Hutchings 2006). Appropriate training is also a crucial element in promoting successful localization, particularly in societies with an under-resourced education system or where there is a serious skills shortfall (Yamani 2000; Harry 2007). In many countries, the major task is not skill training, but rather the development of appropriate behaviour and inculcating a work ethic. The education system of the former Soviet Union, for example, produced people with good technical and professional skills but poor work attitudes. This is well reflected in the aphorism 'employers pretend to pay the staff and the staff pretend to work' (Harry 2006). In Eastern Europe, the traditional emphasis on theory rather than application resulted in poor-quality levels and high scrap rates (Kiriazov et al. 2000). While effective recruitment and training are seen as essential components of effective localization, recent studies, such as Banai and Harry (2004) and Harry and Collings (2006), have highlighted the central role of incumbent expatriates in this process.

The evidence points to a lack of investment in training appropriate to the needs of a new generation of local managers. Possible explanations for this lack of support and investment in management training include the attitude of expatriates to developing local staff, self-interest of the first generation of local managers (who sometimes resent better qualified or more capable younger rivals) and the extent to which the parent company fails to sanction ongoing investment in staff development in order to discredit the localization process and justify the re-employment of expatriate managers (Hailey 1994). Selmer argues that 'effective localization commences with the incumbent expatriates' (2004: 1094). Expatriates, perhaps because they can earn more abroad than at home, can be a serious obstacle to

33

effective localization. The attitude and ability of individual expatriates is crucial in determining the success of the localization process. This is because the expatriate's own self-interest may dictate whether they willingly engage in the localization process (Harry and Collings 2006). Moreover, they may actively attempt to thwart efforts at localization in an attempt to delay their own repatriation and the threat to their career or income (Keeley 1999; Rogers 1999; Law et al. 2004; Selmer 2004).

One of the key roles that expatriates play is a developmental one. In this regard, expatriates must proactively assume a mentoring and coaching role if localization strategies are to be successful (Evans et al. 2002; Law et al. 2004). They can also fulfil an important role by disseminating knowledge about corporate cultures, structures and systems (Gamble 2000). It is imperative that local managers benefit from the knowledge and skills of the expatriate manager if they are to grow and develop and ultimately assume the responsibilities once held by the expatriate. This may be problematic for a number of reasons. First, expatriates may not have the skills or abilities to play a mentoring or coaching role (Nadler 1993). Second, they may be deterred from developing local staff due to the short-term nature of their foreign assignment brief or an over-emphasis on quantitative performance indicators such as return on investment or quality levels. Third, expatriates may also delay localization by painting a picture of local staff being lazy or not motivated, untrustworthy and so too expensive to train and to employ (Selmer 2004). This study concludes by suggesting that, in practice, it is the unwillingness of recalcitrant expatriates that impedes localization rather than inability or lack of skills.

Thus the challenge for organizations deploying expatriates is to select and assign only those who are committed to or who understand the dynamics of developing local staff. Moreover, to give these expatriates additional training to develop their own mentoring skills and design a reward package or incentive scheme that encourages them to develop local counterparts. The role of intrinsic motivators should not be underestimated. Many individuals get satisfaction from passing on skills to others, enjoy learning new skills themselves (such as improving the capability of others in foreign lands) or have the self-satisfaction of a job well done (Banai and Harry 2004). Thus, the challenge for the international HR manager is to develop a compensation system that accommodates these various motivators and encourages appropriate behaviours in expatriate employees.

The expatriate's support is crucial to the success of the localization process. Not only can expatriates transfer skills and knowledge, but they can also set an example and pass on attitudes and behaviours and set standards that local staff can emulate. They can also act as champions for local staff when dealing with head office. However, if expatriates are resistant, cynical or incapable, then effective localization will fail or be postponed. In contrast, if expatriates are supportive, foster a climate of trust and are prepared to play a developmental role then localization strategies are much more likely to succeed (Fryxell et al. 2004; Selmer 2004;

34

Harry and Collings 2006). The evidence suggests that many expatriates have found themselves highly employable because of their ability to train, to advise and to consult on localization programmes (Banai and Harry 2004). The most effective expatriates realize that they are no longer employed as 'doers', but instead as supporters and capacity builders.

CONCLUSION

This chapter has explored some of the contemporary research around localization. It argues that localization is a key human resource issue in its own right with major economic and ethical dimensions, but that all too often it has been overlooked as an issue for research. As such it is one of the 'Cinderella' subjects in the field of international HRM. This is a matter of some concern because the evidence suggests that localization should be seen as an integral strand of any multinational organization's international strategies. The evidence suggests that it would be cheaper and more ethically appropriate for such organizations to phase out, or at least reduce, the use of expatriate managers, place greater trust in local staff and build on their experience, expertise, local knowledge and contacts. Expatriates have a useful role in many global organizations but locals have a crucial role in the success of globalization.

KEY LEARNING POINTS

- This is an area of international HRM which has not attracted much research interest over the years. The lack of research in this area suggests that this is a difficult and sensitive area to study in any depth.
- The chapter has identified the key elements of the strategies that promote successful localization, as well as some of the obstacles that inhibit or constrain the effective implementation of these strategies.
- It is such difficult HR issues that must be addressed on a regular basis and not avoided because they are too complex or culturally sensitive.

REFERENCES

Armstrong, A. (1987) 'Tanzania's expert-led planning: an assessment', *Public Administration and Development* 7, 2:261–271.

Banai, M. and Harry, W.E. (2004) 'Boundaryless global careers: the international itinerants', *International Studies of Management and Organisation* 34, 3:96–120.

Banai, M. and Reisel, W.D. (1999) 'Would you trust your foreign manager? An empirical investigation', *International Journal of Human Resource Management* 10,3: 477–487.

Banai, M. and Sema, L. (2000) 'Ethical dilemmas in MNCs' international staffing policies: a conceptual framework', *Journal of Business Ethics* 25, 3:477–487.

Bedi, H. (1991) *Understanding the Asian Manager*, London: Allen & Unwin.

Black, J.S. and Gregersen, H.B. (1992) 'Serving two masters: managing the dual allegiance of expatriate employees', *Sloan Management Review* 33, 4:61–71.

Black, J.S., Gregersen, H., Mendenhall, M. and Stroh, L. (1999) *Globalizing People
Through International Assignments*, Reading, MA: Addison-Wesley.

Boisot, M. and Child, J. (1999) 'Organisations as adaptive systems in complex environments: the case of China', *Organisation Science* 10:237–252.

Braun, W.H. and Warner, M. (2002) 'Strategic human resource management in western
multinationals in China: the differentiation of practices across different ownership
forms', *Personnel Review* 31:533–579.

Brewster, C. and Scullion, H. (1997) 'A review and agenda for expatriate HRM', *Human
Resource Management Journal* 7, 5:32–41.

Briscoe, D.R. and Schuler, R.S. (2004) *International Human Resource Management*,
London: Routledge.

Child, J. and Yan, Y. (1999) 'Investment and control in international joint ventures: the
case of China', *Journal of World Business* 34:3–15.

Cohen, E. (1977) 'Expatriate communities', *Current Sociology* 24, 3:5–129.

Cohen, J. (1992) 'Foreign advisers and capacity building: the case of Kenya', *Public
Administration and Development* 12, 5:493–510.

Dowling, P.J. and Welch, D.E. (2004) *International Human Resource Management:
Managing People in a Multinational Context* (4th edn), London: Thomson.

Evans, P., Pucik, V. and Barsoux, J.L. (2002) *The Global Challenge: Frameworks for
International Human Resource Management*, Boston, MA: McGraw-Hill.

Forster, N. (1997) 'The persistent myth of high expatriate failure rates: a reappraisal',
International Journal of Human Resourse Management 8, 4.

Forster, N. (2000) 'The myth of the international manager', *International Journal of
Human Resource Management* 10, 5:126–142.

Fryxell, G.E., Butler, J. and Choi, A. (2004) 'Successful localisation in China: an
important element in strategy implementation', *Journal of World Business* 39:
268–282.

Gamble, J. (2000) 'Localizing management in foreign-invested enterprises in China:
practical, cultural and strategic perspectives', *International Journal of Human
Resource Management* 11, 5:883–1004.

Hailey, J. (1994) 'Localizing the multinationals: limitations and problems', in S. Segal
Horn (ed.) *The Challenge of International Business*, London: Kogan Page.

Hailey, J. (1996) 'The expatriate myth: cross-cultural perceptions of expatriate managers', *The International Executive* 38, 2:255–271.

Hailey, J. (1999) 'Localisation, ethics, and internationalisation', in C. Brewster and
H. Harris (eds) *International Human Resource Management: Contemporary Issues
in Europe*, London: Routledge.

Harry, W.E. (2006) 'History and HRM in Central Asia', *Thunderbird International
Business Review* 48, 1:39–53.

Harry, W.E. (2007) 'Employment creation and localisation: the crucial human resource
issues for the GCC', *International Journal of Human Resource Management* 18, 1:
132–146.

Harry, W.E. and Collings, D. (2006) 'Localisation: societies, organisations and employees', in H. Scullion and D. Collings (eds) *Global Staffing Systems,* London: Routledge.

Harry, W.E. and Jackson, K. (forthcoming) 'Globalisation, the wave, and the undertow', *Management Revue.*

Harzing, A.W. (1995) 'The persistent myth of high expatriate failure rates', *International Journal of Human Resource Management* 6, 2:457–475.

Jain, H., Lawler, J. and Morishima, M. (1998) 'Multinational corporations, human resource management and host-country nationals', *International Journal of Human Resource Management* 9, 4:533–566.

Joynt, P. and Morton, N. (1999) *The Global HR Manager,* London: IPD.

Keeley, S. (1999) 'The theory and practice of localisation', in J. Lee (ed.) *Localisation in China: Best Practice,* Hong Kong: Euromoney.

Kiriazov, D., Sullivan, S.E. and Tu, H.S. (2000) 'Business success in Eastern Europe: understanding and customising HRM', *Business Horizons* 43, 1:39–43.

Lassere, P. and Ching, P.S. (1997) 'Human resources management in China and the localisation challenge', *Journal of Asian Business* 13, 4:85–99.

Law, K.S., Wong, C.S. and Wang, K.D. (2004) 'An empirical test of the model on managing the localisation of human resources in the People's Republic of China', *International Journal of Human Resource Management* 15:635–648.

Leach, F. (1993) 'Counterpart personnel, a review of the literature with implications for education and development', *International Journal of Educational Development* 13, 4:315–330.

Lee, J. (ed.) (1999) *Localisation in China: Best Practice,* Hong Kong: Euromoney.

Litvin, D. (2003) *Empires of Profit,* New York: Texere.

McAllister, D. (1995) 'Affect and cognition-based trust as foundations for interpersonal co-operation in organisations', *Academy of Management Journal* 38: 24–59.

Micklethwait, J. (1996) 'The search for the Asian manager', *The Economist* 338, 7956: S3–S5.

Nadler, N. (1993) 'First train the expatriate', *Brussels MEMC Report* 4/93:1.

Nakajima, C. and Harry, W.E. (2006) 'Ethnocentric organisations: how hosts perceive MNCs using HR policies as a means of domination', *EIASM Workshop on International Strategy and Cross Cultural Management,* Toulouse, France.

Potter, C. (1989) 'Effective localisation of the workforce', *Journal of European Industrial Training* 13, 6:25–30.

Rogers, B. (1999) 'The expatriates in China: a dying species?', in J. Lee (ed.) *Localisation in China: Best Practice,* Hong Kong: Euromoney.

Rowley, C. and Benson, J. (eds) (2004) *Management of Human Resources in the Asia–Pacific,* London: Routledge.

Scullion, H. (1995) 'International human resource management', in J. Storey (ed.) *Human Resource Management: A Critical Text,* London: Routledge.

Scullion, H. and Brewster, C. (2001) 'Managing expatriates: messages from Europe', *Journal of World Business* 36, 4:346–365.

Selmer, J. (2004) 'Expatriates' hesitation and the localisation of western business operations in China', *International Journal of Human Resource Management* 15, 6: 1094–1097.

Selmer, J. and Luk, V. (1995) 'Expatriate management succession in foreign business subsidiaries', *Asia Pacific Journal of Management* 12, 1:1094–1107.

Selmer, J., Kang, I.L. and Wright, R.P. (1994) 'Managerial behaviour of expatriate versus local bosses', *International Studies of Management and Organisation* 24, 3: 91–100.

Sparrow, P. (1999) 'International recruitment, selection and assessment', in P. Joynt and B. Morton (eds) *The Global HR Manager: Creating the Seamless Organisation,* London: IPD.

Sparrow, P., Brewster, C. and Harris, H. (2004) *Globalizing Human Resource Management,* London: Routledge.

Stroh, L.S., Gregersen, H.B. and Black, J.S. (2000) 'Triumphs and tragedies: expectations and commitment upon repatriation', *International Journal of Human Resource Management* 11, 4:681–697.

Taylor, B. (1999) 'Patterns of control within Japanese manufacturing plants in China: doubts about Japanization in Asia', *Journal of Management Studies* 36, 6: 853–874.

Vance, C.M. and Paderon, E.S. (1993) 'An ethical argument for host country workforce training and development in the expatriate management assignment', *Journal of Business Ethics* 12, 8:635–641.

Vance, C.M. and Ring, P.S. (1994) 'Preparing the host country workforce for expatriate managers: the neglected side of the coin', *Human Resource Development Quarterly* 5, 4:337–352.

Weir, D. and Hutchings, K. (2006) 'Guanxi and wasta: a review of the traditional ways of networking in China and the Arab world and their implications for international business', *Thunderbird International Business Review* 48, 1:141–156.

Wong, C.S. and Law, K.S. (1999) 'Managing localisation of human resources in the PRC: a practical model', *Journal of World Business* 34: 26–40.

Worm, V., Selmer, J. and de Leon, C.T. (2001) 'Human resource development for localisation: European multinationals in China', in J.B. Kidd, X. Li and F.J. Richter (eds) *Advances in Human Resource Management in Asia,* Basingstoke: Palgrave.

Yamani, M. (2000) *Changed Identities,* London: Royal Institute of International Affairs.

Zeira, Y.E., Harari, I. and Nundi, I. (1974) 'Some structural and cultural factors in ethnocentric multinational corporations and employee morale', *Journal of Management Studies* 12, 1:66–82.

Chapter 3

HR sourcing and shoring

Strategies, drivers, success factors and implications for HR

Paul Sparrow and Werner Braun

SUMMARY

This chapter explores the different strategies that are at play in terms of both sourcing and shoring of HR services. A brief review of theoretical perspectives is followed by a warning that theory tends not to align with the judgements made by the key actors in practice. The chapter explores the range of variables that can be identified and the need to understand parallel developments in the strategic reorientation of the HR function. It is noted that there are continued and substantial international differences in the pursuit and preference for HR outsourcing (HRO). Despite the fact that HRO vendors are building impressive delivery centres and capabilities spanning the globe, their ability to truly optimize HR processes on a global scale remains to be proven but there are significant developments in these areas and the service offerings of vendors are evolving rapidly to address such concerns.

CHAPTER OBJECTIVES

By the end of this chapter, readers will have:

- understood the core strategies pursued as firms make choices about sourcing and shoring of HR services
- identified the variables that need to be measured to assess the effectiveness of each strategy
- reviewed the business drivers for human resource outsourcing and identified the strategic outcomes that should be used to determine success
- considered how the market for sourcing and shoring options is developing by analysing the volume and scale of contemporary deals
- identified useful avenues of research that might help explain international differences in the HRO market

39

- gained a sensitivity to future developments and challenges for HR functions by analysing both vendor strategies and issues for the retained HR business

INTRODUCTION

A wide set of business services can now be delivered through a range of new organizational forms. Abramovsky et al. (2006) differentiate these services into direct IT services (for example, hardware and software consultancy, data processing, maintenance) and IT-enabled services (the much broader range of work including professional services and other diverse activity, of which the various human resource sourcing and shoring strategies examined in this chapter are but one variant).

Mahoney and Brewster (2002) note that while findings from the Cranet survey show that HR service delivery is commonly indicated as one of the key challenges for personnel/HR management, the term 'HR outsourcing' still carries its own intellectual 'baggage'. It is often associated with perceptions about the loss of responsibility and control, reduced importance for the function and a lack of focus from the external service providers. Because HR departments are challenged to be more cost effective while at the same time improving the quality of their service and the value of their overall business contribution, outsourcing of certain activities under appropriate conditions may be a desirable solution. Finding the right balance and solution remains the challenge for many and no organization appears to have yet developed a fully effective way of exploiting the possibilities associated with these recent developments in HR service provision on a global scale (Sparrow et al. 2004). Indeed, there is still considerable confusion about many of the options faced.

CORE STRATEGIC RATIONALES AND CHOICES

The first question that we address therefore is: how can we best distinguish between some of the new organizational forms that have emerged such as insourcing, outsourcing, offshoring and global insourcing? Abramovsky et al. (2006) provide a staged model of these organizational forms. They are all seen as different forms of specialization, whereby activities are moved, under different geographical and sourcing arrangements, to specialized units. For Chakrabarty (2006), there are two strategies at play: 'sourcing' (across organizational boundaries between a client entity and non-client entities such as vendors, suppliers and third parties) and 'shoring' (across either onshore – same country – or wider geographical boundaries). Sometimes offshoring may be further differentiated into nearshoring (shared borders or close institutional and cultural regulatory regimes) and offshoring (used specifically to refer to sourcing across a wide geographical and cultural distance). The taxonomy that follows can be applied to any process, not just HR. Indeed, as a general observation, in order to inform research on HR sourcing and shoring, we need to draw on the general business process outsourcing literature. From this perspective, then, there are four core strategies that might be applied:

1 *In-country insourcing* describes the situation where the supplier–customer relationship is still formalized and contracted and activities are still sent to another (within-country) location (generally for reasons of cost efficiency), but the activities are still performed in-house, for example, in one of the organization's own subsidiaries or a service centre. The responsibility and delegation of tasks to the service provider means that they are still what is called an internalized 'client entity'.

2 *Global insourcing* describes the situation where the redesign and reconfiguration of activities and processes to become more efficient and effective allows some geographical flexibility over the location of the activity. The other location is outside the original country. For economists, ownership of 10% of offshore operations constitutes direct foreign investment between a parent operation and an affiliate.

3 *Outsourcing* describes situations when a third party provider is used to carry out the activity, with the production of services purchased externally, but still within the same country. It is generally aimed at achieving higher profitability by using fewer in-house resources. It is defined as 'a discontinuation of internal production (whether it be production of goods or services) and an initiation of procurement from outside suppliers' (Gilley and Rasheed 2000: 764). Human resource outsourcing (henceforth abbreviated to HRO) involves 'the purchasing by an organization of ongoing HR services from a third-party provider that it would otherwise normally provide by itself' (Hesketh 2006: 1).

4 *Offshoring* describes a particular type of specialization in which the production of services or goods is moved overseas. Offshoring involves a broad range of tasks that are executed by a firm in another country, ranging from the establishment of a foreign subsidiary to a relatively arm's length relationship with another firm (Harrison and McMillan 2006). More arm's length relationships tend to involve a more explicit practice of contracting with individuals or companies in foreign countries to perform work that might reasonably be conducted domestically. Hunter (2006: 2) therefore defines offshoring as 'the act of transferring some of a company's recurring internal activities to outside providers, who are located in a different country and market economy, under a formal service contract'. Offshore transactions also typically involve two parts: a transfer of responsibility for the operation and management of part of an organization; and a guaranteed provision of

41

services to the client organization by the vendor for a particular time period. Given the distances involved in offshoring, the factors of production are rarely transferred to offshore sites, but the services, processes and decision rights are (Hunter 2006).

The risks associated with each of these organizational forms differ, of course. Offshoring is considered to take the benefits and risks of outsourcing to its extremes (Chakrabarty 2006). Moreover, even if the best skills can be found at the lowest cost, the challenges of coordination, communication and control are tested by the cultural divergences.

Three dominant theoretical perspectives have been used to explain the motivation to outsource: models of core–periphery activity and the resource-based view of the firm, transactional cost economics and the decision to make or buy services; and models of HR roles and the shift towards more consultative and strategic activity (Budhwar and Cooke 2008). But the theoretical basis to drive each choice of organizational form is different. As a strategic tool, Hesketh (2006) argues that outsourcing revolves around decisions about: capability (whether to improve or acquire this); scale (providing well-administered services for populations large enough to justify the return on investment); and technology (the benefits of which may be acquired or leveraged through the development of shared services or outsourcing). Outsourcing is therefore typically analysed from a resource-based view (RBV) of the firm. Espino-Rodríquez and Padrón-Robaina (2006) point out, however, that it is not the capabilities or resources that form the source of competitive advantage, but the *exploitation* of these resources through the efficiency and effectiveness of existing business processes.

Offshoring, in contrast, is often analysed from a transaction cost perspective. Traditional supplier relationships often involve the purchase of new services, but offshoring generally involves the movement of already existing in-house activities. The issue therefore is the completion of the same task in a different location, where the costs may be significantly cheaper. Hesketh (2006) notes that decisions about this are driven more by economic theories of labour arbitrage rather than the RBV models of organizational capability that drive thinking about shared service, e-enablement and outsourcing.

Theory, however, rarely aligns with the pragmatic judgements that are made by the strategic actors. One of the challenges that faces all of those working with the decisions that surround the choice of the above four options is neatly summarized by De Vita and Wang (2006: 4):

The question of the extent to which each (core competence) … is singularly both necessary and sufficient to justify the … choice has never been satisfactorily squared … Ambiguity still reigns on how to establish what, and what not, should be seen as core. Is it what we do best? Is it what creates value? Or is it related to the strategic importance of the activity in relation to changing industry requirements?

Not surprisingly then, Kenney and Florida (2004: 1) observe that, once we analyse the strategic paths being pursued, we should not oversimplify our assumptions about globalization:

Globalisation is much more than simply moving employment and activities from developed nations into nations with lower cost forces. Such a simple conclusion obscures the complicated skein of cross-border relationships that have evolved out of firm strategies seeking to balance a kaleidoscope of variables including labor and inventory costs, transportation, quality, concentration of valuable knowledge in clusters and temporal proximity to customers. Understanding firm strategies at a single moment in time is complicated enough, but unfortunately these variables also fluctuate [over time].

DETERMINANTS OF THE EFFECTIVENESS OF STRATEGIC CHOICE AND EXECUTION

The second question to address is: which variables need to be measured to assess the effectiveness of these organizational forms (or assess the strategy used to execute them)? In answering this question, one cannot ignore the role that technology (primarily, through e-enablement) and supporting HR structures (for example, in the form of shared services) play in enabling each of these choices. This is because one of the cornerstones for success in HRO is clarity in terms of desired changes for the future HR operating model. Outsourcing HR activities typically involves moving activities into an outsourced centre of scale (in contrast to an internal shared service centre). In most companies, this triggers a restructuring process of the retained HR organization and organizational design work around the retained organization, including the establishment of service management organizations (SMOs) to manage the client–vendor interface and structural arrangements for the transition and transformation stages. HR outsourcing projects also allow organizations to gain access to cutting-edge HR technology while avoiding ongoing IT investments. In order to maximize the benefits from this access to technology, organizations have to formulate an appropriate IT strategy and architecture approach. This requires a thorough understanding of the vendor's technology, the challenges it creates in terms of appropriate technology interfaces, data compatibility, data security, maximized user buy-in and technology investment for the retained organization.

43

Therefore, although it is beyond the scope of this chapter to discuss the more general developments of the role of IT in HR, in practice solutions such as outsourcing are often combined with the e-enablement of many HR processes and an extension of existing information and communications technology (ICT) systems (CIPD 2005a, 2005b). Indeed, in a study of 64 UK MNCs, Brewster et al. (2005) found that when HR managers ranked items on HR structures and strategies, high outsourcing of business processes loaded on a factor of efficiency alongside high centralization and e-enablement of HR.

In practice, when we consider execution of strategy, responses are far more complex even than suggested by the four organizational forms just considered. This is because each of the four organizational forms – and indeed the hybrid combinations of these forms that are often pursued – offers a different contribution to parts of the value chain (Chakrabarty 2006). Firms therefore make much more differentiated decisions, which involve choices about:

- sourcing (for example co-sourcing with one or multisourcing with multiple vendors)
- different support strategies (for example, fix-and-keep in-house, rehabilitate and retain, enable capability building within the client or indeed the vendor operation, outsourcing with a reverse option, through to complete divestment)
- contractual arrangements, which may be benefits based (whereby payments are linked to realized benefits) or may be co-sourced (where vendor revenues are linked to client performance)
- location of resources, which may be distributed (where the vendor has teams both on shore and offshore) or dyadic (independent client and vendor operations).

There are also multiple regulatory regimes (referred to as contract complexity or density) that can be adopted. Attention is therefore now being given to the nature of governance and risk mitigation that accompanies any particular outsourcing solution (Barthélemy and Quélin 2006). Complexity is required for three reasons:

1 to mitigate opportunistic behaviours by the vendor
2 to avoid over-dependence on the vendor
3 to allow flexible responses to changes in the environment.

In practice, governance arrangements are based on two control mechanisms:

1 formal contractual relations in the form of 'a bundle of obligations, incentives, rewards and penalties' where 'it is not clear that the chosen governance will mitigate all contractual hazards'

44

2 a range of complementary social mechanisms such as trust, reputation and what has been termed 'the shadow of the future' act to ensure self-regulation.

How important a set of variables does contract complexity represent? Barthélemy and Quélin (2006) identified 816 outsourcing agreements from 1992–97 based on searches in ABI/Inform and Reuters. They surveyed 82 of these deals (76% in Europe) in order to assess the link between contract complexity and the aftermath (the impact of hazards on post-deal transaction costs). Denser contracts existed when there were high switching costs, higher strategic centrality of the outsourced activity and higher uncertainty about future needs. Denser contracts were also associated with higher monitoring and enforcement costs. While adapting human assets, surprisingly, bore no relationship to contract complexity, it was associated with higher switching costs. The study also showed that governance was clearly based on a blend of formal contracts *and* relational norms and this raises an important research agenda around the design of outsourcing arrangements, the role of relational versus contractual elements (itself likely to differ across countries or national cultures) and the impact on performance outcomes such as service, innovation and productivity.

What messages does this last section contain for researchers? Given the complexity of sourcing and shoring strategies and contracts, the need to understand how these are combined with other changes (such as centralization or e-enablement) and the range of variables associated with effective execution, beware the writers who take strong ideological positions for or against HRO.

BUSINESS DRIVERS FOR HRO

How important might the different business drivers for sourcing options be? What does analysis of these drivers tell us about the necessary research base that is needed? In this section we look at the business drivers for one of the sourcing options – HRO – to help address these questions. The most common business drivers for companies to consider HRO are:

- cost savings
- improved service quality
- IT investment/access to technology
- improved process efficiencies
- global process harmonization
- strategic reorientation of HR
- improved business agility.

We will review each of these drivers in turn, but first set the broader decision-making context. The decision to outsource reflects a complex amalgam of motivations.

45

Greer et al. (1999) identified a series of competitive and political forces that, by the end of the 1990s, were driving a significant proportion of firms to outsource some or all of their HR activities as they attempted to refocus their businesses, lower costs, increase service levels and improve the capability to respond to future business challenges. These were:

- downsizing pressures in other functions, moving into the HR function itself as calls for reduced costs of HR services increased
- rapid growth through mergers or acquisitions or rapid decline in markets and associated pressure to monitor costs: the former provided the opportunity to decide whether to hold on to or release selected HR activities or was associated with exceptional service demands being outsourced because of limited internal capacity; the latter increased pressure to reduce costs
- globalization, where the move from being sellers of products or services to managing more complex international movements, harmonization of policies or requirements for specialized services led to the standardization of in-house activity or outsourcing to specialist providers
- increased competition and adoption of balanced scorecard approaches, which increased attention to customer and employee measures of service quality and created pressure for more responsive service provision at lowest cost
- mismatches between the demand for more specialized expertise and growing complexity of HR tasks and capabilities of existing specialists, reinforcing pressure to outsource
- desire to reduce HR bureaucracy (perceived) to get in the way of operational efficiency, reinforcing pressures for the shape, size and focus of HR departments to be determined on the basis of market forces rather than procedural processes
- outsourcing enabling unsatisfactorily performing or troublesome HR operations to be 'hidden' from view or passed on to vendors, reducing personal risk to the decision makers.

In addition to descriptions of the political and strategic forces at play, there have also been analyses of the actual management motivations to outsource HR.

> **Text box 3.1**
> **Management motivations to outsource HR**
> Lever (1997) showed that early developments in the outsourcing of HR were driven not just by cost drivers, but by a combination of three factors.

46

Cost reduction

Savings produced by avoiding the need to add new personnel or by reducing existing personnel by hiring experts in specific areas at lower cost.

Higher value created where transactions with external agents are more cost effective than building and maintaining internal capacity.

Better service demonstrated at lower prices through economics of scale and learning curve efficiencies as work from several clients is combined.

Standardization of processes, judicious use of services or reduction of bureaucracy extracting additional cost savings that can be shared with the purchaser.

Risk reduction

Insuring against problematic performance and reducing business risks by transferring productivity and component cost issues to the vendor.

Vendor risk increased because of exposure to client business lifecycles and their profits depending on the client maintaining their business.

Client risk reduced because technological and skills obsolescence/updating issues and day-to-day control/coordination passed on to the vendor.

Competency building

Building organizational capability by focusing on a set of core competencies.

Access to highly skilled specialists and opportunity afforded by outsourcing mundane or infrequent activity used to selectively build internal skills.

Commodity-like and esoteric activity replaced by more value-adding activity.

Cost savings

While buyers are increasingly demanding higher value and incremental business benefits from their HRO engagement, the achievement of significant cost savings is by far the most frequently mentioned reason why companies outsource (Cook and Gildner 2006; Hesketh 2006). The capital outlay, for example, for continuous HR technology investments, can be immense and for many companies HRO provides a real incentive to move towards a variable cost model.

Cost reduction has proved an enduring motivation. The study by Brewster et al. (2005) found that 37% of their sample of MNCs was pursuing an efficiency strategy, combining outsourcing with centralization and e-enablement. Similarly, data from an UNCTAD/Roland Berger Strategy Consultants study (cited in Hunter 2006) show that, in practice, the decisions by Fortune 500 companies to pursue another of the sourcing options – that of offshoring – are driven by (in order of importance): lower wage costs; reduction of other costs; improved service quality; focus on core competences; speeding up the process cycle; avoiding capacity constraints;

47

extending the scope of services; strengthening an existing affiliate; and access to technology and infrastructure.

The typical achievable cost savings through HRO are believed to be in the range of 20-25% (Golas 2005). Hunter (2006) estimates that a typical offshore deal from the UK to India generates cost savings of between 35-45% once offshore overheads (onsite contract management, schedule delays and rework and transition costs) have been accounted for. We caution that such figures need to be read with great care as the achievable cost savings are evidently dependent on a whole range of factors. Some of the most obvious variables are:

- *Previous HR transformation and current HR efficiency rate*: Efficiency savings are typically lower if a company has already established a shared service centre structure.
- *Complexity of HR processes and the extent of transformation and transition work required by vendor*: The more vendor resources need to be tied up during the transition and transformation stage to baseline and untangle 'as-is' HR processes, the more this will impact upon cost savings negatively.
- *Transition and transformation approach and degree of process specificity required by the client*: The more a client is willing to move towards the standardized 'best practice' processes of a vendor, the higher the opportunities for cost savings.
- *Type of processes to be outsourced*: The more transactional and standardized the requested HR processes the larger the possible cost savings.
- *HRO market maturity and degree of competitiveness*: In the past years many vendors in the multi-process HRO market have struggled to build a showcase base of clients. As a consequence, they were willing to guarantee significant cost savings to these clients. The more competitive the market for the requested processes, the bigger the positive impact on cost savings.
- *Cost base to be transferred*: The higher the transferred cost base to a vendor, the higher the possibilities for efficiency savings.
- *The delivery model*: There is a positive association between the degree to which the client is willing to accept an offshore delivery model and the impact on cost savings.
- *Employee transition*: The higher the number of staff needing to be transitioned from client to vendor, the lower the possible cost savings.

There are many hidden costs. Barthélemy and Quélin (2006) draw attention to the problem of escalating commitment. The governance and risk mitigation arrangements mentioned earlier (which themselves bear cost) are necessary because of the switching costs associated with a move to outsourcing and the extent to which the resources that underlie the activity contribute to competitive advantage. There are additional hidden costs associated with adapting the human assets (changes required in the skills and knowledge of employees to work effectively

48

in the new context, the customization required to business processes and so forth) involved in the delivery of services.

The strong focus of companies on cost savings as the main business driver of HRO is therefore intriguing. In addition to hidden costs, it is well known that the costs of the HR function are typically not much higher than 1% of the total operating costs of a company. Efficiency savings achieved through HRO are, therefore, unlikely to influence the overall performance of a company.

What really impacts upon shareholder value, however, are the assumptions that go with HRO in terms of service quality improvement, enhanced strategic focus of the retained HR function, increased alignment of the HR structure for possible merger and acquisition activities.

Improved service quality

Many HR functions that have not yet gone through a significant HR transformation are characterized by Golas (2005):

- excessive amounts of time management spent on transactional administrative issues
- little standardization and harmonization of processes across business units and geographies
- a high degree of exception cases resulting in management acting as 'firefighters'
- limited internal capability to manage change and transformation.

In presenting the arguments in the following sections, therefore, more sceptical observers would argue that the potential benefits presented should be seen as no more than propositions that remain to be tested and evidenced. This is undoubtedly true. More pragmatic observers would argue that strategy tends to follow action and the potential benefits presented will act as proxies for strategic logics and as benchmarks that could be used to evaluate inevitable actions in the area.

Unlike internal HR functions, outsourcing providers must prove themselves in the marketplace (Cook and Gildner 2006). In order to maintain their competitive position, vendors will strive for maximized process efficiencies and the application of best practices. Vendor specialization, company size and market position means that they are typically in a good position to attract HR talent, develop and maintain high professional standards. Indeed, 'best-in-class' vendor companies typically have sophisticated HR metrics systems in place, which they use with client companies. Given the dearth of HR metrics in the average client HR function, the availability of intelligent metrics can drastically improve the way an organization's retained HR organization is perceived by top management. This obviously assumes that a client organization has successfully gone through the appropriate design and implementation of an effective retained HR function that is capable of utilizing a vendor's HR metrics.

49

IT investment/access to technology

In many companies continued investment in HR technology has been a low priority. HR information systems (HRIS) are often in desperate need of upgrades or patching. HR functions are frequently highly fragmented and differentiated across geographies or business units. As a consequence, their HRIS consists of a patchwork of highly customized and incompatible systems with poor data integration qualities with existing enterprise resource planning (ERP) systems and poor analytical and reporting functionalities.

Any internal HR transformation is, therefore, typically linked to immense investments in HR technology. Often a new or updated ERP module is needed and/or investments in adequate employee self-service (ESS) and management self-service (MSS) portal technology and customer relationship management (CRM) systems. Furthermore, ongoing licensing, upgrade and maintenance costs need to be considered. Even after heavy investments, many companies are not using the implemented technology effectively. Experts suggest that most users take advantage of only 10% of what an application provides (Ravi et al. 2006).

Through an outsourced solution, clients can avoid ongoing IT investments. Furthermore, clients gain access to cutting-edge technology. For vendors, continuous investments in their HR technology is a prerequisite to keep up with competition and for many it is a source of competitive differentiation.

Improved process efficiencies and global process harmonization

Historically, many MNCs have structured their HR processes on a country-by-country or regional basis. The assumption was that HR is too idiosyncratic and country-specific to allow global harmonization. Today, MNCs increasingly try to harmonize at least their transactional HR processes (e.g. the administration of payroll, training, performance appraisals) globally. Yet, decades of decentralized HR management have still left redundancies in terms of HR delivery platforms, services and resources. Internal transformations towards global HR structures are therefore always likely to meet strong and continuing internal resistance.

HRO vendors are still in the 'proving' stage of being able to deliver seamless global services, but they are surely developing this capability rapidly (Martorelli 2006). For this reason we discuss international differences in the pursuit of HRO later in the chapter. At this point, however, suffice it to say that for many MNCs, HRO is therefore an option to gain access to consistent global practices that can be delivered via highly efficient platforms. The delivery platforms of vendors are already in place, speeding up the implementation of these processes. During the transition and transformation phase, vendors will share the burden of an intensive change management task and will help the company deal with internal resistance. Furthermore, vendors will control legal risks and ensure compliance of global processes with local/regional laws and regulations (e.g. on issues of data protection).

Strategic reorientation of HR

Increasingly companies want to restructure their HR function so that remaining internal staff are more focused on transformational processes and the delivery of strategic activities, rather than spending the majority of their time on transactional administration. The reasons for this lie in the expressed desire by many senior executives for HR to become more involved in transformational activities such as workforce strategic alignment, the strategic management of workforce costs, the creation of a human capital metrics system that incorporates not only efficiency measures (of the HR function) but also effectiveness and impact measures of HR activities on the workforce (see, for example, the work of authors such as Lawler, Levenson, Boudreau, Huselid and Becker).

Outsourcing transactional HR activities clearly allows companies to pursue this ambition. Yet, once transactional processes are outsourced, a strategic reorientation of HR is only possible if a company is willing to go through a dramatic change process in designing and implementing a world-class retained HR function.

We argue that MNCs need to build an HR business partner structure that is committed to dealing with HR issues impacting upon business units. Implementation of such a structure is hugely complex, even in a domestic setting, especially as in many companies the boundaries of this role are far from clearly defined and existing HR personnel often do not display an adequate set of competencies. Making this operate across national boundaries, where the role of business partners and line managers varies so much, raises its own research agenda.

Parallel to a business partner structure, for the continuous development of HR strategy, policies, processes and services, MNCs have been advised to develop a centres of excellence (CoE) structure. The traditional and evolutionary progression of MNCs has been discussed in the context of the trade-off between global integration and local responsiveness, but as MNCs change their organization design in response to the need to build more international capability, they establish dedicated balancing mechanisms and organizational forms to facilitate this – one of which is the centre of excellence. CoEs are organizational units that embody sets of capabilities that are explicitly recognized as an important source of value creation. They need strategic remits, such as the intention to leverage or disseminate these capabilities to other parts of the firm. While the leadership of a CoE might be vested in a physical location, the centre itself may be virtual, spread across networks of teams in different geographies (Sparrow et al. 2004).

CoEs involve further differentiating the retained HR services into those activities where additional benefits can be obtained if the capability can be leveraged internally. The development and effective use of CoEs therefore demands a clearly

51

defined knowledge management strategy, an understanding of the development stages of CoEs and the establishment of interfaces that structure the exchange of knowledge between the CoEs, business partners and business units as well as corporate HR (Sparrow 2006).

Additionally, companies will need to develop advanced management information (MI) and HR metrics systems. Vendor companies will be able to provide their clients with sophisticated HR metrics related to the outsourced transactional activities. The effectiveness of such metrics, however, is greatly diminished, unless they are combined with metrics generated within the retained function and unless they reach and can be utilised by their appropriate recipients in the business partner roles and the CoEs.

Improved business agility

The argument that HRO produces improved business agility rests on the assumption that a combination of outsourced, centralized and standardized transactional HR processes, combined with a restructured retained HR function and an effective HR metrics system, will greatly improve decision-making support within a company and will enhance control and impact upon measurement of HR activities. Furthermore, outsourced solutions can provide an effective platform for growth, business fluctuation, organizational change and merger and acquisition activities. It is HRO vendors who are in a far better position than an individual company to adjust flexibly to changing patterns in service demand. By operating on a 'one-to-many' service delivery platform, vendors are able to spread their resources flexibly across their clients, without a decrease in service quality.

CONSTRAINTS TO DEVELOPMENT

There are, however, some natural constraints to the pace of the sourcing and shoring options discussed in this chapter. Constraints to offshoring have recently been the focus of discussion in the literature. The demand and supply of appropriate talent is one of these constraints. The McKinsey Global Institute has analysed likely demand for offshore talent in service work within the automotive, financial services, software, pharmaceuticals and retailing sectors as well as the likely supply of offshore talent in 28 low-cost countries (Farrell et al. 2006). They estimate that 11% of service jobs around the world have the potential to be carried out remotely, although this varies across sectors, ranging from 49% in packaged software to 3% in retail. In practice only a small proportion of those jobs that could go offshore actually will – total offshore employment will grow from 1.5 million jobs in 2003 to 4.1 million by 2008 – only 1% of service jobs in developed economies. The main deterrents to larger movements are:

- company-specific considerations such as scale (current fragmentation of work makes it difficult to create sufficient critical mass of activity, and therefore insufficient scale of activity to justify the costs of offshoring)
- structure (large organizations have complex business processes that would require root-and-branch reorganization in order to globalize service delivery; international growth through mergers and acquisitions creates complex interactions and separating out those portions of an operation that could be performed offshore is very difficult)
- management attitudes (senior managers are wary of overseeing operations that are geographically remote and of travel and coordination costs and availability of talent).

SO HOW WILL THE HRO MARKET CONTINUE TO DEVELOP?

Given such constraints, clearly automation or organizational restructuring of existing activity may be a more attractive option than offshoring. Such a comment requires that we enter into a penultimate discussion. In order to identify relevant and sustainable research agendas, we need to consider how the market for sourcing and shoring options is developing. To do this, in this section we review the evidence on developments in the HRO market, by looking at the volume and scale of deals, international differences and the current developments and challenges.

Hesketh (2006) cited research by the Everest Research Group showing spending on HRO increasing from $75 million in 1998 to $1562 million by 2004. Golas (2005) estimates that the HRO market is worth approximately $3.6bn. Much higher estimates are also to be found. According to strategy consultants McKinsey, the potential global market for HR offshoring could be worth £27 billion by 2008, up from £0.6 billion in 2001. Despite their observations about constraints on growth, the amount of 'offshoring' is expected to have shown a rise by an average of 71% each year between 2001 and 2008 – twice the rate of most other business activities. Currently, the USA and UK together generate almost three-quarters of global offshoring activity. However, while legal and cultural differences are still considered to inhibit the transfer of more advisory roles, it has become feasible to move HR administration overseas. Prime candidates for HR 'offshoring' have included payroll, as well as pensions and benefits administration (see Table 3.1).

However, predictions about future growth have to be read very carefully. After much hype in recent years, growth in the HRO market actually slowed somewhat in 2006, although this was believed to be only a temporary slow down. The most

53

Table 3.1 HRO market volume

HRO categories	2005 estimated global market ($m)	2009 estimated global market ($m)	Estimated CAGR (%)
Multi-process HRO	3,600	7,400	20
Payroll administration	8,700	9,800	3
Benefits administration	10,600	15,400	10
Recruiting and staffing	26,100	38,000	10
Workforce development	24,100	29,400	5
Mobility services	10,200	13,300	7
Total	83,300	113,300	8

Source: adapted from Golas (2005)

positive estimates by research institutes claim that over the next 3–5 years, the total HRO market will grow by a compound annual growth rate (CAGR) of between 8 and 10% (Golas 2005; Cook and Gildner 2006). However, within this, 'multi-process HRO' will show a higher CAGR of 10–20% (Rowan 2006).

Significant progress in globalizing HR service delivery has been made through the interrelated developments of sourcing, technology and process streamlining. We have outlined the different sourcing options in the introduction, but in addition there have been developments in technology and in the nature of process streamlining. Arrangements have evolved rapidly and become more complex. Many current multi-process HRO contracts developed out of more traditional single process outsourcing deals for payroll and benefits administration (Martorelli 2006). Although CAGRs for these market segments are estimated to be significantly lower than for multi-process HRO, currently these single-process HRO market segments still outweigh the multi-process HRO market. Payroll administration is estimated to have a global market volume of $9.8bn, whereas benefits administration is believed to represent $15.4bn. When all the single process service areas are included, the global HRO market is estimated to have reached a volume of more than $80bn in 2005 and is expected to rise to well over $100bn by 2009/10 (Golas 2005; Cook and Gildner 2006).

Not only is service provision of HRO moving from single to multi-process, it is changing from the mere provision of bureau, processing and managed services in the more traditional process areas, towards the provision of multiple, fully outsourced end-to-end processes. The market for services has now become quite differentiated.

With the service offerings of vendors evolving, an increasing number of companies are evaluating the feasibility of outsourcing either parts of, or entire end-to-end processes. These developments have been linked in particular to three HR processes: recruitment, training and development, and talent management (Hesketh 2006; Ravi et al. 2006) with a particularly strong and rapidly growing single-process HRO segment in this regard being recruitment and staffing. Golas (2005) estimates the total market for this segment – recruitment process

$USm

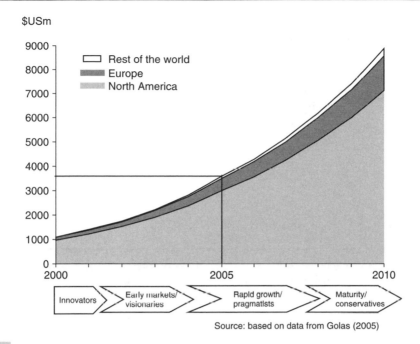

Source: based on data from Golas (2005)

Figure 3.1 *Multi-process HRO market growth.*

outsourcing (RPO) – to have a volume of $26bn with significant growth potential. Although few vendors in the RPO sector are capable of providing a complete end-to-end recruitment and staffing solution (certainly not without entering into other partnerships), they are quickly building their technological and service capabilities and are active in every stage of the recruitment process, i.e. strategic consulting, sourcing, screening, onboarding and benchmarking and surveying (Teng 2006a)(see Figure 3.1).

Text box 3.2
Characteristics of the multi-process HRO industry

The industry can now be characterized by two developments:

1   After a relative lull in so-called 'mega-deals' (i.e. deals exceeding total contract value of $1bn) in this period, recently there has been an increase in such deals, involving firms such as DuPont, Unilever and CVS (Rowan 2006). For example, the Unilever contract signed in June 2006 was the largest multi-process HRO contract to date, on the basis of total contract value, number of employees served and geographic scope. The Unilever contract also suggests that there is a new

---

55

> pattern of activity developing. A number of companies are now follow-
> ing their innovator competitors (in the case of Unilever, this is Proctor &
> Gamble) in entering multi-process HRO contracts.
>
> 2 In 2005 and 2006 the industry also saw a significant increase in the activ-
>   ity in the multi-process HRO mid-market, serving companies outside
>   the Global & Fortune 500 and FTSE 100 MNC categories (Mortland
>   2006). Evidence for this second development can be seen in recent
>   vendor moves. For example, Accenture acquired Savista (a provider of
>   HR and payroll services to the small and mid-market), Aon aligned with
>   Ultimate Software for mid-market platform delivery. In 2005 Gevity,
>   originally focusing on small businesses, announced a mid-market initia-
>   tive moving upmarket (Ravi et al. 2006; Rowan 2006).

What does this analysis of the HRO market show us? There was an initial 'innovator' phase, seen, for example, in the early deals by BP and Bank of America with Exult
in 1999/2000, followed by the recent 'early market phase', in which firms have
moved down the learning curve. In this early market phase, some firms that signed
HRO deals in the innovator phase re-evaluated their contracts and in some cases
recontracted (this happened at firms such as Bank of America and BASF). However,
the multi-process HRO industry has now entered a new phase of rapid growth.

ARE THERE INTERNATIONAL DIFFERENCES IN THE HRO MARKET?

The practitioner literature on market differentiation and volume increasingly suggests then that the world of outsourcing is at an important juncture. The outsourcing
penetration in the MNC market is believed to be about 4% (Teng 2006b).
However, in pointing to evidence that many outsourcing deals collapse before the
contract ends, PricewaterhouseCoopers (2007) highlight contrasting prognoses
whereby:

> Some industry analysts and media pundits ... translate the findings into painful
> trade-offs: cost savings vs. growth, speed vs. quality, and organizational cohe-
> sion vs. knowledge and innovation. Others suggest outsourcing is in a death
> spiral ... a decline fuelled by structural risks, questionable cost savings, and
> multiple complexities while others point to lucrative outsourcing deals,
> impressive benefits and uncapped growth projections and level[s] of strategic
> and operational flexibility unattainable through other means.
>
> (PricewaterhouseCoopers 2007: 2)

Their survey of 226 customers and 66 service providers across nine countries confirmed the growing complexity of options, maturing strategies and innovative partnering. However, 'outsourcing is now as diverse as business itself, differing by country, sector, and company strategy' (p. 3).

In this section, we consider the nature of international differences in HRO by asking (and briefly addressing) five questions:

1 Is there geographical differentiation in HRO expenditure and market volume?
2 Are there different preferences for insourcing versus outsourcing across geographies?
3 What factors are likely to determine international differences in adoption?
4 Are there cultural differences in service perception (and so different pull factors with regard to use of services)?
5 What is the institutional context that surrounds the attractiveness of sourcing and shoring options?

The picture in relation to international differences in the attractiveness of HRO remains a little confused, depending on whether one examines practice at the level of organizations or the size of the market for services. From the former perspective, Mahoney and Brewster (2002) found that approximately one-quarter of European organizations involved in the 1999 Cranet survey used external suppliers for multiple services (three or more HR processes). While the use of suppliers was increasing significantly, 55% of organizations had not changed their use of suppliers in the 3 years prior to 1999. The trend in outsourcing was clearly up but was not yet fundamentally changing the basis on the way in which the HR function was organized. There were important country variations in the outsourcing of HR even though overall the use of outsourcing is widespread across Europe. The results showed that for a majority of countries in Europe, more than 60% of organizations outsourced. Countries outsourcing the most included Sweden, the Czech Republic, Poland and the Netherlands (92%, 86%, 78% and 77% respectively) and countries outsourcing the least included Turkey, Greece and Italy (32%, 46% and 49% respectively). The United Kingdom was just above the average, with 71% of organizations outsourcing. There was also wide variation in the resource levels and cost structures of HR functions throughout Europe and the research evidence did not support the assumption that organizations with a low HR staff to employee ratio used suppliers more or that by using suppliers the headcount in the HR department was lower.

When market volume data are analysed, then there are clear international differences in the market for HRO. There is a geographically differentiated HRO market that reflects the pattern seen in the broader business services market. North America clearly dominates. In the multi-process HRO segment,

57

North America is estimated to represent a market volume of $3bn. In contrast, Europe and the rest of the world have significantly lower market volumes with $500m and $80m respectively. By the same token, growth expectations in Europe and the rest of the world are higher than in North America with 23% and 32% annual respective growth (see Table 3.2).

Within Europe the majority of HRO spending goes to single-process payroll outsourcing (Takahashi 2006) and the total market value in Europe, inclusive of all single and multi-process HRO, is estimated to be approximately $4.8bn. The UK is clearly the most established European HRO market, accounting for approximately 40% of Europe's HRO spending. Germany and France account for approximately 16% and 14% of HRO spending, respectively (Takahashi 2006). The relatively lower HRO market penetration in these two core EU economies has been linked to stronger trade union influence and the legislative complexities associated with HR (Golas 2005). The majority of the remaining European HRO spend is distributed across the Netherlands, Italy and the four Nordic countries. Forrester predicts rapid future growth in the Baltic and Eastern European countries (Takahashi 2006). Indeed, 2006 witnessed an increasingly buoyant European multi-process HRO market, evidenced by the signing of a number of significant deals in firms such as Unilever, BBC, Nestlé, Lloyds and Centrica (McEwen 2006).

However, there is still evidence to suggest that continental European firms continue to favour captive (insourcing) arrangements rather than pure outsourcing scenarios (Golas 2005). Hesketh (2006) argues that HR directors in Europe may see an insourced shared services route as the best stepping stone to future HRO. His research across 28 organizations, such as Crédit Suisse, Deutsche Bank, Royal Bank of Scotland, IBM, Shell and Royal Mail Group showed increased outsourcing of higher value HR processes such as recruitment, use of shared service models and evolution of e-HR activities.

Budhwar and Cooke (2008) concur with this. The complexity of HR operations still makes single-process outsourcing an attractive option and many of the solutions

Table 3.2 Multi-process HRO market by geographies

Region	2005 estimated market size ($m)	2009 estimated market size ($m)	Estimated GAGR (%)
North America	3,000	6,000	19
USA	2,500	4,900	18
Canada	500	1,100	22
Europe	500	1,150	23
UK	220	410	17
Continental Europe	280	750	28
Rest of the World	80	250	32
Total	3,600	7,400	20

Source: adapted from Golas (2005)

that have been adopted are not as radical as some of the practitioner literature suggests. They also draw attention to the persistence of wide international differences in the pursuit of HRO. Asian organizations are not adopting outsourcing to the same extent as found in US and European organizations. They link the current (limited) use of outsourcing by indigenous MNCs or small firms to the size of domestic businesses, the sophistication of HR functions, the extent to which there is a developed local HR outsourcing market, cultural norms and other institutional factors. They examined the specific challenges associated with the offshoring of HR work to India and China, noting that currently the motivation to offshore to each is different. They argue that, unlike IT outsourcing and offshoring, the same decisions in relation to HR work tend to be tied far more closely to the internationalization strategy of the firm and driven by motivations to reduce levels of uncertainty and to gain insight into local market conditions.

IHRM functions face complex decisions and the outcome is clearly likely to vary across national ownership. In a global context, local country managers argue that much of the corporate HR armoury requires deep tacit understanding of the national culture and therefore should not be a candidate either for operation through shared services or indeed for any subsequent outsourcing. Organizations must make sensible assessments of this tacit knowledge constraint.

It is also likely that other national factors will influence the effectiveness that might be achieved in outsourcing (and associated automation) of HR activity. Although not directly looking at HR outsourcing, there is some work that should be of interest to HR researchers. It comes from the international and services marketing literatures and has been carried out looking at international differences in service perceptions. This draws attention to the role of ethics in explaining cultural differences in service perception and could be used to explore the implications of offshore outsourcing for consumer (employee) behaviour and the way in which perceptions, attitudes and behaviours to the new organizational forms may differ internationally: 'Within e-business environment, while there is evidence that the processes of engineering and implementation of … systems are being successfully exported … as a consequence of globalization, the adoption of western social and ethical values … is another matter' (Ruzic 2006: 99).

The work of Ruzic (2006) shows that employee engagement with and usage of e-enabled services is influenced by a series of ethical judgements made about the provision of such services, namely: perceived personal benefit; social benefit; societal consequences; level of benevolence (help to those in need); paternalism (assistance to others to pursue their best interests when they cannot do it themselves); honesty (lack of deceit); lawfulness; autonomy (freedom over action); justice (due process); and rights (to information, privacy and free expression). It would be interesting to see if such factors have any utility in explaining international differences in the attractiveness (or not) of e-enabled HR services that are associated

59

with the organizational solutions that accompany outsourcing (such as shared service centres, centres of excellence and self-service intranets).

Finally, there are also very real problems faced in the calculation of the cost benefit of these decisions, and the cost benefit varies across countries in subtle ways. For example, Pyndt and Pedersen (2006) found that while the direct benefits of offshoring may be easy to understand (and are derived from savings in labour costs, foreign suppliers' import of products or services and repatriation of profits), the indirect benefits of offshoring (which include the value of re-employing the employees in the home country affected by the offshoring) make the calculation of true costs and benefits much more difficult. They point out that in principle, capital savings associated with offshoring can be reinvested in higher value jobs. Achieving these benefits is dependent on the home country's ability to train, upgrade and re-employ the home workers. It immediately becomes clear that the institutional context that surrounds the employment relationship both in the country from which work is outsourced and the new location determines the attractiveness (or not) of offshoring. In Denmark the return on every unit of currency invested in offshoring was 1.15, but in Germany the equivalent return was only 0.8. In part, this figure also reflects the fact that German firms tend to offshore to East European countries, which have higher labour costs.

The pursuit of these processes across countries is a relatively under-theorized one, although recent advances in institutional theory have focused on the causes and nature of the diversity in organizational practices and differing degrees of receptiveness to new technologies (Streeck and Thelen 2005).

WHAT ARE THE FUTURE DEVELOPMENTS AND CHALLENGES?

Having noted the challenges of executing sourcing and shoring strategies on a global scale, we return to a generic discussion of the future developments and challenges for HR functions. It is clear there are performance issues surrounding HRO deals and continuing debates over the shape of HR functions and the focus of HRO measurement and evaluation. In order to address these latter concerns, attention should be focused on five issues:

1 efficiency focus in the delivery of HR services
2 developments in the HRO vendor landscape
3 the need for improved understanding of the outsourcing process
4 the need to see HRO as part of multifunctional outsourcing arrangements
5 understanding the issues involved in the management of multiple vendor relationships.

 60

Continued attention to the first element – that of efficiency – will result because of the idiosyncratic nature of many HR processes and frequent resistance by client companies to offshoring (this resistance applies particularly to voice-related HR processes). As a consequence the HRO business model cannot take full advantage of the cost benefits of offshore labour arbitrage. The real test for HRO providers is their ability to create the necessary economics of scale without jeopardizing service quality (Ravi et al. 2006). Providers are currently relying on streamlining service delivery and processes to create cost savings. But in contrast to experience in finance and accounting outsourcing, where delivery can be judged on a standardized basis, for HR services the delivery challenge is highly complex. Many HRO providers are struggling to deliver immediate cost savings as well as promised service quality improvements (Fersht 2006). Moreover, despite the fact that vendors have built impressive delivery centres and capabilities spanning the globe, their ability to truly optimize HR processes on a global scale remains to be proven (Martorelli 2006).

One way of predicting future developments in HRO, therefore, is to consider a second element. How will vendor HRO strategies develop in response to these challenges? After all, it is their survival that is most at stake. An analysis of their strategies is informative. They have a vital interest in focusing on those HR processes that can be easily adapted to an outsourced model and that eventually allow them to reduce costs through a 'one-to-many' service delivery platform. To create the necessary economies of scale:

- to reduce costs, they will focus on clients who have large transferable cost bases, by offering improved and increased offshore capabilities (including their capabilities for voice-related processes)
- to improve their multishore delivery arrangements, vendors will need to combine on- , near- and offshore delivery in the most cost-efficient way
- to increase acceptance among future clients for offshore delivery, they will develop their communication strategies.

Apart from the classic offshore locations in India, new locations are continuously developing, for example, in Mexico and Jamaica in the Americas or Philippines and Malaysia in Southeast Asia. However, a geographically differentiated HRO market segment should be expected to continue. The country-specific nature of HR means that geographies vary with regard to their client requirements and their current HRO penetration. Vendors currently have, and will continue to develop, differentiated strategies serving particular geographic regions. For example, providers like Fidelity and Hewitt have appealed to US-based clientele with their strong payroll and benefits solution focus (Martorelli 2006; Rowan 2006), providing continued opportunities for new suppliers to enter the market, with, for example, new providers developing out of the current Indian offshore providers.

In contrast, given that a crucial requirement for many MNCs is the need to optimize and harmonize their processes on a global scale (Sparrow et al. 2004), there is a strong demand for pan-regional and global capabilities (payroll is one example of this). Vendors in the multi-process space (such as Accenture, ACS, Convergys, IBM, Hewitt) as well as those in the single-process market (such as ADP and Arinso for international payroll) have responded by crafting HRO strategies that appeal to this MNC market.

A third element is the need to improve understanding of the outsourcing process. HRO clients now understand that many outsourcing agreements have run into difficulties because of lack of upfront investment in the development of a valid business case. HRO clients increasingly understand that the initial baselining of processes and costs and the development of a solid business case is an absolute prerequisite to track future benefits and to monitor an outsourcing arrangement with a vendor. In future, HRO clients will become more advanced in the development of service-level agreements, price and performance mechanisms and the benefits realization process. Understanding and articulating these data and mechanisms on a global scale represents a significant challenge for researchers and practitioners alike.

A fourth element concerns the need to view these processes across functions. As observed by Sparrow et al. (2004), the pursuit of global strategies is leading to increasing convergence of workstreams across HR, IT, marketing and supply chain functions. As business process outsourcing becomes increasingly established in multiple business functions, clients will start integrating HRO as part of what are called 'multi-tower arrangements', i.e. arrangements that also include F&A and IT. As a result, companies will look for ways to capitalize on the synergies of cross-functional outsourcing contracts.

A fifth and final element is that with an increase in outsourcing activity, the need to manage multiple vendors (either as part of a multi-tower deal or existing vendor relationships) will become an increasingly complex task for organizations. This will further increase pressure for converged organizational capabilities (and structures) that sit across HR, IT and F&A functions inside globalizing firms.

CONCLUSION

A number of conclusions with regard to HR functions should be drawn from the analysis of contemporary developments in sourcing and shoring options in this chapter. Within IHRM functions there will be some immediate tactical and reactive challenges. For example, Budhwar and Cooke (2008) have drawn attention to some specific challenges created for corporate IHRM functions, including issues such as problems with the recruitment and retention of local talent, differences in career advancement behaviour, potential for hidden discrimination, a heightened importance of boundary spanning and coordination roles and the fragmentation of HR careers.

In terms of more strategic considerations, HR functions will have to determine whether the desire (of the organization or their internal stakeholders) to outsource an HR activity is driven by its low contribution to core competencies, is influenced by the external environment or reflects poor management of the activity. They will therefore need to demonstrate that performance is more important than low HR department headcounts or lower costs. They will have to consider the tradeoff between different ways in which they may be evaluated. Many of these tradeoffs will be very political in nature. For example, might the need to retain and 'pamper' world-class talented employees through personalized service and with error-free administration outweigh potential cost savings of offshoring? As researchers, how would we help demonstrate the consequences of such tradeoffs?

They will need to avoid excessive deskilling and reliance on single vendors. This means that they will need to assess what the impact might be of learning accruing to the vendor and not to themselves. In turn, this will require that they must decide how much control and organizational learning is needed for various HR activities and whether such control can be retained with outsourcing.

HR functions will therefore have to treat vendor selection with the same due diligence exercised during a planned acquisition. Managing vendor relationships will be as important as joint venture relationships, requiring the development of long-term relationships where continuity of service, learning of corporate culture and development of employee–organization fit will be critical. Such (global) assessments are usual for actuarial or search firms, but will likely be extended to more outsourced activities.

These are all implications for the management of those activities that may be handled through different sourcing and shoring options. But, perhaps the most important question that still needs to be understood in the field of HRO is what is the best way to organize the (surviving) HR operations? We believe that there is an important research agenda around the current roles for international HR professionals in the development of centres of excellence (CoE) and structures for the retained HR business. HR functions need to understand what CoEs can be created within their own activities and how they can build networks of HR experts within these areas of competence on a global basis (Sparrow et al. 2004).

The IHR function has to understand how to link developments in new forms of international working (see Chapter 11) and the international mobility of staff in relation to either geographically remote CoEs or globally insourced service operations. They need to reconfigure their core competencies on a global scale by adjusting talent management strategies. They need the best IHR strategies to coordinate and control such activities. We would endorse the following research questions as useful avenues for research (Sparrow 2006; Brewster and Sparrow 2008):

- What activities, processes and capabilities might constitute a CoE and how should such units be mandated?
- What has to happen in terms of the 'capability-building investments' that are needed? Is it possible to specify capabilities such as decision-making autonomy, requisite levels of connectivity to other sources of competence inside the organization, leadership and processes of knowledge management?
- What are the indicators of success and under what contingencies?
- To what extent do institutional factors preclude or support long-term survival and contribution of CoEs and retained HR structures?

KEY LEARNING POINTS

- Two strategies are at play, involving options of both sourcing and shoring of HR services.
- Different theoretical perspectives tend to have been used to analyse each option but this theory tends not to align with the pragmatic judgements made by strategic actors.
- A complex range of variables can be identified that need to be controlled for when analysing the effective execution of sourcing and shoring strategies.
- Such strategies cannot be analysed without understanding parallel developments in the strategic re-orientation of the HR function.
- There are continued and substantial international differences in the pursuit and preference for HRO.
- Despite the fact that HRO vendors are building impressive delivery centres and capabilities spanning the globe, their ability to truly optimize HR processes on a global scale remains to be proven.
- However, the service offerings of vendors are evolving rapidly to address such concerns.

REFERENCES

Abramovsky, L., Griffith, R. and Sako, M. (2006) *Offshoring Myth and Reality: What the Global Trade in Business Services Means for the UK*, London: Advanced Institute of Management.

Barthélemy, J. and Quélin, B.V. (2006) 'Complexity of outsourcing contracts and ex post transaction costs: an empirical investigation', *Journal of Management Studies* 43, 8: 1775–1797.

Brewster, C. and Sparrow, P.R. (2008) 'Les nouveaux roles et les defis de la GRHI', in C. Barmeyer and M-F. Waxin (eds) *Gestation des Resources Humaines Internationales*, Paris: Les Editions de Liaisons.

Brewster, C., Sparrow, P.R. and Harris, H. (2005) 'Towards a new model of globalizing HRM', *International Journal of Human Resource Management* 16, 6: 949–970.

Budhwar, P. and Cooke, F.L. (2008) 'HR offshoring and outsourcing: research issues for IHRM', in P.R. Sparrow (ed.) *Handbook of International HR Research: Integrating People, Process and Context*, Oxford: Blackwell.

Chakrabarty, S. (2006) 'Making sense of the sourcing and shoring maze: various outsourcing and offshoring alternatives', in H.S. Kehal and V.A. Singh (eds) *Outsourcing and Offshoring in the 21st Century: A Socio-economic Perspective*, London: Idea Group.

CIPD (2005a) *HR Outsourcing: The Key Decision*, London: Chartered Institute of Personnel and Development.

CIPD (2005b) *People Management and Technology: Progress and Potential. Survey Report*, London: Chartered Institute of Personnel and Development.

Cook, M.F. and Gildner, S.B. (2006) *Outsourcing Human Resources Functions*, 2nd edn., Alexandria: SHRM.

De Vita, G. and Wang, C.L. (2006) 'Development of outsourcing theory and practice: a taxonomy of outsourcing generations', in H.S. Kehal and V.P. Singh (eds) *Outsourcing and Offshoring in the 21st Century: A Socio-economic Perspective*, London: Idea Group.

Espino-Rodríquez, T.F. and Padrón-Robaina, V. (2006) 'A review of outsourcing from the resource-based view of the firm', *International Journal of Management Reviews* 8, 1: 49–70.

Farrell, D., Laboissiére, M.A. and Rosenfeld, J. (2006) 'Sizing the emerging global labor market: rational behavior from both companies and countries can help it work more efficiently', *Academy of Management Perspectives* 20, 4: 6–12.

Fersht, P. (2006) *The Great Outsourcing Divide: Where HRO has been Challenged FAO is Blossoming*, Everest Research Institute.

Gilley, K. and Rasheed, A. (2000) 'Making more by doing less: an analysis of outsourcing and its effects on firm performance', *Journal of Management* 26: 763–790.

Golas, S.W. (2005) *Multiprocess HR Outsourcing Market Analysis*, London: Nelson Hall.

Greer, C.R., Youngblood, S.A. and Gray, D.A. (1999) 'Human resource management outsourcing: the make or buy decision', *Academy of Management Executive* 13, 3: 85–96.

Harrison, A.F. and McMillan, M.S. (2006) 'Dispelling some myths about offshoring', *Academy of Management Perspectives* 20, 4: 6–22.

Hesketh, A. (2006) *Outsourcing the HR Function: Possibilities and Pitfall*, London: Corporate Research Forum.

Hunter, I. (2006) *The Indian Offshore Advantage: How Offshoring is Changing the Face of HR*, Aldershot: Gower.

Kenney, M. and Florida, R. (eds) (2004) *Locating Global Advantage: Industry Dynamics in the International Economy*, Stanford, CA: Stanford University Press.

Lever, S. (1997) 'An analysis of managerial motivations behind outsourcing practices in human resources', *Human Resource Planning* 20, 2: 37–47.

65

Mahoney, C. and Brewster, C. (2002) 'Outsourcing the HR function in Europe', *Journal of Professional HRM* 27: 23–28.

Martorelli, W. (2006) *The Forrester Wave: HR BPO Providers, Q1 2006*, Forrester.

McEwen, N. (2006) 'With more and more deals signed, HRO growth is accelerating', *HRO Europe* 4, 2: October.

Mortland, J. (2006) 'The mid-market accelerates', *HRO Today* 5, 9: November.

PricewaterhouseCoopers (2007) *Outsourcing Comes of Age: The Rise of Collaborative Partnering*, London: PwC.

Pyndt, J. and Pedersen, T. (2006) *Managing Global Offshoring Strategies: A Case Approach*, Copenhagen: Copenhagen Business School Press.

Ravi, R., McStravick, P., Bingham, B.J., Rowan, L. and Loynd, S. (2006) *Worldwide and US Business Process Outsourcing 2006–2010 Forecast: Market Opportunity by Horizontal Business Process*, London: IDC.

Rowan, L. (2006) *Worldwide and US HR BPO 2006 Vendor Analysis: The Answer is in the Margin*, London: IDC.

Ruzic, F. (2006) 'New ethics for e-business offshore outsourcing', in H.S. Kehal and V.A. Singh (eds) *Outsourcing and Offshoring in the 21st Century: A Socio-economic Perspective*, London: Idea Group.

Sparrow, P.R. (2006) 'Knowledge management in global organizations', in G. Stahl and I. Björkman (eds) *Handbook of Research into International HRM*, London: Edward Elgar.

Sparrow, P.R., Brewster, C. and Harris, H. (2004) *Globalizing Human Resource Management*, London: Routledge.

Streeck, W. and Thelen, K. (eds) (2005) *Beyond Continuity: Institutional Change in Advanced Political Economies*, Oxford: Oxford University Press.

Takahashi, S. (2006) *European HR BPO Spending Forecast: 2006 To 2011*, Forrester.

Teng, A. (2006a) 'Defining RPO: wading through the hype', *HRO Today* 5, 10: December.

Teng, A. (2006b) 'The year of the mid-market HRO?', *HRO Today*, July/August.

Chapter 4

Transfer of strategic HR know-how in MNCs

Mechanisms, barriers and initiatives

Jaime Bonache and Michael Dickmann

CHAPTER OBJECTIVES

By the end of this chapter, readers will have:

- an understanding of the strategic value of knowledge creation and transfer in MNCs
- an appreciation of the different direction of HR knowledge flows within international organizations, including head office to subsidiaries, subsidiaries to head office and inter-subsidiary flows
- a sensitivity to different strategic roles of subsidiaries related to the degree to which they are involved in creating new and transferring existing HR know-how
- identified challenges and key HR mechanisms for the transfer of HR know-how, distinguishing between bureaucratic, social and personal forms
- explored possible HR initiatives to overcome barriers to efficient HR knowledge management

INTRODUCTION

Knowledge has become the most important asset in economic life. Unlike physical assets, which traditionally have been considered the basis of competitive advantage, knowledge assets are the competitive difference for today's organizations (Miller and Shamsie 1996). A growing number of executives and management theorists have proclaimed in recent years that knowledge management now constitutes the key source of competitive advantage for organizations.

The expression 'knowledge management', however, is usually loosely defined in the literature. There are at least three different aspects of the topic (Sparrow 2006). First, the generation of new knowledge is captured in the concept of knowledge acquisition and creation. Second, organizations need to 'take stock' of their knowledge and understand their knowledge assets and where knowledge resides. This is often depicted as knowledge capture and storage. Finally, it is also possible to discuss the role of knowledge diffusion and transfer: the capacity a firm possesses to distribute knowledge flows among different groups and units of its international network of activities. This chapter will focus especially on knowledge diffusion and transfer.

THE STRATEGIC VALUE OF KNOWLEDGE TRANSFER IN MULTINATIONAL CORPORATIONS (MNCS)

The knowledge to be diffused and transferred refers to that which enables the firm to add value to the incoming factors of production. In fact, knowledge is no more than a recipe that specifies how activities can be carried out (Gupta and Govindarajan 1991; Kogut and Zander 1993). It may refer to input processes (e.g. purchasing skills), throughput processes (e.g. product designs, process engineering, technological and organizational details) or output processes (e.g. marketing know-how, merchandising). Thus understood, knowledge differs from information, which is simply a statement of facts (i.e. external market data about key customers, competitors or suppliers). Our interest lies in HR management so that we conceive knowledge as HR know-how, in other words as a particular way of conducting the HR function within the organization.

The strategic value of knowledge (and, hence, of HR know-how) is highlighted and explained in the resource-based view of the firm (Wernerfelt 1984; Barney 1991; Peteraf 1993; Grant 1996; Argote and Ingram 2000). This view analyses the conditions under which firms can achieve positions of competitive advantage. According to this view, competitive advantage can occur only in situations of firm resource heterogeneity (resources are unevenly distributed and deployed across firms) and firm resource immobility (they cannot be transferred easily from one firm to another). A sustainable competitive advantage is achieved when firms implement a value-creating strategy that is grounded in resources that are valuable, rare, imperfectly imitable and non-substitutable (Barney 1991).

Resources encompass all input factors that are owned or controlled by the firm and enter into the production of goods and services to satisfy human needs (Amit and Schoemaker 1993; Lado and Wilson 1994). They can be both tangible (financial and physical resources) and intangible (technology, know-how, reputation, organizational culture, human resources). It is increasingly recognized that intangible resources are more important to the firm both in value and as a basis for competitive advantage and that knowledge is the most strategically important intangible resource (Grant 1996). Knowledge is the resource that potentially best satisfies the characteristics that are most important in establishing a competitive advantage over rivals (i.e. to be valuable, rare, imperfectly imitable and non-substitutable). Examples of this strategic knowledge will vary, depending on what a particular firm considers its sources of competitive advantage to be (Kostova 1999). Focusing on HRM, for one firm this knowledge might be the way it attracts, retains and motivates its employees to foster innovation and creativity, whereas for another this might be the incentive system for its workforce.

Strategic knowledge can be a key asset for a multinational corporation's expansion. Some HR know-how that provides the company with a competitive advantage in the firm's home country may also be useful in other countries, thus providing the company with an opportunity to derive additional rents in other markets. In addition to opportunities to diffuse and transfer existing knowledge, internationalization also provides learning opportunities through exposure of the company to new cultures, ideas, experiences, etc., which can be used to create new expertise that complements and leverages its current knowledge. Hence, in the resource-based view, the simultaneous efforts to earn income from the diffusion and transfer of knowledge (and other tangible resources) and to generate and create new knowledge to produce future income define the two basic dimensions of multinational expansion (Tallman and Fladmoe-Lindquist 1994).

DIRECTION OF HR KNOW-HOW TRANSFER

During this exploitation and accumulation of HR know-how, not all subsidiaries perform the same function. On the contrary, the literature on corporate internationalization has traditionally pointed out that there is internal differentiation among subsidiaries making up an MNC (Bartlett and Ghoshal 1987; Ghoshal and Nohria 1989; Gupta and Govindarajan 1991; Martinez and Jarillo 1991; Roth and Morrison 1992; Dickmann and Müller-Camen 2006). Thus, for example, Gupta and Govindarajan (1991) have shown that reciprocal knowledge flows are dominant in MNCs indicating that it is important to look at the direction of IHRM knowledge flows.

Based on the extent (low versus high) to which knowledge is created or transferred (i.e. the aforementioned two dimensions of internationalization) into a given subsidiary, we can classify them into four categories: implementer, autonomous unit, learning unit and globally integrated unit (see Figure 4.1).

Implementer subsidiaries apply the HR know-how developed in the headquarters or other units of the organization to a specific geographic area. For example, the international strategy of North American auditing firms was based on exporting their career development management systems and other related HR initiatives to

69

	Transfer of existing HR know-how into the unit	
	High	Low
Creation of new HR know-how for other units — Low	Implementer	Autonomous unit
Creation of new HR know-how for other units — High	Globally integrated unit	Learning unit

Source: adapted from Bonache and Fernandez (1997)

Figure 4.1 *Strategic roles of subsidiaries.*

other countries. This HR know-how was not confined to its place of origin but was also effective across countries, thus providing the opportunity for these firms of developing strategic HR know-how in one location and exploiting it in others.

Autonomous units are much less dependent on the human and organizational resources existing in the rest of the company's international network. In this case, internationalization is based more on the transfer of products or capital than on intangible assets (Gupta and Govindarajan 1991). The reason for this is that their environment is considered to be so idiosyncratic that the subsidiary has to develop expertise internally. This developed knowledge cannot then be transferred to other subsidiaries. Examples of this type of unit would be the Cuban subsidiaries of many multinational firms. The incentive system they develop for the local workforce is completely different from the one they develop in the country of origin.

The *learning unit* acquires and develops new resources that may later be exported to other parts of the organization. An example of this type of unit is the US branch of Maphre, a Spanish insurance company. The reason for its location in the USA is the headquarters' interest in learning from the most competitive markets in order to transfer this knowledge to other units of the organization (including Spain). The Japanese subsidiary of IBM would also fall into this category. Its role is not so much to play a leading position in the local market as to be within a highly competitive environment in order to create new knowledge.

The *globally integrated unit*, finally, develops new expertise but also uses the know-how generated in other subsidiaries or in the headquarters. For example, the electronic product units of Ford Motor Company belong to this category. They are high-tech subsidiaries belonging to the same corporate division and they manufacture car audio systems, airbags, speedometers and other sorts of electronic auto component. These components are used as inputs for other corporate-owned regional auto assembly plants. The company designs different HR practices (e.g. idea suggestion systems) by assuming that ideas and expertise can come from any of these units, not only from headquarters (see Bonache 2000).

70

CHALLENGES AND MECHANISMS FOR THE TRANSFER OF HR KNOW-HOW

It has been argued that, at least in three types of subsidiary of multinational companies (i.e. learning units, globally integrated units and implementer units), there might be an internal transfer of HR know-how. Following Szulanski (1996), this transfer entails a replication of an internal way of conducting a HR function (or a particular practice) that is performed in a superior way in some part of the organization (the source unit) and is to be implemented in another unit (the recipient unit). As argued, these internal transfers are not confined to those from headquarters to foreign subsidiaries, but can occur in various directions within the MNC.

The transfer of HR knowledge has an obvious implication for the way people are managed: when an HR practice (e.g. a selection, training, incentive practice, or the whole HR function) is transferred across the units of a multinational corporation, this practice (or set of practices) becomes standardized (i.e. people will be managed in a similar fashion with respect to this practice). There are several reasons for the standardization of HR policies (Bonache 2000). The first of these reasons concerns the extent to which an MNC's headquarters links a particular HR practice to the firm's attaining competitive advantage. By way of example, take Beechler and Yang's (1994) study of the transfer of Japanese HR practices to industrial subsidiaries in North America. These researchers affirmed that the fundamental source of competitive advantage of firms in Japan was their capability to obtain first-rate products and zero defects and that certain HR practices, such as job flexibility, intensive on-the-job training, teamwork and cooperative relations between management and employees, were essential in achieving this. As a result, work in the North American subsidiaries of these firms was organized according to these practices. In contrast, other HR practices of a more peripheral nature, such as the use of uniforms or of the same restaurant for all the organization's members, were abandoned in some of the subsidiaries.

A second reason for standardizing HR practices concerns high levels of interdependence between various MNC units. The greater the subsidiary's dependence on the resources and capabilities of the headquarters or of other units (e.g. to supply technology, raw materials, production components or management practices), the more influence the headquarters will be able to have over its practices (Rosenzweig and Singh 1991; Rosenzweig and Nohria 1994; Rosenzweig 2006). Similarly, the greater the dependence of headquarters on the subsidiary to supply the resources required for the corporation (e.g. profits, sales), the greater the need to control it. In both cases, headquarters will try to implement management procedures that it is familiar with, a situation that will result in high levels of standardization.

71

A third reason for standardization relates to the MNC's attempts to maintain consistency and internal equity in employee management (Laurent 1986; Rosenzweig and Nohria 1994). This is of particular importance to firms that make extensive use of international assignments of employees, either to control and co-ordinate different sub-units in the corporation (Edström and Galbraith 1977; Bonache and Brewster 2001) or to transfer experience and know-how (Bartlett and Ghoshal 1987; Kamoche 1996).

Finally, and more importantly in our context, a fourth motive for standardization is related to MNCs recognizing the need to facilitate flows of information and knowledge among their different units. As mentioned, in today's MNCs every unit (both headquarters and overseas subsidiaries) can be a source of capabilities, expertise and innovation that can be transferred to other parts of the organizations. If they are managed with a similar logic (i.e. similar marketing, production and HR policies), the transfer of these intangible assets takes place more easily. For this reason, Kobrin (1988) suggested that, when a company wants to facilitate information and knowledge flow between different units, it tends to develop a global approach in management practices.

Yet, as usual in HR management, things are not that easy. Highlighting the strategic importance of knowledge transfer should not lead us to forget other needs and goals an MNC should meet in order to be competitive. In this respect, it should be noted that standardization, by definition, reduces variation. A policy of knowledge transfer is subject to two main constraints:

1 If variation or heterogeneity in practices is fully eliminated, the possibility of global learning, argued by the resource-based view to be a key potential source of competitive advantage for multinational companies, is severely restricted.
2 In each unit, the company should develop a way of attracting, retaining and motivating employees that is well adapted to the values, needs and demands of that particular setting. Therefore, it is necessary to assess the extent to which a given HR practice is really 'superior' and responds to local differences. Thus, for example, it might be the case that a given HR practice is not equally effective across different globally integrated units or across HQ and implementer subsidiaries.

The challenge then for the multinational firm is to identify how it can preserve variety and local adaptation while simultaneously establishing a foundation for global integration and knowledge transfer (Morris, Snell and Wright 2006). This is a difficult challenge. To illustrate it, we will consider the case of a particular company: GlobalCo. The case will help us to identify the main mechanisms a company may implement in order to facilitate knowledge transfer and integration within its international network.

72

Case study 4.1
Knowledge transfer in GlobalCo

The German electrical and electronic engineering company GlobalCo was founded in the first half of the 19th century and started its international expansion shortly afterwards. Today the company operates in 190 countries, has a turnover of more than $45 billion and employs in excess of 300,000 employees, more than one-third of whom work in foreign subsidiaries.

The firm's structure is based on a regional and functional matrix. HR planning is generally local – there is no international setting of HR budgets. Yet, to control this locally designed HR planning, each local HR director reports to the local managing director and to the global HR head. Reporting covers not only general HR expenditure but also a host of other information such as details on training and development. Moreover, the intranet acts as a substantial standardized resource for information, common HR processes and documents that can be accessed throughout the world. In addition to this reporting, there are many formal contacts between head office and subsidiaries with German HR executives having a strong involvement in key local HR initiatives.

These highly formal mechanisms of integration and knowledge diffusion are supplemented by other initiatives aimed at grouping employees from different units to develop common standards. For example, management development pro-grammes attempt to create a common business culture so that leadership princi-ples, core competencies and many HR instruments are taught in internationally standardized seminars. Personal coordination is also intensive. About 1% of employees outside Germany are home-country international assignees with the number of third-country nationals on expatriation increasing rapidly. The com-pany also has one international meeting of top HR executives a year focusing on the development and refinement of international HRM approaches. Some irregu-lar regional meetings are held and frequent informal contacts between HR spe-cialists in the head office and HR personnel abroad take place.

Cross-national projects on the part of HR specialists are also favoured. Initially, ideas are invited from all countries, but then a unilateral development of strategic and international matters on the part of the parent's head office often takes place. The expertise in the development of international HR instruments remains in the head office, which works thus as the company's centre of excellence.

Drawing on all these mechanisms (i.e. in-depth HR communication and bureau-cratic, social and personal coordination activities through HR reporting, manage-ment development, expatriation patterns and the roles and influences of HR specialists from the head office), the company can disperse knowledge around its component parts. On some occasions, the source of knowledge comes from the subsidiaries. For example, instruments such as the US accounting system or Hay-type job evaluations were introduced in the parent country from abroad and have been subsequently implemented worldwide. On other occasions, however, HR innovations originating from the German headquarters received mixed support from local management. For instance, Spanish HRM managers did not object to work within a binational project group set up for the selection and succession of top executives. In this group, they contributed ideas and acted as a testing ground for implementation. And yet the Spanish managers were excluded from the actual development of the international system. They accepted their role as implementers of practices that heavily favoured the head office. However, this ready acceptance of HQ initiatives was not always the case. One example is a 'security-minded' European remuneration system which operated until 1996 in Spain. It was seen as 'not motivating our managers' (by Spanish HR executives) and was replaced by a locally developed compensation system that has a higher risk element geared to the achievement of individually set objectives.

This tension between global standardization and local adaptation is reflected in other instances. For example, the high detail of HR reporting is regarded in Spain as 'bureaucratic' and 'too much effort'. Still, there is no active resistance to reporting measures that local management does not see as beneficial. Ironically, the extensive formal reporting may have led to an information overload in Germany where managers argue that it would be preferable to gather fewer data but to analyse and use them more carefully.

The GlobalCo case illustrates some of the different mechanisms a company can implement in order to integrate its operations and transfer knowledge. They fall into three main categories (Dickmann and Müller-Camen 2006): bureaucratic, social and personal mechanisms.

Bureaucratic mechanisms are based on formal roles and procedures that are monitored and sanctioned: for example, the planning, monitoring and reporting of key HR budgets. Although bureaucratic initiatives are mainly designed for control and coordination purposes (Bartlett and Ghoshal 1987), they also can be implemented for knowledge transfer reasons (Sparrow 2006); for example, the design of computerized HR knowledge management systems (e.g. intranets) to share expertise and to capture and store best practices. This is perhaps the most common initiative for knowledge management. As Nonaka and Konno (1998) have pointed out, when academics and business people refer to 'knowledge management' they often mean 'information technology'. Research evidence confirms this statement. According to a survey by KPMG in 2000, 62% of the main companies in Europe and the USA are taking initiatives to facilitate knowledge transfer and creation in and between their different units. However, most of these initiatives refer to the different technology-based information systems (e.g. intranets, data warehousing, DSS, Lotus Notes, etc.) provided by the company to enable the exchange of explicit knowledge. These findings are consistent with those of Ernst and Young in 1997. This company carried out a study of 432 European and US organizations in order to find out what measures were being implemented to manage knowledge. The study showed that most of these companies limit themselves to introducing technological capacity.

Bureaucratic mechanisms may be a prerequisite for knowledge management but they are not sufficient in themselves (Ferner 2000). They must be supplemented with *social mechanisms* aiming at creating corporate cohesion (Harzing 1999; Ferner 2000) and transferring and generating knowledge. International and globally distributed teams, international assignments, communities of practice and global expertise networks are the main international initiatives falling within this category. They are all aimed at facilitating social interaction among people of different units who have common tasks and who interact and share knowledge with each other, either formally or informally.

Personal mechanisms represent the third integration vehicle. They aim at building intense personal relationships among particular members of the international network of the company. Building these personal relationships is vital as they have positive effects on the frequency of inter-subsidiary and subsidiary–head office communication (Edström and Galbraith 1977; Bartlett and Ghoshal 1987) as well as on the level of knowledge transfer (Bonache and Zárraga 2007). In any case, the importance attributed to the building of these personal relationships will depend on the strategic role of subsidiaries (Birkinshaw and Morrison 1995). For example, 'implementer' subsidiaries make a heavier use of communication vehicles than 'autonomous units' (Martínez and Jarillo 1991). Visits of HR managers from HQ, local HR managers in HQ, and the use of international assignees to transfer tacit knowledge are the main mechanisms falling into this category.

We summarize these mechanisms in Table 4.1. As suggested in the table, they can be assessed for their potential to achieve the two resource-based dimensions of internationalization mentioned earlier (i.e. creation and transfer of knowledge). Thus, while some mechanisms (e.g. IHRM planning and reporting) are expected to be poor on both dimensions, others (e.g. HR centres of excellence) have the potential to both diffuse existing knowledge as well as create new knowledge. We use the word 'potential' deliberately to convey the idea that they are a necessary but insufficient condition for the transfer and creation of knowledge. As will be later explained, many barriers may impede the efficient functioning of these mechanisms.

Table 4.1 also includes some statements regarding the relative importance of these mechanisms for each type of subsidiary. As seen in the case of GlobalCo, a company can use a variety of these mechanisms. Yet it can be argued that they will not be equally important in all units. That is, depending on the strategic role of

Table 4.1 Key mechanisms for HR knowledge management

Type	Mechanisms	Examples	Potential for knowledge transfer	Knowledge generation	A key mechanism in
Bureaucratic	IHRM planning	Vision and mission, corporate culture, IHR strategy, HR principles, underlying competency frameworks, talent management approach etc.	Low	Low	Autonomous units
	IHRM reporting	Global, national, functional HR budgets, actual costs; outcomes	Low	Low	Autonomous units
	HR information systems	Use of common approaches, forms, policy documents etc. that are for instance located on the intranet	High	Low	Implementor units
Social	Communities of practice	International management seminars on HR instruments such as appraisals, employees' opinion surveys etc.	High	High	Globally integrated units
	Globally distributed teams	International project groups (including virtual teams)	Low	High	Learning units
	Expatriation	Expatriation as cultural coordination mechanisms (including international commuters)	High	Low	Implementor units
	HR centre of excellence	Units (with cross-border collaboration) responsible for the design of HR practices, to be exported and standardized across the whole organization	High	High	Globally integrated units
Personal	HR line manager in head office	International assignee who is leader/line manager in host location and who also shapes some part of the 'organizational culture'	High	High	Globally integrated units
	Visits of IHR managers from HQ	Visits and other contacts with HR local professionals (including frequent flyers)	Low	Low	Autonomous units
	Knowledge transferors	International assignees introducing corporate systems and processes (e.g. in performance management) in local operations	High	Low	Implementor units

subsidiaries, some mechanisms will be attributed more or less relevance. Thus, for example, while global centres of excellence will be unlikely to be found in autonomous units (i.e. they design and implement their own HR practices), they will be a key knowledge management mechanism in globally integrated units. In these integrated units, communities of practices, aiming at reinforcing a corporate culture that enables the diffusion of existing knowledge and the acquisition of new learning, will also be a vital mechanism. The degree to which companies make use of these alternative mechanisms depending on the strategic role of subsidiaries is an issue requiring further empirical research.

BARRIERS AND HR INITIATIVES FOR KNOWLEDGE MANAGEMENT

So far we have recognized the importance of knowledge transfer within MNCs as well as the different mechanisms designed for this purpose. However, researchers have shown that transferring knowledge within a firm is far from easy, as several barriers usually appear in this process. Along these lines, two main theoretical models specifying the barriers to the success of the transnational transfer of knowledge within MNCs have been provided, one developed by Szulanski (1996) and another by Kostova (1999).

Szulanski (1996) developed the notion of internal stickiness to refer to the difficulty of transferring knowledge within organizations. He identifies four sets of factors influencing the difficulty of knowledge transfer: characteristics of the knowledge transferred (i.e. causal ambiguity, 'unprovenness'), of the source (i.e. lack of motivation, not perceived as reliable), of the recipient (i.e. lack of motivation, absorptive capacity) and of the context in which the transfer takes place (i.e. barren organizational context, arduous relationship). The findings of his empirical study showed that the major barriers to internal knowledge transfer are the recipient's lack of absorptive capacity, causal ambiguity and an arduous relationship between the source and the recipient.

The second notable theoretical contribution to the analysis of knowledge transfer is from Kostova (1999). Drawing on a variety of theoretical perspectives (organizational behaviour, resource dependence and institutional theory), she proposes an alternative set of factors affecting the success of transfers. Some are social, referring to the degree to which the regulatory, cognitive and normative profiles of the home country and the recipient country are similar or different. Others are organizational, referring to compatibility between the values implied by the knowledge transferred and the values underlying the unit's firm culture, or to the degree to which the unit's organizational culture is supportive of learning, change and innovation. Finally, others are individual, referring to the attitudes of transfer coalition's members (i.e. their commitment to, identity with and trust in the parent company).

It is important to note that these types of barrier may impede the efficient implementation of the mechanisms for knowledge transfer already outlined. If employees are motivated to share knowledge, they may be guided by different logics. For instance, practitioners in the UK and India rated the importance of certain approaches to create competitive advantage fundamentally differently (Sparrow and Budhwar 1997). People may work to different logics (Budhwar and Sparrow 2003). Moreover, it has been shown that individuals often display some reluctance to share knowledge (Moravec et al. 1997). If indeed this is the case (i.e. if employees from the different units are not motivated to share knowledge, in terms of Szulanski's model), the mechanisms implemented for knowledge management will not produce the desired results.

Let us take as an example one of the aforementioned mechanisms to transfer knowledge, the global HR management systems. What may prevent individuals from sharing their knowledge in these systems?

It has been suggested that the problems facing people in situations in which knowledge has to be exchanged and shared can be conceptualized as social dilemmas (Cabrera and Cabrera 2002; Zárraga and Bonache 2005). In these situations, the interests of individual members of a group are at odds with the collective interest of that group (Van Lange et al. 1992), forcing individuals to choose between either self-interest or collective interest. The problem of public goods is a particular social dilemma reflecting the situation of knowledge sharing in global HR knowledge management systems. A public good is a shared resource, made up of the voluntary contributions of some of the members of a collective and from which all its members benefit, whether they have contributed to it or not (Connolly and Thorn 1990). These assets can also work as incentive for some members to take advantage of the collective. In fact, if everybody contributes and shares their knowledge except for one, then this member will benefit from collectively generated knowledge. Contrariwise, if there is only one person who contributes and shares, the situation could well result in a series of costs (loss of power, position of privilege, job etc.) with no benefits in return. In that case, non-contribution becomes the dominant strategy in global HR management systems, where no type of collective knowledge is either transferred or generated.

These problems indicate that mechanisms for knowledge transfer and creation, although widely used, do not always produce positive results. Only under certain conditions will the desired knowledge transfer and creation take place. For example, a company may assign an employee to a given foreign unit to transfer his/her expertise. Yet many factors may impede such a transfer. Local employees may not be motivated or not be able to acquire this new knowledge. Communication between the international assignees and local employees is not easy. Similarly, the international assignee may not be perceived as reliable. If so, poor knowledge transfer will take place.

This suggests that it is vital for a company to examine specific initiatives it can adopt in order to turn knowledge transfer mechanisms into an efficient device. In this respect, HRM practices can play a key role. According to the resource-based view, their goal is to attract, retain and motivate the sorts of skill and behaviour required by the organization to achieve its objectives (Wright et al. 2001). The purpose here is knowledge transfer and creation. However, little is known about the specific HR initiatives a company can implement in order to turn knowledge transfer mechanisms into efficient devices for knowledge sharing and creation. Although some work has recently been produced in this direction (see, for example, Cabrera and Cabrera (2002) for specific initiatives favouring knowledge transfer and creation in global HR management systems), more research is clearly needed.

Figure 4.1 offers a recent model (see Bonache and Zárraga (2007) for a more detailed explanation) of some HR initiatives favouring knowledge transfer (and creation) through international assignees, a typical mechanism for knowledge management.

The model basically assumes that an efficient knowledge transfer through international assignees will take place provided three conditions hold: abilities and motivation of international assignees; abilities and motivation of local staff; and a fertile relationship between them. In turn, the model includes the need to implement certain HR initiatives promoting these three factors. For example, what specific HR initiatives can a multinational company adopt to trigger the first of these factors (i.e. abilities and motivation of international staff to transfer knowledge)?

In this respect, HR initiatives deemed most likely to affect international assignees' abilities, given what is currently known about the subject, include the following:

- Extensive screening of prospective candidates (see Chapter 5). It has been shown that international staff selected on the basis not only of technical competencies but also of other additional abilities will be more effective as knowledge transferrers than those whose selection criteria are limited to assessment of their performance at home.
- Cross-cultural training of international staff (see Chapter 6). The need for such preparation is likely to be determined in part by the type of knowledge to be transferred. At one extreme assignments can involve the transfer of organizational culture. The international staff will have a key representational role, requiring extensive interaction with locals; at the other, there are transfers that may be almost entirely technology or equipment related, with the expatriate living in a tight expatriate community in a capital city or even a specific compound reserved for their compatriots. Most, of course, will fall between these extremes, but the different requirements for preparation are clear (Pickard and Brewster 1995).

79

In addition to the initiatives promoting the abilities of international assignees, motivation also has to be analysed. This is usually described in terms of the basic goals of objectives that drive behaviour (Baron and Kreps 1999). In our context, this means that employees must be motivated to perform their knowledge transfer function efficiently. Some initiatives likely to affect international assignees' motivation include the following:

- Emphasis on the importance of knowledge transfer in the performance evaluation criteria. International assignees' perception of the importance attached by the company to knowledge transfer as a performance evaluation criterion is likely to increase their efforts to transfer (Björkman et al. 2004).
- Reward systems linked to knowledge sharing (see Chapter 8). In general, the greater the direct and indirect perceived rewards derived from knowledge transfer, the more motivated the employee will be.

The specification of performance evaluation criteria and the use of extrinsic rewards may be insufficient to ensure the sorts of efforts required for knowledge transfer. In this regard, it is vital to distinguish between the motivations to participate versus the motivation to produce (March and Simon 1958). An international assignee may be motivated by the extrinsic monetary rewards to take up an international assignment. In contrast, to contribute one's tacit knowledge hinges on intrinsic motivation. International assignees will be intrinsically motivated if they value their activity for its own sake and will appear to be self-sustained.

CONCLUSION

Intrinsic motivation to share knowledge is a crucial issue. However, this cannot be compelled but only enabled under suitable conditions. By its nature, it is always voluntary. Several HR initiatives can be implemented to foster intrinsic motivation; some of them have to do with the recruitment of potential candidates and others with the establishing of the conditions of the assignment:

- Selecting candidates who find engaging in knowledge transfer activities to be inherently satisfying. Not every potential employee has the appropriate temperament and motivational profile to be an effective international assignee. It is important to recruit intrinsically motivated persons for the task at hand, either because it results in personal development and increased esteem or because it involves recognition from local employees or headquarters.
- Establishing psychological contracts based on emotional loyalties and participation. An international assignee may also be intrinsically motivated to efficiently perform his or her tasks because of personal loyalties.

80

An international assignee who is considering making a relatively low effort in transferring knowledge may feel that such behaviour will be disappointing for HQs or for local employees. Alternatively, he or she may feel that his or her competence as an efficient employee will be questioned by either of these two groups. Although these types of personal concern and consideration may be a complex construct, they appear to be potentially important factors here. If a personal relationship strongly raises the intrinsic motivation to cooperate, establishing a psychological contract based on emotional loyalties seems a reasonable HR initiative.

As Figure 4.2 suggests, similar initiatives can be implemented to trigger the other two factors (abilities and motivation of local staff, and a fertile relationship between international and local staff). The key point, however, is that if a company is limited to sending international assignees as a means to transfer HR practices, without taking into consideration the HR practices that aid efficient knowledge transfer, a poor outcome can be expected.

In sum, HR practices are thus not only a key asset to be transferred in MNCs, but also a vital element to promote an adequate internal knowledge transfer within the international network of multinational enterprises.

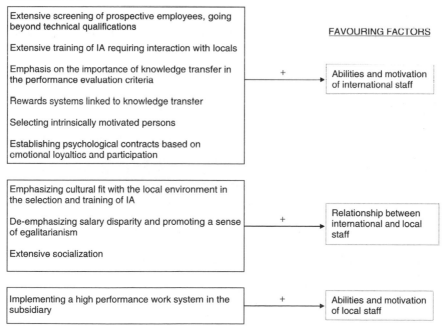

Figure 4.2 *Initiatives to promote knowledge transfer through international assignees.*
Source: adapted from Bonache and Zárraga (2008).

81

KEY LEARNING POINTS

- The transfer and creation of HR know-how is a key strategic goal in MNCs. In fact, in the resource-based view of the firm, internationalization can be conceived as an exploitation and accumulation of strategic HR knowledge.
- Knowledge transfer and creation are not confined to those from headquarters to foreign subsidiaries, but can occur in various directions within the MNC.
- Subsidiaries of MNCs can be classified according to the degree to which they are involved in the transfer and creation of knowledge. Following this criterion, there are four main types of subsidiary: globally integrated units, autonomous units, learning units and implementer units.
- Knowledge transfer is subject to certain constraints and challenges. The main challenge for the multinational firm is to identify how it can preserve variety and local adaptation while simultaneously establishing a foundation for global integration and knowledge transfer.
- Different mechanisms favour knowledge management in MNCs. Some of them favour the transfer of existing knowledge, while others favour the creation of new knowledge.
- The implementation of these mechanisms is a necessary but insufficient condition for knowledge transfer. Research has shown that many barriers make it difficult to ensure their efficient functioning.
- HR initiatives are a key element to overcome those barriers. If they are not taken into consideration, a poor knowledge transfer and creation will likely take place.

REFERENCES

Amit, R. and Schoemaker, P.J. (1993) 'Strategic assets and organizational rent', *Strategic Management Journal* 14: 33–46.

Argote, L. and Ingram, P. (2000) 'Knowledge transfer: a basis for competitive advantage in firms', *Organizational Behaviour and Human Decision Processes* 82, 1: 150–169.

Barney, L. (1991) 'Firm resources and sustained competitive advantage', *Journal of Management* 17: 99–120.

Baron, J.N. and Kreps, D.M. (1999) *Strategic Human Resource Frameworks for General Managers*, New York: John Wiley and Sons.

Bartlett, C.A. and Ghoshal, S. (1987) 'Managing across borders: new organizational responses', *Sloan Management Review* 10: 43–53.

Beechler, S. and Yang, J.Z. (1994) 'The transfer of Japanese-style management to American subsidiaries: contingencies, constraints, and competencies', *Journal of International Business Studies* 25, 3: 467–491.

Birkinshaw, J. and Morrison, A. (1995) 'Configurations of strategy and structure in subsidiaries of multinational corporations', *Journal of International Business Studies* 26, 4: 729–753.

Björkman, I., Barner-Rasmussen, W. and Li, L. (2004) 'Managing knowledge transfer in MNCs: the impact of headquarters control mechanisms', *Journal of International Business Studies* 35: 443–455.

Bonache, J. (2000) 'The international transfer of an idea suggestion system', *International Studies of Management and Organization* 29, 4: 24–44.

Bonache, J. and Brewster, C. (2001) 'Knowledge transfer and the management of expatriation', *Thunderbird International Business Review* 43, 1: 145–168.

Bonache, J. and Fernández, Z. (1997) 'Expatriate compensation and its link to the subsidiary strategic role: a theoretical analysis', *The International Journal of HRM* 8: 457–475.

Bonache, J. and Zárraga, C. (2008) 'Determinants of the success of international assignees as knowledge transferors', *The International Journal of HRM* 19, 1: 1–18.

Budhwar, P.S. and Sparrow, P. (2003) 'Strategic HRM through the cultural looking glass: mapping the cognition of British and Indian managers', *Organization Studies* 23, 4: 599–638.

Cabrera, A. and Cabrera, E. (2002) 'Knowledge sharing dilemmas', *Organization Studies* 23, 5: 687–710.

Connolly, T. and Thorn, B. (1990) 'Discretionary database: theory, data and implications', in J. Fulk and C. Steinfield (eds) *Organizations and Communication Technology*, London: Sage.

Dickmann, M. and Müller-Camen, M. (2006) 'Configuring for IHRM innovation: a typology and empirical assessment of strategies, structures and processes of international HRM', *International Journal of Human Resource Management* 17, 4: 580–601.

Edström, A. and Galbraith, J. (1977) 'Transfer of managers as a coordination and control strategy in multinational organizations', *Administrative Science Quarterly* 22: 248–263.

Ferner, A. (2000) 'The underpinnings of "Bureaucratic" control systems', *Journal of Management Studies* 37, 4: 521–539.

Ghoshal, S. and Nohria, N. (1989) 'Internal differentiation within multinational corporations', *Strategic Management Journal* 10, 4: 323–337.

Grant, R.M. (1996) 'Toward a knowledge-based theory of the firm', *Strategic Management Journal* 17, Winter Special Issue: 109–122.

Gupta, A.K. and Govindarajan, V. (1991) 'Knowledge flows and the structure of control within multinational corporations', *Academy of Management Review* 16, 4: 768–792.

Harzing, A.W. (1999) *Managing the Multinationals – An International Study of Control Mechanisms*, Cheltenham: Edward Elgar.

Kamoche, K. (1996) 'Strategic human resource management within a resource-capability view of the firm', *Journal of Management Studies* 33, 2: 213–221.

Kobrin, S.J. (1988) 'Expatriate reduction and strategic control in American multifunctional corporations', *Human Resource Management* 27, 1: 63–75.

Kogut, B. and Zander, U. (1993) 'Knowledge of the firm and the evolutionary theory of the multinational corporation', *Journal of International Business Studies* 24, 4: 625–645.

Kostova, T. (1999) 'Transnational transfer of strategic organisational practices: a contextual perspective', *Academy of Management Review* 24, 2: 308–324.

Lado, A.A. and Wilson, M.C. (1994) 'Human resource systems and sustained competitive advantage', *Academy of Management Review* 19: 699–727.

Laurent, A. (1986) 'The cross-cultural puzzle of international human resource management', *Human Resource Management* 25, 1: 91–102.

March, J.G. and Simon, H.A. (1958) *Organizations*, New York: Wiley.

83

Martínez, J.I. and Jarillo, J.C. (1991) 'The evolution of research on coordination mechanisms in multinational corporations', *Journal of International Business Studies* 20, 3: 389–514.

Miller, D. and Shamsie, J. (1996) 'The resource-based view of the firm in two environments: the Hollywood film studios from 1936 to 1965', *Academy of Management Journal* 39, 3: 519–543.

Moravec, M., Johannessen, O. and Hjelmas, T. (1997) 'Thumbs up for self-managed teams', *Management Review* 86, 7: 42–47.

Morris, S., Snell, S. and Wright P. (2006) 'A resource-based view of international human resources: toward a framework of integrative and creative capabilities', in G. Stahl and I. Björkman (eds) *Handbook of Research in International Human Resource Management*, Cheltenham: Edward Elgar.

Nonaka, I. and Konno, N. (1998) 'The concept of BA: building a foundation for knowledge creation', *California Management Review* 40, 3: 40–54.

Peteraf, M.A. (1993) 'The cornerstones of competitive advantage: a resource based view', *Strategic Management Journal* 14: 179–193.

Pickard, J. and Brewster, C. (1995) 'Repatriation: closing the circle', *International Journal of Human Resource Management* 4, 2: 45–49.

Rosenzweig, S. (2006) 'The dual logics behind international human resource management: pressures for global integration and local responsiveness', in G. Stahl and I. Björkman (eds) *Handbook of Research in International Human Resource Management*, Cheltenham: Edward Elgar.

Rosenzweig, S. and Nohria, N. (1994) 'Influences on human resource management practices in multinational corporations', *Journal of International Business Studies* 25, 2: 222–251.

Rosenzweig, S. and Singh, J. (1991) 'Organisational environments and the multinational enterprise', *Academy of Management Review* 16, 2: 340–361.

Roth, K. and Morrison, A.J. (1992) 'Implementing global strategy: characteristics of global subsidiary mandates', *Journal of International Business Studies* 23: 715–735.

Sparrow, P. (2006) 'Global knowledge management and HRM', in G. Stahl and I. Björkman (eds) *Handbook of Research in International Human Resource Management*, Cheltenham: Edward Elgar.

Sparrow, P. and Budhwar, P. (1997) 'Competition and change in India: mapping transitions in HRM', *Journal of World Business* 32, 3: 224–242.

Szulanski, G. (1996) 'Exploring internal stickiness: impediments to the transfer of best practice within the firm', *Strategic Management Journal* 17: 27–43.

Tallman, S. and Fladmoe-Lindquist, K. (1994) 'A resource-based model of the multinational firm', paper presented in the Strategic Management Society Conference, Paris, France.

Van Lange, P., Liebrand, W., Messick, D. and Wilke, H. (1992) 'Introduction and literature review', in W.B.G. Liebrand, D.M. Messick and H.A.M. Wilke (eds) *Social Dilemmas: Theoretical Issues and Research Findings*, New York: Pergamon.

Wernerfelt, B. (1984) 'A resource based view of the firm: ten years after', *Strategic Management Journal* 5: 171–180.

Wright, P., Dunfond, B. and Snell, S. (2001) 'Human resources and the resource based view of the firm', *Journal of Management* 27: 701–721.

Zárraga, C. and Bonache, J. (2005) 'The impact of team atmosphere on knowledge outcomes in self-managed teams', *Organization Studies* 26, 5: 661–681.

Part II

HR management of international employees

Chapter 5

Resourcing international assignees

David G. Collings and Hugh Scullion

CHAPTER OBJECTIVES

By the end of this chapter, readers will have:

- considered the context of resourcing international assignees, which, we argue, is more complex than resourcing in a domestic context
- an understanding of the emerging strategic constraints on international resourcing
- identified the key factors that multinational corporations (MNCs) should take into account in resourcing international assignees
- explored international resourcing in practice
- an appreciation of the key means through which MNCs could advance their international resourcing practice in terms of adopting a more strategic perspective

INTRODUCTION

In international business it has long been recognized that organizational 'strategy (the what) is internationalizing faster than the implementation (the how) and much faster than the managers and executives themselves (the who)' charged with its development and execution (Adler and Bartholomew 1992: 52). Indeed, Harvey et al. (2001: 899) posit that: 'Successful formulation and implementation of a corporate strategy for managing global operations requires a commensurate strategy for managing international human resources.'

In this regard, one of the primary means through which MNCs coordinate and control their foreign operations is through the use of international assignees (Edström and Galbraith 1977; Harzing 2004). International assignees are also used as a means of developing organizational competence or indeed for individual management development. However, even allowing for over a quarter of a century since the emergence of some seminal papers around the theme of international assignments, we are left with a very incomplete picture of the effectiveness of these assignees, and indeed their value and continued use in the multinational enterprise has recently been subject to scrutiny and challenge (Collings et al. 2007).

Perhaps the most significant challenge to the continued use of expatriate assignments was (Harzing 1995) – and still remains (Harzing 2002; Harzing and Christensen 2004) – the hotly debated area of expatriate failure, a topic closely related to international resourcing. In the earliest literature on this topic, failure rates of 10 to 45% were commonly cited and failure rates in this range are still frequently cited in the North American literature. In contrast reported failure rates in European and Japanese MNCs tend to be lower. For instance, in the late 1980s and early 1990s Brewster (1988) reported failure rates of below 5% in 72% of his sample. Likewise Scullion's (1991) study of UK and Irish multinationals found that only 10% of these firms had failure rates over 5%. In recent years empirical research on expatriate failure has been limited. Indeed, Harzing and Christensen (2004) have gone so far as to argue that it may be better to abandon the concept of expatriate failure completely and instead focus on analysing the issues around expatriate turnover and performance management. Others have argued for a broader conceptualization of expatriate failure with a particular emphasis on performance (Collings and Scullion 2006). Empirical studies on expatriate failure in emerging economies such as China and India would, however, represent a particularly useful addition to the literature. Discussions around the definition of expatriate failure notwithstanding, it is clear that any significant level of expatriate failure is likely to result in significant cost implications for the organization concerned and also has the potential to considerably impact on the subsidiary operation.

It is also clear, however, that the prospect of working in a foreign environment that may differ significantly from one's home country presents a significant challenge for those concerned. Further, successful adjustment to the host environment is widely considered to be a significant antecedent of expatriate performance and it appears as an underpinning kernel in much of the study of expatriation.

Unfortunately, however, even allowing for the large body of extant literature on the nature of adjustment, we are faced with a number of disparate findings, leading to a number of paradoxes. For instance, in a review of the literature in the field Thomas (1998) points to the contradiction that the very factors that make an expatriate effective also make it more difficult for that expatriate to adjust. While a more in-depth discussion of the adjustment issue is conducted in Chapter 7, it is important to recognize the significance of international assignee and family adjustment in explaining the success of international assignments. A key theme in this literature is the link between expatriate selection and adjustment and in this chapter we focus primarily on the selection issue.

Before we begin our analysis of resourcing international assignees, it is necessary to define the boundaries of our discussion. Specifically we use the term *international assignees*, which we define as employees of an MNC who are sent on secondment to a location outside of their home country. We use this term instead of expatriation, which is often used in quite ethnocentric terms to refer to parent country nationals (PCNs) who are sent to foreign subsidiaries. Our definition also includes the use of third country nationals, nationals from a country other than the parent country who are seconded to a subsidiary in a country other than their home country and inpatriates (Harvey et al. 2001) where assignees from subsidiaries are seconded to the headquarter operation. While traditionally these secondments typically had lasted between 3 and 5 years, we also briefly discuss short-term international assignments (i.e. less than 1 year's duration). Our focus in this chapter is limited to the resourcing of managerial talent from inside the MNC (internal labour market) which can be justified as there is a growing recognition that the success of global business depends most importantly on the quality of management talent available in the multinational (Scullion and Starkey 2000). (For a broader discussion of recruitment and selection in an international context see Scullion and Collings 2006; Sparrow 2006.)

In this chapter, we take a strategic focus rather than focusing in detail on the practicalities of selection of international assignees, which have been covered elsewhere (see Briscoe and Schuler 2004; Dowling and Welch 2004; Scullion and Collings 2006; Sparrow 2007). Our approach is to examine the strategic issues faced by MNCs with regard to resourcing international assignees and we seek to highlight how resourcing staff for international assignments plays an important role in enabling international firms to compete effectively in the international business environment.

CONTEXT FOR RESOURCING INTERNATIONAL ASSIGNEES

The resourcing of international assignees is more complex than resourcing in a domestic context and as such the area presents significant challenges for the international HR professional (Dowling and Welch 2004). In this regard we highlight eight significant challenges:

1   The performance requirements of international assignees are often more complex than their domestic counterparts. This is a result of a number of factors, including the fact that assignees will be expected to reach high performance standards in a different cultural environment that usually involves adapting to varying cultural norms and often also to a different language.

2 We often have little concrete knowledge of how a potential candidate is likely to perform during an international assignment. While managers may have a relatively clear idea of the candidate's competence based on their performance in their home organization, the difficulty is that 'past performance may have little or no bearing on one's ability to achieve a task in a foreign environment' (Dowling and Welch 2004: 99). Thus, high performance in the home country does not always guarantee performance in foreign locations.

3 International HR professionals are often forced to recruit candidates for international assignments in reaction to crises in foreign subsidiaries with little time to systematically and strategically assess the situation and develop an appropriate pool of applicants (Black et al. 1999; Sparrow 2006). Thus HR professionals often face greater temporal pressures in recruiting international assignees.

4 Because international assignments by definition involve relocation to a different country, it is likely that the assignee's family situation will be more significant in their decision to put themselves forward for an assignment and also their decision to accept it than in the domestic context. Thus, international HR professionals will have to take into greater account issues surrounding the potential international assignees' family situation in selection decisions.

5 Legislative requirements in the proposed location of the assignment will also impact on the selection decision. Specifically, assignments in many countries will require visas for international assignees and their spouses and children. In some countries it may be that spouses will find it difficult or even impossible to get a work visa, resulting in further complications as they may be unable to pursue their own careers in the host location.

6 Cultural differences between the home and host country may have to be taken into account. For example, the extent to which females may be accepted as managers of male subordinates in certain Arab countries may have some significance. Also international assignees of specific nationalities may find assignments in certain countries particularly challenging for historic or political reasons. Specifically, English or American assignees in Iraq may find such postings very difficult, due to the perception of certain citizens within that country toward their government's role in the hostilities in the country.

7 Given that assignments often involve spending time in dangerous locations, firms will often have to be more aware of the risks attached to assignments in such countries. For example, there have been a number of high-profile abductions of expatriate oil workers in Nigeria in recent years and also of employees of American firms in countries such as Iraq. On this basis, MNCs will be required increasingly to conduct risk assessments for international assignees.

90

8 MNCs must effectively manage the balance between adopting globally standardized selection criteria and techniques vis-à-vis adapting such criteria and techniques to local countries in selecting international assignees. Two key issues emerge in this respect. First, policies may have to be adapted to account for legislative requirements in varying host countries. Second, MNCs must ensure that techniques and tests do not discriminate against certain employees who may be unfamiliar with the methods or disadvantaged through language skills.

It is clear that international resourcing is a complex and multifaceted task. While a discussion of all of the relevant issues is beyond the scope of the current chapter, we do discuss some of the more pertinent ones. Specifically, we consider the strategic constraints on international resourcing, debates around the characterization of international assignees, some of the issues around the practice of international resourcing and, finally, propose some ideas for the way forward

STRATEGIC CONSTRAINTS ON RESOURCING INTERNATIONAL ASSIGNMENTS

There is an increasing realization that MNCs are experiencing a number of difficulties in staffing foreign positions with traditional parent-country national expatriates and for over a decade this issue has dominated the agenda of international HR managers. These challenges emerge from a number of strategic constraints that international HR professionals face in resourcing international assignees (Collings et al. 2007).

Supply-side issue

Four key trends emerge in this regard – dual-careers issues, the limited participation of women in international assignments, issues around repatriation and weaknesses of talent management at an international level.

Demand-side issues

We point to the rapid growth of emerging markets in countries such as those in Eastern Europe, India and China, which is important in explaining the growing demand for expatriate employees with the specific competences needed to manage in these markets. Further, there is increasing demand for expatriate employees in a far wider range of organizations than the traditional large MNC partly due to the rapid growth of small and medium-sized enterprise (SME) internationalization and international joint ventures (IJVs).

91

Expatriate failure and associated controversies

As noted already, the long-established orthodoxy was that many expatriate assignments ended prematurely as a large percentage of employees returned home due to a failure to adjust to the host environment. Recent analyses, however, indicate that while expatriate performance remains a serious concern for many MNCs, high expatriate failure rates may not have been as widespread as originally believed (Harzing 2002; Harzing and Christensen 2004) although the costs associated with failure in both financial and non-financial terms remain high.

Performance evaluation

The performance of expatriates continues to be problematical for MNCs, which is partly due to difficult challenges faced by expatriates between meeting the often conflicting demands of the HQ and subsidiary operations. Further, several other factors also impact on expatriate performance including adjustment, family adjustment, language competence, etc., although the debate on adjustment and performance has long been open (Thomas 1998).

Costs

Although many firms do not have a true idea of the costs associated with expatriate assignments, it is generally estimated that the cost associated with the international assignment is between three and five times an assignee's home salary in a year. Given increasing cost pressures in many industries, cost issues represent a significant challenge for many MNCs in utilizing PCN expatriates.

As already noted, these developments have two key implications for resourcing international assignees. First, the pool of candidates available to MNCs for assignments is being influenced by two key factors. One factor concerns the problem of a lack of supply of available candidates, apposite to the rapidly increasing demand for those with the competence to work in the international sphere. This means that organizations face a significant recruitment challenge in attracting an appropriate pool of candidates for international assignments. This suggests the increasing importance of global branding for MNCs in attracting an appropriate pool of candidates for international assignments. Further, the importance of developing an appropriate and congruent set of HR policies to support international assignees and encourage candidates to accept these assignments also emerges as key. The second factor is that MNCs are increasingly looking beyond traditional expatriate pools and beyond traditional PCN expatriates in meeting staffing requirements for senior managerial posts in foreign subsidiaries (see Collings et al. 2007; also Chapter 11). Thus the complex challenges involved in recruiting and selecting international assignees is becoming even more demanding owing to three key factors:

92

1 organizations simply have less experience in recruiting for non-traditional forms of international assignments
2 there has been less opportunity to benchmark best practice in this context due to the relatively recent emergence of these alternatives
3 there is little research to guide practitioners in this regard.

Nonetheless, it does appear that more flexible forms of global staffing are increasingly being used as alternatives to traditional expatriate assignment (Collings et al. 2007).

CHARACTERIZING THE INTERNATIONAL MANAGER

While it is generally understood that role specification and resourcing strategies are different for every organization and, indeed, for different international assignments, it is sometimes assumed that the same selection and assessment criteria are valid across the board. However, this is not supported by the research evidence, which suggests that the role of the international manager varies significantly across sectors of the economy (Sparrow 1999b). Despite the obvious variety of requirements placed on international assignees dependent on the nature, duration and location of their assignment, a number of authors have attempted to identify the characteristics and competencies required by the international manager. Early research in the field linked high expatriate failure rates to lack of pre-departure training and spouse adjustment problems perhaps suggesting generic requirements regardless of the nature of assignment or individual. Our knowledge about skills and competencies related to international job changes has increased and attempts have been made to understand the more complex psychological processes involved (Bognanno and Sparrow 1995).

Various studies have identified comprehensive lists of the competencies required for the international manager (see Chapter 6 for a discussion of important antecedent factors such as personality). The main problem is that various studies produce lists with a very large range of competencies for the international manager. For example, by the 1990s two leading specialists in the field of cross-cultural management, Harris and Moran (1996) cited almost 70 dimensions of competency, of which over 20 are seen as most desirable. Other studies identify similarly large lists (Barham and Wills 1992). The practitioner literature also contains many lists of apparently predictive factors, many of which are of questionable validity (see also the more recent contributions of Yamazaki and Kayes 2004; Stroh et al. 2005). There remains a consensus between practitioners that there is a range of specific competencies linked with effective performance in international roles.

However, it was noted that the approach of some organizations was to continue to create lists of potentially relevant dimensions rather than engage with the more

93

challenging task of defining the key generic attributes, which include both personality characteristics and management competencies (Sparrow and Hiltrop 1994). The main reason for this problem is that three main research streams have contributed to our knowledge about effective performance in an international setting (Sparrow 1999a): expatriation studies; international joint venture research and research into the socialization process for international managers (for a discussion of these studies see Sparrow 1999a; Scullion and Collings 2006).

Overly focusing on generic competencies in the selection of international assignees is reflective of four key myths, which, Dowling and Welch (2004: 84-85) argue, have evolved surrounding the recruitment of international managers.

Universal approach to management

This refers to the mistaken belief among some managers that they can apply corporately developed HR policies and practices in a standardized way throughout their foreign subsidiaries. This attitude arguably reflects ethnocentric tendencies within MNCs and ignores a large body of research which shows the challenges of implementing standardized process on a global basis.

Multicultural adaptability and behaviours

This refers to the fact that while some people have an innate ability to adopt culturally appropriate behaviours in foreign countries, not everyone has these skills. International assignments require individuals to have effectiveness skills (the ability to successfully translate technical or managerial skills into the foreign environment) and coping skills (the ability to settle in or at least survive in the foreign environment). Not all people possess these skills.

Characteristics shared by successful international managers

While acknowledging that there are some characteristics shared by those who are successful in international assignments, many explanations ignore the significance of other factors including how an individual might react to the foreign location.

Impediments to mobility

Despite MNCs' preference that employees be globally mobile and willing to relocate as per corporate requirements, a number of issues emerge with regard to the extent to which people will actually consider relocating. Key issues here include dual-career and family issues, career concerns, concerns over repatriation, etc.

94

DOWLING AND WELCH'S FACTORS OF EXPATRIATE SELECTION

In seeking to build a more comprehensive understanding of the factors which should be considered in international assignee selection, Dowling and Welch (2004) point to six key, interrelated factors which should be considered in the process. This work builds on earlier studies in the area. For example, Tung's (1981) review of the literature identified four groups of variables that can contribute to expatriate success and thus should influence selection decisions. These were technical competence, personal traits or related abilities, ability to cope with environmental variables and family situation. Three of Dowling and Welch's factors, technical ability, cross-cultural suitability and family requirements, are particular to the individual while the other three, country/cultural requirements, language and MNC requirements are specific to the assignment/situation. Dowling and Welch's contribution is useful in that, in contrast to studies which produce endless lists of specific competencies that are required by international managers, they point to some overarching principles that should guide the international selection decision. Thus, the emphasis is on the general rather than the specific – an approach that, we argue, is more appropriate given the wide variety of role requirements of international assignees. We now briefly review these characteristics.

Individual factors

Technical ability

Clearly, any potential assignee will require a base level of technical competence for performance in an international assignment. This is particularly significant when the assignment is posited on a position-filling rationale. Indeed, there is a large body of empirical evidence that highlights the significance managers place on technical competence in selecting expatriate employees. This is hardly surprising as technical competence is relatively easy to measure based on past performance particularly for international assignees sourced from the internal labour market. However, a key disjuncture emerges in this debate. Past performance may not be an accurate indicator of one's ability to perform similar tasks in a foreign country. As Dowling and Welch (2004: 99) surmise: 'Technical skills are critical [in completing international assignments], but success depends on how the individual handles the situation.'

Cross-cultural suitability

As already indicated, above there are some personal characteristics associated with expatriates' successful performance in a foreign culture. A large body of largely

95

US literature focuses on the big five personality characteristics (extroversion, agreeableness, conscientiousness, emotional stability and openness or intellect) as predictors of performance in foreign cultures (see, for example, Caligiuri 2000). Broader skills that are posited to represent higher levels of cross-cultural competence include *inter alia* cultural empathy, adaptability, diplomacy, language ability, openness and, more recently, cultural intelligence. The challenge from a resourcing perspective however is, as Dowling and Welch (2004) note, that it is very difficult to define such competencies, not to mention assess a candidate's competence in relation to them.

Family requirements

Family requirements have a number of impacts on the decision of an expatriate to accept an assignment and further their adjustment and ultimately perhaps performance while on assignment. First, dual-career issues emerge. International assignees are no longer necessarily males who are sole breadwinners with spouses who are willing and able to relocate to a foreign location to further their husband's career. Increasingly, the decision to accept an international assignment is conditioned by the impact on spousal careers. Linked to this, potential international assignees are often reluctant to uproot children from schools for the purposes of accompanying them on assignment. Poorly and ageing parents may also mean that candidates are reluctant to accept assignments. Indeed, family issues were cited as the most important reason for refusing international assignments in a recent study (GMAC 2006: 14). Finally, there is a large body of literature which has highlighted the link between spousal adjustment and expatriate adjustment; however, the extent to which spouses are included in the selection decision is limited in practice. An interesting explanation for this failure in the European context could be that legislative requirements in certain countries mean it is illegal to discriminate against employees on the basis of marital status. Thus, if marital status were raised in the selection process in a country such as Ireland, and a married candidate was not offered a job while the successful candidate was unmarried, the appointment could be challenged on the basis of discrimination due to marital status under the Employment Equality Acts 1998 and 2004.

Situational factors

Country/cultural requirements

This factor has two key influences on the selection decision. First, the host location may represent a particularly politically volatile or dangerous country and thus the assignment may be considered a 'hardship posting'. This may mean that the MNC may find it difficult to get a candidate to accept the assignment or indeed the

MNC may choose not to use an expatriate based on their risk assessment of the assignment. Second, increasingly many countries place restrictions on the percentage of foreign employees in key positions. The employment of host-country employees may also be key in building mutually beneficial and sustainable relationships between the MNC and the host government. This may cause MNCs to re-evaluate the balance of foreign and host employees in subsidiaries. The issue of working permits and visas for international assignees and their spouses is also a key consideration for MNCs. Clearly, acquiring visas is more difficult in some countries than in others and the problem is less relevant when MNCs transfer European Union (EU) passport holders within the EU.

MNC requirements

Operational issues in specific circumstances may affect the selection decision in certain MNCs. For example, Collings et al. (2008) note that MNCs which internationalize at an early stage may suffer from a lack of available managerial talent within the international labour market and thus may have to recruit from the external labour market in filling key positions in new subsidiaries. Second, as noted earlier, operating subsidiaries in politically volatile countries may mean that MNCs are forced to look beyond traditional PCN expatriate pools to fill these positions. Dowling and Welch (2004) also point to the mode of operation, suggesting that selecting staff for international joint ventures will be informed by different criteria than those in traditional subsidiaries. They also note the importance of the duration of the assignment. Specifically, family issues will be different for short-term assignments (less than 1 year) than in longer assignments. Finally, they note that the degree of knowledge transfer required by the job should impact on the selection process. Where a key role of the expatriate is upskilling local staff, training skills may be a competence emphasized in the selection decision.

Language

Dowling and Welch (2004) classify language competence as a situational factor as opposed to an individual factor in terms of its importance in the selection decision. Although acknowledging the fact that the significance of language competence for international assignees varies dependent on the nature of the assignment and the level of interaction with host employees, some level of competence in the host language is required for almost all assignments. This factor is, however, underestimated in selection in many instances despite the fact that research has demonstrated the advantages attached to language proficiency in operating in a foreign location (Björkman and Gertsen, 1992). This may be a factor of the growth in common corporate languages. Thus, if the assignee is competent in the common corporate language (often English), the MNC may underestimate the importance

97

of host-language competence and the selection decision may be overly focused on competence in the corporate language.

Having outlined some of the key factors that should be considered in expatriate selection, the following section explores the practice of expatriate selection.

PRACTICE OF INTERNATIONAL SELECTION

Much of the literature suggests the emphasis in international recruitment should be on softer skills, such as personality characteristics, cross-cultural and language competence, family situation and the like. In practice, however, it appears that the focus in selection is very much on technical skills and past performance, which, as we have already indicated, may not always easily transfer to the foreign location. There are a number of reasons for this focus on technical skills (Franke and Nicholson 2002; Anderson 2005):

1 The majority of international assignments are concerned with filling a position.
2 It is relatively easy to quantify the past performance of those employed in the organization.
3 The difficulty of identifying and measuring the relevant interpersonal and cross-cultural skills.
4 Selectors will seek to minimize the personal risk involved by selecting a candidate who is unlikely to fail for technical reasons.

Apposite to this, family issues, which we noted earlier were identified as a key factor in explaining expatriate success in the global assignment, tend to be one of the factors least considered in the selection decision (Franke and Nicholson 2002; Anderson 2005; GMAC 2006). This paradox is difficult to explain and in advancing the utility of international assignees, IHR professionals need to address this issue.

Further, the literature suggests that despite rhetoric around the significance of certain competencies required in successfully completing international assignments, in practice many selection decisions are taken informally. Earlier research highlighted the importance of personal recommendations and informal methods for expatriate selection and the suggestion was that the outcome of selection interviews may often be pre-determined before the actual interview (Brewster 1991). This means that the potential pool of applicants available to the recruiter is often limited to employees who are well known to the recruiters (Harris and Brewster 1999; Linehan and Scullion 2001). Harris and Brewster (1999) develop this notion of informality in expatriate selection further in an important article 'The coffee machine system: how international selection really works'. They provide a typology of expatriate selection systems based on the distinction between open and closed systems and formal and informal systems. The closed/informal system was the dominant one used in the UK organizations studied by Brewster and Harris. The typology of selection systems is shown in Table 5.1 and helps to explain variations found in the way expatriate selection is conducted. They show that expatriate selection, in practice, is often an ad hoc process and they suggest that the selection process can be started through a casual conversation about an assignment between executives chatting around the coffee machine. Recent research on short-term internal assignments confirms that informal selection is the rule rather than the exception in sourcing short-term international assignees (Tahvanainen et al. 2005).

It is suggested that an MNC's organizational processes are used to legitimize the decision that has already been taken informally at the coffee machine. There are, however, several disadvantages of this type of selection system. Not only are candidates not formally evaluated against agreed criteria, in addition the pool of potential candidates is highly restricted and in general it reflects a reactive rather than strategic approach to the management of expatriation (Harzing 2004). A consideration of these and other factors has resulted in Anderson (2005) concluding that international assignee management, and selection in particular, is often more a function of good luck than good management.

Linked to the preceding point a final theme which emerges in relation to the resourcing of international assignees is that recruitment of pools of candidates is often ad hoc and reactive. International HR managers are often faced with the challenge of finding suitable candidates in response to a crisis in a foreign operation or to fill a key skills gap in such an operation (Black et al. 1999; Sparrow 2006). As Sparrow (2006: 10) notes: 'Another challenge today [in international recruitment] is the speed at which the need to recruit internationally develops

Table 5.1 Harris and Brewster's selection typology

Formal	Informal
Open	
■ Clearly defined criteria	■ Less defined criteria
■ Clearly defined measures	■ Less defined measures
■ Training for selectors	■ Limited training for selectors
■ Open advertising of vacancy (internal/external)	■ No panel discussions
	■ Open advertising of vacancy
■ Panel discussions	■ Recommendations
Closed	
■ Clearly defined criteria	■ Selectors' individual preferences determine selection criteria
■ Clearly defined measures	
■ Training for selectors	■ No panel discussions
■ Panel discussions	■ Nominations only (networking/reputation)
■ Nominations only (networking/reputation)	

Source: adapted from Harris and Brewster (1999)

99

and the volatility of the activities that are involved.' This means that they do not have sufficient time to adequately define the parameters of the role, design role and person specification or adequately source a pool of candidates. It also reinforces the significance of the emphasis on technical skills in the selection process and also the focus on a limited pool of candidates known to the recruiter.

This trend has some noteworthy implications for international HR practice. A key US study (Miller 1972) found that in situations where one, or more, technically qualified candidates were quickly identified by recruiters, they often terminated their search at an early stage meaning they often overlooked potential candidates with similar technical skill sets but superior cross-cultural skills. However, paradoxically, when a suitable candidate was not immediately identified, recruiters tended to more coherently define the skill set required for the assignment, to consider the performance requirements of the role, to search more aggressively and broadly throughout their organizations and indeed to request more assistance from HR professionals (see also Black et al. 1999 for a discussion). Given that much of this research is somewhat dated, research which explores the impact of more sophisticated human resource information systems (HRIS) and talent management systems on the selection decision in the MNC would be a useful contribution to the literature. Specifically, research which explores the extent to which selectors still quickly gravitate towards visible, technically proficient candidates in the context of integrated talent management systems and HRIS and further search behaviour in HRIS would be particularly timely.

While this work gives some key insights into the selection systems for international managers it is important not to generalize as selection processes can be influenced by factors such as the maturity of the multinational, its stage in the internationalization process and its size and industry sector (Dowling and Welch 2004).

THE WAY FORWARD

In moving beyond the limitations commonly associated with resourcing international assignments, MNCs could focus on a number of key issues. First, in expanding the pool of potential candidates available for international assignments in the context of the key supply and demand issues identified earlier, HR professionals should look beyond traditional PCN expatriate pools and even beyond traditional assignments. In this regard, Collings et al. (2007) point to the emergence of a portfolio of alternatives to the traditional international assignment including short-term assignments, commuter assignments, international business travel and virtual assignments which MNCs can consider alongside the conventional expatriate assignment. The short case vignette that follows highlights some of resourcing issues in the case of DrinksCo international (see Chapter 11 for a related discussion of modern forms of international working).

Case study 5.1
Flexible resourcing in Drinks Co. International

Drinks Co. International is a UK-based multinational which has expanded rapidly into European markets over the past decade through acquisitions and joint ventures. As a result, the character of the company was fundamentally altered and for the first time in their history the group had more business by turnover and profit from international activities than in the UK. However, due to the very rapid growth in the pace of internationalization, shortages of international managers had emerged as a significant problem. The implementation of the global strategy was increasingly constrained by shortages of international management talent that threatened to constrain corporate efforts to expand abroad.

As a result, the company undertook a strategic review of the requirements of resourcing key positions in international operations. This review suggested that the company should shift away from a reliance on traditional expatriate assignments and towards a more flexible form of resourcing international assignments through the introduction of shorter term assignments (assignments of less than 1 year's duration), international commuter assignments (staff commute from home base while family remains at home) and frequent flyer assignments (staff undertake frequent international business trips but do not commute).

These changes have been broadly successful and facilitated the company's expansion in Europe and the contribution of international operations to revenues continues to expand. Corporate executives indicate that they feel this success would have been constrained without the introduction of more flexible international staffing arrangements.

The situation highlighted that a sensible approach to the work–life balance and the adaptation and support of the partner were key factors for the success of managers on these more flexible alternative forms of assignment. One important advantage of these flexible assignments was the relative lack of disruption to the career paths of the managers because they were not required to change jobs. Another advantage was that managers were not faced with the messy problems associated with the repatriation process. By the same token, more flexible assignments also had some significant disadvantages. First, managers had often to travel to many different countries, which can put strain on work and domestic relationships. In addition, the requirement to develop a wide range of networks and personal relationships in a wide range of countries can be highly stressful.

Question

1 What factors will influence the success or failure of flexible alternative forms of international assignments?

In selecting international assignees, the key to success is adopting a more strategic focus. In this regard the challenge is not just strategy formulation, which many organizations do relatively well (Tahvanainen and Suutari 2005), but also to translate strategic planning to the operational level, through the development of HR policies and practices aimed at ensuring congruence between employees' work behaviours and the organizational strategy. International HR managers, in conjunction with line managers, must begin by defining the requirements of the role in the foreign subsidiary. Then they must decide on the most appropriate employee type, host-country national (HCN) or international assignee or an alternative form of international work. If an international assignee is deemed suitable then the objectives for the assignments must be codified. The achievement of these objectives will be improved if the individual expatriate is selected and supported through a congruent set of HR policies throughout the expatriate cycle (Collings et al. 2007). This begins with appropriate selection criteria and techniques that are related to the role and that expand on simple measures of technical competence that have been shown empirically to be poor indicators of managers' performance while they are on assignment.

CONCLUSION

In addressing the reactive nature of international resourcing throughout this chapter and suggesting a more strategic role for international resourcing, it is important to highlight the significance of related debates about talent management systems in MNCs. In an international context talent management is concerned with the strategic integration of resourcing and development at the international level and involves the proactive identification, development and strategic deployment of high-performing and high-potential strategic employees on a global scale. Thus, it goes beyond HR planning international assignments for international managers and high-potential managers. It also focuses on talent identification, development and deployment and also succession planning for key positions within the MNC (Sparrow 2006). A key challenge in this respect is managing the *talent pipeline* and *recruiting ahead of the curve* as opposed to the recruitment of international assignees on a reactive basis (Sparrow et al. 2004; Sparrow 2007). Sparrow et al. (2004) highlight that a major challenge facing organizations seeking to coordinate their talent pipelines on a more global basis at the operational level is the need to consider the cross-cultural relevance and fairness of the tools and techniques that are employed.

Paradoxically, however, despite the hype about talent management in recent years there is little evidence to suggest that many organizations do it in a coordinated and efficient manner (Scullion and Starkey 2000). A recent study reported that under 20% of senior managers strongly agreed that their organization brought in highly talented people, under 10% thought that they retained all their high performers,

102

while under 5% thought that their organization developed people quickly and effectively or removed low performers (Michaels et al. 2001). Also, many companies are frequently unaware of where their best talent is located (Evans et al. 2002).

Future research could move the debate forward and address the extent to which talent management systems can help to resolve the historical problems associated with international assignee selection. Specifically, as noted earlier, it would be useful to explore the extent to which HR information systems and talent management systems have resulted in a shift away from an overemphasis on technical competence in the international selection decision. Research could also explore whether talent management systems result in a closer alignment between international selection and corporate strategic objectives. Further, it would be interesting to explore the extent to which sophisticated talent management systems facilitate the development of truly global internal talent markets within MNCs and hence minimize the potential for regional or business unit silos that retard global resourcing within the MNC (see Collings et al. 2008).

In summary, this chapter has highlighted some of the strategic challenges associated with resourcing international assignees. It should be clear from our discussions that resourcing for international assignments is more complex than recruiting in a domestic context. We also explored the strategic constraints on the resourcing of international assignees. Next we attempted to profile the skill requirements of international assignees and considered the practice of international resourcing. Finally, we discussed some initiatives that MNCs could consider in adopting a more strategic view of resourcing international assignees. We identified talent management as a key initiative in this regard.

KEY LEARNING POINTS

- The resourcing of international assignees is more complex than resourcing in a domestic context due to a number of factors.
- Organizations face a number of emerging strategic constraints on international resourcing.
- While it is difficult to characterize an international manager, there are some factors that can aid organizations in selecting international assignees.
- In practice, resourcing international assignees tends to be overly focused on technical competence with a lack of emphasis on softer skills and family issues that paradoxically have been identified as key in explaining expatriate adjustment while on assignment.
- MNCs can advance their international resourcing practice in terms of adopting a more strategic perspective. In particular, their efforts could focus on expanding traditional expatriate pools and developing their international talent management practice.

103

REFERENCES

Adler, N.J. and Bartholomew, S. (1992) 'Managing globally competent people', *Academy of Management Executive* 6, 3: 52–65.

Anderson, B.A. (2005) 'Expatriate selection: good management or good luck?', *International Journal of Human Resource Management* 16: 567–583.

Barham, K. and Wills, S. (1992) *Managing Across Frontiers*, Asridge: Asridge Management Centre.

Björkman, I. and Gertsen, M. (1992) 'Selecting and training Scandinavian expatriates', *Scandinavian Journal of Management* 9:145–164.

Black, J.S., Gregersen, H.B., Mendenhall, M.E. and Stroh, L.K. (1999) *Globalizing People through International Assignments*, Reading, MA: Addison-Wesley.

Bognanno, M. and Sparrow, P.R. (1995) 'Integrating HRM strategy using culturally defined competencies at British Petroleum: cross-cultural implementation issues,' in J.M. Hiltrop and P.R. Sparrow (eds) *European Casebook on Human Resource and Change Management*, London: Prentice-Hall.

Brewster, C. (1988) 'Managing expatriates', *International Journal of Manpower* 9 (2):17–20.

Brewster, C. (1991) *The Management of Expatriates*, London: Kogan Page.

Briscoe, D. and Schuler, R. (2004) *International Human Resource Management*, London: Routledge.

Caligiuri, P.M. (2000) 'The big five personality characteristics as predictors of expatriate's desire to terminate the assignment and supervisor-related performance', *Personnel Psychology* 53:67–88.

Collings, D.G. and Scullion, H. (2006) 'Global staffing', in G.K. Stahl and I. Bjorkman (eds) *Handbook of Research in International Human Resource Management*, Cheltenham: Edward Elgar.

Collings, D.G., Morley, M.J. and Gunnigle, P. (2008) 'Composing the top management team in the international subsidiary: qualitative evidence on international staffing in US MNCs in the Republic of Ireland', *Journal of World Business*, in press.

Collings, D.G., Scullion, H. and Morley, M.J. (2007) 'Changing patterns of global staffing in the multinational enterprise: challenges to the conventional expatriate assignment and emerging alternatives', *Journal of World Business* 42, 2: 198–213.

Dowling, P.J. and Welch, D.E. (2004) *International Human Resource Management*, 4th edition, London: Thompson.

Edström, A. and Galbraith, J.R. (1977) 'Transfer of managers as a coordination and control strategy in multinational organizations', *Administrative Science Quarterly* 22:248–263.

Evans, P., Pucik, V. and Barsoux, J.L. (2002) *The Global Challenge: Frameworks For International Human Resource Management*, New York: McGraw-Hill-Irwin.

Franke, J. and Nicholson, N. (2002) 'Who shall we send? Cultural and other influences on the rating of selection criteria for expatriate assignments', *International Journal of Cross Cultural Management* 2:21–36.

GMAC (2006) *Global Relocation Trends: 2005 Survey Report,* Woodridge, IL: GMAC.

Harris, H. and Brewster, C. (1999) 'The coffee machine system: how international selection really works', *International Journal of Human Resource Management* 10: 488–500.

Harris, P.R. and Moran, R.T. (1996) *Managing Cultural Differences*, 4th edn, Houston, TX: Gulf Publishing Company.

Harvey, M., Speier, C. and Novicevic, M.M. (2001) 'A theory-based framework for strategic global human resource staffing policies and practices', *International Journal of Human Resource Management* 12:898–915.

Harzing, A.W.K. (1995) 'The persistent myth of high expatriate failure rates', *International Journal of Human Resource Management* 6:457–475.

Harzing, A.W. (2002) 'Are our referencing errors undermining our scholarship and credibility? The case of expatriate failure rates', *Journal of Organizational Behavior* 23: 127–148.

Harzing, A.W.K. (2004) 'Composing an international staff', in A.W.J. Harzing and J. Van Ruysseveldt (eds) *International Human Resource Management*, London: Sage.

Harzing, A.W. and Christensen, C. (2004) 'Expatriate failure: time to abandon the concept?', *Career Development International* 9:616–626.

Linehan, M. and Scullion, H. (2001) 'Selection, training and development for female international executives', *Career Development International* 6:318–323.

Michaels, E., Handfield-Jones, H. and Axelrod, B. (2001) *The War for Talent*, Boston, MA: Harvard Business School Press.

Miller, E. (1972) 'The selection decision for an international assignment: a study of the decision-maker's behaviour', *Journal of International Business Studies* 4: 45–65.

Scullion, H. (1991) 'Why companies prefer to use expatriates', *Personnel Management* 23:32–35.

Scullion, H. and Collings, D. (2006) 'International recruitment and selection', in H. Scullion and D.G. Collings (eds) *Global Staffing*, London: Routledge.

Scullion, H. and Starkey, K. (2000) 'The changing role of the corporate human resource function in the international firm', *International Journal of Human Resource Management* 11:1061–1081.

Sparrow, P.R. (1999a) *The IPD Guide on International Recruitment, Selection and Assessment*, London: Institute of Personnel and Development.

Sparrow, P.R. (1999b) 'International recruitment, selection and assessment', in P. Joynt and B. Morton (eds) *The Global HR Manager: Creating the Seamless Organization*, London: Institute of Personnel and Development.

Sparrow, P.R. (2006) *International Recruitment, Selection and Assessment*, London: CIPD.

Sparrow, P.R. (2007) 'Globalisation of HR at function level: four case studies of the international recruitment, selection and assessment process', *International Journal of Human Resource Management* 18, 5:845–867.

Sparrow, P.R. and Hiltrop, J.M. (1994) *European Human Resource Management in Transition*, London: Prentice-Hall.

Sparrow, P.R., Brewster, C. and Harris, H. (2004) *Globalizing Human Resource Management*, London: Routledge.

Stroh, L.K., Black, J.S., Mendenhall, M.E. and Gregersen, H.B. (2005) *International Assignments: An Integration of Strategy, Research and Practice*, London: Lawrence Erlbaum.

Tahvanainen, M. and Suutari, V. (2005) 'Expatriate performance management in MNCs', in H. Scullion and M. Linehan (eds) *International Human Resource Management: A Critical Text*, Basingstoke: Palgrave.

Tahvanainen, M., Welch, D. and Worm, V. (2005) 'Implications of short-term international assignments', *European Management Journal* 23:663–673.

105

Thomas, D.C. (1998) 'The expatriate experience: a critical review and synthesis', *Advances in International and Comparative Management* 12: 237–273.

Tung, R.L. (1981) 'Selection and training of personnel for overseas assignments', *Colombia Journal of World Business* 23:129–143.

Yamazaki, Y. and Kayes, C. (2004) 'An experiential approach to cross-cultural learning: a review and integration of competencies for successful expatriate adaptation', *Academy of Management Learning and Education* 5:362–379.

Chapter 6

An integrative framework for expatriate preparation and training

Ina Ehnert and Chris Brewster

CHAPTER OBJECTIVES

By the end of this chapter, readers will have:

- an understanding of recent developments on expatriate preparation with a particular focus on European organizations and research
- an appreciation of existing research into expatriate preparation and its impact on expatriate success, performance and adjustment
- identified the need for an integrative view on selection, training and preparation of expatriates
- become familiar with the literature on expatriate training and evaluation, with particular emphasis on alternatives to training, the value of training and development in the host country and the need for pre-return preparation
- explored an integrative framework for expatriate preparation

INTRODUCTION

Multinational corporations (MNCs) in Europe, as elsewhere, face increasing pressures to ensure efficiency and effectiveness in their expatriation practices. At the same time, investments in the development of high-quality talents are required. The significance of expatriates has increased in recent years (Scullion and Brewster 2001), with their numbers remaining steady or even rising. Rises in numbers are seen for smaller and newer international organizations and for self-initiated expatriation (GMAC 2005; Bonache et al. forthcoming). Identifying potential expatriates and developing these is seen as key to international success, particularly with the acknowledgement of expatriates as crucial for knowledge transfer within the organization (Bonache and Brewster 2001; Mäkelä forthcoming) (see Chapter 4). This development has been made easier for organizations by the spread of self-assessment tools that help firms to create candidate pools (Caligiuri and Tarique 2006). Additionally, expatriation is regarded as an important step in career development from the perspective of potential candidates themselves (Stahl et al. 2002; Bonache et al. forthcoming; Jokinen et al. forthcoming).

Although the importance of developing global talent and expatriates as a source for competitive advantage has been widely recognized, MNCs face an overall pressure for cost effectiveness and efficiency to compete in the international business arena. This challenge – the requirement for investment in high-quality talent development on the one hand and the simultaneous need for efficient practices on the other – has led these organizations to take a sharp look at their policies for expatriates. International organizations have responded by increased use of other options, such as relying more heavily on locally recruited staff, short-term transfers, more frequent international travel, international commuting or even teleconferencing (Mayerhofer et al. 2004; Harris and Dickmann 2005; see also Chapter 12). And, MNCs have also attempted to increase the cost effectiveness of their expatriates. A key element in this has been a growth in the attention organizations are paying to appropriate preparation for the assignment.

This chapter explores this issue: examining in turn the importance of preparation, what we know about it, what can be done to improve it and proposing a new integrative framework for understanding it.

IMPORTANCE OF EXPATRIATE TRAINING AND PREPARATION

Attention to preparation is linked to research into factors that contribute to expatriate success, job performance and international adjustment. There is an assumption that preparation for the posting will assist in adjustment to the new host location and in success in operating there, thereby indirectly reducing replacement costs associated with assignment failure. It is worth reminding ourselves, therefore, of what is known about adjustment and success. Individual factors, environmental (or contextual) factors and organizational factors have been suggested as leading to successful expatriate assignments (for reviews see Mendenhall et al. 2002; Bhaskar-Shrinivas et al. 2005; Holopainen and Björkman 2005).

Individual antecedents of expatriate success include personality characteristics, prior international experience and language skills (Caligiuri and Tarique 2006). The research on personality characteristics and skills for successful expatriation has received considerable attention. In this literature, extensive lists of personality characteristics necessary for successful and well-adjusted expatriates have been produced (for example, Torbiörn 1982; Mendenhall and Oddou 1985; Black et al. 1991; Kealey 1996; Caligiuri 2000a, 2000b). This stream of research assumes that certain generalizable personality traits are of importance for expatriate success and adjustment across different cultures and contexts (for reviews see Holopainen and Björkman 2005; see also Chapter 7). These personality characteristics facilitating cross-cultural adjustment include stress tolerance (Black 1988), relational skills (Tung 1981) and communication skills (Mendenhall and Oddou 1985). Caligiuri and Tarique (2006) assert that the five widely accepted personality factors ('the Big Five'), i.e. extroversion, agreeableness, conscientiousness, emotional stability and openness or intellect, have been found repeatedly to be related to expatriate success (for example, Ones and Viswesvaran 1997; Caligiuri 2000a). Personality characteristics are not susceptible to training and are an important issue in selection (but see Chapter 5 for a critique of the role of personality and competencies).

Empirical results are also mixed with regard to prior international experience, a factor that has been found to facilitate adjustment but which has its limits when it comes to relocating the expatriate to a new cultural environment (see Caligiuri and Tarique 2006). Louis (1980), Jones (1983) and Nicholson (1984) suggest that employees who are frequently mobile learn how to cope with and adjust to new work settings, as each successive transfer helps them become comfortable and productive faster and more easily. However, empirical studies have found inconsistent results: Parker and McEvoy (1993) found that prior international experience was significantly correlated with general adjustment; Pinder and Schroeder (1987) found no relation between frequency of prior transfers and capacity in the new country; Black (1988) found that prior international experience facilitates general adjustment, but not interaction and work adjustment.

In addition to the factors that cannot be taught, language skills have been identified as individual antecedents for expatriate success (Torbiörn 1982) although little agreement exists on its relative importance in comparison to other factors (Caligiuri and Tarique 2006). These authors conclude that, for some positions, language skills are more important than for others and that, where possible, expatriates with appropriate language skills should be selected. Language skills facilitate social integration, which has been identified as an effective expatriate coping strategy for adjustment (Stahl and Caligiuri 2005). More positive effects of language skills are the opportunity to profit from communicational abilities which have been found to be vital for expatriate performance (Holopainen and Björkman, 2005), to show an interest in the host culture and its members, to build professional and private relationships and to facilitate general adjustment to a new cultural environment. Language skills, of course, can be taught.

Organizational factors linked to success include, for example, job variables, organizational support, selection and, of central importance to this chapter, preparation, training and development. Important job variables are the nature of the job, the degree of interaction with host nationals, the objective and type of assignment. In European MNCs, a trend towards more developmental assignments can be observed, i.e. assignments that form an integral part of an organization's

109

international management development programme (Harris and Dickmann 2005). Organizational support at headquarters and in the host country has also been proposed to have a positive influence on expatriate success and commitment (Aycan 1997). This support includes, for example, pre-departure preparation, support during an assignment, pre-return preparation and logistical help.

Much of the work on the preparation and training that will assist this adjustment (for reviews, see Mendenhall et al. 2004) is built on the importance of the ability of the expatriate to understand the clues and cues being presented by the new environment, by new behaviours of others, etc. and to develop behaviours different to those that were 'natural' at home (see Chapter 7). Attention has been given recently to the role of cultural intelligence (CQ) in this regard – an attitude and skill that enables individuals to adapt effectively across cultures (Earley and Ang 2003; Earley and Mosakowski 2004; Earley and Peterson 2004). It is argued that this enables an individual to interpret unfamiliar and ambiguous gestures in ways as accurately as a national compatriot could.

However, this is a complex process. The expatriate has at the same time both to adjust to the environment and maintain the distinguishing characteristics that they are intended to bring in to the host country (Brewster 1995b). It remains unclear how much adjustment is needed for an expatriate to perform well and to balance between an organization's global demands and local responsiveness. Therefore, preparation itself becomes a complex process. Additional complexity is added when expatriates are sent to different destinations and do not return to their headquarters between these sojourns (see Chapter 10 for a discussion of career expatriation) or when preparation requirements for new types of assignment are considered. It remains important to note here that the purpose of an assignment is not expatriate adjustment and well-being in itself, but rather expatriate success and performance.

The link between preparation, adjustment and performance is crucial but tenuous, in part due to difficulties in determining the criteria by which to measure expatriate performance. The causal relationship between adjustment and performance has not yet been clarified because high levels of adjustment do not necessarily lead to high performance (Holopainen and Björkman 2005). Clearly the three major variables affecting performance are the personality characteristics of the individual, the environment and the job requirements (Schuler et al. 1991). Failure can result from there being a lack of fit across any combination of these three factors. Any misalignment in the first factor can be addressed through recruitment and selection and misalignments in the other two through preparation.

However imperfect training may be as a substitute for actual foreign living experience, it is still valuable if it can raise awareness of differing cultural norms and reduce the often painful and agonizing experience of adjusting to another culture. This would, in turn, help the organization to avoid the great damage that culture shock and cultural misunderstanding can do to its operating relationship (Robock and Simmonds 1983: 562).

110

It has been suggested that a realistic preview of what the expatriate has to expect in an unfamiliar cultural and job environment facilitates expatriate adjustment and contributes to job performance. Numerous authors (for example, Tung 1998; Caligiuri et al. 2001; Kühlmann 2001; Caligiuri and Tarique 2006) have pointed out the important role of training in creating realistic expectations. However, organizations undertaking training and development programmes for expatriates have found that the process is complex.

UNDERSTANDING EXPATRIATE TRAINING AND PREPARATION

Four problems make training and development for international assignments more complex than for domestic assignments. First, the expatriate has to adjust not only to a new job and a new role, but also to a new culture (Mendenhall and Oddou 1985). Second, many potential critical incidents and cultural paradoxes cannot be foreseen before an assignment, raising the need for individualized expatriate in-country support (Mendenhall and Stahl 2000). Third, since the stress associated with a foreign assignment falls on all family members (Harris and Moran 1979; Harvey 1985) the issue of training programmes for the partner and family need to be addressed. A fourth problem concerns the problem of repatriation. This has only been recognized more recently, but is now developing an extensive literature (see Chapter 9). Many MNCs seem to perform poorly with regard to retaining their expatriates on return and thus face the danger of losing their investments when the high-skilled managers that they have developed at considerable cost leave the organization (see, for example, Stahl et al. 2002; see also Chapter 9).

The four problems together indicate that the tasks surrounding international assignments   such as expatriate training and preparation – have become critical HRM activities in MNCs. Caligiuri and Tarique (2006: 302) assert that:

> Given the criticality of their roles and the associated challenges of living and working in another country, maximising the cross-national effectiveness of international assignees has become an increasingly important function for researchers and human resources (HR) practitioners alike.

Expatriates themselves are very positive about the value of training programmes (Harris and Brewster 1999; GMAC 2005). In the past, evidence has been provided that European and Japanese firms tend to use pre-departure training programmes more often than US MNCs (Torbiörn 1982; Tung 1982). Compared to US MNCs, European companies have a longer history of moving managers around the world (Hamill 1989) and this may explain that finding to some extent.

Cross-cultural training has long been advocated as a means of facilitating effective cross-cultural interactions (Brislin 1986), yet in practice there still seems to be a gap between the training provided even by European MNCs and the perceived needs of expatriates for training and preparation before, during and after an assignment (for example, Stahl et al. 2002). Today, many MNCs prepare their expatriates for assignments (GMAC 2005), but these practices are by no means common in all organizations (Harris and Brewster 1999). Other forms of preparation – briefing, shadowing, learning by doing, self-study – are more frequent than formal training programmes (Mayrhofer and Scullion 2002) and may be more cost effective.

Models of training and development for expatriate managers, developed over the last three decades, consider the task, the individual and the environment before deciding the depth of training required (Tung 1981; Rahim 1983). Tung's (1981) framework for selecting cross-cultural training methods identified two main dimensions:

1 the degree of interaction required in the host culture
2 the similarity between the expatriate's home culture and the host culture.

Mendenhall and Oddou (1986) developed this framework by grouping training methods according to their level of rigour and by discussing the duration of time for each type of training programme corresponding to the degree of interaction and culture similarity. This framework consisted of three levels:

1 information-giving approaches (e.g. factual briefing and awareness training)
2 affective approaches (e.g. culture assimilator training, critical incidents and role plays)
3 immersion approaches (e.g. assessment centres, field experience and simulations).

Black and Mendenhall (1991) further refined those frameworks by using Bandura's Social Learning Theory to make assumptions explicit about why cross-cultural training is effective and about which training method is appropriate for which situation.

Mendenhall et al. (1995) make the point that while these models are well known among academics, to date few human resource directors use them when selecting and designing cross-cultural training programmes for their companies. They argue that the design of such training programmes is still done informally, with little regard to findings in the research literature.

Numerous training programmes have been developed to help expatriates operate more quickly and more effectively in the new country. Many of these have been drawn up by experienced expatriates who have moved into management

112

development and training roles or by consultancies or colleges drawing on the same base of experienced expatriates. In many cases their experience will have been gained at a time when the pressures on cost reduction and performance were much lower. As a result the programmes are usually strong on what might be termed the cultural hygiene factors – ensuring, usually anecdotally, that the potential expatriate does not make immediately embarrassing or insensitive cultural mistakes and that they can handle the issues raised by living in the country. They are rarely focused on resolving business problems. These programmes tend to take as models the picture of middle-aged, confident, male professionals moving from a developed Christian country to a less developed area with noticeably different religions and social customs such as Africa or the Middle East (Pickard and Brewster 1992).

DISAGGREGATING THE POPULATION

The requirement and opportunities for preparation will vary considerably and the expatriate community needs to be disaggregated in order to identify appropriate training and preparation. Some basic issues will have a considerable effect on the requirement for preparation. Thus, the job that the person undertakes will have a considerable impact: if it is a senior management job or a sales job, understanding governmental and institutional arrangements and interacting with locals may be crucial, i.e. preparation for this will be needed. If the job is very technical and involves little interaction, less of that kind of preparation will be required. If the country the expatriate is going to is familiar (from holidays, for example) or is near home, there will be a different requirement than if the country were far away and very different in terms of culture, religion, customs, etc. Whether the expatriate is accompanied by their family will have an effect. Similarly, how the expatriate will live (in a 'compound' with other expatriates, in a big multicultural city or 'up-country') will have an impact on the required type of preparation (Pickard and Brewster 1992). The expatriates' background (ethnicity, education and experience) will be considerations. And so will their language skills (see Figure 6.1).

Opportunities for preparation will also have an effect. The evidence is that about half of the European MNCs in one study (Mayrhofer and Scullion 2002) generally managed to give their expatriates less than 3 weeks between the decision to expatriate and departure; figures ranged from a minimum of immediate start (0 days) to a maximum of 120 days, with the expatriates receiving on average 12 days to prepare themselves for the assignment. This means that the time available for preparation was very limited – particularly in view of the pressures of completing current work, making family, home and other arrangements and organizing the move itself. An earlier survey of Finnish expatriates (Suutari and Brewster 1998) found that they had more time – 3½ months on average. Instructively, this earlier

113

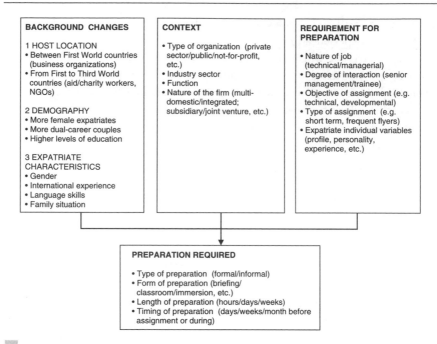

Figure 6.1 *Disaggregating the population.*

survey found a clear statistical correlation between those expatriates who had a short time to make the move and those who were dissatisfied with their preparation.

The world of the expatriate is changing rapidly in at least two significant areas. First, there are important changes in host location. It is necessary, here again, to disaggregate the expatriate population. While it appears that among MNCs expatriation is increasingly between wealthy First World countries, in recent years there has been a commensurate growth in expatriation from the rich First World to the poor Third World among aid and charity workers and people working for international intergovernmental organizations. Even here, the pressures for performance are increasing: the new United Nations Task Group on efficiency within the organization is a clear, but by no means the only, example (see Chapter 14).

Equally, changes in the demographic profile (younger, more women – see Chapter 13), dual-career couples and higher levels of education of expatriates will affect traditional patterns of expatriation and will create demands for a clearer focus on the assignment as part of career progression and a means of developing broader senior management capabilities. Expatriates may, in the future, demand explicit guarantees about their subsequent careers.

While some personality characteristics of successful domestic and international managers have been suggested to be universal (for example, Phillips 1993; Trompenaars 1993) and are not susceptible to training, many researchers propose that particular skills that can be developed are needed for success in cross-cultural encounters (for example, Mendenhall and Oddou 1985; Kealey and Protheroe 1996; see also Lievens et al. 2003). The reasons are that successful development of international business demands a higher level of skills and qualities than for managing in a domestic market and that managers working overseas will be involved in a wider range of activities, roles and responsibilities than those required in the home market. The international manager needs additional skills to reconcile the cultural problems created by the international environment. Possessing an awareness of the difficulties is not enough in this situation.

In these circumstances the need for pre-departure preparation has become crucial for MNCs to save their 'investments' in expatriate managers by reintegrating them successfully into the host country or to a new assignment. Preparation is not the same as training. Indeed, it may be that some of the alternatives are more expedient and more cost effective. They include a variety of different approaches. We adapt a broad notion of preparation and include the period before and during an expatriate's sojourn. First, however, we discuss different training and preparation scenarios and their effectiveness.

EFFECTIVENESS OF CROSS-CULTURAL TRAINING

The objectives of cross-cultural training are to facilitate, first, expatriates' effective interactions across different cultures, second, their adjustment to cultural and work environments and, third, high-quality job performance. Depending on the type of assignment, building social networks in the host country can also be of importance (see Harris and Dickmann 2005). Learning objectives for formal training programmes have often been categorized into cognitive, affective and behavioural dimensions (see Gertsen 1990).

This is based on two assumptions (see Kealey and Protheroe 1996):

1 Expatriates need to be provided with knowledge about the host culture, that they need to learn how to make cultural attributions, how to cope with negative emotions that could result from stressful experiences in an unfamiliar cultural context, and how to exhibit new behaviours that are problem-solving oriented, appropriate and accepted in the host culture.
2 Cross-cultural training can provide expatriates with the qualities and skills desired such as intercultural sensitivity or communication skills (for a review on these qualities and skills see Hannigan 1990).

While the first assumption has been confirmed repeatedly as indicated in the earlier sections of this chapter, the latter has initiated an ongoing debate about whether and which cross-cultural training methods lead to the outcomes desired

115

(see the previous mention of cultural intelligence). The choice of learning objectives needs to be tailored to individual training needs and to organizational demands, which influences also the choice of adequate training methods or preparation scenarios.

Traditionally, various formal training methods have been suggested for preparing expatriates for an assignment (for reviews see Fowler and Gudykunst 2004; Blohm et al. 1996). These include lectures, written materials (e.g. books), videos or films, case studies, cultural assimilators or critical incidents, role playing, culture contact simulation games, video analysis, and intercultural exercises (individual or group). Available training methods have been categorized according to their main training approach (didactic, experiential or mixed) and main focus (culture general, culture specific or mixed) (Gertsen 1990). The training methods mentioned are neither equally efficient nor equally effective with regard to expatriate adjustment and performance.

A number of largely US-dominated and quantitative studies have focused on evaluating the effectiveness of cross-cultural training. The results have been compared and summarized in reviews (Black and Mendenhall 1990; Bhagat and Prien 1996; Kealey and Protheroe 1996; Bhawuk and Brislin 2000; Ehnert 2004; Mendenhall et al. 2004) and meta-analyses (Deshpande and Viswesvaran 1992; Morris and Robie 2001). The impact of cross-cultural training in these reviews is considered from being very strong and positive (for example, Deshpande and Viswesvaran 1992) to just slightly positive (Kealey and Protheroe 1996; Morris and Robie 2001; Mendenhall et al. 2004). In these reviews, attention to European research on expatriate training and effectiveness is limited (for exceptions see Mendenhall et al. 2004). Each of the reviews has looked at cross-cultural training effectiveness from a different perspective (Mendenhall et al. 2004), and not all reviews have differentiated between different training methods.

Black and Mendenhall (1990) compared the effects of cross-cultural training on the dependent variables of adjustment, performance and development of cross-cultural skills on three dimensions, i.e. the self, relationship and perceptual dimension. As the authors found primarily positive results on all three dependent variables in the studies reviewed they proposed 'that cross-cultural training has a positive impact on cross-cultural effectiveness' (Black and Mendenhall 1990: 120). In their meta-analysis, Deshpande and Viswesvaran (1992) reviewed nearly the same set of studies evaluating cross-cultural training for the 'real effects' on the development of cross-cultural skills, adjustment and performance. They come to the conclusion that cross-cultural training is effective but point out the limitation that a large number of studies were conducted with student and military training participants and not with expatriate managers. This is one of the shortcomings of studies evaluating cross-cultural training, raising doubts concerning the generalizability of the results.

116

More criticism on methodological shortcomings in the research on evaluating cross-cultural training has been mentioned in the reviews of Bhagat and Prien (1996), Kealey and Protheroe (1996) and Mendenhall et al. (2004). Kealey and Protheroe (1996) point out that previous reviews have compared the impact of different cross-cultural training methods without differentiating between categories such as informational, area studies and culture awareness training. These authors also assert that the methodological quality of the evaluation studies of cross-cultural training is insufficient and they suggest criteria for improving experimental studies that aim at examining the short- and long-term impact of cross-cultural training on the performance of expatriate managers: control groups, pre/post-tests of dependent variables, randomization of training and control groups, measurement of on-the-job performance, etc. (Kealey and Protheroe 1996).

LANGUAGE TRAINING

Learning a new language requires the expatriate's willingness and ability to dedicate time and resources to the training. Operating in any kind of managerial capacity where one does not know the language is definitely not impossible – there are many examples of successful managers who never learn the language of the country in which they operate. This is particularly the case in recent years when many European MNCs based in what might be termed 'non-English-speaking' countries, such as Germany, Spain and Portugal, have adopted English as the company's language of business. Despite this, those who learn even a basic level of language skills find the benefits to be significant and those who become fluent have an additional skill that will not only make them more effective in their role in the host country but will last them for the rest of their career. Apart from straightforward issues of communication and understanding, language learning shows a willingness to adapt that is appreciated by local employees and customers and provides a degree of confidence when 'side conversations' in the local language take place during meetings.

Language training can be provided before or during an assignment by formal training programmes or interactive self-learning tools on CD-ROM (Mendenhall and Stahl 2000). The benefits of language training seem to be clearer and less equivocal than general cross-cultural training, but the costs in terms of money and particularly time are considerable.

Formal training has come under attack in recent years for being expensive and not very cost efficient. Questions have been raised about whether the learning is really internalized, whether the learning is easily transferred into practice and whether it is appropriate for expatriates with limited time, in different circumstances and with different learning styles, to meet together for this form of classroom-based training (see also Earley and Peterson 2004). In conclusion, here, it

117

seems that even in cross-cultural research the complexities involved in these formal learning processes are sometimes underestimated: the difficulty of learning and sensemaking for someone exposed to a new culture may be much greater than has sometimes been assumed in cross-cultural comparative research, which usually operates by overly simplifying cultures to bipolar dimensions (see Osland and Bird 2000; Earley and Peterson 2004). In fact, of course, cultures are complex amalgams of multidimensional variation and as such difficult to encompass in formal training programmes in ways that are likely to match the experiences of international transferees.

Alternatives to formal training programmes

Formal training programmes can be particularly useful before going abroad but alternative problem-solving oriented and individual solutions have been suggested for both before and during the period the expatriate spends in the country. Mendenhall and Stahl (2000) have been among those scholars identifying the need for 'in-country, real-time training' arguing that expatriate pre-departure training is not enough and that cross-cultural training might be more effective when provided in the host country at an early stage of an assignment. While the authors also propose the use of formal training programmes for this real-time training, they admit that an important limitation of this approach remains; every expatriate gets the same training although individual needs and urgencies might differ substantially (see also Earley and Peterson 2004).

Expatriate managers need immediate answers to questions that arise from confusing cross-cultural encounters, so that problems do not fester and launch widespread negative ripple effects in relationships with employees, clients, government officials, customers or suppliers (Mendenhall and Stahl 2000: 254). More flexible solutions are needed to provide individuals with answers in critical intercultural situations and to generate problem-oriented solutions. These alternatives to formal training programmes include, for example, informal briefings, look-see visits, overlaps, shadowing, cultural coaching and mentoring.

INFORMAL BRIEFINGS

Brewster (1995a) found that two-thirds of European organizations use informal briefings for expatriates. Arguably, the chance to meet and discuss the host country with people who know it well, perhaps other employees of the company who are from that country or who have just returned from there, is among the cheapest and best forms of preparation. If the whole family is involved this can be particularly useful. These briefings can be arranged easily, fit in with the hectic schedules of the 'soon to move' and can provide the sort of information and even

118

contacts not available elsewhere. Many expatriates make their own arrangements of this sort. Properly managed they can be even more valuable. It is easy for the putative expatriate to meet with one or two people who have limited knowledge and miss some important aspects of living and working in the host country or to meet with individuals who may have an unwarrantedly prejudiced and jaundiced view of the country – or an impossibly romantic one. Careful selection of the briefers, so that they provide a rounded and comprehensive view, makes the process more effective.

LOOK-SEE VISITS

Some companies provide look-see visits. The costs here are obviously higher, particularly if, as one might hope, the family was included. However, the payoff can be substantial. Increasing numbers of the larger MNCs seem to be using this approach (two-thirds in a survey of Finnish MNCs; Suutari and Brewster 1998). It is obviously a good way for the expatriate or the family to prepare. They arrive in the country knowing something about it; having had some, however limited, experience of living there; knowing the work environment; and having made contacts both at work and in the community that can be activated when they make the transfer. Some MNCs have found, however, that such visits need to be carefully managed. They are to a degree unreal. On look-see visits the expatriates and their families will meet important people and be on their best behaviour; they will stay in the best hotels and eat at the best restaurants – their image of the country may take a hard knock when they arrive 'for real'.

OVERLAPS

Handovers from one expatriate to another are common and in some organizations are extended to ensure an overlap, particularly for managers. This has the significant advantages of allowing one to brief the other, to introduce them to key clients, government officers and so on and to 'show them the ropes' in the working environment. However, such overlaps are expensive, difficult to organize and can lead the local staff to be unclear about who is actually in charge.

SHADOWING

In some cases, particularly where the expatriates have been working in head office, it is possible for them to 'shadow' the country concerned – being responsible for the reports, communications with and results of the country concerned. They may

119

visit the country, meet with members of the staff there when they visit HQ and generally get a good feel for the country's issues, concerns and performance, at least as far as the MNC is concerned.

COMPUTER-BASED TRAINING (SELF-/E-LEARNING)

Recent years have seen a growth in computer-based training and development programmes. Apart from the commercially available options, some companies have been putting their own programmes on to the company intranet for expatriates (or even those who would like to be expatriates) to access in their own time. Since expatriates, particularly those without a family with them, are known to spend long hours on work-related matters, this makes a lot of sense. The flexibility of these systems too, with learners able to explore specific issues as they arise, is considerably greater than many other forms of development — and the costs, once established, are considerably lower (Mendenhall and Stahl 2000). The drawbacks of e-learning are that the expatriate is isolated in his learning experience, while cultures are better learned in an experiential way and in direct contact with host-country nationals.

CULTURAL COACHING

The growth of e-learning in recent years is part of a wider trend for expatriates to undertake self-directed learning. This includes development on-the-job and work-based learning in the host country. This has become increasingly popular as this form of support allows the tailoring of development to individual needs (for examples, see Bolten 2005; Harris and Dickmann 2005). Cultural coaching provides the expatriate with advice from external personal consultants or advisers (Mendenhall and Stahl 2000). In the host country, expatriate managers might find themselves confronted with behaviours and conflicts they do not understand and which their previous learned scripts do not help them to understand. Having a coach familiar with the new culture can be of significant help.

The objectives of cultural coaching are to assist the expatriate managers to identify the dilemmas they are facing, to help assess the expatriate's job and private situation, to provide confidential space for reflective and individualized learning processes and to show different possible avenues for problem-oriented action (Mendenhall and Stahl 2000; Barmeyer 2002). Follow-up coaching can be supported with e-coaching, i.e. support by e-mail and telephone and e-learning (Bolten 2005). Cultural coaches can support expatriates' sensemaking processes, allowing them a better understanding of unfamiliar cultural situations and making it easier to acquire additional knowledge and skills.

120

While empirical evidence for the effectiveness of cultural coaching remains anecdotal (for example, Mendenhall and Stahl 2000; Barmeyer 2002), it seems that this is a promising instrument for developing highly qualified international managers and global leaders (Mendenhall and Stahl 2000; see also Evans et al. 2002). However, the availability of suitable cultural coaches is a major concern (Bolten 2005) and the service can involve high costs. A more cost-effective possibility might be the use of cultural mentors.

CULTURAL MENTORING

For expatriate managers, mentoring relationships are of great importance as mentoring can facilitate adjustment during and reintegration after an assignment. Feldman and Bolino (1999) found that 'on-site' mentoring was positively associated with expatriate socialization. However, this instrument is rarely used by European MNCs. In a study by Mayrhofer and Scullion (2002), about one-quarter of the respondents (23%) had a mentor providing them with support, but those expatriates rated the assistance as the most helpful support instrument provided to them. Mentors can provide their protégés with task-related assistance, social support, career advice and can act as role models (see Feldman and Bolino 1999). Ideally, mentors will have been faced with the same challenges as their protégés. Potential mentors could be senior managers of the organization, trained host-country managers or returning expatriates – a much under-utilized resource (Mendenhall and Stahl 2000). Seeing that problem-focused expatriate coping strategies have a positive impact on their cultural adjustment (Stahl and Caligiuri 2005), it seems to be important that this knowledge and experience is transferred from repatriates to future expatriates. Some scholars see a similarity between formal post-arrival cross-cultural training and cultural mentoring, since the advantage of both is a more problem-oriented approach to expatriate preparation (Mendenhall and Stahl 2000; Selmer 2001).

PRE-RETURN PREPARATION

Pre-repatriation preparation is just begining to grow in popularity (see Chapter 9; Kühlmann and Stahl 1995; Linehan and Scullion 2002; Suutari and Brewster 2003). As is pointed out in Chapter 9, repatriation is increasingly being viewed less as the end of an assignment and more as a stage in a career. In that light, and in view of the loss of experience, expertise and global thinking that occurs with the loss of employees after repatriation, organizations are becoming more aware of the need to manage repatriation effectively: and that includes a significant element of preparation before and training after return (Black et al. 1999).

121

AN INTEGRATIVE FRAMEWORK

The literature proposes viewing expatriate selection, training and preparation from an integrative perspective in order to enhance the cost effectiveness of international assignments and the success of training efforts (Caligiuri 2000b; Caligiuri et al. 2001; Lievens et al. 2003). Harris and Brewster (1999) suggested an integrative framework for expatriate selection and preparation. This framework includes the selection of expatriates according to job and individual variables such as family considerations.

The proposal is to use the framework (see Figure 6.2) during the selection process in order to make a full assessment of the individual's current level of competence in the areas of international adjustment. MNCs might also be able to attempt to ascertain the level of learning obtained from previous assignments. Leading on from this assessment, an evaluation of preparation needs can be developed for the expatriate and partner/family and a suitable preparation scenario produced.

Differing degrees of cross-cultural training will need to be provided depending on the extent to which each of these variables is present in the expatriate assignment.

We should conclude this chapter by returning to the challenge with which we started: the tension in the management of expatriates between efficient practices (which argues for reducing costs) and the requirement for high-quality talent development (which implies serious investment). The tension will remain but is perhaps partly resolved by the notion of cost-effective HRM practices. Mendenhall

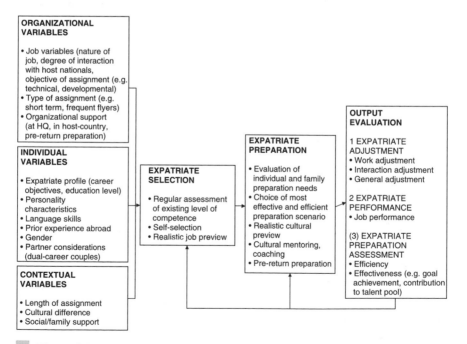

Figure 6.2 An integrative framework for expatriate performance.

122

and Stahl (2000) have made the point that maximum learning for expatriates might occur if they are plunged into their new environment without any preparation or support: but this is a risky way to ensure such learning and few organizations are ready to take such chances. The importance of satisfactory completion of the work comes before the assumed advantages of significant learning.

The importance of organizational and contextual factors for successful assignments has been underestimated in practice and research (Aycan 1997). However, in the case of expatriates there seems to be a growing body of evidence that preparation reduces the time it takes for expatriates to become effective. Preparation does not need to be – indeed perhaps is better not – formal training programmes: there are many other cheaper and more effective options, including mentoring. If formal training programmes are chosen these should be customized. Ongoing, post-arrival support and training may be particularly beneficial (see Selmer 2001). The focus in expatriate preparation should be on supporting the expatriate in making sense of the new cultural situation and on supporting the development of individual coping and problem-solving strategies (see Stahl and Caligiuri 2005).

Case study 6.1
Educating Alex?

Alex Nichols has just found out that his company is sending him from the headquarters operation in Scotland to the new subsidiary in St Petersburg for around 3 years. Despite his natural caution, Alex is quite keen on the idea: as an expatriate he will get paid considerably more than he is being paid now; as a single man, now is a good time to be taking such a step; and his career after the assignment should be enhanced. He has never been to Russia but he has seen pictures of St Petersburg and it looks a wonderful place. Alex has always been one of those people who prepared meticulously for each new job and he thinks that this recognition of his skills is a reward for that – and he intends to use the month or so that he has before going to Russia to wind up his current project, organize his affairs at home and prepare for his time in Russia. He has come to you as the company's HRM specialist to advise him on how he can prepare.

Questions
1 What does Alex need to be made aware of before he goes?
2 What would you suggest Alex does to prepare himself, in the circumstances?
3 What help do you think the company should be ready to give him?
4 How would you, in the time available, arrange a valuable and cost-effective preparation programme for Alex?

CONCLUSION

Overall, the evidence is that preparation and training for international assignments is effective in decreasing time to proficiency in the new assignment, in helping expatriates and their families adjust to their new lives and that employees feel that it is beneficial. By contrast, most international assignees still go to another country with little or no preparation at all. The reasons are probably a rather messy combination of a lack of understanding of the value of such preparation, a shortage of time between the appointment and the transfer to the foreign country, rather than the cost of the preparation, which is usually cheap compared to the importance of the assignment.

It is clear that, where preparation is undertaken, it is variable in nature. There is an extensive range of options available and all of them are used in some settings. This is in one way as it should be: there is a huge range of circumstances, countries and people involved and it is inappropriate to assume that 'one size will fit all'. By the same token, there is little evidence that the variety is a response to the variety of circumstances: rather it seems that different organizations tend to adopt particular patterns (with some always sending people to places like Farnham Castle that run such programmes while others rely on look-see visits, etc.). The implication of the research findings to date is that expatriate preparation would be significantly improved with careful evaluation of the needs and the options.

KEY LEARNING POINTS

- Recent developments in expatriation and in international business have given rise to an increased importance for effective expatriate preparation in order to ensure adjustment and performance.
- Expatriate adjustment and performance is influenced by various individual, contextual and organizational factors.
- As these factors mutually influence each other we propose an integrative view on expatriate preparation which includes expatriate selection, pre-return preparation and evaluation of expatriate adjustment and performance.
- The choice of the 'right' form of expatriate preparation should be tailored according to an expatriate's individual needs in the context of organizational, cultural and social requirements.

REFERENCES

Aycan, Z. (1997) 'Expatriate adjustment as a multifaceted phenomenon: individual and organizational level predictors', *International Journal of Human Resource Management* 8, 4:434–456.

 124

Barmeyer, C.I. (2002) 'Interkulturelles Coaching', in C. Rauen (ed.) *Handbuch Coaching*, Göttingen: Hogrefe.

Bhagat, R.S. and Prien, K.O. (1996) 'Cross-cultural training in organisational contexts', in D. Landis and R.S. Bhagat (eds) *Handbook of Intercultural Training*, Thousand Oaks, CA: Sage.

Bhaskar-Shrinivas, P., Harrison, D.A., Shaffer, M.A. and Luk, D.M. (2005) 'Input-based and time-based models of international adjustment: meta-analytic evidence and theoretical extensions', *Academy of Management Journal* 48, 2:257–281.

Bhawuk, D.P.S. and Brislin, R.W. (2000) 'Cross-cultural training: a review', *Applied Psychology* 49, 1:162–191.

Black, J.S. (1988) 'Work role transitions: a study of American expatriate managers in Japan', *Journal of International Business Studies* 30, 2:119–134.

Black, J.S. and Mendenhall, M. (1990) 'Cross-cultural training effectiveness: a review and a theoretical framework for future research', *Academy of Management Review* 15, I:113–136.

Black, J.S. and Mendenhall, M.E. (1991) 'A practical but theory-based framework for selecting cross-cultural training methods', in M.E. Mendenhall and G.R. Oddou (eds) *International Human Resource Management*, Boston MA: PWS-Kent Publishing Company.

Black, J.S., Mendenhall, M. and Oddou, G. (1991) 'Toward a comprehensive model of international adjustment: an integration of multiple theoretical perspectives', *Academy of Management Review* 16, 2:291–317.

Black, J.S., Gregersen, H.B., Mendenhall, M.E. and Stroh, L.K. (1999) *Globalizing People Through International Assignments*, New York: Addison-Wesley-Longman.

Bolten, J. (2005) 'Interkulturelle Personalentwicklungsmaßnahmen: Training, Coaching und Meditation', In G.K. Stahl, W. Mayrhofer and T.M. Kühlmann (eds) *Internationales Personalmanagement*, Munich: Rainer Hampp.

Bonache, J. and Brewster, C. (2001) 'Knowledge transfer and the management of expatriation', *Thunderbird International Business Review* 43, 1: 145–168.

Bonache, J., Brewster, C. and Suutari, V. (forthcoming) 'International mobility, knowledge and careers: editorial', special edition, *International Studies in Management and Organization* Fall, 37, 3.

Brewster, C. (1995a) 'Effective expatriate training', in J. Selmer (ed.) *Expatriate Management: New Ideas for International Business*, Westport, CT: Quorum Books.

Brewster, C. (1995b) 'The paradox of expatriate adjustment', in J. Selmer (ed.) *Expatriate Management: New Ideas for International Business*, Westport, CT: Quorum Books.

Brislin, R.W. (1986) 'The wording and translation of research instruments', in W.J. Lonner and J.W. Berry Fidel (eds) *Methods in Cross-cultural Research*, Beverly Hills, CA: Sage.

Caligiuri, P. (2000a) 'The Big Five personality characteristics as predictors of expatriate success', *Personnel Psychology* 53: 67–88.

Caligiuri, P. (2000b) 'Selecting expatriates for personality characteristics: a moderating effect of personality on the relationship between host national contact and cross-cultural adjustment', *Management International Review* 40, 1: 61–80.

Caligiuri, P. and Tarique, I. (2006) 'International assignee selection and cross-cultural training and development', in G. Stahl and I. Björkman (eds) *Handbook of Research in International Human Resource Management*, Cheltenham: Edward Elgar.

125

Caligiuri, P., Phillips, J., Lazarova, M., Tarique, I. and Bürgi, P. (2001) 'The theory of met expectations applied to expatriate adjustment: the role of cross-cultural training', *International Journal of Human Resource Management* 12, 3: 357–372.

Deshpande, S.P. and Viswesvaran, C. (1992) 'Is cross-cultural training of expatriate managers effective? A meta analysis', *International Journal of Intercultural Relations* 16, 3:295–310.

Earley, P.C. and Ang, S. (2003) *Cultural Intelligence: Individual Interactions across Cultures*, Stanford, CA: Stanford University Press.

Earley, P.C. and Mosakowski, E. (2004) 'Cultural intelligence', *Harvard Business Review* 82, 10:139–146.

Earley, P.C. and Peterson, R.S. (2004) 'The elusive cultural chameleon: cultural intelligence as a new approach to intercultural training for the global manager', *Academy of Management Learning and Education* 3, 1:100–115.

Ehnert, I. (2004) 'Die Effektivität von interkulturellen Trainings: Überblick über den aktuellen Forschungsstand', Hamburg: Dr. Kovac.

Evans, P.A.L., Pucik, V. and Barsoux, J. (2002) *The Global Challenge: Frameworks for International Human Resource Management*, Boston, MA: McGraw-Hill-Irwin.

Feldman, D.C. and Bolino, M.C. (1999) 'The impact of on-site mentoring on expatriate socialization: a structural equation modelling approach', *International Journal of Human Resource Management* 10, 1:54–71.

Fowler, S.M. and Blohm, J.M. (2004) 'An analysis of methods for international training', in D. Landis, J.M. Bennett and M.J. Bennett *Handbook of Intercultural Training,* Thousand Oaks, CA: Sage.

Gertsen, M.C. (1990) 'Intercultural competence and expatriates', *International Journal of Human Resource Management* 3, 1:341–362.

GMAC Global Relocation Services/Windham International (2005) *Global Relocation Trends: 2005 Survey; Report,* New York: GMAC Global Relocation Services/Windham International; http://www.gmacglobalrelocation.com.

Gudykunst, W.B., Guzley, R.M. and Hammer, M.R. (1996) 'Designing intercultural training', in D. Landis and R.S. Bhagat (eds) *Handbook of Intercultural Training,* Thousand Oaks, CA: Sage.

Hamill, J. (1989) 'Expatriate policies in British multinationals', *Journal of General Management* 14, 4:18–33.

Hannigan, T. (1990) 'Traits, attitudes, and skills that are related to intercultural effectiveness and their implications for cross-cultural training: a review of the literature', *International Journal of Intercultural Relations* 14, 1:89–111.

Harris, H. and Brewster, C. (1999) 'An integrative framework for pre-departure preparation', in C. Brewster and H. Harris (eds) *International HRM - Contemporary Issues in Europe,* London: Routledge.

Harris, H. and Dickmann, M. (2005) 'International management development: a CIPD guide to help companies deliver effective international management development', *Chartered Institute of Personnel and Development (CIPD)*; http://www.cipd.co.uk/NR/rdonlyres/79BCFBA3-B9A9-451C-9FD8-6B1A32EE3ABE/0/intmandev1205.pdf.

Harris, P.R. and Moran, R.T. (1979) *Managing Cultural Differences,* 2nd edn, Houston, TX: Gulf.

Harvey, M.G. (1985) 'The executive family: an overlooked variable in international assignments', *Columbia Journal of World Business* 20, 1:84–92.

Holopainen, J. and Björkman, I. (2005) 'The personal characteristics of the successful expatriate: a critical review of the literature and an empirical investigation', *Personnel Review* 43, 1:37–50.

Jokinen, T., Brewster, C. and Suutari, V. (forthcoming) 'Career capital during international work experiences: contrasting self-initiated expatriate experiences and assigned expatriation', *International Journal of Human Resource Management.*

Jones G.R. (1983) 'Psychological orientation and the process of organizational socialization: an interactionist perspective', *Academy of Management Review* 8:464–474.

Kealey, D.J. (1996) 'The challenge of international personnel selection', in D. Landis and R.S. Bhagat (eds) *Handbook of Intercultural Training*, Thousand Oaks, CA: Sage.

Kealey, D.J. and Protheroe, D.R. (1996) 'The effectiveness of cross-cultural training for expatriates: an assessment of the literature on the issue', *International Journal of Intercultural Relations* 20, 2:141–65.

Kühlmann, T.M. (2001) 'The German approach to developing global leaders via expatriation', in M.E. Mendenhall, T.M. Kühlmann and G.K. Stahl (eds) *Developing Global Business Leaders: Policies, Processes, and Innovations*, Westport, CT, London: Quorum Books.

Kühlmann, T.M. and Stahl, G.K. (1995) 'Die Wiedereingliederung von Mitarbeitern nach einem Auslandseinsatz: Wissenschaftliche Grundlagen', in T.M. Kühlmann (ed.) *Mitarbeiterentsendung ins Ausland: Auswahl, Vorbereitung, Betreuung und Wiedereingliederung*, Göttingen: Verlag für Angewandte Psychologie.

Lievens, F., Harris, M.M., Van Keer, E. and Bisqueret, C. (2003) 'Predicting cross-cultural training performance: the validity of personality, cognitive ability, and dimensions measured by an assessment center and a behavior description interview', *Journal of Applied Psychology* 88, 3:476–489.

Linehan, M. and Scullion, H. (2002) 'Repatriation of European female corporate executives: an empirical study', *International Journal of Human Resource Management* 13, 2:254–267.

Louis, M.R. (1980) 'Surprise and sense making: what newcomers experience in entering unfamiliar organisational settings', *Administrative Science Quarterly* 25: 226–251.

Mäkelä, K. (forthcoming) 'Knowledge sharing through expatriate relationships: a social capital perspective', *International Studies in Management and Organization* Fall, 37, 3.

Mayerhofer, H., Hartmann, L.C., Michelitsch-Riedl, G. and Kollinger, I. (2004) 'Flexpatriate assignments: a neglected issue in global staffing', *International Journal of Human Resource Management* 15, 8:1371–1389.

Mayrhofer, W. and Scullion, H. (2002) 'Female expatriates in international business: empirical evidence from the German clothing industry', *International Journal of Human Resource Management* 13, 5:815–836.

Mendenhall, M.E. and Oddou, G. (1985) 'The dimensions of expatriate acculturation: a review', *Academy of Management Review* 10, 1:39–48.

Mendenhall, M.E. and Oddou, G. (1986) 'Acculturation profiles of expatriate managers: implications for cross-cultural training programs', *Columbia Journal of Business* Winter: 73–79.

Mendenhall, M.E., Punnett, B.J. and Ricks, D. (1995) *Global Management*, Cambridge, MA: Blackwell.

Mendenhall, M.E. and Stahl, G.K. (2000) 'Expatriate training and development: where do we go from here?', *Human Resource Management* 39, 2/3:251–265.

Mendenhall, M.E., Kühlmann, T.M., Stahl, G.K. and Osland, J.S. (2002) 'Employee development and expatriate assignments', in M.J. Gannon and K.L. Newman (eds) *The Blackwell Handbook of Cross-cultural Management*, Oxford: Blackwell.

Mendenhall, M.E., Stahl, G.K., Ehnert, I., Oddou, G., Osland, J.S. and Kühlmann, T.M. (2004) 'Evaluation studies of cross-cultural training programs: a review of the literature from 1988 to 2000', in D. Landis, J.M. Bennett and M.J. Bennett (eds) *Handbook of Intercultural Training*, Thousand Oaks, CA: Sage.

Morris, M.A. and Robie, C. (2001) 'A meta-analysis of the effects of cross-cultural training on expatriate performance and adjustment', *International Journal of Training and Development* 5, 2:112–125.

Nicholson N. (1984) 'A theory of work role transitions', *Administrative Science Quarterly* 29: 172–191.

Ones, D. and Viswesvaran, C. (1997) 'Personality determinants in the prediction of aspects of expatriate job success', in Z. Aycan (ed.) *Expatriate Management: Theory and Practice*, Greenwich, CT: JAI Press.

Osland, J.S. and Bird, A. (2000) 'Beyond sophisticated stereotyping: cultural sense-making in context', *Academy of Management Executive* 14, 1:65–79.

Parker, B. and McEvoy, G.M. (1993) 'Initial examination of a model of intercultural adjustment', *International Journal of Intercultural Relations* 17: 355–379.

Phillips, N. (1993) 'Cross-cultural training', *Journal of European Industrial Training* 17, 2:32–34.

Pickard, J. and Brewster, C. (1992) *Evaluation of Expatriate Training*, Farnham Castle: Centre for International Briefing.

Pinder, C.C. and Schroeder K.G. (1987) 'Time to proficiency following job transfer', *Academy of Management Journal* 30, 2:336–353.

Rahim, A. (1983) 'A model for developing key expatriate executives', *Personnel Journal* 62, 4:312–317.

Robock, S.H. and Simmonds, K. (1983) *International Business and Multinational Enterprises*, Homewood, IL: Irwin.

Schuler, R.S., Fulkerson, J.R.K. and Dowling, P.J. (1991) 'Strategic performance measurement and management in multinational corporations', *Human Resource Management* 30:365–392.

Scullion, H. and Brewster, C. (2001) 'The management of expatriates: messages from Europe', *Journal of World Business* 36, 4:346–365.

Selmer, J. (2001) 'The preference for predeparture or postarrival cross-cultural training: an exploratory approach', *Journal of Managerial Psychology* 16, 1:50–58.

Stahl, G.K. and Caligiuri, P. (2005) 'The effectiveness of expatriate coping strategies: the moderating role of cultural distance, position level, and time on the international assignment', *Journal of Applied Psychology* 90, 4:603–615.

Stahl, G.K., Miller, E.L. and Tung, R.L. (2002) 'Toward the boundaryless career: a closer look at the expatriate career concept and the perceived implications of an international assignment', *Journal of World Business* 37, 3:216–227.

Suutari, V. and Brewster, C. (1998) 'The adaptation of expatriates in Europe: evidence from Finnish companies', *Personnel Review* 27, 1/2:89–103.

Suutari, V. and Brewster, C. (2003) 'Repatriation: empirical evidence from a longitudinal study of careers and expectations among Finnish expatriates', *International Journal of Human Resource Management* 14, 7:1132–1151.

Torbiörn, I. (1982) *Living Abroad: Personal Adjustment and Personnel Policy in the Overseas Setting*, New York: Wiley.

Trompenaars, F. (1993) *Riding the Waves of Culture*, London: Economist Books.

Tung, R.L. (1981) 'Selection and training of personnel for overseas assignments', *Columbia Journal of World Business* 16, 1:68–78.

Tung, R.L. (1982) 'Selection and training procedures of US, European and Japanese Multinationals', *California Management Review* 25, 1: 57–71.

Tung, R.L. (1998) 'A contingency framework of selection and training of expatriates revisited', *Human Resource Management Review* 8, 1:23–31.

Chapter 7

Expatriate adjustment

A more nuanced view

Arno Haslberger

CHAPTER OBJECTIVES

By the end of this chapter, readers will have:

- an understanding of the issues pertinent to adjustment success and failure
- an appreciation of the factors that shape 'culture shock'
- insights into the process of adjustment of individuals to foreign environments and overseas work contexts
- sensitivity to cross- and spillover effects in the adjustment of international assignees and their families in various domains
- information on changes to expatriates' identity triggered by experiences abroad
- an understanding of support activities given by organizations to facilitate expatriate adjustment

INTRODUCTION

For people hired from overseas, the single largest reason for failure is the inability of their families, particularly non-working 'trailing partners', to adjust to living conditions, says Mr Everhart [a senior partner at Korn/Ferry]. This is especially true for companies that have built operations in rural areas of China, far from big cities.

(*Economist* 21 September 2006)

67% of respondents reported that family concerns were the dominant cause of early return from an assignment, and spouse/partner dissatisfaction was cited as the top reason for assignment failure.

(GMAC Global Relocation Services 2006)

From these quotes it seems that the most important issues in expatriate adjustment concern avoiding 'failure' by focusing on families. But what is 'failure' to adjust? Is it only premature return or is it also poor performance of the expatriate, long bouts of homesickness, a dangerous increase in the consumption of alcohol or perhaps the inability to communicate in the local language even after several years in the foreign country?

A focus on 'failure' – however defined – puts the spotlight on a small minority of expatriate employees. In the past, high failure rates were assumed. But a careful study of the adjustment literature has demonstrated high failure rates to be a myth stemming from poor referencing practice (Harzing 1995).

Family problems often come first in lists of adjustment issues generated from surveys of managers and HR professionals. There are several possible reasons for this:

1 Families actually have the most difficult time adjusting.
2 Families are most likely to press for an early return.
3 Blaming families allows the most significant players in the expatriation to save face.

Looking briefly at the last reason, if the family takes the blame, the likely damage to the expatriate's career is minimized. The manager of the expatriate and the human resources department come out fine – the expatriate family is not their (prime) responsibility. And finally, the managers who selected the expatriate did not choose an unsuitable candidate. In reality, therefore, a variable mix of the three reasons is likely to be responsible for the prominent role of families in accounting for adjustment problems.

A different approach is needed. An exclusive focus on avoiding failure creates a poor mindset in the search for what influences expatriate adjustment. This chapter tries to give a more balanced view, taking into account the tremendous potential for learning and growth that comes with a foreign posting. As in any change of circumstances, and an international assignment is a big one, there will be driving factors easing adjustment and restraining factors that provide challenges to be overcome. Trying to avoid failure focuses our attention on minimizing the restraining forces and forgets about the potential in building and reinforcing drivers. The juxtaposition in the quotes of the expatriate on the one side and family on the other can be equally misleading because it mixes levels of analysis. This chapter deals with adjustment first on the level of the individual, be it the expatriate, the accompanying partner or a child and then looks at adjustment at an aggregate level, by taking the family as a system. Adjustment of an expatriate family is not the sum of the adjustment outcomes of each individual family member; rather it is the result of a dynamic interplay of the family members in their attempt to adjust to the new environment.

131

WHAT IS ADJUSTMENT?

Any change in a person's life brings with it a requirement to adjust – whether it is entering university, joining the labour force or changing jobs, moving in with a partner, having a child or retiring. Change is principally a positive force in life; it provides stimulation. Too little or too much change, though, can constitute a problem. The former creates under-stimulation and boredom; the latter leads to overload and inability to cope. Adjustment is the outcome of a learning process that enables the individual to be more effective and content in new circumstances. For Gerrig and Zimbardo (2002), learning has three constitutive elements. First, it is a change in behaviour or behavioural tendencies. Second, that change is relatively consistent over time. Finally, it is based on experience, i.e. experiences stored in memory influence the reaction to stimuli. Expatriate adjustment, therefore, is a lasting change in behaviour or behavioural tendencies that originates in relevant past experiences and enables the expatriate to be more effective in the new environment. Adjustment has three components: first, it involves behaviour or behavioural tendencies; second, it involves information processing and memory, i.e. cognitions; and third, it involves emotions. Roth (1996), a neurobiologist, calls emotions 'concentrated experiences'. Emotions, therefore, form part of learning and adjustment.

The term 'adjustment' is most commonly used to describe expatriates. A similar term that is sometimes used interchangeably in this context is 'adaptation'. Adjustment involves the learning of a new culture, i.e. 'acculturation'. Individuals first learn their native culture when they grow up. This includes learning language(s), values, norms and assumptions. In order to be effective in a new culture, the expatriate has to learn some of the specifics of the local culture. Adjustment also includes learning the rules necessary for successful interaction with people, i.e. 'socialization'. Every social entity has particular rules that govern interactions within its boundaries. A new employee undergoes a process of organizational socialization. As an expatriate joins the office and other organizations abroad, he or she must follow relevant rules or suffer ineffectiveness or isolation. The expectation is that highly adjusted expatriate employees perform well at work (Bhaskar-Shrinivas et al. 2005). Yet some experts find that the relationship is weak and sometimes non-existent (Thomas and Lazarova 2006). Empirical research on the link between adjustment and performance is scant and the relationship moderated by other variables such as job satisfaction, organizational commitment and strain (Hechanova et al. 2003). Much depends on the conceptualization of both adjustment and performance and their facets. Kraimer et al. (2001), for example, found that work adjustment influenced task performance while interaction adjustment influenced contextual performance, i.e. the cross-cultural aspects of the expatriate's job. The definition of 'good performance', finally, varies with the purpose of the assignment. If the purpose is corporate control, good performance may

132

require a certain distance from the local operation. Hence, the optimal level of adjustment may be different from and lower than in an assignment where the goal is knowledge transfer or selling to the local market.

When, then, is an expatriate adjusted? Adjustment has an internal and an external component. On the internal side, expatriates may regard themselves adjusted if they experience a satisfactory level of effectiveness in dealings in their new environment (behaviour), are sufficiently clear about the various aspects of the new culture (cognitions) and feel neither overly stressed nor a preponderance of negative emotions. From an external perspective, an expatriate may be regarded as adjusted if the external world, by and large, perceives him or her as adjusted. Different segments of the expatriate's social environment may come to different conclusions: other foreigners may regard the expatriate as adjusted in comparison to themselves or the expatriate community as a whole, while members of the local culture may regard the same individual as still lacking. The expatriate's family may have yet another take on its member's state of adjustment. To call someone adjusted presumes a criterion against which the expatriate's level of adjustment is measured. The level of behavioural effectiveness, knowledge of the host culture and emotional well-being expected naturally varies among observers and among expatriates themselves, too. On a more abstract level, is the expatriate supposed to assimilate the new culture, integrate home and host cultures or is happy segregation in the environmental bubble of an expatriate community enough (Brewster and Pickard 1994; Berry 1997; Ward et al. 2001)? Finally, an expatriate may have differing levels of adjustment to different life domains (Navas et al. 2005): the expatriate as employee may be well adjusted to the new work environment, but not quite as well adjusted in various aspects of private life such as social contacts with neighbours and in the local community or shopping for goods and services. The definition of an adjusted expatriate can take many different forms, depending on the aspects one wants to stress. For expatriate employees, an appropriate definition might be as follows. Expatriates shall be called adjusted if they are subjectively and in the view of significant local (in the case of expatriate employees, work-related) contacts effective in dealings in the new location, perceive themselves as adequately knowledgeable about the local culture and feel neutral or positive emotions overall.

Much of the research on expatriate employees over the last decade and a half has followed one particular conceptualization of expatriate adjustment. This conceptualization distinguishes three facets of adjustment: interaction, general and work adjustment (Black 1988; Black and Stephens 1989). Interaction adjustment refers to speaking, interacting and socializing with host nationals in- and outside work. General adjustment includes living conditions in general, housing conditions, food, shopping, cost of living, entertainment and recreation and healthcare facilities. Work adjustment, finally, denotes performance standards

133

and expectations, specific job responsibilities and supervisory responsibilities. These three facets of adjustment formed the core around which Black et al. (1991) developed their model of international adjustment. The model was very successful and triggered numerous studies that used it as the theoretical underpinning. A 2003 meta-analytic review of 42 studies was based on the three-facet conceptualization of adjustment (Hechanova et al. 2003). In 2005 a meta-analytic review of 66 studies found support for the Black et al. model and suggested some extensions to incorporate the newest findings in expatriate research (Bhaskar-Shrinivas et al. 2005). With such strong empirical support, what is the catch?

The three facets of interaction, general and work adjustment were originally found in a two-country study based on 67 responses (Black 1988). The original questionnaire contained 11 items that were developed specifically to measure the three hypothesized facets. The three facets were hypothesized without a strong recourse to prior research and theory. A larger scale study of 220 expatriates rephrased parts of the original questionnaire and expanded it by three questions (Black and Stephens 1989). The resulting 14-item questionnaire has been used more or less unaltered in studies since. But this instrument for the measurement of expatriate adjustment has three weaknesses (cf. Thomas and Lazarova 2006):

1 It is not rooted in theory; rather it is the outcome of an attempt to measure three loosely defined, and overlapping, facets of adjustment.
2 It may as a result systematically exclude facets of adjustment.
3 It measures adjustment as one-dimensional along a scale of unadjusted to adjusted. As the following discussion will show, this combines discrete dimensions of adjustment.

Therefore, while the three facets have appeared consistently in many studies, the shortcomings of the instrument that produces them make it unlikely that they capture expatriate adjustment correctly or in its entirety.

Another conceptualization of expatriate adjustment distinguishes psychological and socio-cultural adjustment (Searle and Ward 1990; Ward and Kennedy 1999). Psychological adjustment denotes an expatriate's emotional well-being and experiences of stress. Socio-cultural adjustment of expatriates refers to the behavioural dimension, indicating the learning of effective social skills. More recently, Ward et al. (2001) have added a cognitive dimension by looking at social identity in cross-cultural contact. This model of adjustment outcomes is theoretically sounder than the one previously described (Thomas and Lazarova 2006). It has exerted little influence on the field, although it dates from the early 1990s like the other model.

134

TO WHAT DO WE NEED TO ADJUST?

Any transition or move requires a person to adjust to some extent. The more different the new environment is, the bigger the need for adjustment. Even domestic moves from one end of the country to the other or from the inner city to a near rural suburb change a person's routines and demand some learning. An international move brings with it additional challenges and opportunities to learn. These include such aspects as a different: language and culture, public administration setup or business practices and markets. In essence, the environment sets the type and difficulty of demands to which an individual must adjust. For analytical purposes, it is helpful to distinguish the immediate or micro-environment from the society at large or the macro-environment. While the two are linked and influence each other, the expatriate's experience of the two differs. The macro-environment is a given and is not open to influence by the expatriate. Elements of micro-environments, contrariwise, are somewhat malleable. Sometimes they can be exchanged for more congenial ones. An expatriate family may, for example, move house to live in a different neighbourhood. Table 7.1 lists a few relevant variables in micro- and macro-environments (cf. Bhaskar-Shrinivas et al. 2005):

Table 7.1 *Driving and restraining forces in adjustment*

Macro-environmental variables	Micro-environmental variables
Culture	**Work**
Business practices	Clarity of objectives/reporting lines
Openness to/view of foreigners	Role discretion
Administrative burdens, e.g. difficult-to-obtain work permits	Role novelty
	Role conflict
Level of security	Level of difficulty
Religious/political systems	Support by supervisor/co-workers
Health and medical system	Logistical support
Level of socio-economic development including housing standards, utilities, etc.	Mentor or coach
Environmental protection/pollution	**Private life**
Climate and weather patterns	Partner and family:
	■ level of adjustment
	■ motivation to stay
	■ resilience
	■ parochialism/cosmopolitanism
	Schooling
	Socio-economic situation
	Networks
	Friends
	Availability of desired or familiar food
	Shopping facilities and opening hours

Text box 7.1
Activity

Review the driving and restraining forces in adjustment (in Table 7.1). Discuss which ones, if any, are unambiguous drivers or restraints. For the ambiguous variables, state under what conditions they turn into drivers or restraints. Give examples of each driver/restraint.

Some of these variables constitute challenges that hamper adjustment, while others facilitate it. Clear objectives or a well-adjusted partner, for example, are conducive to expatriate adjustment; the opposites make it harder. The extent to which the adjustment challenges are met depends on the individual expatriate's personal characteristics and resources. Wise selection for the right personal characteristics and background (see Chapter 5) and appropriate preparatory and in-country training (see Chapter 6) can increase the chances that the expatriate succeeds.

The perception of the adjustment challenge faced varies depending on the expatriate's desire to go abroad. Not all candidates for expatriate assignments crave a foreign assignment. Many companies tell their employees and the public that the only way to the top of the management ladder includes a stint abroad. It is doubtful this is true in all cases. But the likely response to such statements is that some managers will reluctantly apply for and accept an assignment abroad, 'because it's good for my career'. Some family members may also be apprehensive. An assignment-related career break of one partner in a dual-career couple is sometimes welcome, but often it is not. Children vary in their support of an international move. Teenagers especially tend to resent being torn away from their friends and peers. The expatriate's motivation for taking an international assignment influences the energy he or she has available to actively adjust and cope with the unavoidable challenges.

PROCESS OF ADJUSTMENT

The expatriate has to do most of the adjusting to the challenges provided by the new environment and overall situation. But how does the process of adjustment progress? Take a single male expatriate manager, John, as an example.[1] After selection and pre-departure training, he arrives abroad. John has only rudimentary knowledge of the local language. He has taken several business trips to the country. This is John's first assignment abroad. He was eager to go and actively pursued the opening in discussions with his manager. There are, of course, many more variables that have a bearing, but for now we have enough to start the discussion of a possible adjustment process.

As John steps off the plane, he can already perform a few of the essentials because of his experience in the country on past business trips. He can hail a taxi that will take him to his hotel, which will be his temporary housing for a month. At the restaurant, he can identify and order drinks and a few of the dishes he likes. He has also mastered a number of other useful skills. He is confident and excited to have finally arrived. But now that he is here more permanently, he needs to learn some new skills and become self-sufficient. A company representative will no longer pick him up from the hotel every morning. He quickly discovers that many of the things he did back home automatically now take much longer to accomplish and he is not as effective. Buying groceries is a chore; finding the right ingredients is time consuming and frustrating. Getting things done is harder than anticipated. Sometimes he wonders whether the 'locals' really cannot understand him or whether they ignore him deliberately. John's experience is, of course, nothing out of the ordinary. Some of the difficulties he had expected, but many came as a surprise. An Austrian sociologist who emigrated to the USA in 1939 pointed out that the mental representation of the host culture of a new arrival was developed from a distance, by consensus with members from his home culture, and not with the intent to guide effective behaviour in the new environment (Schütz 1944). Preparatory training will improve this, but not set it right completely. John, therefore, will feel right from the start that his behaviours in interactions with host nationals are less than adequate and that he needs to become more effective. Every day he will make progress, learning as he goes along. Expatriates sometimes feel like they are children again during the first few weeks and months in their new environment. They are not aware of all the rules for social interaction, are sometimes not taken quite as seriously as members of the host community. They are learning by leaps and bounds every day. To summarize, behaviours start out below adequate; accelerated learning takes place initially; later the learning curve will become flatter as represented in Figure 7.1.

John arrives with a lot of energy and confidence in his knowledge about his new environment. Prior business trips have been successful; he was able to pick up a fair amount of useful information. As part of his preparation, he has also acquired essential knowledge about the history, political and economic system of the new country as well as of its cultural background and behavioural norms. Therefore, the extent to which his behavioural effectiveness is lacking comes as a surprise. This deals a blow to his confidence. He soon realizes that his knowledge about the country is rather superficial. Unlike his behavioural effectiveness, John's cognitive confidence is high at first, but it dips below adequate soon after arrival as shown in Figure 7.1. John suffers from two shortcomings in his cognitive frame of reference for interaction with the hosts. First, old and new elements of knowledge about how to act recommend incompatible behaviours in some situations leading to cognitive inconsistency. Second, in novel situations he has no knowledge available to guide his behaviour, leading to cognitive ambiguity (Grove and Torbiörn 1985).

137

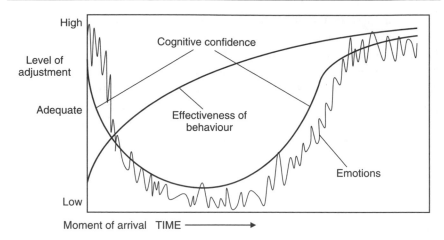

Figure 7.1 *Adjustment curve including 'culture shock'.*

We have assumed that John has sought the assignment and was highly motivated to go. Many expatriates like John are excited when they finally set foot in a new country. John feels very positive about his move. During the first weeks of the assignment, he feels happy, almost euphoric. Sure there are some mishaps, when his actions do not lead to the desired results. Occasionally, he is unsure and does not know how to act. This makes him feel bad at times, but not for long. Overall, he regards these episodes as part of a passing phase, a challenge to be overcome. Researchers have long called this the 'honeymoon' stage (Oberg 1960). Not every expatriate experiences it, but John certainly does. He explores the sights of the new city and the surrounding areas on weekends. He has long days at work, but in the evening he treats himself to a trip to a new restaurant or bar. This exciting life eventually makes him tired, though. After a few weeks, he starts to feel drained. He begins to feel that it is time for the 'holiday' to end so that he can return to his normal life. He also misses his friends; there is no one to share his excitement with. Sometimes he feels as if he goes out only to combat his own increasing loneliness. And after trying every variation of the local food he can get hold of, he craves his regular Sunday meal from home. Slowly but surely the feeling sets in that this is not going to be as easy as it first seemed. Sure, he is making progress. Every day he is learning to become more effective, but he is still far from the threshold that marks adequate for him. What was exciting in the beginning is now stressful. John slides imperceptibly into what is commonly termed 'culture shock' (Oberg 1960; Ward et al. 2001) as behavioural inadequacy and cognitive uncertainty wear him down. Even if expatriates feel good at first, like John, they sometimes hit the emotional doldrums. John's feelings will return to normal only after he adequately masters interactions with members of the host culture and thus regains confidence in his knowledge about his new environment. This emotional rollercoaster is represented in the third curve in Figure 7.1. The emotions curve looks like a fever chart because emotions and feelings are volatile, varying over short intervals. There is also an underlying long-term trend. If someone shouts at John because he committed a faux pas, he will feel bad for a while. A friendly smile, by way of contrast, will lift his spirits for an hour. Yet neither of these episodes in isolation will change the long-term pattern of his emotions as he adjusts to his new life. Cumulatively, they will.

John's example shows a typical adjustment process as represented in Figure 7.1. There are, of course, many variations possible. We turn to some of these now.

Expatriates with recent significant experience in the host culture may be less likely than others to suffer from culture shock (Takeuchi et al. 2005). In this case adjustment curves may resemble a J-curve or linear trends (Black and Mendenhall 1991) similar to those depicted in Figure 7.2. Yet prior expatriate experience may also undermine adjustment. Nicholson and Imaizumi (1993) found that Japanese expatriates in Britain who had prior expatriate experience suffered more adjustment difficulties. The authors speculated that prior experience lessened the 'excitement' factor for these individuals. A move from a home culture that is similar to the host culture and poses a small rather than a large language barrier, e.g. from Ireland to England, from the United States to English-speaking Canada, or from Germany to Austria, is more likely to resemble the dynamics in Figure 7.2 than that in Figure 7.1.

Personal characteristics (see e.g. Caligiuri 2000) influence the process of adjustment. An optimistic outlook known as positive affectivity, realistic expectations, openness to new experiences, ability to speak the local language and willingness to interact with members of the host culture to name but a few may all influence the process of adjustment. Optimism may help an expatriate reach an adequate level on the emotions curve more quickly. Realistic expectations from good advance

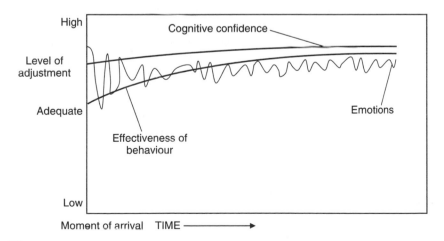

Figure 7.2 *Smooth adjustment curve.*

preparation may protect expatriates from hard knocks to their confidence. Language skills, openness and a desire to interact may accelerate the learning of new behaviours. A lack of motivation to go may prevent the expatriate from experiencing any 'honeymoon' period at all. Bad feelings and stress may have the upper hand right from the beginning; emotional adjustment would then start below adequate. In contrast, expatriates with the ability to replace cherished activities that are unavailable in the new environment – such as an Australian surfer taking up snowboarding when in Switzerland – may experience less stress and quicker affective adjustment.

The discussion shows that selecting expatriates for variables other than track record and technical expertise and supporting them through anticipatory and in-country training and coaching can improve the chances for speedy adjustment (compare Chapters 5 and 6). So far we have treated adjustment holistically, as if an expatriate adjusts to a new culture as a whole. In reality, expatriates must adjust to different life domains (Navas et al. 2005). Most significantly, expatriate employees have to adjust to the new job and work environment. In addition, they have to establish relationships outside of work with neighbours and friends. They have to adjust to a different system of public order; for example, expatriates from Britain and the United States who live in Germany are sometimes amazed that there are restrictions as to when one can mow the lawn in the garden. And anyone who learned to drive on the right side of the road has quite a bit of adjusting to do when moving to the British Isles or Japan. Expatriates also have to get used to a different economy, including shopping for goods and services. It can take weeks to get a landline phone, TV cable and broadband internet set up in some countries. Expatriates from Britain find the practices of 'non-queuing' in many countries frustrating and exhausting. Expatriates' adjustment may proceed at differing speeds and may show differing patterns in the various domains. However, researchers have found significant spillover effects between adjustment domains (Takeuchi et al. 2002).

There may also be differing requirements regarding the style the expatriate is supposed to use when adjusting (Zimmermann et al. 2003). Is the expatriate supposed to shoulder all the burden of adjustment or may he or she expect the members of the local culture to do some of the adjusting? Is there any tolerance for non-conformist behaviour by expatriates? In some Arabic countries, western women are supposed to wear a headscarf in public. Yet in some Asian cultures western women are not subject to the same rules as local women; they are treated first and foremost as foreigners, to whom different rules apply (Adler 1987). Clearly, expatriates will adjust more easily if they have the leeway to retain more of their familiar ways of interacting with others than if they must adhere to all the local rules. In the workplace, incoming expatriates tend to enjoy an elevated status, which may allow them to mould their environment rather than just assimilate. But the perks that often come with assignments abroad such as a housing subsidy that allows the expatriate to live in community beyond the means of their local peers can have a detrimental effect on relations with local co-workers (Toh and DeNisi 2005; and see Chapter 2). The perceived inequitable treatment may create tensions between expatriates and local employees. The jealousy of local co-workers may make it harder for expatriates to adjust or, at least, dry up sources of support that would have made adjustment easier. A housing subsidy may have another effect on adjustment: expatriates may be able to move into an expensive expatriate 'ghetto' (Brewster and Pickard 1994). In the short run, this will make adjustment in several domains easier, for example, in the areas of shopping or relationships with neighbours. But, in the longer run, the expatriate will not learn as much about how to interact in the local culture with possible detrimental effects for relationships with local co-workers, business partners and government officials. By the same token, corporations may happily accept this potential drawback in order to ensure that the expatriate will not 'go native'.

So far, we have only considered expatriates as individuals. Since at least half of expatriates move abroad with others, it is necessary to broaden our perspective and look at the dynamics of family adjustment.

FAMILY ADJUSTMENT

By studying the family unit, we raise the analysis to a new level. Organizational studies generally take a three-tiered approach; they study the individual, groups and the organization as a whole. Each layer adds complexity and insight. Similarly, it is necessary to study adjustment as an individual and as a group phenomenon. The dynamic interplay of adjustment efforts of family members may have a beneficial or a detrimental effect on the adjustment outcomes of individuals. Over the years studies have found significant moderating crossover effects among expatriates and their partners (Shaffer et al. 1999; Takeuchi et al. 2002; Bhaskar-Shrinivas et al. 2005;). But no theoretical framework yet exists that goes beyond these isolated effects and takes a systemic view of family adjustment.[2] Here is a description of some of the dynamics that expatriate families encounter.

Each of the family members has to adjust to their various life domains abroad such as work or school, shopping and entertainment, making and interacting with friends and acquaintances, general rules of conduct and public order. While individuals adjust to these domains separately, the domains are interconnected and impact upon each other (Takeuchi et al. 2002). A teenager's ability to make friends abroad may influence motivation and school success. At the same time, the teenager's parents will react to their child's state of adjustment: a tough time with friends or school also makes their adjustment more difficult. This might follow the lagged pattern of behavioural, cognitive and affective adjustment depicted in Figure 7.1 or it could directly correlate with one of the dimensions. The parents' attempts to interact with the school may not bring the desired reactions by school officials (behavioural ineffectiveness). Perhaps the rules they know from home to deal with school officials are incompatible with what they have been told about local practice (cognitive inconsistency). They may just empathize with their child's difficulties and feel bad (negative emotions). This works on the positive side, too. Children and adolescents often adjust with remarkable speed, gaining fluency in the local language in a matter of months. A child's successes may prop up the parents, lightening their adjustment load. It may not only make them feel better, it may provide them with useful information. Teenagers may pick up important cross-cultural knowledge, which they share with parents. They may also coach parents in cross-cultural interactions, helping them with shopping or ordering at a restaurant.

The crossover among the members of the expatriate family may take various forms (Westman et al. 2006). It may be a direct outcome of the interaction between family members leading to behavioural or cognitive crossover. It may also be empathetic sharing of emotions. Sometimes the same external factor impacts upon each family member. This in itself is not crossover, though, and the effects could be explained on the level of the individual. We can only speak of crossover when the external factor results in reinforcing empathy with each other leading to a stronger effect in the family than it would have on an individual alone. The latter is an analytical distinction that will be difficult to observe empirically in the field. Crossover may be one-directional, e.g. the teenager's adjustment impacting upon the parents, but not vice versa. It could also be bidirectional, e.g. the parents' reaction to the teenager's adjustment feeding back and reinforcing the teenager's trend. Crossover can be positive, leading to better adjustment, or negative.

To summarize, Table 7.2 shows examples of effects among family members and domains. The arrows indicate spillover (vertical connection between domains) and crossover (horizontal connection between family members). The diagonal arrow shows a combination of crossover and spillover, e.g. if the expatriate's successful adjustment at work helps the partner's adjustment in the social sphere, either by sharing knowledge about how to develop relationships with members of the local culture or by providing opportunities to meet people. Cross- and spillovers may be one- or bidirectional as indicated by the arrows. In principle, all cells may be

Table 7.2 Cross- and spillover in adjustment

Domains	Expatriate	Spouse	Child (1 … n)
Work/school Social relations Public life and order Shopping and entertainment Other domains			

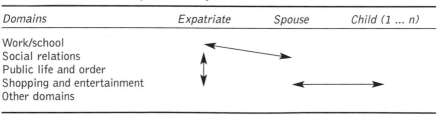

connected, although some effects will be more common than others. Work/ school and social relations may show more interactions with other domains than, say, public life and order.

After this brief look at the dynamics of family adjustment we now turn to questions of cultural identity in expatriation.

EXPATRIATE ADJUSTMENT AND IDENTITY

The adaptation of the newcomer to the in-group which at first seemed to be strange and unfamiliar to him is a continuous process of inquiry into the cultural pattern of the approached group. If this process of inquiry succeeds, then this pattern and its elements will become to the newcomer a matter of course, an unquestionable way of life, a shelter, and a protection. But then the stranger is no stranger any more.

(Schütz 1944: 507)

Those expatriates who live in another country for a number of years will in all likelihood change their views and ways of thinking in subtle ways. At the same time their own country does not stand still. Therefore, on return some expatriates may experience a gap between themselves and their friends or fellow citizens and find that aspects of their cultural identity have changed.

The process of adjustment leads to a change in identity that replaces some of the elements of the home with those of the host culture and combines others in novel ways. This leads to a third cultural identity separate from either home or host culture. Szalay and Inn (1988) studied Puerto Ricans living in New York. Cross-cultural adjustment and the resulting change in cultural identity fluctuated in time. A person does not develop in linear fashion towards a different identity. Adjustment is also an experience of personal growth. The expatriate does not simply replace one set of cultural elements with another. Rather, expatriates will develop new views and attitudes (Szalay and Inn 1988) and expand their understanding and set of available behaviours.

To speak of one identity is a simplification, though. People have multiple role identities depending on the social context in which they find themselves (Earley and Ang 2003). One of the sources of variation in salient identities is the adjustment domain. At work, the expatriate's identity as an employee becomes central; at home, the identity as friend or a family member in the form of parent, partner, etc. dominates. Since the extent of adjustment may vary by domain, the change of identity and the extent of the gap experienced between the expatriate on a home visit or during repatriation will vary accordingly. For example, how one makes friends differs considerably by culture (see Text box 7.2). The Austrian in the example may take on the habit of inviting people over to his home, causing similar confusion back home with fellow Austrians. Similarly, German speakers distinguish

143

> **Text box 7.2**
> **Cultural niceties**
>
> A young Austrian moved to the United States to teach at a university. He was delighted when, early on in his stay, a colleague invited him and other colleagues over to his house for a barbecue. He had not realized their friendship was deep enough to warrant such a personal invitation. In Austria, only close friends would normally be invited over to one's home. The week following the party, his delight turned to chagrin. The colleague remained polite and friendly, but the relationship was not particularly warm. It was only then, as he reflected in his third month in Texas, that the Austrian realized the invitation to the barbecue was not yet the sign of a close, warm relationship. It was an initial overture.
> Source: Esarey and Haslberger (2005: 4)

carefully between people with whom they are on a first-name basis and others. After a few years in the USA, our Austrian will probably feel awkward on returning home because he has grown accustomed to using first names.

The changes in attitudes and behaviours that expatriates like our Austrian go through may have a lasting impact on their identities. They may feel less tightly bound to some aspects of their culture. The Austrian may feel more cosmopolitan rather than Austrian in the future. Some expatriates on successive assignments also report the development of a 'portable lifestyle' that fits with only minor adjustments in many different environments, e.g. metropolitan areas in industrialized countries. Naturally, identities change as a result. On return to the home culture a blending-back-in process will start. For some expatriates, the newly developed multicultural aspects of identity will fade in time and memories may be all that remain. For others, blending back in is impossible. They may decide to leave again to become permanent expatriates or immigrants in their chosen new home. A third group may become boundary-spanning persons with multicultural identities (Adler 1996).

One aspect of identity that the company sending an expatriate employee particularly cares about is the identification with and allegiance to parts of the organization. Not all expatriates are required or expected by their employers to adjust well to the host culture (Brewster 1995). If the purpose of the assignment is corporate control, e.g. a financial manager is sent to provide corporate oversight for an otherwise local management board, the corporation would not want the manager to adjust fully to life in the host country. Continued and undivided allegiance to the home office is essential. If the purpose is a boundary-spanning activity such as knowledge transfer or enhancing communications, dual allegiance is desirable. If the expatriate's assignment focuses on building the local business, allegiance to

144

the host organization is probably most appropriate, which has as a likely correlate a high level of adjustment to the host location.

A company can do a number of things to ease the transition for the expatriate employee and the accompanying family members. The conclusion lists those that can be provided on arrival abroad. Other support measures such as in pre-departure preparation are discussed in Chapter 6.

CONCLUSION

The literature on expatriate adjustment has long focused exclusively on the negative side, highlighting 'failure' and how to avoid it. This chapter has tried to give a more balanced view of expatriate adjustment showing the undeniable challenges of expatriate life, but also including the rewarding side that leads to personal growth and learning.

Every person experiences expatriation and adjustment in a different way. What provides just the right amount of challenge and excitement for one may be too much for another. Therefore, companies should provide flexible support in addition to standard items such as assistance in house hunting, finding schools or obtaining work and residency permits:[3]

- Follow up pre-departure training with on-the-ground cross-cultural training and language classes. Both types of training may actually prove more effective when delivered abroad because of their immediate applicability. John, the new expatriate from earlier, would benefit from an opportunity to improve his ability to speak the local language and to learn more about the local culture and the country. Now he needs to get menial day-to-day things done such as buying groceries and has to work with lower level local employees other than his contacts from his earlier business trips. Now he is also more interested to learn about civics and history.
- Set up local 'buddies' for expatriates and partners to help them acclimatize. Buddies could be other expatriates and their partners who have lived in the location for a while or local employees and partners. Buddies provide informal support and can accelerate the process of building a new social support network. John enjoys exploring the local restaurant scene on his own. After a while, though, his excitement wanes. With a local buddy right from the start, he might still get homesick, but the headstart his buddy provides in building his new network would make the bouts of homesickness more manageable. John's buddy could also supplement the ongoing training by providing a local view on his experiences with members of the host culture.

- Organize a home office mentor for the expatriate. A mentor keeps the expatriate from feeling marginalized by offering a line to the home office and combats the 'out-of-sight, out-of-mind' syndrome. Mentors help expatriates stay informed about home office developments. John's mentor will keep him apprised of changes in the home office. While John still gets the regular newsletter, he has no direct way to sense the subtle changes in climate that occur in every organization over time. His mentor can also be on the lookout for the next job back home and bring up his name in informal discussions about up-and-coming talent in the organization.

- Support partners in carving out meaningful roles for themselves. Such help could come in the form of job placement assistance or, where work restrictions apply, job-like or charitable activities.

- Provide an employee assistance programme (EAP) for those expatriates and partners who experience 'culture shock' and train local managers in recognizing symptoms. John is making good progress and he is well on course to good adjustment. He has not once considered calling the EAP, but he feels reassured that he has the number in his pocket.

- Ensure that local employees feel supportive of the expatriate employee (Toh and DeNisi 2005). Local employees, especially HR employees responsible for expatriate support, need to understand the adjustment process and also learn how to adjust to cultural differences themselves. They may have misconceptions about expatriate compensation packages and perks, resulting in feelings of jealousy and lack of desire to cooperate with the expatriate. John's peers have learned about his cultural background and about the process expatriates go through when they move to another country. They are still sometimes puzzled by his approach to work, but they do not attribute this to his being odd nor do they avoid him. They understand that in his culture his actions would be appropriate and they are now more likely to explain to him how things are done locally.

Company support for expatriates should resemble that for circus acrobats on a highwire act. The organization should provide them with all the skills and tools required to adjust and perform well. Then it should stand back and let them do their adjusting act without undue interference. Most expatriates are quite capable of learning and growing without handholding provided that the cornerstones for success have been put in place. Careful selection, clarity of objectives and reporting lines, logistical support, adequate training and assignment planning are essential to success (see Chapters 5, 6, 9 and 12 for further information). But just like in the circus, the company should provide a reliable safety net to cushion the fall, in case the expatriate stumbles.

KEY LEARNING POINTS

- Adjustment is the outcome of a learning process.
- Macro- and micro-environmental variables determine the overall adjustment challenge the expatriate has to master.
- Adjustment consists of behaviours (behavioural effectiveness), knowledge (cognitive confidence) and emotions (affective evaluation).
- Adjustment takes place in different life domains such as work, systems of public order, social life including friends and neighbours, consumption of goods and services.
- Expatriates have multiple roles in the different domains; adjustment levels may vary from one role to another. There is spillover of adjustment among domains and roles.
- The adjustment of an expatriate family is the result of the dynamic interplay of adjustment efforts by family members. There is crossover of adjustment among family members.
- The adjustment process may but does not have to include 'culture shock'.
- Any long-term stay in a foreign country has the potential to effect a lasting change in a person's identity (or identities).
- Companies should provide flexible support to expatriates.

NOTES

1   According to the GMAC Global Relocation Services 2005 survey 76% of expatriates were male (and see Chapter 13). The historical average is even higher at 86%. Based on the same survey, roughly 50% of expatriates were married and accompanied by a partner. The presence of family complicates the discussion of the adjustment process. Therefore, we shall focus on single expatriates here and discuss families later in the chapter. Similarly, after the description of John's case, other courses of adjustment will be highlighted.
2   Some researchers are beginning to incorporate a systemic view of family adjustment into theories on expatriation, e.g. Haslberger, A. and Brewster, C., 'Expatriate adjustment – systematic extensions to theory' and Westman, M., Shaffer, M. A. and Lazarova, M., 'Work–family interface among expatriates: an integrative framework'. Both papers presented at the ACREW 2006, *Socially Responsive, Socially Responsible Approaches To Employment And Work*, Monash University, Prato Centre, Italy.
3   The following information is taken from Esarey and Haslberger 2005.

REFERENCES

Adler, N.J. (1987) 'Pacific Basin managers: a gaijin, not a woman', *Human Resource Management* 26, 2:169–191.

147

Adler, N.J. (1996) *International Dimensions of Organizational Behavior*, 3rd edn, Mason, OH: South Western College Publishing.

Berry, J.W. (1997) 'Individual and group relations in plural societies', in C. Skromme Granrose and S. Oskamp (eds) *Cross-cultural Work Groups*, Thousand Oaks, CA: Sage.

Bhaskar-Shrinivas, P., Harrison, D.A., Shaffer, M.A. and Luk, D.M. (2005) 'Input-based and time-based models of international adjustment: meta-analytic evidence and theoretical extensions', *Academy of Management Journal* 48, 2:257–281.

Black, J.S. (1988) 'Work role transitions: a study of American expatriate managers in Japan', *Journal of International Business Studies* 30, 2:277–294.

Black, J.S. and Mendenhall, M. (1991) 'The U-curve adjustment hypothesis revisited: a review and theoretical framework', *Journal of International Business Studies* 22, 2: 225–247.

Black, S.J. and Stephens, G.K. (1989) 'The influence of the partner on American expatriate adjustment and intent to stay in Pacific Rim overseas assignments', *Journal of Management* 15, 4:529–544.

Black, J.S., Mendenhall, M. and Oddou, G. (1991) 'Toward a comprehensive model of international adjustment: an integration of multiple theoretical perspectives', *Academy of Management Review* 16,2:291–317.

Brewster, C. (1995) 'The paradox of expatriate adjustment', in J. Selmer (ed.) *Expatriate Management – New Ideas for International Business*, Westport, CT: Quorum Books.

Brewster, C. and Pickard, J. (1994) 'Evaluating expatriate training', *International Studies of Management and Organization* 24, 3:18–35.

Caligiuri, P.M. (2000) 'Selecting expatriates for personality characteristics: a moderating effect of personality on the relationship between host national contact and cross-cultural adjustment', *Management International Review* 40, 1:61–80.

Earley, P.C. and Ang, S. (2003) *Cultural Intelligence: Individual Interactions Across Cultures*, Stanford, CA: Stanford University Press.

Esarey, S. and Haslberger, A. (2005) *Moving People Abroad: A Guide to Successful Transitions*, Berkhamsted: Ashridge.

Gerrig, R.J. and Zimbardo, P.G. (2002) *Psychology and Life*, 16th edn, Boston, MA: Allyn & Bacon.

Grove, C.L. and Torbiörn, I. (1985) 'A new conceptualization of intercultural adjustment and the goals of training', *International Journal of Intercultural Relations* 9: 205–233.

Harzing, A-W.K. (1995) 'The persistent myth of high expatriate failure rates', *International Journal of Human Resource Management* 6, 2: 457–474.

Hechanova, R., Beehr, T.A. and Christiansen, N.D. (2003) 'Antecedents and consequences of employees' adjustment to overseas assignment: a meta-analytic review', *Applied Psychology* 52, 2:213–236.

Kraimer, M.L., Wayne, S.J. and Jaworski, R.A. (2001) 'Sources of support and expatriate performance: the mediating role of expatriate adjustment', *Personnel Psychology* 54, 1:71–99.

Navas, M., Garcia, M.C., Sánchez, J., Rojas, A.J., Pumares, P. and Fernández, J.S. (2005) 'Relative acculturation extended model (RAEM): new contributions with regard to the study of acculturation', *International Journal of Intercultural Relations* 29:21–37.

Nicholson, N. and Imaizumi, A. (1993) 'The adjustment of Japanese expatriates to living and working in Britain', *British Journal of Management* 4: 119–134.

148

Oberg, K. (1960) 'Cultural shock: adjustment to new cultural environments', *Practical Anthropology* July-August: 177–182.

Roth, G. (1996) *Das Gehirn und seine Wirklichkeit*, Frankfurt-am-Main: Suhrkamp.

Schütz, A. (1944) 'The stranger: an essay in social psychology', *American Journal of Sociology* 49,6:499–507.

Searle, W. and Ward, C. (1990) 'The prediction of psychological and sociocultural adjustment during cross-cultural transitions', *International Journal of Intercultural Relations* 14:449–464.

Shaffer, M.A., Harrison, D.A. and Gilley, K.M. (1999) 'Dimensions, determinants, and differences in the expatriate adjustment process', *Journal of International Business Studies* 30, 3:557–581.

Szalay, L.B. and Inn, A. (1988) 'Cross-cultural adaptation and diversity: Hispanic Americans', in Y. Y. Kim and W. B. Gudykunst (eds) *Cross-cultural Adaptation – Current Approaches*, Newbury Park, CA: Sage.

Takeuchi, R., Yun, S. and Tesluk, P.E. (2002) 'An examination of crossover and spillover effects of spousal and expatriate cross-cultural adjustment on expatriate outcomes', *Journal of Applied Psychology* 87, 4:655–666.

Takeuchi, R., Tesluk, P.E., Yun, S. and Lepak, D.P. (2005) 'An integrative view of international experience', *The Academy of Management Journal* 48, 1:85–100.

Thomas, D.C. and Lazarova, M.B. (2006) 'Expatriate adjustment and performance: a critical review', in G.K. Stahl and I. Bjorkman (eds) *Handbook of Research in International Human Resource Management*, Cheltenham: Edward Elgar.

Toh, S.M. and DeNisi, A.S. (2005) 'A local perspective to expatriate success', *The Academy of Management Executive* 19, 1:132–146.

Ward, C. and Kennedy, A. (1999) 'The measurement of sociocultural adaptation', *International Journal of Intercultural Relations* 23, 4:659–677.

Ward, C., Bochner, S. and Furnham, A. (2001) *The Psychology of Culture Shock*, 2nd edn, London: Routledge.

Westman, M., Shaffer, M.A. and Lazarova, M. (2006) 'Work–family interface among expatriates: an integrative framework', paper presented at the ACREW 2006, *Socially Responsive, Socially Responsible Approaches to Employment and Work*, Monash University, Prato Centre, Italy.

Zimmermann, A., Holman, D. and Sparrow, P. (2003) 'Unravelling adjustment mechanisms: adjustment of German expatriates to intercultural interactions, work, and living conditions in the People's Republic of China', *International Journal of Cross Cultural Management* 3, 1:45–66.

Chapter 8

Rewards for internationally mobile employees

Marion Festing and Stephen J. Perkins

CHAPTER OBJECTIVES

By the end of this chapter, readers will have:

- an outline of a sophisticated approach to framing the problem of determining rewards for internationally mobile employees
- an appreciation of intersecting perspectives on the issue, informed by strategic management and social science commentary
- a sensitivity for the search for connections between expatriate compensation and organizational effectiveness on a multinational scale, as well as an appreciation of evaluating contemporary practice; in doing so, the various roles played by individuals and groups within multinational corporations (MNCs) are discussed
- the skills to take more effective decisions for practice, by ensuring that consequences are more systematically weighed prior to action
- an understanding of the importance to evaluate practice in context, incorporating explicit assumptions that have influenced practice but have previously been unexplored and therefore have not been subject to critically informed reflection

INTRODUCTION

Outlining a more sophisticated approach to rewards for internationally mobile employees is acknowledged to be a complex and challenging task (Harvey 1993; Suutari and Tornikoski 2001; Dowling et al. 2005; Bonache 2006). Literature in this area has been criticized for being overly descriptive and normative (Bonache and Fernández 1997; Chen et al. 2002; Phillips and Fox 2003). This chapter aims to combine intersecting perspectives, informed by strategic management and social science commentary.

 150

Reward (or 'compensation' or 'remuneration') may be defined generally as 'the way employees are rewarded at the workplace' (Kessler 2005: 317). And *extrinsic* reward, in the form of tangible monetary and non-monetary payments – wages and fringe benefits – may be specified as a 'bundle of returns offered in return for a cluster of employee contributions' to the organization (Bloom and Milkovich 1992: 22). Hence the notion of an 'effort–reward bargain', forming a central pillar of the employment relationship (Kessler 2001).

A FRAMEWORK TO INFORM ANALYSIS

At present, it can be argued that normative commentary on expatriate compensation draws on a conceptualization (albeit unstated) that is static and unidimensional. It fails to account for the range of interest groups involved and the social nature of the interaction – exchange – taking place between them. It therefore fails to capture the assumptions and other 'baggage' interested parties bring with them, so limiting scope to anticipate how policies are received/interpreted and applied and to explain why outcomes occur as they do. Thus, expatriate compensation needs to be analysed, paying attention to the stakeholders that might have an interest in the design and in the outcome of expatriate compensation systems.

We have identified four levels of analysis: the individual, the organization, the HR department, as well as the environment, which is especially complex in a multinational organization. Furthermore, in this context there are social exchange relationships, which must also be considered if an encompassing picture of expatriate compensation is to be drawn.

As this chapter primarily addresses HR practitioners and academics, the analysis starts from a perspective derived from the HR literature on employee mobilization across international boundaries. We then place the organizational perspective, with its focus on the strategic orientation of the firm, in the centre of consideration. The effects of expatriate compensation from the viewpoint of the individual are then analysed. When discussing the organizational and individual perspectives, questions about the *interrelationships* between both perspectives and between different individuals and groups of individuals arise. The focus is on 'exchange relationships', which is our next level of analysis. Finally, we address the external context of the multinational, which has an impact on all of the previous levels: the organizational perspective, at the level of HR practice, individual behaviour and exchange relationships. By focusing explicitly on the dimension of the environment we follow a contextual paradigm perspective on expatriate compensation (Brewster 1999). This is in contrast to the often dominating universalist approach to this topic that concentrates on best practices. The proposed levels of analysis are summarized in Figure 8.1.

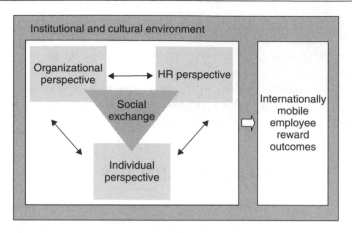

Figure 8.1 *Levels of analysis of expatriate compensation.*

In the following sections, we discuss causes and effects of expatriate compensation based on a variety of theoretical approaches on the different levels already identified. We concentrate on those relationships that seem to be most salient for deriving implications about expatriate compensation. To begin, we briefly describe the different types of international assignment and the different approaches to expatriate compensation, surfacing possible areas of tension, comprehension of which may benefit from the application of a more critical lens such as that outlined in the framework sketched earlier.

APPROACHES TO EXPATRIATE COMPENSATION

The principle of 'keeping the expatriate whole' (Phillips and Fox 2003: 470) in reward terms has governed reported thinking and practice on expatriate compensation: 'The intention is not to "reward" assignees as such, but rather to compensate them for changes in lifestyle, enduring "hardship", etc.' (Perkins and Shortland 2006: 185). First, this is expressed in terms of pay package design intended to preserve existing relativities with peers in the 'home' location (generally the country of origin of the MNC). Second, the expressed ambition is to maintain 'purchasing parity' – so that the expatriate may enjoy the same living standards as at home (Fenwick 2004; Dowling et al. 2008). This approach, known as the home-based/salary build-up, or 'balance sheet' (ORC 2004), augments basic pay with a 'foreign service premium' (Dowling et al. 2008), as well as cash supplements to compensate for 'hardships' (e.g., working in remote locations, those affected by political instability or with limited social infrastructure). Housing and children's education costs are reimbursed, extending the 'kept whole' principle to the employee's family members. In addition to salary adjustments to neutralize cost of living differences, other allowances may include home leave, relocation, spouse assistance/dual career allowances and so on (Fenwick 2004; Perkins and Shortland 2006). The principle of 'tax equalization' generally accompanies balance sheet expatriate compensation. Hypothetical tax the employee would have paid at home is deducted from the home base pay to arrive at a net salary. Allowances and premiums are then added to that amount and the organization pays any tax falling due within host jurisdiction on the total of the remuneration package.

Figure 8.2 gives an example of such a compensation scheme for expatriates from a German multinational company (MNC). Here, the salary is determined based on a comparison with the net salary that would have been payable in the home country. The comparative net domestic salary serves then as the basis for the further calculation of the expatriate salary. In calculating the expatriate salary, differences in cost of living, living standards and housing standards are taken into account. In the case of this particular MNC the employee is guaranteed the calculated net expatriate salary, subject to annual exchange rate adjustment. The host unit will perform a gross-up for taxes and pay the taxes in the host country.

The *cost of living adjustment* is used to balance the differences in cost of living between the home country and the host country. The cost of living adjustments allow the consumption of goods and services of the same type, quality and amount in the host country. The cost of living index is calculated based on a home country basket of goods and the exchange rate used for compensation calculation. In this particular MNC, the cost of living allowance (COLA) is applied to 65% of the comparative net domestic salary. This percentage corresponds to a statistical value of the typical proportion of income required for daily expenses. The cost of living allowance usually receives high attention in expatriate compensation schemes. Often this allowance is difficult to determine, so companies may use the services

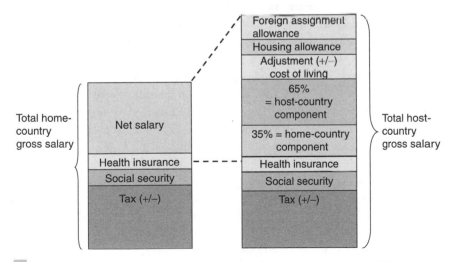

Figure 8.2 *Compensation scheme for expatriates from a German MNC.*

of organizations such as ORC Worldwide (a US-based firm) or ECA International (based in Britain). These firms specialize in providing COLA information on a global basis, regularly updated, to their clients.

The *housing allowance* means that the host unit either carries rental costs directly or authorizes a rental budget, which the expatriate receives in the expatriate salary calculation (host-country rent). In return, an amount equivalent to the normal housing cost in the home country (home-country rent) may be deducted in the expatriate salary calculation. In the case of this particular German MNC, the actual housing costs of the expatriate are not considered: 'Other alternatives include company-provided housing, either mandatory or optional; a fixed housing allowance; or assessment of a portion of income, out of which actual housing costs are paid. Housing issues are often addressed on a case-by-case basis, but as a firm internationalizes, formal policies become more necessary and efficient' (Dowling et al. 2008).

The *foreign assignment allowance* recognizes the mobility of the expatriate. This allowance takes into account intangible difficulties as well as material hardships that cannot be considered in the cost of living adjustment. This includes issues such as personal safety, distance, language, cultural and climatic differences, economic conditions as well as the political and social environment. Sometimes, this issue is also discussed under the heading of hardship allowances.

According to one large-scale survey, around 85–95% of organizations in the USA and Japan continue to favour the balance sheet approach and in Europe the figure is about 70% (ORC 2002). Despite this, experimentation has been reported as MNCs find the high cost of balance sheet packages incompatible with cost containment goals (Wentland 2003). The best-known alternative to the balance sheet, for application to employees assigned abroad for periods of 1 year and over is described by Dowling et al. (2008) as the 'going rate' approach, reflective of salary structures in force in the host country. Region-based arrangements represent a variant of this 'destination'- rather than 'home'-facing orientation (Fenwick 2004). Here the equity benchmark is between the assignee and local/regional peers, with the emphasis on integration (Watson and Singh 2005), although if the location is in a low-pay country, the multinational usually supplements base pay with additional benefits and payments (Dowling et al. 2008). Hybrid systems (Suutari and Torknikoski 2001), combining elements of home and host approaches, as well as individually tailored packages, apply in some multinationals.

Short-term assignment terms are generally intended to be less complex, and less expensive, than arrangements applied to long-term expatriation, although there is evidence against generalizing in this regard. While those assigned for 6 months or less tend to receive reduced terms compared with long-term assignees, the same source reveals that for those abroad for between 6 months and 1 year (after which long-term assignment terms generally apply), 'services, incentives, hardship compensation, housing, transportation, relocation allowances [and] trips home' continue to be provided to assignees (ORC 2006: 12). The commuter assignment, sometimes referred to as 'flexpatriation' (see Chapter 11), does not really fit in with the traditional expatriation reward policy categories. Commuters may engage in international assignments on weekly or monthly terms, or for some other duration, leaving family members at home. Expenditure will be less on groceries and transportation but more on restaurant meals and travel home. Commuter packages therefore tend to be home based and contain elements primarily relating to reimbursement of travel (air fares paid) and serviced accommodation costs. While simplifying international mobilization, on the one hand, complications in taxation (as well as visa issues) may arise in administering policies applicable to this group of international workers, on the other (Perkins and Shortland 2006). And the trend may mitigate against transnational organizational designs, signalling a return to ethnocentric management that inhibits expatriate acculturation (Phillips and Fox 2003) and concomitant sense of interdependency between expatriate and key local employees.

International assignments are important investments for MNCs. Besides the direct costs of employee salaries, taxes, housing, shipment of household goods, education assistance for dependants, spouse support, cross-cultural training, goods and service allowances, repatriation logistics and reassignment costs, the administrative costs of running an international assignment programme should not be neglected. These include home-based HR support (assignment planning, selection and compensation management), assignment location- or host-based HR support, post-assignment placement costs as well as post-assignment career tracking costs (see Chapters 9 and 13). Furthermore, adjustment costs of the expatriates have to be taken into account. While many of these figures are hardly quantifiable, it is even more difficult to assess the return on investment of international assignments (for an overview and discussion see Dowling et al. 2008). In a study conducted by Cranfield School of Management and PricewaterhouseCoopers (Dickmann et al. 2006: 18–19) it was reported that the average costs per annum for an expatriate amounted to US$311,000. This includes the direct compensation costs and the costs to the organizations of managing their international assignments programme. At US$22,378 the latter accounted for 7% of the total assignment costs. While more and more firms are interested in measuring a return on investment in international assignment, to date only 14% are addressing this complex task mainly looking at the definition and respective fulfilment of assignment objectives (GMAC 2006).

Having summarized expatriation approaches and related compensation practice, we now turn our attention to theoretical perspectives related to the various levels illustrated in Figure 8.1. In this way we set the scene for addressing the question of how expatriate compensation outcomes (the dependent or 'outcome' variable in this analysis) may be influenced by a series of independent variables,

155

in dynamic interaction with one another and with the environmental context(s) in which international employee mobilization may occur.

HR perspective

Two aspects in particular may influence the HR perspective on expatriate effort–reward determination:

1 Ideas of 'best practice' and related normative commentary on policies and practices that MNCs should adopt: a 'functional' lens focusing the HR viewpoint.
2 The role and interests of the HR function likely to affect HR specialists' interpretations of alternative approaches to expatriate compensation determination: a 'political' orientation.

Administering the compensation of expatriate employees has been an important concern for international HR specialists, accounting for over 50% of their time (Perkins and Hendry 2001). Changes in the nature and duration of international employee mobility, not necessarily of HR's making but which need an HR response, condition the context for HR strategies to address the attendant compensation policy and practice implications. Reynolds (1997) cites evidence that in the USA 10% of companies have outsourced expatriation administration, with a further 9% considering doing so. It is not self-evident that the HR perspective will have caught up with these trends, for functional and political reasons.

In functional terms, corporate management may be assumed to have delegated to HR specialists the task of ensuring the consistent application of international assignment policy: setting and monitoring practice against standards in pursuit of efficient administrative practices, controlling costs, and safeguarding equity of treatment across groups (Dowling and Welch 2004). Emerging changes in the character of expatriation may undermine the HR function's ability to discharge this accountability both in practical terms (keeping track) and in terms of their authority to ensure line management compliance with corporate standards. Further complications may be anticipated – not only in terms of non-conventional expatriates. Recognition of the contribution of key locally recruited employees raises a requirement for sensitive treatment of reward differentials to avoid de-motivating either group. Recently observable corporate efforts to standardize at least pay policy *principles* across the multinational (Perkins 2006) in pursuit of overall cost effectiveness and with an accent on relating pay outcomes to performance requirements aligned to corporate priorities, add still further to emergent complexities.

An institutionalized set of arrangements for managing the complexities of traditional expatriate compensation (Briscoe and Schuler 2004) offers fairly junior

HR specialists a status likely to elude their peers in the mainstream HR function. HR contracts managers also have opportunities to reinforce their relative status as skilful intermediaries in negotiations between individuals identified for expatriation, their assigning manager and possibly the receiving manager in the host location. Status may also be derived from HR specialists' proximity to senior expatriate managers, as 'support services' providers. The shifting landscape of international mobility may threaten these positions reinforced, for example, by line management administrative 'self-service' facilitated by investment in HR IT infrastructure (Perkins 2006).

HR professionals aspiring to be in the vanguard of performance management strategy aligned with corporate business goals, may expect to fare better. Greater attention to corporate monitoring infrastructure to overcome top management frustration with a 'deals culture' around international mobility (Perkins 2006) may reinforce the status of HRM. Multinationals that have made significant investments in 'IT networked HR solutions' cite the requirement for a refreshment of HR teams given the changes in the skill sets required under the new corporate HR infrastructure.

Organization perspective

Ideas from the social science literature designed to evaluate the problems of organization, conceptualized in terms of economic institutions and also as social communities, may be combined with empirically derived commentary to inform the organization perspective on expatriate compensation. Organizations come into being as 'instruments to serve some purpose: a conscious arrangement of material and human resources required for the achievement of a defined objective' (Jones 1996: 4). One reward policy imperative to support that ambition may be 'to secure skills cost-effectively' (Hendry 2003: 1433). If expatriates are viewed as economic self-maximizing agents (Roberts 2001), managerial intervention may be focused on containing the transactional costs (Williamson 1996) of acquiring skills for international assignment. While having the merit of being very theory driven, an economics bias has the drawback, at least in the context of HRM analysis, of being 'very narrow and simplistic' (Guest 2001: 1093).

If expatriates are perceived as valuable, rare, non-substitutable and inimitable resources (Barney 1991; Boxall and Purcell 2003), and socially embedded culture and meaning systems are highlighted (Whitley 1992, 2000; Swedberg and Granovetter 2001), then managerial attention may be directed to *processual* aspects of expatriate compensation. The accent may be not only on what is included, but also on how outcomes are arrived at (Cox 2000). Common experiences of being justly treated in the process of reward management may help build sustainable relationships between expatriates and other members of the organization community, even when vastly different levels of economic development across the countries in

157

which multinationals operate mean that disparity in the substantive employee compensation, outcomes compared to local peers, is unavoidable (Chen et al. 2002).

Complementing these theoretical lenses, an empirical starting point for an organization perspective on expatriate compensation is the claim that international managers accentuate knowledge – its generation and mobilization to units and locations where it will add the greatest value leading to profitable investment returns. If value-generating knowledge is tacit – carried in the minds of experienced and skilled individuals and groups (Nonaka and Takeuchi 1995; Hall 2006) – deploying 'human capital' inputs (Madsen et al. 2002), may require migrating from hierarchical structures to organization designs that foster and activate transnational knowledge-centred network relationships. An explicit connection between compensation for 'global champions' (Perkins and Hendry 2001) and MNC performance goals may be anticipated as a priority (Phillips and Fox 2003). Reward practices that develop 'global mindsets' (Milkovich and Bloom 1998) have been advocated.

The messages communicated to expatriates in traditional expatriate compensation designs may be perceived as incompatible with contemporary organizational concerns. The explicit association of reward with employee performance appears absent or at best understated in the mainstream literature. In fact, it may be argued that, from the organization perspective, approaches such as the balance sheet have failed to keep in step with the changing priorities of corporate senior managers and their customers and financial investment principals. Some international compensation architects have begun talking about a future focus away from the 'deals culture' (Perkins 2006). But 'there is so little research to identify what works best' (Briscoe and Schuler 2004: 331), assuming we have generally agreed indicators for what 'working best' means across dynamic contexts.

Agency or transaction cost-based thinking would imply a recalibration of expatriate compensation to eliminate practices that introduce costs not validated by reference to external market comparisons and/or measurable performance contribution (Zingheim and Schuster 2000). Case study research findings in large western multinationals such as Cadbury Schweppes, Citibank, Honeywell and Unilever signal early initiatives in this direction. And some multinationals have invested in e-enabled transnational HR and performance monitoring, as well as corporate brand-oriented organizational redesign to increase management accountability at the corporate level while devolving pay-for-performance decision taking beyond a traditional HR 'black box' (Perkins 2006). It would be imprudent to generalize from this evidence at present. Performance-linked expatriate pay determination informed by transnational performance monitoring systems might be explicitly aligned with active engagement in knowledge sharing. But given the tacit nature of much employee-mediated knowledge, there may be problems in designing objective reward management arrangements that will effectively satisfy this aim. Actions demonstrating commitment to knowledge diffusion across the

158

transnational structure, engaging workforce members from all sources (expatriate or local) and in all relevant locations may be reinforced by corporate recognition of collective success through collectively delivered reward such as profit-sharing and 'gain-sharing' schemes.

A resource-dependency lens (Pfeffer and Salancik 1978; Pfeffer 1981; Wright and McMahan 1992) may also be used to scrutinize proposals emerging from resource-based theory. If organizations are perceived as sites of contestation over valuable, scarce, inimitable and non-substitutable resources, the balance of bargaining power in calibrating expatriate performance and reward determination may reside with those able to control transnational skill sets. Where managers are constrained in their choice of individuals to accept international assignments, in contexts where the options for alternative human resources are limited or non-existent, decision takers may acquiesce to demands from expatriates for 'fully loaded' packages, rather than seeking to negotiate more economic deals. Informed by institutional economics theory, an argument can be made that expatriation remains a cost-effective solution (Bonache and Fernández 2005). Corporate management may be unwilling to entrust safeguarding the value of the corporate brand to individuals recruited from local external labour markets, where attitudes to corporate governance and wider cultural values may contrast with the organizational priority. The transaction costs associated with expatriate remuneration may thus be equivalent to or even lower than those accompanying an external hire (Bonache and Fernández 2005). The time and other resources consumed in integrating a manager recruited from one of the local economies in which subsidiary operations are located may be incompatible with the need to achieve early returns on the investment in subsidiary operations.

Individual perspective

Employee rewards can affect employee recruitment and retention, motivate individuals and groups, impact on people's satisfaction and work behaviour and directly impact on employees' motivation and thus increase their performance (Armstrong and Murlis 1991; Burke and Terry 2004; McClenahen and Purdum 2004). This simple set of assumptions is lacking in much expatriate compensation literature. Only two aspects are discussed in this context: costs and retention. For example, Suutari and Tornikoski (2001) mention only that a well-designed and maintained programme can ensure that costs are controlled and that expatriates remain motivated and productive. Reward practices need to fit with other expatriate policies and with international performance management practices (Bonache and Fernández 1997).

Postulating a strategic role for expatriate compensation, Bonache and Fernández (1997) also emphasize the strategic fit between reward emphases and type of subsidiary within the multinational network in which the expatriate is located.

159

In the case of *local innovator* or *implementer* they expect a high emphasis on extrinsic rewards, while anticipating the more intensive use of intrinsic rewards in *global innovators* and *integrated players*. Similar hypotheses are developed with respect to the criterion used to evaluate performance (behavioural or results-based criteria) and the unit of reference (individual or group based).

Related to the notion of intrinsic and extrinsic rewards is the question of the return on an international assignment. Milkovich and Bloom (1998: 21) differentiate between financial return and relational returns:

> Relational returns may bind individuals more strongly to the organization because they can answer those special individual needs that cannot be met as effectively with economic returns (e.g., providing for childcare via the non-economic return of flexible work schedules versus the financial return of salary to pay for childcare; the flexible schedule puts a parent, not a caregiver at home).

Fish and Wood (1994) argue that the expectation would be for internationally mobile employees to be rewarded for demonstrating, additionally to expertise, intercultural and strategic competencies required for success in operating across international boundaries. The question then arises: how can compensation arrangements help support expatriate success?

Employee *contribution* implies not only individual performance outcomes but also the ways in which these are achieved consistent with organizational objectives. However, as well as skill- and competency-based pay, the diversity of interrelationships with peers, investors, etc., and hence the comparisons and tradeoffs that are likely to be made, add a further dimension to be accounted for. Simply reading off from a competency-based pay template would not offer a solution. The same applies in terms of setting, monitoring and appraising performance outcomes – and a wider range of people may be involved (business partners, local supervisors/peers, as well as corporate management) in arriving at a view of what (good) performance is assessed to be.

Bonache (2005) has drawn attention to another research stream that has analysed the impact of expatriate compensation on the satisfaction of international managers, i.e. a positive emotional state: 'Intrinsic satisfaction is related to work performance and feelings of accomplishment and self-actualisation. Extrinsic satisfaction, on the other hand, is related to rewards received by the employee (i.e., recognition, compensation and advancement)' (Suutari and Tornikoski 2001: 394). Empirical evidence on the sources of satisfaction and dissatisfaction among Finnish expatriates revealed that:

> The major sources of satisfaction were the lower level of taxation, the higher total salary level and allowances (in particular the car allowance). Furthermore, in the majority of cases the expatriates reported that the companies had clear

160

compensation principles, that they had enough prior information to negotiate, and thus the contract-making situation was not perceived to be very difficult.

(Suutari and Tornikoski 2001: 389)

Social exchange relationship perspective

Forms of contract underlying the exchange between employer and employee can be described using different theoretical lenses that emphasize different aspects:

Whereas ... [agency theory] focuses on the opportunistic tendency of economic agents, and thus ex ante prevention from it, the [psychological contract] focuses on the psychological state of the individual and his or her perception of the organization's action in accordance with the individual's initial expectation. The interaction or conjuncture between the theories, however, is that the parties involved in an employment relationship, such as an international assignment, are directed by multiple motives ... the parties pursue their self-interests (opportunism) and strive to keep their commitment (thus remaining as legitimate players) simultaneously.

(Yan et al. 2002: 377)

In this section, we will discuss the impact of both perspectives on expatriate compensation, before turning to equity considerations introducing the variable of the social referent in the social exchange relationship.

There is evidence that the compensation system has a clear impact on the psychological contract of employees (Gaertner and Nollen 1989; Rousseau and Greller 1994; Guest 2004). The psychological contract is 'an individual's belief in mutual obligations between that person and another party such as an employer (either a firm or another person)' (Rousseau and Tijoriwala 1998: 679). The expatriate compensation strategy can be part of the system creating expectancies and obligations (Rousseau 1995): 'It sends clear messages to members of the organization, informing them about expected attitudes and behaviours' (Suutari and Tornikoski 2001: 390). According to an empirical study by Guzzo et al. (1994) financial inducements are of primary importance within expatriates' psychological contracts.

Rousseau (1995) differentiates between relational, i.e. open-ended employment relationships characterized by a high mutual interest, and transactional psychological contracts, which can be well described by the statement 'a fair day's work for a fair day's pay' (Rousseau 1995: 91). According to Guzzo et al. (1994), psychological contracts are far more likely to be relational than transactional (for empirical evidence with respect to international careers see also Festing and Müller 2006). In the field of IHRM this could lead to the unplanned expatriate retention problems and economic losses due to de-motivation reported in the literature

161

(e.g., Black et al. 1992; Stroh 1995; Black and Gregersen 1999; Festing and Müller 2006). Furthermore, the psychological contract is contingent on the organization's philosophy and other corresponding IHRM practices (Guzzo et al. 1994; Festing and Müller 2006). A firm valuing international experience would want rather long-term relationships with experienced international managers in order to be able to amortize high investments in human capital (Yan et al. 2002). With respect to psychological contract research, this would imply a relational contract.

However, these economic arguments can also be further differentiated through the lens of new institutional economics (Festing 2006). Transaction cost theory (Williamson et al. 1975, 1984, 1985)[1] as well as agency theory (Pratt and Zeckhauser 1985; Eisenhardt 1989) offer explanations concerning the exchange relationship between employer and employee using the concept of transaction or agency costs. Under the transactional costs lens, due to the parties' self-interest and in the case of low verifiability of the employee's behaviour, firms need to create relational team employment relationships (Williamson 1984) or – embracing agency theory – strong incentive and control systems. While career development is an important, if not *the* most important, long-term incentive for the international manager (Yan et al. 2002), compensation issues are of high importance as well. The integration of expatriate reward within the total compensation system is critical. It should facilitate administrative processes, guarantee transparency of the compensation system and should indicate future developments contingent on the performance of the international manager.

Whether the reasoning is based on a relational psychological contract, a relational team or a specific relationship between principals and agents, the offer of an attractive international employment proposition not only at the point of mobilization abroad, but also facilitating reintegration into the compensation system following the international assignment, is significant. However, the control of expectations is limited. This is especially the case with international assignments because these include unfamiliar circumstances. It is important to specify clearly the expatriate compensation strategy in order to avoid dysfunctional effects. Suutari and Tornikoski (2001) provide evidence that at least some European multinationals seem to have made progress in this field (see also Reynolds 1997).

While psychological contract research as well as new institutional economics focuses on the exchange relationship between employees and the organization, ideas following an equity perspective address another dimension. They add the dimension of the 'social referent' and suggest that individuals compare input/output ratios of themselves with those of social referents and evaluate the organization's reward system on this basis (Adams 1963, 1965). 'Equal ratios lead to perceived fairness, but unequal ones may lead to perceived unfairness, as the comparer feels either under- or overcompensated' (Chen et al. 2002: 808). In the case of perceived unfairness, managers may try to manipulate their input or their output including

162

processes and results that are not favourable for the organization. In the case of international assignments, social referents can be expatriates of the same nationality, expatriates of a different nationality and locals – i.e. multiple referents (Bonache 2006). Taking these equity arguments into consideration, different expatriate compensation approaches have different effects. The home-country approach results in salary differentials between the expatriate of a specific country and local managers. Furthermore, expatriates of different nationalities get different salaries also. The effect might be that locals or expatriates from different national backgrounds with a lower pay level may perceive the system as unfair and reduce their performance (Toh and Denisi 2003). Another option would be that they engage in negotiation processes for a salary increase, albeit a more difficult response. In contrast, the host-country approach links expatriate compensation to the salary structure of the host-country environment (Phillips and Fox 2003; Bonache 2006). 'This approach aims not only at reducing salary inequalities perceived by the employees of the same subsidiary but also at reducing the high costs of expatriate treatment to their minimum for the company' (Suutari and Tornikoski 2001: 391). However, here, inequities between expatriates and their colleagues at headquarters may occur, leading to a low motivation for accepting international assignments. Thus, another major challenge in the design of expatriate compensation systems is the reduction of perceived inequalities between employee referent groups.

In summary, it seems that a differentiated analysis of the exchange relationship between the organization and the expatriate is useful to shed light on a variety of factors that might otherwise be neglected. A number of practical steps follow from this and the preceding elements of the differentiated analysis of expatriate compensation that has been discussed.

IMPACT OF THE INSTITUTIONAL AND CULTURAL ENVIRONMENT

The argument in the following section derives from the notion that national cultures and institutions are different and that this is manifested in organizational cultures and in the individuals working for them (Ferner 1997). We discuss the impact of the cultural and institutional context on expatriate compensation issues. The analytical framework in Figure 8.1 includes the assumption that the external environment influences each of the interacting levels and perspectives outlined.

Cultural theory and new institutional theory offer insights and evidence to help understand these relationships. The significance of national culture for expatriate compensation practices is underlined by Hofstede's (1991) statement that most inhabitants and most organizations of a country share the same mental programme and thus have similar ideas and perceptions of compensation practices. The new institutional perspective (Zucker 1977; DiMaggio and Powell 1983; Powell and

DiMaggio 1991) focuses on the relationships between the organization and its 'institutional environment' and the way in which they shape the organization's internal structures. Such characteristic 'clusters' of national institutional variables, which induce organizational behaviour, constitute the *national business system* of a country (Whitley 1992).

Since Hofstede's (1980) study many other researchers have recognized the importance of culture and its impact on HR and compensation issues (Rogovsky et al. 2000). Following the national culture approach means that 'compensation and reward policies must be aligned with and reinforce attributes of national culture' (Milkovich and Bloom 1998: 18). Exemplifying institutional factors affecting reward expectations, the: 'scope of labour legislation and its recency of codification creates new codes of conduct through issues such as sex discrimination, equal pay for equal work, and minimum wages' (Sparrow 2004: 103). In this context expatriate compensation becomes a complex challenge. Different cultural and institutional backgrounds in the headquarters and in the foreign subsidiaries collide. Often the attitudes and customs of the home country and the host country are conflicting (see e.g. Ferner 1997). Thus, expatriate compensation has to accommodate these differences to assure appropriate and attractive packages. Discussing the cultural and institutional embeddedness of the individual expatriate and the embeddedness of the organization, at the headquarters and the subsidiary level, may elucidate the issues.

The expatriate is embedded in the country in which he/she has acquired most of his/her work experiences – in general this is in the home country (Rosenzweig and Nohria 1994; Dowling and Welch 2004). Sparrow (2004) has identified cultural influences on reward behaviour such as 'different expectations of the manager–subordinate relationship and their impact on performance management

---

Text box 8.1
Ten practical steps for firms in designing reward approaches for expatriates

1 Ensure initiatives for consistency in expatriate compensation do not exacerbate multi-local compensation differentials, which may appear illogical and inequitable among local core workforce members on whom multinational joint ventures and strategic alliances, as well as local market embedding aspirations increasingly depend.

2 Don't assume homogeneity of interest perceptions among the parties to expatriate compensation determination – not only comparing specialists and generalist managers, but also even among HR function members. Consider whether HR competencies need refreshing matched to progressive compensation priorities and systems.

3 Evaluate corporate priorities to minimize expatriation transaction costs over securing the release of potential among valuable, rare, inimitable, and non-substitutable expatriate resources, where attention to procedural justice as much as substance may be required.

4 Audit the extent to which expatriate compensation practices enable or constrain development of a global mindset, possibly shifting the emphasis from expatriate-centred 'wholeness' preservation to one of balancing the needs and priorities of a range of stakeholders.

5 Consider the ways expatriate compensation may be calibrated to align with multidirectional knowledge sharing, exploring the optimum balance between individual and collective performance.

6 Pay attention to the social referents influencing expatriate expectations and behaviours in setting more performance oriented expatriate compensation, acting on opportunities for greater openness and transparency compared with 'black box deal making'.

7 Apply a return-on-investment lens to judge the value of fully loaded expatriate packages, factoring in consideration of corporate governance risks of premature devolution of the corporate brand to local recruits.

8 Supplement attention to securing and retaining expatriates with consideration of motivational features not only of the quantum but also the mode of delivery of expatriate compensation, emphasizing organizational effectiveness contribution and how that is made.

9 Weigh alternative approaches to structuring and delivering expatriate compensation contingent on the extent to which managers are expected to operate in local innovation (with limited infrastructure) or local implementation mode, where extrinsic reward may be preferred, compared with a priority for behaviour attuned to global innovation and/or global integration. In the last case, career incentives coupling short-term intrinsic (developmental experience) reward with longer term extrinsic reward through vertical post-assignment career progression may be preferred.

10 Pay attention to the expatriation psychological contract, as a mechanism for dialogue around mutual expectations and obligations, but beware of over-emphasizing unwritten promises (e.g. the career incentives in item 9) if operational considerations are likely to inhibit fulfilment. Be prepared to answer the question honestly as to whether a transactional or relational relationship is desired and/or feasible and work through the consequences in structuring the expatriate package of tangible and intangible rewards.

and motivational processes' (Sparrow 2004: 105). A more holistic balancing of intrinsic and extrinsic rewards may be valued in societies where work is based on more integrated personal social 'relationships', while in cultures characterized by personal independence and isolation ('individualism'), as well as rapidly changing personal and social contexts, extrinsic rewards may be emphasized (Frey 1997; Triandis 2002). Dowling and Welch (2004) name the service of a chauffeur as another example for an element of the compensation package that might be evaluated differently by individuals in distinct countries.

With respect to country-specific attractiveness of variable pay, a study by Lowe et al. (2002) indicates that employees in the USA, Taiwan, Mexico and Latin America prefer variable pay incentives while their counterparts in Australia and Japan only moderately emphasize this kind of pay. Research shows that seniority-based pay in terms of a fixed salary is more likely to be found in countries with higher levels of uncertainty avoidance such as Greece, Portugal and Guatemala (Schuler and Rogovsky 1998). If the cultural dimension of uncertainty avoidance (Hofstede 1980) is taken into account, the extent to which people are risk averse or are prepared to take risks is highlighted. Risk-taking managers are probably ready to accept large incentive payments while risk-averse managers are not prepared to accept high levels of income variability (e.g. performance-based pay).[2]

Different socialization processes experienced by expatriates and local co-workers may lead expatriates to respond differently to incentives offered by the host country than their colleagues. Consequently, expatriate compensation might be based on compensation standards in the expatriate's home country and reflect similar patterns in order to attract and retain staff in the areas where the multinational has needs and opportunities (Dowling and Welch 2004).

Organizations as social institutions are likewise embedded in their institutional and cultural environments. In order to operate effectively, their managements must take into consideration significant national variables when formulating business strategies (Ferner 1997). Thus, institutional rules and cultural norms necessarily feature in compensation decisions to avoid problems in attracting and retaining employees, labour relations conflicts or ineffective employee behaviour (Armstrong and Murlis 1991; Grønhaug and Nordhaug 1992; Milkovich and Bloom 1998; Bradley et al. 1999; Bloom et al. 2003; Sparrow 2004; Schuler and Jackson 2005). The characteristics of the industrial relations system as part of the national business system, including the importance placed on labour unions, can have significant effects on pay systems. And Pendleton et al. (2002) identify considerable differences among the member states of the European Union in the areas of employee profit sharing and share ownership, which 'correlated broadly with the extent of differences in legislative and fiscal support for them' (p. 21). Festing et al. (1999) confirm this and argue that the complexity of German law, the formalized German workplace industrial relations system and the government attitudes have led to the fact that financial participation schemes are not very

166

common in the German context. The empirical results give examples indicating how organizational pay strategies are influenced by external factors. As MNCs are operating in multiple environments, subsidiaries often follow different (multi-centric) approaches to be effective in every country. For this reason, MNCs that try to standardize pay strategy at a global level often provide room for flexible adaptation to local conditions (Festing et al. 2006).

CONCLUSION

While not made explicit in the literature, description of the determination of reward for internationally mobile employees reflects a market-clearing assumption from economics combined with a policy focus on 'keeping expatriates whole', possibly the legacy of 'welfare capitalist' management (Jacoby 2005: 37). Although changes may be perceived as the corporate governance and competitive context for international organization and employee mobility overseas has evolved, the response reported in the empirical literature seems to be simply one of trimming back on the duration and level of compensation applicable to expatriate assignments. We have argued in this chapter that to lay the foundations for a more root-and-branch review of internationally mobile employee reward management a more complex amalgam of perspectives – and their interaction – needs to be considered. Rewards applied to internationally mobile employees (the dependent variable) therefore need to be analysed in terms of their relationship with a series of interacting independent variables (that also interact with the dependent variable) that include perspectives from the organization and line managers who administer it, the HR function, individual expatriates, contextual conditions and the relationship around exchanging labour, willingly deployed in a foreign country, for remuneration.

In summary, the independent variables that appear to influence the policies and processes for setting compensation for internationally mobile employees reward outcomes (dependent variables) may be viewed as stemming from multiple sources with a stake in the project.

KEY LEARNING POINTS

- Corporate management wants to resource achievement of business strategic goals and governance priorities.
- Senior operational managers wish to be able to delegate line accountability to experienced, knowledgeable people whom they feel they can rely on to act and control the resources devolved to them in ways that help the supervising line manager to contribute to achievement of corporate goals.

167

- HR people have a stake in acting on behalf of corporate and line managers (depending on their own location and alliances in the organizational structure) to facilitate the mobilization, to ensure corporate and divisional HR policies are implemented in ways that will keep the parties to the effort–reward relationship content, while sustaining consistency in applying reward policies so as not to attract criticism through unfavourable comparisons among other employees or in terms of impact on corporate costs and to assure administrative efficiency.

- Individuals approach the internationally mobile effort–reward bargain with their own needs and expectations. They may be able to leverage their market influence increasingly, the more the firm is dependent on that individual to fill the role. These factors lie outside the internal policy-making framework – they are 'controlled' by the employee. Representatives of the employer are in a position where they may proactively make an offer, but this may be subsequently judged over-generous.

- Cultural values such as those outlined by Hofstede (1980) as well as institutional factors including employment regulations, the economic state of the employer and stage of international growth and, in turn, interaction between expatriate and local peers, are likely to have an influence on expatriate compensation decisions. Corporate actors' interpretations of these contextual factors need to feature in any analysis of the decision-making process.

- The perspectives summarized in the framework of Figure 8.1 could lead to challenging new avenues for future theoretical and, especially, empirical research that could further enrich our knowledge in the field of expatriate compensation.

To sum up, using the framework outlined in this chapter, academic analysts and management decision-takers would have a more effective understanding about the range of factors that influence expatriate compensation if they understood how they interact with other determinants of expatriate compensation. Ideas about this interactive process may challenge some assumptions but would lead to better outcomes.

NOTES

1 Based on transaction cost theory, Festing (1997) as well as Bonache and Pla (2005) discuss the relative costs inherent in the use of expatriates and argue that the result is contingent on the firm's internationalization strategy.

2 However, this distinction cannot only be made according to country-specific cultural values but also with respect to industry-specific features, e.g. firms belonging to high-tech industries or the so-called new economy have seen more risk-taking managers than traditional firms (Gomez-Mejía and Welbourne 1988, 1991).

REFERENCES

Adams, J.S. (1963) 'Toward an understanding of inequity', *Journal of Abnormal and Social Psychology* 67:422–436.

Adams, J. (1965) 'Inequity in social exchange', in L.L. Berkowitz (ed.) *Advances in Experimental Social Psychology*, 2nd edn, New York: Academic Press.

Armstrong, M. and Murlis, H. (1991) *Reward Management: A Handbook of Remuneration Strategy and Practice*, London: Kogan Page.

Barney, J. (1991) 'Firm resources and sustained competitive advantage', *Journal of Management* 17, 1:99–120.

Black, J.S. and Gregersen, H.B. (1999) 'The right way to manage expats', *Harvard Business Review* 77, 2:52–63.

Black, J.S., Gregersen, H.B. and Mendenhall, M.E. (1992) 'Toward a theoretical framework or repatriation adjustment', *Journal of International Business Studies* 23: 737–760.

Bloom, M. and Milkovich, G. (1992) 'Issues in managerial compensation research', in C. Cooper and D. Rouseau (eds) *Trends in Organizational Behavior*, Chichester: Wiley.

Bloom, M., Milkovich, G. and Mitra, A. (2003) 'International compensation: learning from how managers respond to variations in local host contexts', *International Journal of Human Resource Management* 14, 8:1350–1367.

Bonache, J. (2005) 'Job satisfaction among expatriates, repatriates and domestic employees: the perceived impact of international assignments on work-related variables', *Personnel Review* 34, 1:110–124.

Bonache, J. (2006) 'The compensation of expatriates: a review and future research agenda,' in G. Stahl and I. Björkmann (eds) *Handbook of Research in International Human Resource Management*, Cheltenham: Edward Elgar.

Bonache, J. and Fernández, Z. (1997) 'Expatriate compensation and its link to the subsidiary strategic role: a theoretical analysis', *International Journal of Human Resource Management* 8, 4:457–475.

Bonache, J. and Fernández, Z. (2005) 'International compensation: Costs and benefits of international assignments', in H. Scullion and M. Linehan (eds) *International Human Resource Management: A Critical Text*, Basingstoke: Palgrave Macmillan.

Bonache, J. and Pla, J. (2005) 'When are international managers a cost effective solution? The rational of transaction cost theory applied to staffing decisions in MNCs', *Journal of Business Research* 58, 10:1320–1329.

Boxall, P. and Purcell, J. (2003) *Strategy and Human Resource Management*, Basingstoke: Palgrave Macmillan.

Bradley, P., Hendry, C. and Perkins, S.J. (1999) 'Global or multi-local? The significance of international values in reward strategy', in C. Brewster and H. Harris (eds) *International HRM: Contemporary Issues in Europe*, London: Routledge.

Brewster, C. (1999) 'Strategic human resource management: the value of different paradigms', *Management International Review* 39:45–64.

Briscoe, D.R. and Schuler, R.S. (2004) *International Human Resource Management*, 2nd edn, New York: Routledge.

Burke, L.A. and Terry, B. (2004) 'At the intersection of economics and HRM: an argument for variable pay schemes', *American Business Review*, January: 88–92.

Chen, C.C., Choi, J. and Chi, S.C. (2002) 'Making justice sense of local-expatriate compensation disparity: mitigating by local referents, ideological explanations and interpersonal sensitivity in China-foreign joint ventures', *Academy of Management Journal* 45, 4:807–817.

Cox, A. (2000) 'The importance of employee participation in determining pay system effectiveness', *International Journal of Management Reviews* 2, 4:357–375.

Dickmann, M., Doherty, N. and Johnson, A. (2006) 'Measuring the value of international assignments, report for the International Mobility Initiative', London: PricewaterhouseCoopers.

DiMaggio, P.J. and Powell, W.W. (1983) 'The iron cage revisited: institutional isomorphism and collective rationality in organizational fields', *American Sociological Review* 48:47–160.

Dowling, P.J. and Welch, D.E. (2004) *International Human Resource Management: Managing People in a Multinational Context*, London: Thomson.

Dowling, P.J., Engle, A., Festing, M. and Müller, B. (2005) 'Complexity in global pay: a meta-framework', *Proceedings of the 8th Conference on International Human Resource Management*, Cairns, Australia.

Dowling, P.J., Festing, M. and Engle, A.D. (2008) *International Human Resource Management*, 5th edn, London: Thomson Learning.

Eisenhardt, K.M. (1989) 'Agency theory: an assessment and review', *Academy of Management Review* 14:57–74.

Fenwick, M. (2004) 'International compensation and performance management', in A.W Harzing and J. Van Ruysseveldt (eds) *International Human Resource Management*, 2nd edn, London: Sage.

Ferner, A. (1997) 'Country of origin effects and HRM in multinational companies', *Human Resource Management Journal* 7, 1:19–37.

Festing, M. (1997) 'International human resources management strategies in multinational corporations: theoretical assumptions and empirical evidence from German firms', *Management International Review* 1, Special Issue: 43–63.

Festing, M. (2006) 'International human resource management and economic theories of the firm', in G. Stahl and I. Björkmann (eds) *Handbook of Research in International Human Resource Management*, Cheltenham: Edward Elgar.

Festing, M. and Müller, B. (2006) 'International careers and psychological contracts', unpublished manuscript, Berlin: ESCP-EAP European School of Management.

Festing, M., Eidems, J. and Royer, S. (2006) 'Strategic issues and local constraints in transnational compensation strategies. An analysis of cultural, institutional and political influences', unpublished manuscript, Berlin: ESCP-EAP European School of Management.

Festing, M., Groening, Y., Kabst, R. and Weber, W. (1999) 'Financial participation in Europe – determinants and outcomes', *Economic and Industrial Democracy* 20:295–329.

Fish, A.J. and Wood, J. (1994) 'Integrating expatriate careers with international business activity: strategies and procedures', *International Journal of Career Management* 6, 1: 3–13.

Frey, B. (1997) *Not Just for the Money: An Economic Theory of Personal Motivation*, Cheltenham: Edward Elgar.

Gaertner, K.N. and Nollen, S.D. (1989) 'Career practices, perceptions of employment practices, and psychological commitment to the organization', *Human Relations* 42, 11:975–991.

GMAC Global Relocation Services in conjunction with US National Foreign Trade Council Inc and SHRM Global Forum (2006) *GMAC Global Relocation Trends*, 2005 survey report.

170

Gomez-Hejia, L.R. and Welbourne, T. (1988) 'Compensation strategy: an overview and future steps', *Human Resource Planning* 11, 3:173–189.

Gomez-Mejía, L.R. and Welbourne, T. (1991) 'Compensation strategies in a global context', *Human Resource Planning* 14, 1: 29–41.

Grønhaug, K. and Nordhaug, O. (1992) 'International human resource management: an environmental perspective', *International Journal of Human Resource Management* 3, 1:1–14.

Guest, D.E. (2001) 'Human resource management: when research confronts theory', *International Journal of Human Resource Management* 12, 7: 1092–1106.

Guest, D.E. (2004) 'The psychology of the employment relationship: an analysis based on the psychological contract', *Applied Psychology: An International Review* 53, 4: 541–555.

Guzzo, R., Noonan, K. and Elron, E. (1994) 'Expatriate managers and the psychological contract', *Journal of Applied Psychology* 79, 4: 617–626.

Hall, M. (2006) 'Knowledge management and the limits of knowledge codification', *Journal of Knowledge Management* 10, 3:117–126.

Harvey, M. (1993) 'Empirical evidence of recurring international compensation problems', *Journal of International Business Studies* 24, 4: 785–799.

Hendry, C.N. (2003) 'Employing systems theory to the analysis of national models of HRM', *International Journal of Human Resource Management* 14, 8: 1430–1442.

Hofstede, G. (1980) *Culture's Consequences: International Differences in Work Related Values*, Beverly Hills, CA: Sage.

Hofstede, G. (1991) *Culture and Organizations – Software of the Mind*, London: McGraw-Hill.

Jones, F.E. (1996) *Understanding Organizations: A Sociological Perspective*, Mississauga, Ontario: Copp Clark Ltd.

Kessler, I. (2001) 'Reward system choices', in J. Storey (ed.) *Human Resource Management: A Critical Text*, 2nd edn, London: Thomson.

Kessler, I. (2005) 'Remuneration systems', in S. Bach (ed.) *Managing Human Resources: Personnel Management In Transition*, 4th edn, Oxford: Blackwell.

Lowe, K., Milliman, J., DeCieri, H. and Dowling, P. (2002) 'International compensation practices: a ten-country comparative analysis', *Human Resource Management* 41, 1: 45–66.

Madsen, T.L., Mosakowski, E. and Zaheer, S. (2002) 'The dynamics of knowledge flows: human capital mobility, knowledge retention and change', *Journal of Knowledge Management* 6, 2:164–176.

McClenahen, J. and Purdum, T. (2004) 'Making variable pay pay', *Industry Week* 253, 9:72.

Milkovich, G.T. and Bloom, M. (1998) 'Rethinking international compensation', *Compensation and Benefits Review* 30, 1:15–23.

Nonaka, I. and Takeuchi, H. (1995) *The Knowledge-creating Company: How Japanese Companies Create the Dynamics of Innovation*, Oxford: Oxford University Press.

ORC Surveys (2002) 'Balance sheet remains leading international pay approach', *Worldwide Survey Of International Assignment Policies and Practices*.

Organization Resource Counselors (ORC) (2004) *2004 Worldwide Survey of International Assignment Policies and Practices*, New York: ORC Worldwide.

Organization Resource Counselors (ORC) (2006) *Survey of International Short-term Assignment Policies*, New York: ORC Worldwide.

171

Pendleton, A., Poutsma, E., Brewster, C. and van Ommeren, J. (2002) 'Employee share ownership and profit sharing in the European Union: incidence, company characteristics and union representation', *Transfer* 8, 1:47–62.

Perkins, S.J. (2006) *Research Report: International Reward and Recognition*, London: CIPD.

Perkins, S.J. and Hendry, C.N. (2001) 'Global champions: who's paying attention?', *Thunderbird International Business Review* 43, 1:53–75.

Perkins, S.J. and Shortland, S.M. (2006) *Strategic International Human Resource Management: Choices and Consequences in Multinational People Management*, London: Kogan Page.

Pfeffer, J. (1981) *Power in Organisations*, Marshfield, MA: Pitman.

Pfeffer, J. and Salancik, G.R. (1978) *The External Control of Organizations – A Resource Dependence Perspective*, New York, Hagerstown, San Francisco, London: Stanford University Press.

Phillips, L. and Fox, M. (2003) 'Compensation strategy in transnational corporations', *Management Decision* 41, 5:465–476.

Powell, W.W. and DiMaggio, P.J. (1991) *The New Institutionalism in Organizational Analysis*, Chicago and London: University of Chicago Press.

Pratt, J.W. and Zeckhauser, R.J. (1985) 'Principals and agents: an overview', in J.W.Pratt and R.J. Zeckhauser (eds) *Principles of Agents: The Structure of Business*, Boston MA: Harvard Business School Press.

Reynolds, C. (1997) 'Expatriate compensation in historical perspective', *Journal of World Business* 32, 2:118–132.

Roberts, J. (2001) 'Trust and control in Anglo-American systems of corporate governance: the individualizing and socializing effects of processes of accountability', *Human Relations* 54, 12:1547–1572.

Rogovsky, N.G., Schuler, R.S. and Reynolds, C. (2000) 'How can national culture affect compensation practices of MNEs?', *Global Focus* 12, 4:35–42.

Rosenzweig, P.M. and Nohria, N. (1994) 'Influences on human resource management practices in multinational corporations', *Journal of International Business Studies*, 2nd quarter: 229–251.

Rousseau, D.M. (1995) *Psychological Contracts In Organizations*, Thousands Oaks, CA: Sage.

Rousseau, D.M. and Greller, M.M. (1994) 'Human resource practices: administrative contract makers', *Human Resource Management* 33, 3:385–401.

Rousseau, D. and Tijoriwala, S. (1998) 'Assessing psychological contracts: issues, alternatives and measures', *Journal of Organizational Behaviour* 19, 7:679–695.

Schuler, R.S. and Jackson, S.E. (2005) 'A quarter-century review of human resource management in the U.S.: the growth in importance of the international perspective', *Management Revue* 16, 1:11–35.

Schuler, R. and Rogovsky, N. (1998) 'Understanding compensation practice variations across firms: the impact of culture', *Journal of International Business Studies* 29, 1: 159–177.

Sparrow, P. (2004) 'International rewards systems: to converge or not to converge?', in C. Brewster and H. Harris (eds) *International HRM: Contemporary Issues in Europe*, London: Routledge.

Stroh, L.K. (1995) 'Predicting turnover among repatriates: can organizations affect retention rates?', *International Journal of Human Resource Management* 6:443–456.

Suutari, V. and Tornikoski, C. (2001) 'The challenge of expatriate compensation: the sources of satisfaction and dissatisfaction among expatriates', *International Journal of Human Resource Management* 12, 3:389–404.

Swedberg, R. and Granovetter, M. (eds) (2001) *The Sociology of Economic Life*, Boulder, CO: Westview Press.

Toh, S.M. and Denisi, A.S. (2003) 'Host country national reactions to expatriate pay policies: a model and implications', *Academy of Management Review* 28, 4:606–621.

Triandis, H. (2002) 'Generic individualism and collectivism', in M. Gannon and K. Newman (eds) *The Blackwell Handbook of Cross-cultural Management*, Oxford: Blackwell.

Watson, B.W. and Singh, G. (2005) 'Global pay systems: compensation in support of a multinational strategy', *Compensation and Benefits Review* 37, 1:33–36.

Wentland, D.M. (2003) 'A new practical guide for determining expatriate compensation: the comprehensive model', *Compensation and Benefits Review* 35, 3:45–50.

Whitley, R.D. (1992) *European Business Systems: Firms and Markets in Their National Contexts*, London: Sage.

Whitley, R. (2000) *Divergent Capitalisms: The Social Structuring and Change of Business Systems*, Oxford: Oxford University Press.

Williamson, O.E. (1984) 'Efficient labor organization', in F. H. Stephen (ed.) *Firms, Organization and Labour*, London: Macmillan.

Williamson, O.E. (1985) *The Economic Institutions of Capitalism*, New York and London: Free Press.

Williamson, O. (1996) *The Mechanisms of Governance*, Oxford: Oxford University Press.

Williamson, O.E., Wachter, M.L. and Harris, J.E. (1975) 'Understanding the employment relation: the analysis of idiosyncratic exchange', *Bell Journal of Economics* 6: 250–278.

Wright, P.M. and McMahan, G.C. (1992) 'Theoretical perspectives for strategic human resource management', *Journal of Management* 18, 2: 295–320.

Yan, A., Zhu, G. and Hall, D.T. (2002) 'International assignments for career building: a model of agency relationships and psychological contracts', *Academy of Management Review* 27, 3:373–391.

Zingheim, P.K. and Schuster, J.R. (2000) *Pay People Right: Breakthrough Reward Strategies to Create Great Companies*, San Francisco, CA: Jossey-Bass.

Zucker, L. (1977) 'The role of institutionalization in cultural persistence', *American Sociological Review* 42:726–743.

Chapter 9

Repatriation

The end or the middle?

Noeleen Doherty, Chris Brewster, Vesa Suutari and Michael Dickmann

CHAPTER OBJECTIVES

By the end of this chapter, readers will have:

- an appreciation of the integral nature of the expatriation and repatriation experiences
- an understanding of the multitude of factors impacting on the perceived outcomes of repatriation – organizational and individual
- gained sensitivity to the importance of time and timing in repatriation
- explored some practical guidance on managing repatriation

INTRODUCTION

International working has been likened by some to a heroic journey (Campbell 1968), a notion taken from the Parsifal myth common in many European countries: themes of heroism as a cycle of going out from a familiar home base to foreign realms, following a call for adventure, encountering and confronting challenges along the way, learning and experiencing transformations, before returning with new knowledge and understanding to share, an authority on two worlds. The idea that travel can broaden the mind is not new but being globally mobile and able to develop a global outlook has considerable currency. However, the return from such a journey may be far from epic, as much research suggests that the repatriation element of an international expedition can be fraught with difficulties. This chapter explores some of the individual and organizational challenges involved in the repatriation phase of international mobility. These insights are related to practical implications for managing repatriation.

It is now taken for granted that the internationalization of business and of work is increasing apace and that this, in turn, has led to an increasing need for managers with global competence (Oddou et al. 2000; Evans et al. 2002).

For many years research on expatriation seemed to be following the expatriate cycle itself, with early attention paid to criteria for selection, which gradually developed into a debate about the antecedents of and methods for such selection; and to compensation and benefits. This led on to research into the adaptation of expatriates. Eventually, the final phase of the expatriation process – repatriation – came under the spotlight.

Research into repatriation has, in turn, tended first to follow the employers' agenda: exploring the issues related to the problems that arose when the expatriate returned. More recently, led by researchers in Europe, there are the beginnings of an attempt to understand the careers of expatriates and how the repatriation process fits into that. This has signalled a move from seeing repatriation as the end of the process of expatriation to seeing repatriation as another stage in the career of the employee. We explore these perspectives here.

REPATRIATION AS THE END OF THE ASSIGNMENT

The end of the expatriate assignment was initially, perhaps, assumed to be unproblematic. The expatriate would return home, pick up a new job with their employer and continue their career. It became apparent that that was not what happens; rather repatriation has been described as 'the toughest assignment of all' (Hurn 1999).

In fact, surveys show that repatriation is the area of highest dissatisfaction of expatriates with respect to organizational policies (Stahl and Cerdin 2004). Many expatriates never get that far and leave the organization before the end of their assignment (GMAC 2005). Research evidence shows that 10–25% of expatriates leave their company within 1 year of repatriation (Black 1992; Solomon 1995). This figure is notably higher than for equivalent non-expatriates (Black and Gregersen 1999). Longer term, between one-quarter and one-third of repatriates leave their firms within 2 years of returning (Suutari and Brewster 2003). Since nearly half the respondents in some of these surveys did not keep records of the career outcomes of repatriates the true figure is likely to be higher. In a sample of Finnish expatriates, even among those who stayed with the same employer, well over half had seriously considered leaving (Suutari and Brewster 2003): twice as many do so in the first year among the repatriated population as among those who have never been on an international assignment (Dickmann et al. 2006). Attrition and the potential exit of repatriates give cause for concern, certainly for organizations where a key imperative for the use of international assignments is the development of global talent.

The outcomes of an international assignment (henceforth abbreviated to IA), as commentators have pointed out, are far from a straightforward win–win scenario. A number of factors have a bearing on how an expatriation assignment ends. These include how the IA has been positioned by the organization, how well the person and their family adjust to the return home, the impact that the expatriation experience has had on shaping the employees' expectations of the job they return to and the longer term career expectations that they have developed. We consider these factors next.

What's on offer?

From the organizational perspective, there has been much discussion of the need to develop international/global mindsets (Kobrin 1994; Bonache et al. 2001). This is seen as an important source of competitive advantage for multinational corporations (MNCs) (Bartlett and Ghoshal 1997). It has been argued that strategic capability is dependent on the 'cognitive processes' of international managers and the ability of the organization to create a 'matrix in the minds of managers' or a global mindset (Bartlett and Ghoshal 1989: 195). MNCs increasingly understand the value of the creation and absorption of knowledge inside the organization in the international context (Czinkota and Ronkainen 2005). Expatriates are important mechanisms of knowledge transfer (Bonache and Brewster 2001; see Chapter 4) and this may now be one of the main reasons for sending people on such assignments (Bossard and Peterson 2005). This international orientation depends, among other things, on the length and the quality of international experience. Large MNCs consider expatriation as a key means to achieving global leadership development as the number one human resource priority of chief executives in MNCs (Evans et al. 2002). So to meet this growing need for mobility, organizations regularly position an IA as a developmental opportunity.

However, although companies have indicated that opportunities for IAs are on the rise, this comes at a time when employees are becoming increasingly discerning about committing to an IA (GMAC 2005; Dickmann et al. forthcoming). Employees appear keenly focused on their own development and the likely career opportunities and career progression as outcomes of a foreign posting as well as personal development. Dickmann et al. (forthcoming) suggested that the decision to take an IA is strongly influenced by an employee's anticipation of positive skills development and career progression outcomes.

It has been argued that the potential consequences of an international experience can be mutually beneficial for employee and employer (Larsen 2004). But if this is a powerful developmental tool, it is also an expensive one. According to Reynolds (1997) expatriates cost employers, on average, two to five times more than home-country counterparts. As a consequence, expatriates are among the most expensive of an organization's human resources. For that investment to

176

'pay off' it is necessary to retain the repatriates in the organization and to have them satisfied and performing well.

The recurrent argument has been that it is the company that suffers when repatriates leave. Failure to successfully repatriate implies high costs for the international companies: not only is there the loss of key employees and their unique experience if they leave the organization but also the possibility of recruiting new candidates for expatriations is reduced, as other employees may be more reluctant to accept foreign assignments when they see negative effects on career advancement (Brewster and Scullion 1997; Bossard and Peterson 2005). This can also alter the international growth planning of the companies.

A hero's return?

The organizational context to which repatriates return these days has undergone many changes. No longer do companies offer guarantees of employment or the prospect of career progression in the form of promotion in general (Baruch 2006) – if they ever did. This applies just as much to expatriate populations. Although those who expatriate enjoy heavy investment, both financial and managerial, in their administration, organizations increasingly operate on a 'no-slack' basis, where there are not necessarily appropriate jobs for the expatriate to return to (Dickmann et al. 2005). These changing organizational contours frame the context faced by repatriates on their return journey.

The quality of the repatriation journey is impacted by a variety of factors including the individual's expectations and their receptivity to working abroad. Previous research has highlighted the central role of the expatriate's expectations in the repatriation process (Black 1992; Forster 1994; Pickard 1999; Riusala and Suutari 2000). International assignees optimistically hope for a holistic process that gives them an early indication of their next position and an adequate prospect of further career advancement. They look for opportunities to re-establish old contacts in the corporate centre (in the months before return), hope to be mentored in the changed realities at the head office, expect to be debriefed and find honesty important. Most expatriates expect the return to enhance their career prospects and their return to be exciting and/or challenging (Tung 1998; Pickard 1999; Suutari and Brewster 2003).

Thus, repatriates form a set of work-related expectations, including how they will be treated by management and by other employees after repatriation. They have expectations regarding the job position after repatriation, the standard of living they will achieve and their longer term career prospects. Typically, the repatriates expect to be rewarded with high-level jobs and opportunities to utilize skills acquired while abroad. They also expect that their supervisors and colleagues will be interested in their international experiences and support them through the repatriation process.

177

Positive expectations are more likely to be held by those on their first IA than among more experienced expatriates. A positive mindset to the idea of a foreign work experience is a characteristic important to willingness to work abroad (Tharenou 2003). Receptivity to working abroad, it is suggested, is a relatively stable characteristic and, therefore, it is likely to be an enduring trait. It has also been suggested that expectations of gaining valued outcomes from relocating increase receptivity. This is an indication that assisting employees who are receptive to have a good experience would encourage future mobile behaviour. This powerful feedback loop of clear expectations and good experience feeding positive attitudes to mobility is a key area of focus for companies.

Effectively managing the expectations of repatriation starts at the pre-assignment stage where organizational goals and individual aspirations need to be informed, formed and integrated. It is at this stage that the expectations for during and after the assignment are set, therefore clarification of goals and objectives is key to managing outcomes. Company X (see Case study 9.1) employs a process in which the early stage planning of an IA involves an agreement of goals and outcomes, an approach that can help to pre-empt potential problems not only while on assignment but, importantly, on return.

Case study 9.1
Pre-departure – communicating parameters, setting goals and formalizing processes in Company X

The importance of setting clear assignment goals and having processes in place to help deliver on these is important to the outcomes of an international assignment for both an organization and the individual assignee. In fact, it is positioned as a critical element in the management of an international assignment. Communicating these in a comprehensive, digestible format can guard against the potentially detrimental impacts of role ambiguity on adjustment, objectivity in the appraisal of expatriate performance or premature return due to poor performance.

Within Company X, the combination of comprehensive pre-departure information with a process and format that facilitates discussions between the individual, the home and the host, helps to clarify roles and responsibilities before, during and after the assignment. A focused set of questions around the assignment objectives, managerial objectives for the assignment and a business rationale for the duration of the assignment form the basis of an agreement that must be reached before the assignment can start. This format and process explicitly clarifies assignment objectives, identifies the added value of the assignment and facilitates individual career planning.

Questions

1 How can Company X link the assignment goals to their repatriation policy?
2 Develop three scenarios:
   i   an IA to develop the expatriate
   ii an IA to quickly fill a skills gap
   iii an IA to transfer knowledge to a local unit and explore ideas and activities to increase repatriate retention.

Although this may result in a longer than average time to the start of an assignment, an integrated discussion of business goals (home and host) and individual objectives can provide an essential tripartite forum to facilitate synergy in goal setting and clarity in expectations, stated good practice in the current international HRM literature.

The process of returning home can be as much of a culture shock as leaving (see Chapter 7). Rather than the anticipated hero's return, repatriates often experience an intense shock because the return home is not as expected, a 'reverse culture shock'. It has been argued that the longer the repatriates are on an IA, the higher the difficulties they will find when returning to their parent company (Harvey 1982). It is assumed that the longer the time spent abroad, the more the individual will be used to the foreign country and organizational culture and the higher the degree of adjustment to that country. The result will be increased difficulty adjusting back to the home country. This relation has received empirical support in the studies of Black and Gregersen (1992) and Gregersen and Stroh (1997).

Managing expectations

Empirical evidence indicates that repatriates are often disappointed. A sample of British repatriates found that 23% of repatriates' expectations were fully matched, 42% matched to some extent and 25% only a little or not at all (Forster 1994). Pickard (1999) also found that 69% of UK expatriates expected the return to enhance their career prospects and 55% expected their return to be exciting and/or challenging. Among US expatriates, a majority of them expected the assignment to be positive for their career development and to have a positive impact on subsequent career advancement either in their current organization or elsewhere (Tung 1998). Another European study found that 78% of expatriates expected that their new skills would be useful in jobs back home and 63% of them expected to find a job that matched their present qualifications (Riusala and Suutari 2000). The majority (74%) also generally believed that their international experience would be valued in their organization and that IAs would promote their future career development (62%).

179

Unfortunately, these expectations frequently go unfulfilled. Stroh et al. (1998) found that only 39% used their international skills at home, more than two-thirds of expatriates are not content with the repatriation approach of their firms and up to 75% of expatriates consider leaving their employer either during or after their work abroad. Supporting the relevance of discussion around expectations, lower levels of organizational commitment appeared among respondents whose expectations were not met. Conversely, Black (1992) has reported that individuals whose expectations are met report the highest level of repatriation adjustment and job performance.

Thus, readjustments to work, community, the environment and culture are shaped by individual attitudes, values and needs, work characteristics (of both the job and the organization), organizational policies and non-work variables (Black 1992; Suutari and Välimaa 2002). This makes for a complex mix of factors which can affect how the repatriate readjusts and reintegrates on return.

Status

Returning to the home country often implies a downward shift in repatriates' social status and provokes disappointment, disillusion and adjustment problems (Gregersen and Stroh 1997). Repatriates often move from a senior work role in a foreign subsidiary, where they are a 'big fish in a small pond' to being once again a 'cog in the wheel' back in the home country. More than 30 years ago it was shown that individuals' adjustment to work and organization can be negatively influenced by a loss of autonomy after their repatriation (Cagney 1975) and the situation hasn't changed (Black et al. 1999). In most cases, repatriates will also experience a loss, often significant, of income and a change to their lifestyle.

Family

It is not just the repatriate who will have difficulties but a raft of relocation issues has been shown to have an impact on repatriation. These include such matters as cost of living differentials, financial and housing allowances, family education continuity, life and culture differentials and forced spouse career change (Gomez-Mejia and Balkin 1987). The family may also find it difficult to adjust. The children, who may be out of touch with fashions at home may not find it easy to fit in back at school and will have learnt different things from their erstwhile classmates. The family as a whole may be having problems readjusting. Expectations are likely to be based on the home-country situation as it was before the assignment began, rather than based on the current reality (Pickard 1999). The repatriates are returning to a society and organization that has changed during their absence; typically, despite the modern communications, they are not fully up to date with these changes. And they have changed too (see Chapter 7). Added together, these problems can create real stress.

Job on return

There is often a lack of clarity about the job situation after the repatriation and increasingly repatriates may find themselves in a position where there are no guarantees of a job on return (Dickmann et al. 2005). They find themselves, like aeroplanes over a busy airport, in a 'holding pattern', waiting to find a way back in. Or they may find themselves put into a new position with less authority than they had while abroad (Selmer 1999; Dowling and Welch 2004). The uncertainty and potential downshifting involved can create disillusionment and disaffection among repatriates.

Use of acquired skills

Organizations offer the expatriation experience often as a conduit to the development of individual competencies in the preparation of future global leaders. Yet recent research suggests that companies are lacking in the ability to track individuals following assignment (Dickmann et al. 2006). Repatriates can be disappointed and disaffected by the lack of opportunities to use their newfound skills after an assignment (Gomez-Mejía and Balkin 1987). They may suffer job shock and feel a loss of status, loss of autonomy, loss of career direction and a feeling that their international experience is undervalued by the company (Peltonen 1997). Colleagues who stayed close to the political centre at home may have progressed in their careers, leaving those who went abroad lagging in the 'career race' (Dickmann and Harris 2005). These difficulties are likely to have an influence on their performance, their satisfaction and the desire of these individuals to leave the company (Black et al. 1999; Lazarova and Caligiuri 2001).

Attrition

It has been argued that work adjustment will directly affect turnover of repatriates (Shaffer et al. 1999). Problems arise when returnees, dissatisfied because their expectations remain unmet, work ineffectively and are likely to leave the organization (Forster 1994; Pickard 1999). Embedding the international mindsets within the organization will not, of course, be achieved if the international assignees leave as soon as they have completed their assignment. Worse, from the organizational viewpoint, is that people do not often change sectors, so not only may the departing repatriates leave the company that spent a lot of money developing their global mindset, they are likely to join the competition.

It has also been argued that these levels of turnover probably represent a considerable degree of disillusionment within an organization these people have served well; and certainly represents a considerable loss to the organization of expensively created experience and knowledge. It will also, perhaps, have the effect of making others less likely to accept such assignments. Stroh (1995) reports that three variables were found to be significant predictors of turnover among repatriates: corporate values related to the importance of an IA to the organization; whether the organization had a career development plan for repatriates; and the perceived impact of corporate turbulence on the organization's capacity to place repatriates adequately on their return. If part of the aim of an international assignee policy is to foster internationalism and the transfer of knowledge (Bonache and Brewster 2001; Chapter 4), the loss of these repatriates is a significant problem.

There seems to be a lack of coherence in the research findings to date, although the tendency is to report a gloomy picture with organizations losing a lot of talented and experienced international staff at or shortly after repatriation. There is an assumption that this 'fallout' rate is partly the result of dissatisfaction among expatriates whose careers are blighted by their negative experience and who have to rebuild those careers elsewhere, if they can. The literature on the career development of expatriates is still rather unclear. For example, both Tung (1998) and Welch (1998) argue that too little is known about the effect of IAs on the career advancement of expatriates; what happens to them following repatriation. However, Suutari and Brewster (2003) found that even when employees leave their organization, they are generally positive about their international experience and its effect on their careers.

REPATRIATION AS THE MIDDLE OF A CAREER

Increasingly, research into repatriation is less concerned with viewing it as the end of the assignment and more concerned with setting it in its career context. Repatriation is seen as part of the career process rather than a conclusion. Careers are seen as pivotal to repatriation (see e.g. Solomon 1995; Stroh 1995; Riusala and Suutari 2000; Suutari and Brewster 2003). As numerous European authors have pointed out, our understanding of the career impact of an IA – including the process of repatriation – is still far from clear (Bonache et al. 2001; Stahl and Cerdin 2004; Dickmann and Harris 2005). Research has provided a foundation for understanding three key issues:

1 the development of career capital
2 the alignment of expectations
3 career outcomes.

We review each in turn.

Although IAs are seen as a powerful developmental experience for the individuals concerned and as a key tool for developing international managers, the positive connection between such assignments and career progress has been questioned. Being out of the mainstream of advancement can lead to stagnated career development opportunities (Gomez-Mejia and Balkin 1987; Napier and Peterson 1991). The personal and professional isolation from the domestic office during foreign assignments may cause poor integration to the home unit personnel (Harvey 1982; Peltonen 1997). Recent research (Dickmann and Harris 2005) highlighted that the benefits of IAs, in terms of capital accumulation, can be equivocal for expatriates and the organization (see Chapter 12). In addition, a number of authors have pointed out that, with respect to career management, individual and organizational needs are not always in total harmony (Thomas et al. 2005).

Yan et al. (2002) addressed the issue of alignment in organizational and individual expectations of an assignment and argued that these included individual and organizational benefits across short- and long-term time perspectives. Success criteria for the individual incorporated task performance, learning, job satisfaction, development, promotion and future assignments. For the organization, benefits covered the achievement of organizational tasks and objectives, retention and utilization of repatriates and their skills and the transfer of expertise.

Findings among US repatriates indicate that around one-quarter (29% Derr and Oddou 1991; 23% Oddou and Mendenhall 1991) were promoted while one-fifth (20% Derr and Oddou 1991; 18% Oddou and Mendenhall 1991) faced downward career mobility. Things appear to be more positive in Europe: 46% of British repatriates reported positive effects on their career prospects, with 54% reporting negative effects (Forster 1994). Peltonen (1999) reports that among Finnish expatriates working in projects organized by the Finnish International Development Agency, 27% reported positive career impacts and 10% negative impacts. The career status outcomes were on average positive with 68% of the repatriates reporting positively on the change in their organizational status. Few face a lower salary level than before the assignment. Dickmann et al. (2005) found few repatriates were guaranteed a 'right' of passage home and very few (15%) guaranteed a role at the same level on return. Around one-third were promoted and less than one-tenth demoted. These findings are much more positive than those reported elsewhere.

Repatriate retention, performance and promotion

Measuring the value of global assignments is a difficult task. The investment in sending employees on IA can be substantial but the majority of organizations believe that the benefits of international forms of working outweigh the considerable costs (Sparrow et al. 2004). It is, however, not clear on what basis organizations assess the costs and benefits as the data captured and evaluation tends to be poor (Harzing and Christensen 2004; McNulty and Tharenou 2004). Thus, many organizations remain unclear about the benefits and they struggle to determine the

183

return on investment of IAs since there are few indices available to facilitate this (Elias and Scarbrough 2004). A key question becomes 'do the benefits outweigh the costs'?

The value of an IA is linked to:

- the purposes of the assignment
- the success of the international work, which in turn is relative to the context of the organization
- the performance (or other meaningful comparators) of non-expatriated peers.

An assessment of value implies knowing both costs and benefits of these elements. The importance of repatriation in the cycle of international working has attracted more attention recently as both organizations and individuals recognize that the potential benefits of the experience happen not only during the assignment but short term immediately following an assignment and long term well after the assignment has ended.

Although a time dimension is included in the model of repatriate adjustment developed by Black et al. (1999), the extant research does not usually include a temporal element. Only the study by Eschbach et al. (2001) collected information regarding the adjustment of repatriates at two moments of time, at 2 and at 9 months after they had returned home. Sánchez Vidal et al. (2007) replicated this with repatriates to Spain and confirmed that the repatriation adjustment process is a dynamic phenomenon and its effects vary over time. Adjustment to work after 2 months impacts positively on performance and has a key effect on later adjustment. Adjustment after 9 months is correlated with a higher satisfaction and intention to stay with the firm.

Table 9.1 outlines some key individual and organizational value indicators in expatriation and can serve as a short overview and summary of this chapter. The first column distinguishes between indicators of value and loss for both the expatriate and their employers. The second column takes account of the different motivations that individuals pursue in seeking or accepting work abroad and the diverse kinds of rationale that organizations have when using international mobility. The table constitutes a simplified picture of mobility drivers as there are a multitude of interlinked motives for both individuals and their organizations. A depiction as exposed in Table 9.1 is not able to take sufficient account either of the various strengths of the motivations in the complicated process of finding international assignees (or of them agreeing to expatriation) or of the complex weighing of decision-influencing variables (cf. Dickmann et al. 2008). Column three spells out some of the key peer comparators. Relative knowledge about the cost and benefits of expatriation can only be derived with data on meaningful peer groups. Finally, the fourth column outlines different time considerations; again, linked into

Table 9.1 Some individual and organizational value indicators in expatriation

Value indicator	Reason for IA	Peer group comparison	Time dimension
Individual indicators of value	Linked to the mix of motives why the IA was accepted: e.g. career progression, higher remuneration, advantages for family (e.g. better education), personal motives (such as seeking adventure, individual curiosity); ability to use career capital after return, high status of IA and in next job	Depends on the behaviour and attitudes of relevant peer groups: Relative career progression, remuneration increase, status, etc. superior to non-expatriated peers	Depending on the primary reasons for IA: realized family advantage, higher remuneration or achieved personal motives often during the assignment. For positive career and development impact most benefits are likely to accrue after the assignment
Individual indicators of loss	Linked to the mix of motives why the IA was accepted: e.g. career demotion, job insecurity during IA or after return, inability to successfully adjust or readjust after return, family disadvantages (e.g. insecurity, health, education), inability to use career capital acquired overseas, low status of IA and in next job	Depends on the behaviour and attitudes of relevant peer groups: relative job insecurity, career, family attributes, status inferior to non-expatriated peers	In relation to the primary reasons for IA: non-realized family advantage, lower remuneration or personal motives that were not achieved often during the assignment. Negative or neutral career and development impacts are most likely to accrue after the assignment

Table 9.1 Some individual and organizational value indicators in expatriation—cont'd

Value indicator	Reason for IA	Peer group comparison	Time dimension
Organizational indicators of value	Related to the strategic and operational intent of the IA: development of global mindset; high performance, high retention, career progression, skills gap filling, successful control and coordination, finding local successor, application of ethical business practices, etc.	Related to the behaviour and achieved results of relevant peer group: higher performance than local peers, higher retention than global peers, quicker career progression than peers in sending unit	Depending on the primary reasons for IA: for example, for developmental assignment long-term career capital increase, for skills filling short-term application of the necessary capabilities, for control and coordination medium- and long-term use of ethical company (reporting) systems
Organizational indicators of loss	Related to the non-achievement of strategic and operational intent of the IA: low performance (e.g. lost business, underperformance), expatriate turnover, incidents of loss of control (e.g. use of bribery, non-application of company policies, etc.), sometimes low quality of local activities	Related to the behaviour and achieved results of relevant peer group: lower performance than local peers, lower retention than global peers, slower career progression than peers in sending unit, use of more unethical practices than global/home-country peers	Depending on the primary reasons for IA: for example, for developmental assignment inability to use acquired career capital over long term, for skills-filling inability to find and utilize the appropriate skills, for control and coordination medium and long-term non-use of ethical company (reporting) systems

the primary rationale for international mobility; over which the cost/benefits of expatriation can be assessed.

There is considerable evidence and good practice advice on how the planning of an IA can impact on the outcomes at the repatriation stage. In order for the organ ization and the individual (in career terms) to recoup the investment in an IA, alignment of expectations and longer term outcomes become paramount. Therefore, any assessment of 'return on investment' or other value must be time sensitive as it is linked into the first of these elements, i.e. purpose. For instance, while skills gap filling may have its payback during an IA, much of the benefits of a developmental assignment will accrue to the organization after return. Thus, the retention of individuals who are viewed as global leaders of the future becomes crucial. Dickmann et al. (2006) found that while performance on assignment gen- erally increased, performance increase on repatriation was lower, with a substan- tial variance in performance on repatriation.

These data indicate that rather than the smooth transition from assignment to heroic return to home base as a well-informed, internationally seasoned and valued employee, the repatriation experience is much more of a rollercoaster ride for the individual and potentially for the organization in terms of return on investment.

CONCLUSION

Although there are many areas of research that are still untapped, we do have a considerable amount of information to help formulate some practical steps for the management of repatriation.

In this chapter, we have suggested that companies should develop better repa- triation support practices which could help the expatriates to develop a more real- istic picture of their repatriation (Birdseye and Hill 1995; Stroh et al. 1998; Sánchez et al. 2007).

We also argue that practitioners could devote more attention to helping man- agers develop realistic expectations about their work and non-work lives before repatriation.

Companies and expatriates would benefit from pre-departure career discus- sions (Pickard 1999; Riusala and Suutari 2000; Suutari and Brewster 2001) and repatriation job planning, including longer term career planning support (Gomez- Mejía and Balkin 1987; Forster 1994, Stroh 1995; Riusala and Suutari 2000).

The importance of a named contact person in the home country has been high- lighted (Napier and Peterson 1991; Riusala and Suutari 2000); re-entry coun- selling and family repatriation programmes (Harvey 1982; Gomez-Mejía and Balkin 1987); employee debriefings (Gregersen and Black 1995; Solomon 1995); succession planning (Derr and Oddou 1991; Gregersen and Black 1995;

187

Gregersen et al. 1998; Tung 1998); and performance appraisals including related development rewards (Solomon 1995; Pickard 1999).

Finally, McCaughey and Brunning (2005) revisited the HR strategies for foreign assignment success, outlining best practice to improve expatriate experiences. These include having a repatriation plan that embraces career planning, opportunities to capitalize on newly acquired skills, strategies for knowledge transfer and enhancing post-assignment job satisfaction. In addition, Bonache and Zárraga-Oberty (forthcoming) argue that HR practices such as emphasizing the cultural fit with the local environment in selection of expatriates, extensive training, linking knowledge transfer to performance evaluation and rewards, de-emphasizing salary disparity and extensive socialization would create a more fertile relationship for knowledge transfers and aid the achievements of corporate goals in international mobility (see Chapter 4).

KEY LEARNING POINTS

- The repatriation element of international working has until recently received the least amount of attention/research focus.
- Connecting the rationale for expatriation with the repatriation phase highlights many areas where there is a lack of joined-up thinking.
- Time and timing are important factors in the repatriation process.
- Longer term outcomes for both organizations and individuals are central to reaping rewards in the repatriation phase.

REFERENCES

Bartlett, C.A. and Ghoshal, S. (1989) *Managing Across Borders*, Cambridge, MA: Harvard Business School Press.

Bartlett, C.A. and Ghoshal, S. (1997) *The Transnational Organisation*, Chicago: Richard D. Irwin Inc.

Baruch, Y. (2006) 'Career development in organizations and beyond: balancing traditional and contemporary viewpoints', *Human Resource Management Review* 16: 125–138.

Birdseye, M.G. and Hill, J.S. (1995) 'Individual, organizational work and environmental influences on expatriate turnover tendencies: an empirical study', *Journal of International Business Studies* 22:787–813.

Black, J.S. (1992) 'Coming home: the relationship of expatriate expectations with repatriation adjustment and job performance', *Human Relations* 45, 2:177–192.

Black, J.S. and Gregersen, H.B. (1992) 'Towards a theoretical framework of repatriation adjustment', *Journal of International Business Studies* 4:737–760.

Black, J.S. and Gregersen, H.B. (1999) 'The right way to manage expats', *Harvard Business Review*, March/April:52–61.

Black, J.S., Gregersen, H.B., Mendenhall, M.E. and Stroh, K.L. (1999) *Globalizing People through International Assignments*, Reading, MA: Addison-Wesley.

Bonache, J. and Brewster, C. (2001) 'Knowledge transfer and the management of expatriation', *Thunderbird International Business Review* 43, 1:145–168.

Bonache, J. and Zárraga-Oberty, C. (forthcoming), 'Determinants of the success of international assignees as knowledge transfers: a theoretical framework', *International Journal of Human Resource Management*.

Bonache, J., Brewster, C. and Suutari, V. (2001) 'Expatriation: a developing research agenda', *Thunderbird International Business Review* 43, 1:3–20.

Bossard, A.B. and Peterson, R.B. (2005) 'The repatriate experience as seen by American expatriates', *Journal of World Business* 40, 1:9–28.

Brewster, C. and Scullion, H. (1997) 'A review and agenda for expatriate human resource management', *Human Resource Management Journal* 7, 3:32–41.

Cagney, W.F. (1975) 'Executive re-entry: the problems of repatriation', *Personnel Journal* September:487–488.

Campbell, J. (1968) *The Hero with a Thousand Faces*, New York: Bollingen Foundation.

Czinkota, M.R. and Ronkainen, I.A. (2005) 'A forecast of globalization, international business and trade: report from a Delphi study', *Journal of World Business* 40, 2:111–123.

Derr, B.C. and Oddou, G.R. (1991) 'Are US multinationals adequately preparing future American leaders for global competition?', *International Journal of Human Resource Management* 2, 2:227–244.

Dickmann, M. and Harris, H. (2005) 'Developing career capital for global careers: the role of international assignments', *Journal of World Business* 40, 4:399–408.

Dickmann, M., Doherty, N. and Johnson, A. (2006) *Measuring the Value of International Assignments*, PricewaterhouseCoopers.

Dickmann, M., Doherty, N. and Mills, T. (2005) *Understanding Mobility – Influence Factors in the Decision to Accept an International Assignment, Repatriation Issues and Long-term Career Considerations*, PricewaterhouseCoopers.

Dickmann, M., Doherty, N., Mills, T. and Brewster, C. (forthcoming) 'Why do they go? Individual and corporate perspectives on the factors influencing the decision to accept an international assignment', *International Journal of Human Resource Management*.

Dowling, P.J. and Welch, D.E. (2004) *International Human Resource Management*, 4th edn, London: Thomson.

Elias, J. and Scarbrough, H. (2004) 'Evaluating human capital: an exploratory study of management practice', *Human Resource Management Journal* 14, 4:21–40.

Eschbach, D.M., Parker, G.E. and Stoeberl, P.A. (2001) 'American repatriate employees' retrospective assessments of the effects of cross-cultural training on their adaptation to international assignments', *International Journal of Human Resource Management* 12, 2:270–287.

Evans, P., Pucik, V. and Barsoux, J.L. (2002). *The Global Challenge: Frameworks for International Human Resource Management*, London: McGraw-Hill.

Forster, N. (1994) 'The forgotten employees? The experiences of expatriate staff returning to the UK', *International Journal of Human Resource Management* 5,2:405–425.

GMAC (2005) http://www.gmacglobalrelocation.com.

Gomez-Mejía, L. and Balkin, D.B. (1987) 'The determinants of managerial satisfaction with the expatriation and repatriation process', *Journal of Management Development* 6, 1:7–17.

189

Gregersen, H. and Black, J. (1995) 'Keeping high performers after international assignments: a key to global executive development', *Journal of International Management* 1, 1:3–21.

Gregersen, H.B. and Stroh, L.K. (1997) 'Coming home to the Arctic cold: antecedents to Finnish expatriate and spouse repatriation adjustment', *Personnel Psychology* 50, 3:635–654.

Gregersen, H.B., Morrison, A.J. and Black, J.S. (1998) 'Developing leaders for the global frontier', *Sloan Management Review* Fall:21–32.

Harvey, M. (1982) 'The other side of foreign assignments: dealing with the repatriation dilemma', *Columbia Journal of World Business* 17, 1:53–59.

Harzing, A.W. and Christensen, C. (2004) 'Expatriate failure: time to abandon the concept?', *Career Development International* 9, 7:616–626.

Hurn, B.J. (1999). 'Repatriation: the toughest assignment of all', *Industrial and Commercial Training* 31, 6:224–228.

Kobrin, S. (1994). 'Is there a relationship between a geocentric mind-set and multinational strategy', *Journal of International Business Studies* 25, 3:493–512.

Larsen, H.H. (2004), 'Global career as dual dependency between the organization and the individual', *Journal of Management Development* 23, 9:860–869.

Lazarova, M. and Caligiuri, P. (2001) 'Retaining repatriates: the role of organizational support practices', *Journal of World Business* 36, 4:389–402.

McCaughey, D. and Brunning, N.S. (2005) 'Enhancing opportunities for expatriate job satisfaction: HR strategies for foreign assignment success', *Human Resource Planning* 28, 4:21–29.

McNulty, Y. and Tharenou, P. (2004) 'Expatriate return on investment: a definition and antecedents', *International Studies of Management and Organization* 34, 3:68–95.

Napier, N. and Peterson, R. (1991) 'Expatriate re-entry: what expatriates have to say', *Human Resource Planning* 14, 1:19–28.

Oddou, G.R. and Mendenhall, M.E. (1991) 'Succession planning for the 21st century: how well are we grooming our future business leaders?', *Business Horizons* 34, 1:26–35.

Oddou, G.R., Mendenhall, M.E. and Ritchie, J.B. (2000) 'Leveraging travel as a tool for global leadership development', *Human Resource Management* 39, 2/3:159–172.

Peltonen, T. (1997) 'Facing rankings from the past: a tournament perspective on repatriate career mobility', *International Journal of Human Resource Management* 8, 1:107–123.

Peltonen, T. (1999) 'Repatriation and career systems: Finnish public and private sector repatriates in their career lines', in C. Brewster and H. Harris (eds) *International HRM: Contemporary Issues in Europe*, London: Routledge.

Pickard, J. (1999) *Repatriation: Factors Related to Individuals' Expectations of International Assignments*, Cranfield: Cranfield University Press.

Reynolds, C. (1997) 'Expatriate compensation in historical perspective', *Journal of World Business* 32, 2:118–132.

Riusala, K. and Suutari, V. (2000) 'Expatriation and careers: perspectives of expatriates and spouses', *Career Development International* 5, 2:81–90.

Sánchez Vidal, M.E., Sanz Valle, R., Barba Aragón, M.I. and Brewster, C. (2007) 'Effective repatriation management: evidence from Spanish workers', *International Journal of Intercultural Relations* 31, 3:317–337.

Selmer, J. (1999) 'Career issues and international adjustment of business expatriates', *Career Development International* 4, 2:77–87.

Shaffer, M., Harrison, D. and Gilley, M. (1999) 'Dimensions, determinants and differences in the expatriate adjustment process', *Journal of International Business Studies* 31, 3:557–582.

Solomon, C.M. (1995) 'Repatriation: up, down or out?', *Personnel Journal* 74, 1:28–37.

Sparrow, P., Brewster, C. and Harris, H. (2004) *Globalizing Human Resource Management*, London: Routledge.

Stahl, G.K. and Cerdin, J. (2004) 'Global careers in French and German multinational corporations', *Journal of Management Development* 23, 9:885–902.

Stroh, L.K. (1995) 'Predicting turnover among repatriates: can organisations affect retention rates?', *International Journal of Human Resource Management* 6, 2: 443–456.

Stroh, L.K., Gregersen, H.B. and Black, J.S. (1998) 'Closing the gap: expectations versus reality among expatriates', *Journal of World Business* 11, 4:681–697.

Suutari, V. and Brewster, C. (2001) 'Expatriate management practices and perceived relevance: evidence from Finnish expatriates', *Personnel Review* 30, 5:554–577.

Suutari V. and Brewster, C. (2003) 'Repatriation: empirical evidence of a longitudinal study from careers and expectations among Finnish expatriates', *International Journal of Human Resource Management* 14, 7:1132–1151.

Suutari, V. and Välimaa, K. (2002) 'Antecedents of repatriation adjustment: new evidence from Finnish expatriates', *International Journal of Manpower* 23, 7: 617–634.

Tharenou, P. (2003) 'The initial development of receptivity to working abroad: self-initiated international work opportunities in young graduate employees', *Journal of Occupational and Organizational Psychology* 76:489–515.

Thomas, D.C., Lazarova, M.B. and Inkson, K. (2005) 'Global careers: new phenomenon or new perspectives', *Journal of World Business* 40, 4:340–347.

Tung, R.L. (1998) 'A contingency framework of selection and training of expatriates revisited', *Human Resource Management Review* 8, 1:23–38.

Welch, D. (1998) 'The psychological contract and expatriation: a disturbing issue for IHRM?', paper presented at 6th Conference on International Human Resource Management, University of Paderborn, 22–25 June.

Yan, A., Zhu, G. and Hall, D. (2002) 'International assignments for career building: a model of agency relationships and psychological contracts', *Academy of Management Review* 27, 3:373–391.

Chapter 10

Careers and expatriation

Jean-Luc Cerdin

CHAPTER OBJECTIVES

By the end of this chapter, readers will have:

- an understanding of the development of managers through expatriation
- insights into the willingness of individuals to go abroad
- an appreciation of individual career characteristics and their impact on both the type of career pursued internationally and international adjustment
- information about the impact of flexpatriation and foreign experience on career development
- explored the relationship between career and repatriation
- sensitivity to the relationship between career success and international assignment success

INTRODUCTION

Career management today finds itself at a crossroad of two perspectives, that of individuals and that of organizations. For individuals, career management consists of managing one's own career in order to fulfil personal aspirations. For organizations, career management contributes to the accomplishment of human resources objectives. Inkson and Arthur (2001) underline that career management from the traditional perspective of the organization requires creating consistency between individual and organizational objectives. Expatriation may be important to career management from both the individual and organizational perspective. From the individual perspective, it may be an important part of their career development and from the organizational perspective, it may be necessary to the organization's international development.

Today, concepts of career and expatriation hold multiple meanings. Numerous career perspectives are applicable to expatriation, such as protean careers (Hall 1996) or boundaryless careers (Arthur and Rousseau 1996). What these two career perspectives have in common is the fact that they both define individuals' careers as becoming more independent of their organizations. To address the issue of expatriates' careers, we turn to the literature on careers and the literature on expatriation. Expatriates are generally defined as employees who temporarily leave their home-country organization for an assignment lasting a few years in a foreign subsidiary with the intention of returning to their home country once the assignment is completed (Guzzo 1997). Alongside this traditional expatriation develop such forms of international assignment as self-initiated expatriation (Inkson et al. 1997; Suutari and Brewster 2000), international commuter assignments and frequent international business trips (Mayerhofer et al. 2004). Whatever the type of international assignment, career success remains a fundamental consideration. The issue of career success is a central theme in the literature on careers. The evaluation of career success necessitates taking into account the context in which careers develop (Heslin 2005). In this chapter, we consider international assignment as a particular stage in a career, both for the individual and the organization.

There are multiple definitions of career success (see Arthur et al. 2005). In the context of expatriation, what may be considered success by individuals may not be considered as such by an organization and vice versa (Lazarova and Cerdin 2007). Arthur et al. (2005) underline that career success can be defined both in objective terms, where success is measured by quantifiable rewards such as growth in salary or frequency of promotion, and in subjective terms, where the principal indicator of career success is the intrinsic satisfaction of individuals with their careers. The objective/subjective career distinction corresponds with the distinction between the internal and external career (Hall 1996). From the perspective of the internal career, the criteria for determining career success are subjective and correspond to individual aspirations. These criteria for measuring career success are unique for each individual. From the perspective of the external career, the criteria for career success are objective in the sense that they are defined 'outside of' the individual, for example, by the organization or by society. Tung (1998) proposes that individuals are increasingly viewing expatriation as an enhancement of their internal career rather than an enhancement of their external career. For example, in the context of boundaryless careers (Arthur and Rousseau 1996; Parker and Inkson 1999), individuals associate expatriation with personal development, skills acquisition and career advancement. However, if individuals are sceptical about their opportunities for advancement within their own organization, they may consider leaving the organization on return from their expatriation or even during their expatriation.

In this chapter, we refer to the literature on both careers and expatriation. We begin the chapter with the importance of the international development of managers for the organization. Next, we address the willingness of individuals to work abroad, examining in particular their attitude towards expatriation, their motivations and the issue of dual careers. We consider individual career characteristics and their impact on both the type of career that individuals pursue internationally and international adjustment. We then look at two types of international assignment, 'flexpatriation' and foreign experience, and their impact on career development. As the issue of repatriation can be considered a risk in terms of career, we examine the link between career and repatriation. We finish the chapter by considering the link between career success and international assignment success.

DEVELOPMENT OF MANAGERS THROUGH EXPATRIATION: A STRATEGIC PERSPECTIVE

McCall and Hollenbeck (2002) underline organizations' need for a proactive policy in terms of the development of global executives. Expatriation can be one of the ways for the organization to achieve this development.

Purpose of expatriation

Drawing on the work of Edström and Galbraith (1977) carried out in European multinational firms, Hocking et al. (2004) argue that expatriation assignments are organized into three major purpose categories, namely business application, organization application and expatriate learning.

The first purpose category, business application, corresponds to the organization's inability to fill positions using local skills. Organizations cannot always find the required skills locally, so they must bring in expatriates in order to fill positions. In this context, the organization's need to fill positions may take precedence over its management of individuals' careers. This approach by the organization can create difficulties for individuals in terms of their careers, which may materialize during repatriation.

The second purpose category, organization application, corresponds to the organization's international development. This development depends in part on the control and coordination of foreign subsidiaries' activities and relies on a flow of information between the headquarters of the organization and its various subsidiaries. Expatriates are critical in this process. As this purpose is part of the organization's long-term strategy, the organization is more likely to integrate expatriation into its management of individuals' careers.

The third purpose category, expatriate learning, corresponds to the organization's development of its managers. The organization may use expatriation as a means of achieving this development. In this context, expatriation is an important stage in managers' career advancement within the organization, in that expatriation is intended to test managers and place them in situations where they can acquire the skills necessary for this advancement.

194

Organization application and expatriate learning are both strategic purposes of expatriation. Brief sojourns are insufficient for the expatriate learning purpose, as the development of skills in an intercultural context necessitates living in another country for a sufficient period of time. This period of time in general lasts between 1 and 3 years, depending on the country. For example, individuals who are expatriated to a European country with a similar culture to that of their own country may require a shorter period of time to develop their skills. The expatriate learning purpose is particularly important for the development of high-potential employees. The expatriation of high-potential employees is likely to be part of the organization's career management strategy. In the case of success, the repatriation of employees whose expatriation purpose is expatriate learning is not likely to create problems in terms of career, as the expatriation of these individuals is part of organizational career management. Expatriation is a career stage that is likely to be favourable to these individuals' career advancement within the organization.

International approaches to career management

A concern for organizations is the management of individuals' careers, which is primarily achieved through organizational career planning. Organizations may include expatriation in their career planning in order to ensure the development of individuals' skills, which then contributes to individuals' career advancement within the organization. Therefore, individuals may need to complete at least one expatriation in order to advance within the organization. However, all organizations do not integrate expatriation to the same extent into their organizational career management. Career management can be defined in relation to the four classic international approaches proposed by Perlmutter (1969).

Organizations who assume an ethnocentric approach to career management tend to recruit employees from the parent country for international positions. This approach offers managers from the parent country great career opportunities, but limits the career opportunities of employees of other nationalities.

Organizations that follow a polycentric approach try to develop the competences of local employees in the various countries in which their subsidiaries are located. Careers are managed at a local level and therefore expatriation is not central to career planning.

Organizations that follow a geocentric approach adopt a transnational approach to human resource management and therefore do not favour any one nationality in their career management. Skills take precedence over nationality in career management. Some organizations may combine different approaches. For instance, the transnational approach can be used for top potential seen to be the global leaders of the future while the regiocentric approach can be targeted at high potentials envisaged to be lower ranking leaders (Dickmann and Harris 2005).

195

The regiocentric approach resembles the geocentric approach but is limited to a regional level. Career management takes place within one particular geographical zone and therefore individuals' expatriations are likely to be limited to countries within this zone. For example, if an organization's career management takes place within the eurozone, there is little likelihood of the individual being expatriated to a country outside eurozone Europe.

Individuals' careers are shaped in part by the organization's approach to international career management and therefore the structural career model can be applied to this context. In this structural model, individuals' careers are primarily 'structured' by organizational policies, as opposed to the individualistic model, where individuals themselves are the principal agents of their career advancement (Rosenbaum 1993). Whether individuals' careers are shaped by the organization or by individuals themselves, an important issue in the link between career and expatriation is the willingness of individuals to take on an expatriation and integrate it into their careers.

Willingness of individuals to work abroad

To study the willingness of individuals to work abroad, we need to examine:

1 individuals' attitudes towards expatriation
2 motives of individuals in taking on an expatriation
3 issue of dual careers.

These three issues should also be taken into account by organizations in their career management and in their selection of potential candidates for expatriation.

Individuals' attitudes towards expatriation

Individuals can be divided into three categories based on their attitudes towards expatriation (Cerdin 2002):

1 unconditionally non-mobile individuals, whatever the circumstances
2 conditionally mobile individuals, depending on circumstances such as the expatriation's location or the individual's age, family situation or career stage
3 unconditionally mobile individuals, whatever the circumstances.

Because individuals' attitudes towards expatriation can change over time, in particular the attitudes of conditionally mobile employees, the organization should assess their willingness to go abroad from the recruitment stage and should reassess this willingness regularly over the course of individuals' careers. By taking into account individuals' willingness to work abroad, the organization can respect their freedom of choice regarding expatriation. Individuals' freedom of choice to accept an expatriation has fundamental implications for both career success and international assignment success. For example, in his model of international adjustment, Cerdin (2002) includes the freedom to accept or turn down an expatriation as an explanatory factor of expatriate adjustment: researching French expatriates, he found that a chosen assignment is likely to be more favourable to their adjustment than an imposed assignment. Expatriates who establish a connection between career advancement and expatriation adjust better than those who do not establish this connection. This finding is in line with the findings of Feldman and Thomas (1992).

In career management, being aware of individuals' willingness to work abroad allows organizations to formulate suitable career paths. The organization can plan ahead by implementing development programmes for individuals who are open to the possibility of expatriation. This approach can offer at least two advantages. The first is the ability to rapidly recruit employees for expatriation when this is required by the organization. The second advantage is that this development programme obliges the organization to formalize the system of expatriate recruitment and selection. Harris and Brewster (1999) describe the 'coffee machine' selection system in British MNCs where an individual emerges as a potential candidate for expatriation from a conversation around a coffee machine, without going through any formal selection process. Planning ahead by the organization should render this type of recruitment largely obsolete.

Individuals' motives in taking on an expatriation

There are a multitude of influences on the decision of individuals to seek or accept international work experiences. Dickmann et al. (forthcoming) explore the importance of more than two dozen motives for and barriers to expatriation, including influence factors such as security, adventure, life disruption, family, financial impact, career development, social capital impact and development. Borg (1988) finds three principal motives among managers in accepting their first expatriation, namely, in order of importance, desire for new experiences, better financial rewards and career advancement. Torbiörn (1976) found these same motives from a sample of employees that includes categories other than managers. However, career advancement was given a higher rank in this study. In his study of French expatriate managers Cerdin (2002) identifies similar motives to work abroad. The three main motives of French managers in taking on an expatriation are career advancement, financial reward and personal goals such as the exploration of another culture. Stahl and Cerdin (2004) asked French and German expatriates to rank, out of 12 considerations in their decision to accept an international assignment, the five most important. The results show that French and German expatriates have many of the same motives in common in accepting an expatriation. Professional development and personal challenge seem to be the most important motives.

197

> **Text Box 10.1**
> **Expatriation motives**
>
> Stahl and Cerdin (2004) show that the most common motives among French and German employees in taking on an expatriation appear to be professional and personal development.

Future opportunities for career advancement or financial considerations appear to be slightly less important. The importance of professional development compared to future opportunities for career advancement confirms the predominance of the internal career over the external career in expatriation.

Individuals' motives in taking on an expatriation can affect expatriation success. 'Negative' motives, for example, the desire to escape from personal or professional problems, do not bode well for the success of an international assignment (Phatak 1989). 'Positive' motives are those where the individual seeks an intrinsic reward from the expatriation, such as the exploration of another culture. In his study of French expatriates, Cerdin (2002) found that negative motives are linked negatively to international adjustment, in particular work adjustment, whereas positive motives are linked positively to international adjustment.

Dual-career couples

Individuals' willingness to work abroad is also influenced by their family situation. Harvey and Novicevic (2001) identify six family considerations, namely:

1 the current stage of the individual's family lifecycle
2 the number of children and their stage of education
3 specific concerns such as special education needs of children, health-related issues for family members and extended family considerations such as elderly parents
4 the family's previous experiences abroad
5 the career/professional development of the individual's partner
6 the employment potential of the individual's partner.

These last two considerations are linked to the issue of dual careers.

The issue of dual careers is becoming more and more of a challenge in the process of expatriation (Smith and Still 1999). Brett et al. (1993) show that the willingness of individuals to relocate depends strongly on the attitude of their partners towards this relocation. This is a major issue for the organization, as the expatriation of individuals can mean disrupting the careers of their partners. The type of couple that individuals belong to may have an impact

198

on their willingness to work abroad. In terms of career, we look at three types of couples:

1 the traditional couple where one partner works and the other stays at home
2 the dual-income couple where both partners work but where one of the incomes is supplementary
3 the dual-career couple where both partners work and share a similar career level and commitment.

The willingness of the partner to relocate could have less of an influence in the traditional or dual-income couple than in the dual-career couple. The 'balance of power' within a couple, expressed in terms of status and level of income, seems tipped in favour of the partner who works and has a career compared to the partner whose income is supplementary or who has no income at all. In a dual-career couple, in which both partners are equally committed to their career, the power is generally more balanced.

Dual-career couples may be characterized by both a professional and a family commitment. Hall and Hall (1979) suggest that there is no single role structure for dual-career couples, but rather that there are various categories for this type of couple. For example, the category 'allies' corresponds to a couple where both partners share a dedication to either their family or their career. Their priorities are identical and do not cause conflicts. If their identity is defined in relation to the family and their relationships, expatriation will be likely to create difficulties for both partners. If their identity is defined in relation to career, they may accept that one of them works abroad while the other pursues his/her own career at home. Living and working in the same place may not be the top priority for these couples. 'Eurocommuting' (for example, working in Madrid during the week and rejoining one's partner in Paris at the weekend) could be an option for this type of couple. The issue of dual careers is likely to become more and more important with the development of *homogamy* (a marriage or partnership between individuals of the same status, in terms of having qualifications of the same level) (Forsé and Chauvel 1995).

A continuum can be used to show the range of policies used by organizations to address the issue of dual careers in the context of expatriation. At one extreme there is complete non-intervention and, at the other extreme, taking complete charge of the partner's situation. Between these two extremes, there are many policies that the organization can implement. The extent of the organization's involvement depends on the needs of partners, which vary according to factors such as gender, previous international experience and work-related expectations (Punnett 1997). For example, the organization could consider compensating part of partners' lost income in the case that they give up their jobs to accompany expatriates. The organization can further support partners by helping them to find

199

employment abroad. Large organizations depend in general on their international network to help partners pursue their careers. They do this mainly by circulating international vacancies among themselves. Recently, some larger organizations have created 'clubs' where such vacancies can be advertised to all members. Organizations may even hire partners when they possess the necessary skills. However, the legislation of the host country, in particular legislation regarding work permits, and its economic and social environment may impose strong constraints on the organization's endeavours to assist the partner. The organization can help partners to formulate their plans for the future, professional or otherwise, through outplacement. Expatriation can give partners the opportunity to do voluntary work or to start or resume their studies. It can also be seen as an opportunity for a career break or the realization of a creative project such as starting a business. The more important an individual's expatriation is to the organization, the more substantial the help it is likely to offer the individual's partner in terms of career. Beyond a strong message of recognition, helping partners to adjust to expatriation can contribute to the success of the expatriation.

Individual career characteristics and expatriation

Some career characteristics such as career stages and career anchors may help to explain both the type of career that people pursue internationally and their international adjustment. In an attempt to explain the international adjustment of French expatriates, Cerdin (2002) developed the international adjustment model of Black et al. (1991) by adding explanatory variables linked to career theories, such as career plateaux and career anchors. To date, theories from the literature on careers have been little integrated into studies of either the types of international career that individuals pursue or their international adjustment.

Career stages and expatriation

Hall (1976) created a linear model that divides individuals' careers into four stages, namely:

1 exploration period, where individuals search for their career path
2 career establishment and advancement, defined by a series of actions such as promotions
3 growth, maturity or stagnation corresponding to mid-career
4 period of gradual detachment where individuals gradually withdraw from their careers.

Hall and Mirvis (1996) re-examine this linear model and propose a recursive model composed of a repeating succession of these four stages over periods that

 200

correspond to an individual's career age. This model captures the growing discontinuity of new careers better. Each expatriation can thus correspond to a career age.

Certain career stages seem more favourable to expatriation than others. From a sample of French expatriates, Cerdin (2002) finds that 10.4% are in the first stage, 38.1% in the second, 48% in the third and 3.5% in the fourth stage. From the point of view of the development of skills and organizational development, expatriation generally requires individuals to belong to the establishment or mid-career stage. Stahl and Cerdin (2004) find that a large majority of French and German expatriates are in the stage of career advancement, while about one-quarter are in the stage of career establishment. For a minimal percentage of expatriates, expatriation corresponds to a period of progressive withdrawal. These percentages may reflect more the organization's expatriation policy than individuals' own preferences regarding expatriation.

Certain career stages may correspond to career plateaux for individuals. According to Borg (1988), reduced career possibilities in the home company negatively affect international adjustment. A plateaued manager who chooses an international assignment in order to escape from this situation may have more difficulty adjusting than a manager who is not plateaued. Cerdin (2002) showed, from a sample of 293 French expatriates in 44 countries, that managers who had plateaued before expatriation had lower levels of international adjustment than non-plateaued managers.

Career anchors and expatriation

Schein (1978, 1990) defines eight career anchors that guide and influence individuals in their choice of career. Individuals anchored by technical/functional competence are particularly interested in the technical dimensions of their work, whereas individuals anchored by managerial competence are stimulated by management per se, and consider technical specialization to be a trap. Individuals with the anchor autonomy/independence have a desire to become their own boss and to work at their own pace. Individuals anchored by security and stability seek a career that provides them with stability, predictability and long-term employment. Those with the creativity anchor are entrepreneurs in their attitude and seek work environments where their creativity can be expressed. Service/dedication anchored individuals have a desire to make the world a better place by helping others. Individuals anchored by pure challenge are driven by the desire to overcome obstacles and solve problems that are supposedly unsolvable. Finally, individuals with the lifestyle anchor try to integrate their career with their lifestyle and vision of the world. Suutari and Taka (2004) propose a ninth anchor, the internationalism anchor, to be added to Schein's typology. This anchor characterizes individuals who wish to explore new countries and cultures by working in an international environment.

201

Career anchors may help to explain the type of international career that individuals choose. For example, individuals anchored by service/dedication may orientate their international careers towards humanitarian work. Individuals anchored by technical/functional competence may believe an international assignment will enhance their technical expertise. Whatever individuals' career anchors may be, they may choose to pursue international careers, perhaps with the exception of individuals anchored by security and stability, as these individuals appear to be conceptually opposed to the uncertainty that is inherent to an expatriation. Nevertheless, certain anchors are generally more present than others in individuals who take on expatriation. For example, individuals anchored by internationalism prefer to develop their skills in an international environment. A recent study of Finnish expatriates reveals that global careers are most associated with people with the anchors of internationalism, managerial competence and pure challenge (Suutari and Taka 2004).

Career anchors may not only influence the type of international career that individuals choose, but also how these individuals adjust during their expatriation. Some anchors, such as the security anchor and the lifestyle anchor are not likely to be favourable to adjustment during expatriation, as individuals characterized by these anchors appear to be conceptually opposed to the uncertainty that is inherent in the context of expatriation. Other anchors seem more favourable to international adjustment. For example, as expatriation often offers individuals greater autonomy (Dunbar 1992), individuals anchored by autonomy are likely to adjust more easily than other individuals.

Case study 10.1
Paul Bertin

Paul Bertin was identified as a 'high-potential' employee in the early years of his career in a French insurance company, FIC, based in La Défense business district of Paris. After studying business in a French *grande école*, he was particularly attracted by the international career prospects offered by FIC. For Paul, expatriation would allow him to develop his skills so that he could take on positions with more important managerial responsibilities.

Since being hired by FIC, Paul has met Anna, a Russian who always wanted to live in France. After studying engineering in Russia, she decided to look for a job in France. She found a job in a large industrial company in Paris and has blossomed in this job, which enables her to keep developing her technical expertise. Anna is delighted to be in France and her adjustment has been a success.

Paul and Anna have been married for several months when FIC offers Paul an assignment in one of its most important subsidiaries located in Spain. The human resources director informs Paul that this assignment is crucial if he wants to advance within the organization. When Paul comes home that evening and announces his news, Anna does not seem to share his enthusiasm. She even asks him to turn down the assignment.

Questions

1 What are Paul and Anna's career characteristics?
2 What can FIC do to ensure that Paul accepts the international assignment and, if he accepts it, how can they help him succeed?

Types of international assignment and career development

There are numerous types of international assignment, including expatriation initiated by the organization, flexpatriation (e.g. Mayerhofer et al. 2004a; Mayerhofer et al. 2004b) and self-initiated expatriation or foreign experience (e.g. Inkson et al. 1997; Suutari and Brewster 2000; see also Chapter 11). Whatever the type of international assignment, individuals are generally given the opportunity to gain new knowledge, skills and abilities during their international experience, which can prove beneficial to their careers.

There are many skills that individuals can develop during their international assignments. For example, Harvey and Novicevic (2004), using the theoretical frame of political influence theory, suggest that expatriation or impatriation may lead to the acquisition of valuable political skills and political capital. Expatriation may also greatly contribute to the development of individuals' knowledge, skills, abilities and other personality characteristics (KSAOs) although personality characteristics and cognitive ability are relatively immutable (Caligiuri 2006). Indeed, possessing certain personality characteristics such as emotional stability may be necessary for individuals to experience the developmental benefits from an expatriation (Caligiuri 2006).

Flexpatriation and career development

Mayerhofer et al. (2004b), referring to research carried out by Cranfield University's Centre for Research into the Management of Expatriation (CReME), present a new trend in international assignment, namely 'flexpatriate' assignments (see also Chapter 11). Flexpatriation differs from expatriate assignments (individual and family move to host country for more than 1 year) and short-term assignments (individual moves to host country for less than 1 year, perhaps with family) in that flexpatriates undertake frequent international business trips but do not relocate abroad. Mayerhofer et al. (2004a) suggest that flexpatriate work may

203

facilitate both the development of global competence and a global understanding of company operations more effectively than a long-term placement in one location.

Compared to expatriates, flexpatriates appear to have less choice in terms of accepting international work (Mayerhofer et al. 2004a). Flexpatriation does not appear to be a career choice on the part of the individual, but rather an integral part of the job. Mayerhofer et al. (2004a) find that expatriate assignments are perceived by individuals to be more favourable to career success than flexpatriate assignments. As HR involvement in flexpatriation is not as high as involvement in expatriation, flexpatriation may be riskier in terms of career success. Nevertheless, flexpatriates are generally self-managing and proactive in dealing with both career issues and the family and personal demands that may be linked to their international assignment.

Foreign experience and career development

Individuals may choose to work abroad because they believe this may have a positive impact on their career advancement. Inkson et al. (1997) propose two models that explain how an international assignment is initiated and how it is used to contribute to career advancement. The first model corresponds to a traditional expatriation, where the initiative for expatriation comes from the organization. A successful expatriation should allow individuals to develop their skills and to complete their mission abroad. The second model, named 'overseas experience' by Inkson et al. (1997) and 'foreign experience' by Suutari and Brewster (2000) corresponds to an expatriation where the initiative for expatriation comes from the individual. According to Inkson et al. (1997), an overseas experience 'is, by definition, a personal odyssey, initiated and resourced by the self' (p. 352). The objectives are quite diffuse and include 'seeing the world' or 'trying something different'. Table10.1 compares these two approaches and shows that the literature on international assignment is mostly dedicated to traditional expatriation and overlooks foreign experience. Individuals may go abroad on a traditional expatriation and later move on to another international assignment in the form of a foreign experience or vice versa.

Table 10.1 Contrasting qualities of expatriate assignments

	Expatriate assignment	Overseas experience
Initiation	Company	Individual
Goals	Company project (specific)	Individual development(diffuse)
Funding	Company salary and expenses	Personal savings and casual earnings
Career type	Organizational career	Boundaryless career
Research literature	Large	Nil

Source: Inkson et al. (1997: 352).

As Yan et al. (2002) specify, the mutual expectations of expatriates and the organization that were determined at a given point in time can change and later become invalid. According to the authors, when working in a multinational company that operates in distinct markets, expatriates can become very specialized in a local market. If the multinational pulls out of this market, expatriates may become concerned about their career advancement within the multinational and go 'native' by pursuing their careers in other host-country organizations. Based on a study of a sample of Finnish graduates, Suutari and Brewster (2000) propose four categories of individuals who go to work abroad on their own initiative, namely young opportunists, job seekers, officials and localized professionals. 'Gone native' individuals belong to the localized professionals category. Officials are those who work within international organizations such as the European Union. Job seekers are those who sought work abroad because they were unemployed or who were not satisfied with their career in their home country. Young opportunists, getting overseas experience in the words of Inkson et al. (1997), are just at the beginning of their career and work most commonly in foreign companies or subsidiaries located in Europe. University exchanges facilitate the mobility of young people to foreign countries where they can choose to stay for a certain period of time after their studies. In France, *Volontariat International en Entreprise* (International Volunteering in Corporations) is a scheme that allows organizations to expatriate young people for a period of between 6 to 24 months at a much lower cost than traditional expatriation. Even though these individuals work for the organization, the French Agency for the International Development of Enterprises (UBIFRANCE) acts as an intermediary between the two parties. This scheme gives young people the chance to 'kickstart' an international career and to develop their international skills. In this way, they can start to accumulate crucial information and knowledge for their future careers, seen as a repository of knowledge (Bird 2001). Organizations often use this scheme with ultimate recruitment as an objective. Individuals can participate in this scheme even if they have not finished their studies. In the context of boundaryless careers, individuals prefer to study full time abroad in order to develop skills that will be valuable to them in the labour market, be it the labour market in their home country or abroad.

The combination of increasingly boundaryless careers and an emerging global economy could result in self-initiated foreign experience becoming a more prevalent form of expatriation. In the context of boundaryless careers, Inkson et al. (1997) see both expatriation and foreign experience as fundamental building blocks in the development of skills at the individual, organizational and national level. Bird (2001) underlines that 'often the experience is so powerful that it has a transformative effect on the manager' (p. 29). The author, among others (e.g. Osland 1995; McCall and Hollenbeck 2002), emphasizes the fact that managers often return to their home country metamorphozed. Bird (2001) proposes three

205

aspects of foreign experience that can explain the fundamental change that occurs at the individual level:

1 International experience involves many different experiences, both within and outside work, in particular when a family is involved in expatriation.
2 It leads to a proliferation of 'mental maps'.
3 It also leads to a significant loss, both loss of knowledge of some working aspects of the organization's home country and the waning of personal relationships.

International experience may not just be a period of growth and development, but also a period of loss. It is an experience that is likely to bring significant changes in individuals perceptions of themselves and their environment.

Expatriation may be seen as a maturation opportunity for individuals (Cerdin and Dubouloy 2004). In its function as a 'transitional space', the expatriation experience begins well before departure and continues well after return. As Cerdin and Dubouloy (2004: 977) state, 'acceptance of reality and construction of a career plan that integrates the benefit of the expatriation for the individual, particularly psychic maturation, continues after the expatriate has returned'. The benefits of expatriation for the individual appear to last beyond the expatriation itself. Organizations may facilitate this maturation by encouraging individuals to ask themselves the right questions before expatriation, which should help individuals to make a decision appropriate to their personal situation and their long-term plans, in particular their long-term career plan. Nevertheless, the individual and not the organization is responsible for finding the answers to these questions. This maturation may allow individuals to 'paste' themselves into the organization. The organization may therefore benefit from this maturation both during expatriation and repatriation, as individuals who have matured during their expatriation are likely to be more capable of adjusting on repatriation and are therefore more likely to transfer what they have learned during their expatriation. However, the study of Berthoin Antal (2001), carried out on two organizations in Germany, reveals a weak utilization of expatriates as a resource in the organizational learning process. The author notes that the organizations studied have little capacity to profit from expatriates' broadened state of mind on their return.

Career and repatriation

In the literature on international assignment, repatriation is often presented as a risk in terms of career (e.g. Baruch and Altman 2002). Drawing on the literature on career and international assignment, Lazarova and Cerdin (2007) propose that repatriation can be considered from two perspectives. Repatriation can either be seen as a career risk (traditional view) or as a career opportunity (emerging view).

 206

Traditional view

The traditional view presents repatriation as a source of frustration and concerns, both personal and professional, for individuals. The three principal concerns and personal difficulties related to repatriation are:

1   reverse culture shock for individuals and their families
2   changes in lifestyle along with loss of social status, which worsens reverse culture shock
3   changes in financial situation due to both the loss of expatriation-linked benefits and financial costs associated with relocation to the home country.

In addition to these personal difficulties, there are three professional concerns linked to repatriation, namely:

1   under-utilized skills
2   lack of recognition
3   restricted career opportunities.

Repatriation could then potentially be a career disaster for individuals who accept an international assignment (Baruch and Altman 2002).

According to the traditional view, organizations are responsible for the bleak state of repatriation retention. Lazarova and Cerdin (2007) find that repatriation support provided by the organization is negatively related to the intention to leave after repatriation. The failure to provide repatriates with adequate support may prove to be costly for organizations as it may result in the loss of skills due to repatriates' departure from the organization. Competitors thus gain skills that they did not help to develop and organizations do not fully profit from individuals' international experience. Weak retention rates and the frustrations of repatriates may negatively affect a potential expatriate's decision to accept an international assignment. Indeed, potential expatriates could turn down an assignment when they encounter repatriates who express their frustration about their situation on return, especially disappointment regarding their unmet expectations related to career advancement.

Caligiuri and Lazarova (2001) propose a range of practices, including career management practices, that organizations can use to facilitate repatriation. The French repatriates from the sample of the study carried out by Lazarova and Cerdin (2007) provide insight into the implementation of these career management practices in 10 French multinationals. The study also shows how important French repatriates consider these practices to be for repatriation success. In the sample, 70% of repatriates consider career planning sessions, where they can discuss their career-related concerns with management before repatriation, to be extremely important for repatriation success. Another practice judged to be

207

Text box 10.2
Practices in career management

Three practices in career management are considered important for repatriation success by French repatriates: career planning sessions, demonstration by the organization that it values international experience and formal mentoring programmes. However, according to the repatriates sampled, these practices are not implemented to a large extent by their organizations (only 49% use career planning sessions, 25% claimed that the organization demonstrated that it values international experience and 2% of organizations use formal mentoring programmes).

---

extremely important for repatriation success is the demonstration by the organization that it values international experience, thus showing individuals that expatriation can be beneficial to their career. This practice is deemed to be extremely important by 65% of repatriates, yet only 25% of the organizations sampled implement it. For French repatriates, a successful international assignment depends particularly on their perception of future career advancement prospects on return. They are particularly concerned about job opportunities on return and about building their careers over the long term, which is consistent with the conclusions of Yan et al. (2002). According to these repatriates, formal mentoring programs are almost non-existent in the 10 French MNCs sampled. However, 20% of the repatriates consider them to be important. The mentoring system has the advantage of maintaining a link between expatriates and their home organizations. Individuals can follow developments in the organization during their expatriation and remain potential candidates for career advancement opportunities. The literature on careers emphasizes the important role of mentoring and access to information on career success (Seibert et al. 2001b).

Emerging view

In addition to the traditional approach, which is centred on the frustration of repatriates, Lazarova and Cerdin (2007) propose an emerging view centred on individuals' proactivity regarding their repatriation. The emerging view is consistent with current research on careers, in particular boundaryless careers and protean careers. It is also in line with recent studies that examine expatriation or repatriation from a career perspective (Inkson et al. 1997; Tung 1998; Riusala and Suutari 2000; Suutari and Brewster 2001; Leiba-O'Sullivan 2002; Stahl et al. 2002; Suutari and Brewster 2003; Stahl and Cerdin 2004).

Stahl et al. (2002) report German expatriates' dissatisfaction with their organizations' management of the repatriation process, yet many of the expatriates were

208

'nonchalant' regarding the outcome of their repatriation. Stahl and Cerdin (2004) find that one-third of their sample of French and German expatriates were sceptical about the positive impact that their international assignment would have on their career advancement within their current organizations. However, an overwhelming majority were confident that it would have a positive impact on their future career opportunities among other possible employers. In their study of Finnish expatriates, Riusala and Suutari (2000) report that the major concerns of these expatriates were related to their exact responsibilities after repatriation, rather than their general career expectations after repatriation. Likewise, in examining the experiences of repatriated Finnish engineers, Suutari and Brewster (2003) found that most respondents reported that their international assignments had a positive impact on their career advancement, albeit not necessarily in the organization that expatriated them. Finally, Leiba-O'Sullivan (2002) suggests that proactive personality characteristics drive proactive behaviours that, in turn, are favourable to the success of the repatriation.

Building on the empirical findings and theoretical arguments of career research, Lazarova and Cerdin (2007) suggest that:

- What individuals do to accomplish personal career objectives may be central to understanding repatriation retention.
- Career development opportunities may exist within an individual's current organization but may also be offered by external employers.

From their sample, which consists of a majority of French repatriates, they find that the availability of alternative employment opportunities is positively related to the intention to leave after repatriation. They also find that proactive career development behaviours are significantly related to the intention to leave after repatriation.

Their results also show that the traditional and emerging views of repatriation can be combined. Both organization provided repatriation support and the availability of alternative employment opportunities contribute independently to the intention to leave after repatriation. Nevertheless, repatriation support in itself is a significant predictor of the intention to leave, but when considered in the presence of career activism (actions taken by an individual to take charge of or be in control of one's career) it does not contribute additional variance to the intention to leave.

Lazarova and Cerdin (2007) propose that these results have practical implications for individuals' careers on repatriation. Integrated repatriation support practices appear to be effective in reducing unwanted turnover. However, these practices may not be enough for retaining repatriates, as there are influences on repatriate retention that are outside the control of organizations. Organizations must also recognize that they cannot retain their repatriates at any cost. From the

209

perspective of boundaryless careers, repatriates may have their own career agenda, and their career activism may lead them to pursue their career outside the organization that expatriated them.

CAREER AND INTERNATIONAL ASSIGNMENT: A PERSPECTIVE OF SUCCESS

The success of an international assignment encompasses the stages of both expatriation and repatriation and affects both individuals and organizations. Yan et al. (2002) propose two dimensions for measuring the success of an international assignment (Table 10.2). One dimension takes into account the interests of the individual and the organization. The other dimension takes into account the stages of expatriation and repatriation, where expatriation success is measured from a short-term perspective and repatriation success is measured from a longer term perspective. An international assignment may be a success in the short term during expatriation but a failure in the long term on repatriation and therefore may be considered a mitigated success (Yan et al. 2002). The authors also emphasize the fact that individuals and organizations each have different success criteria for international assignments.

The literature on international assignments proposes numerous criteria for expatriation success from both the individual and organizational perspective. International assignment success from the individual perspective may be defined in terms of individual career success. This individual career success can be measured according to one subjective or intrinsic career outcome, career satisfaction and two objective or extrinsic career outcomes, promotion and pay increase (Seibert et al. 2001a). Other variables such as job satisfaction, perceived international

Table 10.2 *Possible success criteria for international assignments*

	Benefits	
	Individual	*Organizational*
Expatriation (shorter term)	■ Task performance	■ Accomplishment of organizational tasks
	■ Skill building, learning, growth	■ Achievement of key organizational objectives
	■ Job satisfaction	
	Assignment stage	
	■ Continual development	
	■ Attractive future assignments	■ Retention of repatriated employee
Repatriation (longer term)	■ Promotion	■ Utilization of new expertise
	■ Enlargement of responsibility	■ Transfer of expertise

Source: Yan et al. (2002: 378)

210

knowledge, skills and abilities acquisition and perceived network and relationship building can also define international assignment success from the individual perspective. Drawing on Yan et al. (2002) and Harzing and Christensen (2004), we can propose measuring international assignment success from the organizational perspective by four criteria: performance (in terms of the achievement of key organizational objectives and the accomplishment of organizational tasks), transfer of expertise, network and relationship building and retention of employees.

International adjustment usually features as a criterion for international assignment success in the research on expatriation (e.g. Black et al. 1991; Bhaskar-Shrinivas et al. 2005). This research contributes to the understanding of international assignment success by using two outcomes of international adjustment as international assignment success criteria, namely performance at work and completion of an assignment in its totality. However, this research generally overlooks variables linked to individuals' careers. It could be worthwhile in future studies to further examine the congruence between certain career variables such as career anchors and the characteristics of an international assignment.

CONCLUSION

International assignment should be considered as an integrated process that takes the perspective of both the individual and the organization into account, combines different theoretical approaches and considers both the stage of expatriation and repatriation (Yan et al. 2002). Much of the difficulty of career management lies in taking into account the perspectives of the different parties involved. This is particularly relevant in the context of international assignment, as individuals and organizations may pursue different objectives in terms of career. As a result, career management and international assignment success can have different meanings for the individual and the organization.

International assignments are becoming more and more diverse, not only in terms of their length, location and the career stage during which they take place but also in terms of who initiates the international assignment. Individuals can consider international assignment as a particular period in their careers. Each career period spent abroad can happen as a short-term assignment (1 year or less), medium term assignment (2 to 3 years), or long-term assignment (over 3 years). In the case that individuals' families relocate with them abroad, these may be considered traditional expatriations. In addition to these traditional expatriations, less traditional forms of international assignment have developed; for example, international commuter assignments and flexpatriate assignments, where neither individuals nor their families relocate abroad. The time that individuals spend working abroad can range from less than 1 year to spending their whole career abroad. Their careers abroad can encompass multiple forms of international assignment.

211

These international assignments can be carried out in the employment of one organization or of several. They can take place in one geographic zone or numerous regions. These various forms of international assignment create many different career paths for individuals and thus result in many different definitions of career success (Cerdin and Bird 2008).

In their aspiration to succeed in their careers, individuals may integrate international assignments into their careers. These assignments can contribute to their career success, however they define this success. In their endeavour to develop internationally, organizations may consider developing the careers of their employees, in particular the careers of talented employees, through the different forms of international assignment that are available to them. This chapter examined the link between career and expatriation in considering expatriation as a particular stage in a career. It also aimed to both advance the understanding and encourage further study of the link that appears to exist between international assignment success and career success.

KEY LEARNING POINTS

- The extent to which the organization integrates expatriation into its career management policies varies according to the purpose of expatriation. Career management also depends on the organization's international approach.
- Being aware of individuals' willingness to go abroad means organizations can avoid 'coffee machine selection'. This same awareness on the part of individuals can help them to choose the type of assignment that they are best suited to.
- Career stages and career anchors are important career characteristics that can help to explain both the type of career that individuals choose and international adjustment.
- With the development of boundaryless careers, flexpatriation and self-initiated foreign experience have become more common. The traditional expatriation model may therefore no longer be the main path to international experience and career development.
- The repatriation stage of an international assignment can pose a career risk for individuals. However, for individuals who display career activism, it can be a career opportunity.
- International assignment success may lead to career success and career success may be one measure of international assignment success. Therefore, career success and international assignment success are intrinsically linked.
- International assignment success encompasses the stages of both expatriation and repatriation. It is evaluated both from the point of view of the individual (development of skills and career development) and from the point of view

 212

of the organization (performance, in terms of the achievement of key organizational objectives and the accomplishment of organizational tasks; transfer of expertise; network and relationship building and retention of employees).

REFERENCES

Arthur, M.B. and Rousseau, D.M. (1996) *The Boundaryless Career: A New Employment Principle for a New Organizational Era*, New York: Oxford University Press.

Arthur, M.B., Khapova, S.N. and Wilderom, C.P.M. (2005) 'Career success in a boundaryless career world', *Journal of Organizational Behavior* 26:177–202.

Baruch, Y. and Altman, Y. (2002) 'Expatriation and repatriation in MNCs: a taxonomy', *Human Resource Management* 41,2:239–259.

Berthoin Antal, A. (2001) 'Expatriates' contributions to organizational learning', *Journal of General Management* 26, 4:62–84.

Bhaskar-Shrinivas, P., Harrison, D.A., Shaffer, M.A. and Luk, D.M. (2005) 'Input-based and time-based models of international adjustment: meta-analytic evidence and theoretical extensions', *Academy of Management Journal* 48, 2:257–281.

Bird, A. (2001) 'International assignments and careers as repositories of knowledge', in M. Mendenhall, T. Kuehlmann and G. Stahl (eds) *Developing Global Business Leaders: Policies, Processes and Innovations*, Westport, CT: Quorum Books.

Black, J. S., Mendenhall, M. and Oddou, G. (1991) 'Toward a comprehensive model of international adjustment: an integration of multiple theoretical perspectives', *Academy of Management Review* 16, 2:291–317.

Borg, M. (1988) *International Transfers of Managers in Multinational Corporations*, Acta Universitatis Upsaliensis, Studia Oeconomiae Negotorium, 27, Uppsala.

Brett, J. M., Stroh, L. K. and Reilly, A. H. (1993) 'Pulling up roots In the 1990s: who's willing to relocate?', *Journal of Organizational Behavior* 14: 49–60.

Caligiuri, P.M. (2006) 'Developing global leaders', *Human Resource Management Review* 16: 219–228.

Caligiuri, P. and Lazarova, M. (2001) 'Strategic repatriation policies to enhance global leadership development', in M. Mendenhall, T. Kuehlmann and G. Stahl (eds) *Developing Global Business Leaders: Policies, Processes and Innovations*, Westport, CT: Quorum Books.

Cerdin, J.L. (2002) *L'expatriation*, 2nd edn, Paris: editions d'Organisation.

Cerdin, J.L. and Bird, A. (2008) 'Careers in a global context', in M. Harris (ed.) *Handbook of Research in International Human Resources*, Mahwah, NJ: Lawrence Erlbaum.

Cerdin, J.L. and Dubouloy, M. (2004) 'Expatriation as a maturation opportunity: A psychoanalytical approach based on "copy and paste"', *Human Relations* 57, 8:957–981.

Dickmann, M. and Harris, H. (2005) 'Developing career capital for global careers: the role of international assignments', *Journal of World Business* 40, 4:399–408.

Dickmann, M., Doherty, N., Mills, T. and Brewster, C. (forthcoming) 'Why do they go? Individual and corporate perspectives on the factors influencing the decision to accept an international assignment', *International Journal of Human Resource Management*.

Dunbar, E. (1992) 'Adjustment and satisfaction of expatriate U.S. personnel', *International Journal of Intercultural Relations* 16: 1–16.

213

Edström, A. and Galbraith, J.R. (1977) 'Transfer of managers as a control and coordination strategy in multinational organizations', *Administrative Science Quarterly* 22: 11–22.

Feldman, D.C. and Thomas, D.C. (1992) 'Career management issues facing expatriates', *Journal of International Business Studies* 23: 271–293.

Forsé, M. and Chauvel, L. (1995) 'L'évolution de l'homogamie en France', *Revue Française de Sociologie* 36:123–142.

Guzzo, R.A. (1997) 'The expatriate employee', *Trends in Organizational Behavior* 4: 123–137.

Hall, D.T. (1976) *Careers in Organizations*, Santa Monica, CA: Goodyear.

Hall, D.T. (1996) 'Protean careers of the 21st century', *Academy of Management Executive* 10:8–16.

Hall, D.T. and Mirvis, P.H. (1996) 'The new protean career: psychological success and the path with a heart', in D.T. Hall and Associates (eds) *The Career is Dead – Long Live the Career*, San Francisco: Jossey–Bass.

Hall, F.S. and Hall, D.T. (1979) *The Two–Career Couple*, Boston, MA: Addison-Wesley.

Harris, H. and Brewster, C. (1999) 'The coffee-machine system: how international selection really works', *International Journal of Human Resource Management* 10,3:488–500.

Harvey, M. and Novicevic, M.M. (2001) 'Selecting expatriates for increasingly complex global assignment', *Career Development International* 6, 2:69–86.

Harvey, M. and Novicevic, M.M. (2004) 'The development of political skill and political capital by global leaders through global assignments', *International Journal of Human Resource Management* 15, 7:1173–1188.

Harzing, A.W. and Christensen, C. (2004) 'Expatriate failure: time to abandon the concept?, *Career Development International* 9, 7: 616–626.

Heslin, P.A. (2005) 'Conceptualizing and evaluating career success', *Journal of Organizational Behavior* 26:113–136.

Hocking, J.B., Brown, M. and Harzing, A.W. (2004) 'A knowledge transfer perspective of strategic assignment purposes and their path-dependent outcomes', *International Journal of Human Resource Management* 15, 3:565–586.

Inkson, K. and Arthur, M.B. (2001) 'How to be a successful career capitalist', *Organizational Dynamics* 30, 1:48–61.

Inkson, K., Arthur, M. B., Pringle, J. and Barry, S. (1997) 'Expatriate assignment versus overseas experience: contrasting models of international human resource development', *Journal of World Business* 32, 4:351–368.

Lazarova, M, and Cerdin, J.L. (2007) 'Revisiting repatriation concerns: organizational support vs. career and contextual influences', *Journal of International Business Studies*.

Leiba-O'Sullivan, S. (2002) 'The protean approach to managing repatriation transitions', *International Journal of Manpower* 23, 7:597–616.

Mayerhofer, H., Hartmann, L. and Herbert, A. (2004a) 'Career management issues for flexpatriate international staff', *Thunderbird International Business Review* 46, 6: 647–666.

Mayerhofer, H., Hartmann, L.C., Michelitsch-Rield, G. and Kollinger, I. (2004b) 'Flexpatriate assignment: a neglected issue in global staffing', *International Journal of Human Resource Management* 15: 1371–1389.

McCall, M.W. and Hollenbeck, G.P. (2002) *Developing Global Executives*, Cambridge, MA: Harvard Business School Press.

214

Osland, J. (1995) *The Adventure of Living Abroad: Hero Tales from the Global Frontier*, San Francisco: Jossey-Bass.

Parker, P. and Inkson, K. (1999) 'New forms of career: the challenge to human resource management', *Asia Pacific Journal of Human Resources* 37: 76–85.

Perlmutter, H. (1969) 'The tortuous evolution of the multinational corporation', *Columbia Journal of World Business* 4, 1: 9–18.

Phatak, A.V. (1989) *International Dimensions of Management*, Boston, MA: PWS-Kent Publishing Company.

Punnett, B.J. (1997) 'Towards effective management of expatriate spouses', *Journal of World Business* 32, 3:243–257.

Riusala, K. and Suutari, V. (2000) 'Expatriation and careers: perspectives of expatriates and spouses', *Career Development International* 5, 2:81–90.

Rosenbaum, J.E. (1993) 'Organization career system and employee misperceptions', in M.B. Arthur, D.T. Hall and B.S. Lawrence (eds) *Handbook of Career Theory*, Cambridge: Cambridge University Press.

Schein, E.H. (1978) *Career Dynamics: Matching Individual and Organisational Needs*, Reading, MA: Addison-Wesley.

Schein, E.H. (1990) *Career Anchors: Discovering Your Real Values*, San Diego, CA: Pfeiffer & Company.

Seibert, K.M., Kraimer, M.L. and Crant, J.M. (2001a) 'What do proactive people do? A longitudinal model linking proactive personality and career success', *Personnel Psychology* 54, 4:845–874.

Seibert, S.E., Kraimer, M.L. and Liden, R.C. (2001b) 'A social capital theory of career success', *Academy of Management Journal* 44, 2:219–238.

Smith, C.R. and Still, L.V. (1999) 'Managing the dual-career expatriate', Workshop on Expatriation, EIASM, September, Madrid.

Stahl, G.K. and Cerdin, J.L. (2004) 'Global careers in French and German multinational corporations', *Journal of Management Development* 23, 9:885–902.

Stahl, G.K. Miller E.L. and Tung, R.L. (2002) 'Toward the boundaryless career: a closer look at the expatriate career concept and the perceived implications of an international assignment', *Journal of World Business* 37, 3:216 227.

Suutari, V. and Brewster, C. (2000) 'Making their own way: international experience through self-initiated foreign assignment', *Journal of World Business* 35, 4: 417–436.

Suutari, V. and Brewster, C. (2001) 'Expatriate management practices and perceived relevance', *Personnel Review* 30, 5/6:554–577.

Suutari, V. and Brewster, C. (2003) 'Repatriation: empirical evidence from a longitudinal study of careers and expectations among Finnish expatriates', *International Journal of Human Resource Management* 14, 7:1132–1151.

Suutari V. and Taka, M. (2004) 'Career anchors of managers with global careers', *Journal of Management Development* 23, 9:833–847.

Torbiörn, I. (1976) *Att Leva Utomlands – En Studie av Utlandssvenskars Anpassning, Trivsel och Levnadsvanor* [*Living Abroad – A Study of the Adjustment of Swedish Overseas Personnel*], Stockholm: SNS.

Tung, R.L. (1998) 'American expatriates abroad: from neophytes to cosmopolitans', *Journal of World Business*, 33, 2:125–144.

Yan, A., Zhu, G. and Hall, D.T. (2002) 'International assignment for career building: a model of agency relationships and psychological contracts', *Academy of Management Review* 27, 3:373–391.

215

Strategic challenge or situational response?

Chapter 11

Modern forms of international working

Wolfgang Mayrhofer, Paul Sparrow and Angelika Zimmermann

CHAPTER OBJECTIVES

By the end of this chapter, readers will have:

- an appreciation of the demand and supply factors that have led to modern forms of international working beyond expatriation
- an understanding of the main characteristics and consequences for organizations of these different forms of international working
- a picture of an organizational example of best practice in managing issues of intercultural training across these more diverse forms of working
- a sensitivity to the issues that determine whether these developments represent a fragmentation of international resourcing or a coherent strategy
- an idea of the issues that could form a future research agenda around these developments

INTRODUCTION

International assignments – traditionally seen as the management of expatriates and various aspects of the expatriation process – are an established element of international human resource management (IHRM) in academia and practice. Consequently, related literature flourishes. It ranges from overview and textbook contributions about expatriates and global leaders (Mendenhall et al. 2000; Dowling et al, 2008) to detailed analyses and recommendations about different elements of expatriation such as recruitment and selection (Guthrie et al. 2003), adaptation and acculturation processes (Ward 1996) or repatriation (Linehan and Mayrhofer 2005). In practice, expatriation is a substantial part of IHRM activities, too. A recent survey (GMAC 2005) suggests that in 2005 47% of the organizations surveyed expected growth in the size of their expatriate workforce.

However, there have been shifts in both supply and demand factors that have brought substantial changes in the area of working internationally. A number of other forms of international working with labels such as flexpatriation, frequent travelling, or international commuting (Harris et al. 2005) have gained importance. Despite some differences, they have one thing in common: they deviate from classic expatriation and the respective expatriation cycle. Three influencing factors are responsible for the emergence of these modern forms.

First, a changing macro-environment creates new demands for working beyond national borders. Globalized business processes, efforts to create markets with few barriers for business transactions through legal frameworks such as the GATT, or emerging supra-national institutions such as the European Union (EU) have changed the economic situation and stimulated exchange of goods, services and people worldwide. Supporting international mobility is on the political agenda in many countries. For example, in 2002 the European Commission proposed a plan to make it easier for Europe's workers to find and move to jobs anywhere around the continent. The EU also proposed making the tax, pension and social security systems across the EU more compatible and to increase immigration from outside the EU. Programmes such as SOCRATES, Leonardo da Vinci or TEMPUS support European exchange of people and create informal networks of understanding and contacts and lead to insight into different ways of living.

Second, organizations create additional demand for an international workforce themselves. For Salt and Millar (2006), three demand factors have fuelled growth in modern forms of international working: the need for skilled international employees to help build new international markets; temporary and short-term access to specialized talent in sending countries to assist the execution of overseas projects; and the need for highly mobile elites of managers to perform boundary-spanning roles to help build social networks and facilitate the exchange of knowledge. Businesses operating across national borders see individuals' willingness to follow the work demand across national borders as part of the implicit – and often explicit – work contract. In a similar way, project dominated organizational forms often require working internationally (Harris 2000).

Third, career concepts and profiles of individuals interested in working internationally have changed substantially, due to changing individual concepts of work and career in general, e.g. alternatives to traditional work arrangements such as boundaryless (Arthur and Rousseau 1996) or protean careers (Hall and Mirvis 1996), a greater diversity of work arrangements beyond 40 hours/5 days a week, and a variety of different career patterns such as patchwork or spiral careers (Brousseau et al. 1996). The profile of the people working abroad has changed and now includes:

- a rising number of individuals from outside the headquarters country such as 'third-country nationals', i.e. not from the home or the host country

 220

- inpatriates, i.e. people brought into headquarters; often aiming at improving the capabilities and networks of people working abroad (cf. Chapter 12)
- an increasing number of women who still face substantial barriers in their international careers (see Chapter 13)
- the more frequent occurrence of dual-career couples where both partners pursue an occupational career of their own: in this case one of them does not merely act as 'trailing partner' during an international assignment (cf. Chapter 10).

Summarizing this, Briscoe and Schuler (2004: 223) observe that the definition of 'international employee' inside organizations has continued to expand: 'The tradition of referring to all international employees as expatriates – or even international assignees – falls short of the need for international HR practitioners to understand the options available ... and fit them to evolving international business strategies.' There are now a wide range of options that can enable the global resourcing of work in organizations.

In this chapter, in order to understand the context of resourcing work on an international basis, we include research on what at first sight appears to be a fragmentary group of individuals, ranging from contract expatriates; assignees on short term or intermediate term foreign postings; permanent cadres of global managers; international commuters; employees utilized on long-term business trips; international transferees moving from one subsidiary to another; self-initiated movers who live in a third country but are willing to work for a multinational; international employees active in cross-border project teams; immigrants actively and passively attracted to a national labour market; domestically based employees in a service centre but dealing with overseas customers, suppliers and partners on a regular basis; and skilled individuals working in geographically remote centres of competence or excellence, i.e. serving global operations. The core of this chapter will outline their major characteristics and analyse individual and organizational consequences.

DIFFERENT FORMS OF INTERNATIONAL WORKING

International commuters and employees utilized on extended business trips

International commuters and extended business trips are widespread modifications of the full-scale expatriation process (Peppas 2004; Harris et al. 2005). International commuter assignments involve a specific workplace abroad to which employees travel on a regular basis, most often weekly or bi-weekly. While the employee works abroad, spouse and family – if existent – stay at home.

221

Extended business trips, often also termed frequent traveller or flexpatriate assignment (Mayerhofer et al. 2004b), deviate from 'normal' trips in terms of duration or frequency. Individuals do not relocate, but visit their work place abroad during business trips undertaken very often or lasting longer than usual.

The following two examples illustrate both forms of working abroad. In 2004, OMV, the Austrian oil company, bought the majority of shares of Petrom, the national Romanian oil company with roughly 50,000 employees at that time. In the immediate aftermath of the acquisition, about 80 experienced Austrian headquarter managers were expatriated to Romania following the classical expatriation format. However, some key positions were filled through international commuting. For example, between 2004 and 2006 the senior vice-president of corporate human resources located at the OMV headquarters in Vienna spent 3 days a week at the operations in Romania. The German clothing industry provides an example for extended business trips used for 'quality engineers' dealing with several countries and the local operations in low-cost countries. The quality engineers have to secure that the products meet the required standards set by the parent company and are delivered on time. They spend a considerable or most of their working time abroad, yet do not move permanently because they regularly have to be at headquarters to report and receive updated information (see Mayrhofer and Scullion 2002).

Compared to classical expatriation, these forms of working internationally have the following consequences for the individuals and organizations involved (for a more detailed view see Mayerhofer et al. 2004b). First, at the individual level they affect the lives of the persons profoundly. The involved working patterns are frequently incompatible with familiar daily routines. In addition, frequent and often little predictable absences can conflict with the established social routines both within the family and in the broader social context. In the long run, this can entail the danger of stress and burnout. Contrariwise, being a boundary-spanning person regularly living in more than one location also has a number of secondary gains. This includes the broadening of the mindset due to the great variety of impressions, an increasing competency of quickly adapting to changing environments or a reflective distance to occurrences at one's base which is supported by leaving also physically. Second, these forms of working internationally affect a greater number of employees. While classical expatriation often is limited to key positions requiring substantial administrative support and financial resources, both international commuting and extended business trips can be used across a broader spectrum of employees. At the same time, the total cost involved is potentially lower since specific procedures for selection, training, financial incentives, etc. are less required or obsolete. Third, both alternative forms offer greater flexibility for the organization. Duration of the arrangement, geographical scope or content of work can more easily and at comparatively short notice be changed. In turn, this promises cost savings and short reaction times. Fourth, they affect different parts of the

222

organization. In classical expatriation, HR departments play a key role in all parts of the process. International commuting and extended business trips are less prone to standardized central procedures and large parts of it are handled without HR specialists. This constitutes some risk since some of the issues involved such as handling cultural differences or coping with constantly changing work and social environments require HR expertise. Nevertheless, it also helps to simplify the process of working abroad. Fifth, less involvement of the HR specialist puts more emphasis on individual employees' abilities to cope with the situation on their own or to get access to supporting resources such as information, coaching or peer networks (Mayerhofer et al. 2004a). Finally, less involvement of HR specialists and central coordination poses the danger of greater fragmentation, less consistency over time and less knowledge flow between various parts of the organization dealing with these forms of working internationally.

International transferees

Individuals moving from one international assignment to the next are not new for IHRM (see also Chapters 5 and 12). In the diplomatic service, for example, they are the rule rather than the exception. In companies operating across national borders, this group traditionally consisted of classical expatriates not returning to their home organization after their foreign assignment. They were certainly not a large-scale phenomenon and partly seen more as a liability than an asset. Again, the situation has changed considerably over the past decades. Mainly related to an accelerating speed of internationalization, the creation of an international orientation within crucial members of the organizational management team is regarded as essential: 'Developing a multicultural, international management is considered to be one of the primary requisites of competing in the global marketplace successfully' (Harvey et al. 1999a: 39). Increasing the number of managers with international work experience and management teams with a mixed cultural background are important measures for achieving this goal.

Two groups of individuals contribute to these efforts. Inpatriate managers are closely familiar with more than one culture due to their personal or job history. Coming from countries other than the home-country organization, they are assigned to the home country on a semi-permanent or even permanent basis (Harvey et al. 1999b). Global managers take the international career orientation one step further and opt for 'aspatial careers' (Suutari 2003: 189ff.). For them, differentiations between home, host- or third-country designation become meaningless as they are no longer attached to specific countries. Rather, they commit themselves to a longer period of international positions irrespective of the specific country, either by consecutive international positions or interrupted only briefly by their 'return' to a basis, e.g. organizational headquarters. Organizations can use them wherever staffing needs arise worldwide. In terms of their personal career anchors (Schein 1978), developing management expertise and looking for challenges seem to be crucial (Suutari and Taka 2004).

Examples of inpatriates managers abound in European companies enlarging into formerly communist countries in eastern Europe. Managers of newly acquired companies or founded subsidiaries were transferred for considerable periods of time to headquarters operations. For example, during the late 1990s, Flextronics, a leading global player in the original equipment manufacturing business, transferred key people of their newly founded subsidiaries in Hungary to longer established subsidiaries to support professional socialization, transfer of cultural values in both directions and increase the global mindset of its employees. At about the same time, Fluor Corporation, one of the world's largest publicly owned engineering, procurement, construction, and maintenance services companies based in the USA, reorganized its staff to achieve a greater potential of internationally capable managers. It developed mobile global managers working in multiple offices and facilities worldwide, thus connecting dispersed operations and forming matrix teams (Stanek 2000).

These forms of working internationally have a number of consequences. First, while inpatriation combines several positive aspects of expatriation and working with locals, some of the problems arising are strikingly similar to classical expatriation. Examples include acting as boundary-spanning persons, coping with cultural and/or economic distance between countries involved, stress due to acculturation processes or adapting to the local organizational culture. Although these topics are familiar for IHRM, their concrete form of appearance is new since many of the structural characteristics of inpatriation clearly differ from expatriation (e.g. the relative internal importance of the sending and receiving organizational unit or the ascribed social status of inpatriates). Second, early international assignments are crucial when trying to build a cadre of internationals. A study of Finnish global managers (Suutari 2003) shows that while roughly half of them had a global orientation from the outset, half of them changed to a long-term international career orientation after their first assignment abroad. Third, inpatriates can be used as 'linking pins' between various parts of the organizations as well as between the organization and the environment. This contributes to a more strategic global HRM response in a turbulent global environment (Harvey et al. 1999b).

Self-initiated movers who live abroad but are willing to work for a multinational organization

Classical expatriation is usually initiated by the organization. Employees can express their interest in jobs abroad, but, by and large, organizational demands determine the 'when', 'where' and 'how'. Self-initiated movers deviate from this pattern. They go abroad on their own initiative and emphasize individual, often diffuse goals when looking for self-initiated work experience (Inkson et al. 1997).

224

Compared to classical expatriates, self-initiated movers are characterized by a number of specifics. Personal agency has been shown to be important in the development of their career attitudes to international mobility. In a longitudinal study about self-initiated movers – full-time employees who had graduated from Australian business schools – Tharenou (2003) shows that the initial development of receptivity to international careers was driven by a combination of personal agency (beliefs about capability to work in foreign cultures), home barriers (low family influence) and work environment opportunities (a clearly understood international focus shifted receptivity in younger but not older employees). A Finnish study contrasts self-initiated movers with expatriates (Suutari and Brewster 2000). Being slightly younger, there are more females and more singles among them. They typically work in a local private company or in international organizations; the organizations they work for are less international and more project based; and they work more frequently on temporary contracts and at lower organizational levels with an expert status. Interest in international issues and poor employment situation at home are mentioned more frequently as primary triggers and motives for going abroad. Self-initiated movers typically have no return guarantee and often no plans to return to their home country. Instead, they are more willing to accept another period of working abroad or even a permanent stay abroad. Their compensation levels vary more and they less frequently have access to typical expatriation benefits such as hardship, housing or education allowances and travel insurance.

Self-initiated movers typically fall into two categories. The first group consists of young people looking for a job abroad on their own immediately after finishing their education. As part of a national pattern – 'every year, tens of thousands of young Australians and New Zealanders make their pilgrimage to London, as a starting point for what they call, in local vernacular, "the big OE" (overseas experience) – a period of travel, exploration, and personal development' (Inkson and Myers 2003: 171) – or individual decision making, they regard their stay abroad as part of a personal development experience that might or might not lead to a longer term occupational career. The second group consists of more experienced people beyond the establishment phase of their careers.

Self-initiated movers lead to a number of issues for organizational HRM. First, they provide an easily accessible pool of international workforce that can be attracted with comparatively little cost and outside typical expatriation schemes. Second, while they are easily accessible, they usually – at least at the beginning – lack any organization-specific track record. Hence, all the risks of external recruitment are linked with hiring from this group. Third, personnel planning is difficult since the availability of this group is hard to predict in case of organizational demand. Finally, it is likely that members of this group have distinct motivation patterns that drive them (e.g. a greater sense of initiative, independence and internal locus of control). Tapping into this source of the labour pool requires attraction

225

mechanisms taking into account these specifics. In addition, the issue of keeping valuable employees gets a new facet in relationship to a group that has a noted record for moving abroad on their own.

Immigrants actively and passively attracted to a national labour market

The opportunity for broader patterns of international resourcing strategies – and types of international working – has increased markedly due to two recent developments:

1 Certain labour markets have themselves become globalized (Ward 2004), for example, healthcare markets (Clark et al. 2006).
2 Levels of international mobility, especially migration, have increased, impacting upon the domestic HR strategies of firms and offering new opportunities to international firms (Salt and Millar 2006).

Historically, the level of mobility within the EU has been low. Before the incorporation of the new accession countries less than 0.5% of Europe's 350 million citizens moved from one member state to another. EU accession has increased levels of mobility and reduced the need for many organizations to rely on specialized cadres of international employees. The UK and Ireland – together with Sweden – allowed open labour markets, causing significant recruitment effects.

In the UK, the proportion of domestic employers recruiting from abroad rose from 28% in 2004 (Czerny 2004) to 38% in 2005. Of those recruiting overseas, 53% expected this activity to increase (CIPD 2005). HR practitioner discussion about this passive and active attraction of foreign labour has included concerns about disincentives for employers to invest in domestic training; negative reputational impacts on host organizations in terms of shifts in resourcing policy and impacts on donor countries; training for managers in the cultures of immigrant employees and insights into the use of own language versus English language and perceptions of customer service; the requirement for passive, active and strategic recruitment activities; and problems of indirect discrimination within selection systems. A number of issues arise from the international migration of talented labour. These include: establishing where professional expertise and technical insight lies; deciding whether initiatives require targeted campaigns or longer term strategic moves to sourcing from specific countries or regions; understanding and establishing base technical competence of recruitees and setting up assessment processes where necessary; considering the ethical and reputational issues associated with campaigns; ensuring infrastructure in local receiving units to handle increasing workforce diversity; and building reputations of receiving units, operations or locations into internationally competitive sites.

226

In Ireland, the open economic model, in which multinationals have been encouraged to locate production and invest on the basis of European demand and cost competitiveness, has seen attention given to societal impacts of immigration. Barrett et al. (2006) examined the impact of Irish immigration policy on high- and low-skilled wages and levels of GNP per head. Overall high-skill policies have been shown to be beneficial, but education–occupation discrepancies exist and attention has turned to industrial relations consequences of international mobility, with large-scale immigration from Poland and from potential EU applicant countries bringing the voluntarist system of workplace relations under pressure and creating debates about national minimum wage systems (Frawley 2006).

The Irish experience of complementary high- and low-skilled immigration has also presented employers with an opportunity to adopt novel global labour supply strategies. Cities such as Dublin or London have become 'magnets' for a category of international self-initiated movers, with new support structures being developed to support employers with multicultural workplaces. Sparrow (2007) uses the example of Barclaycard International to demonstrate how the development of a multicultural workforce in one location can be used to seedcorn new models of internationalization. Its call centre in Dublin acted as a platform and nursery for future international expansion, growing from 10 to 360 people from 1997 to 2006 primarily on the basis of recruiting both immigrants and self-initiated movers in the city. Intended to support non-UK operations, it grew to serve eight countries including Botswana, France, Germany, Greece, Ireland, Italy, Portugal and Spain. The seedcorning of other overseas locations through the development of protocols to manage a multicultural workforce in Dublin operations, and then the 're-export' of both these protocols and (some of) the people to other operations, was a major component of the strategy to build a platform of people management processes (processes, structures and frameworks) that brought stability, governance and control to newly established overseas operations. Active and passive resourcing strategies targeted at residents of large global cities in Europe have produced a useful mix of immigrant and more transient self-initiated movers, capable of assisting effective international working.

The question of effectiveness has seen attention turn to the issue of competencies. For immigrants, employment integration is a significant issue. As with self-initiated movers, personal agency skills have been shown to be important, but they are of a more collective nature. It is fair to say that self-initiated (non-company backed) foreign workers likely also have to – or do – rely on collective agency skills where they form part of a large diaspora. Where there has been reliance on immigrants (as, for example, with the recent large movement of Polish employees to the UK) the mass of like-situation people creates more rapid and easily accessible social structures. Immigrants have to learn by observation, enabling them to acquire knowledge, attitudes, values, emotional proclivities and competences through the information that is conveyed. They develop three important 'agency skills'

227

(Bandura 2001, 2002): direct personal agency to manage their own lives and bring influence to bear directly on themselves and their own environment; proxy agency skills for those spheres of people's lives where they have no direct control over the social and institutional practices that affect everyday life and so rely on others – and must influence others – to act on their behalf and secure personally desired outcomes; and collective agency skills where people act in concert with other people to shape their future by pooling knowledge, skills and resources, forming alliances, and acting in mutual support to secure that which they cannot accomplish on their own.

International employees active in virtual, cross-border teams

With the increase of international collaborations at all hierarchical levels, and through the explosive development of electronic communication media, cross-border, virtual teams abound. These teams face the challenges of working not only across cultures, but also across different national offices, often around the globe. For example, 103 companies in a study of McDonough et al. (2001) estimated that 22% of their product development teams would be distributed globally within the next years. Such international constellations are set up to achieve an international presence while reducing expenses for travelling. However, the success of such collaborations is unlikely to be obtained without careful management attention. Managers have to keep in mind that intercultural process losses can be augmented by the difficulties of virtual cooperation and vice versa.

One of the most persistent problems is that of virtual intercultural communication. To understand the meaning of a message, it is necessary to understand its context to some degree. This is, however, even more the case in high-context cultures, where the larger part of the message is unspoken and can only be understood by knowing the context, such as a Japanese colleague's obligations towards his hierarchical network at home. The potential for misunderstandings is, of course, increased if communication is via less rich media, such as email. These media, by the same token, can decrease misunderstandings when used for documenting facts or decisions. For these reasons, managers have to ensure that the communication form and pattern is adjusted to the purpose of the communication.

Cultural differences and virtuality can also challenge the quality of interpersonal relationships within the teams (Axtell et al. 2004). Due to the lack of social interactions and background knowledge of the other person, affective trust may be more fragile or harder to develop within virtual teams. There is also a propensity to develop separate subgroup identities according to location and nationality, which can make it harder to achieve team identity and cohesion. Team fractures can be further increased by power struggles and by pressures team members experience from their local unit, superiors or customers (Zimmermann and Sparrow 2007).

228

A fundamental choice therefore has to be made regarding the general approach to dealing with the differences in the team. Janssens and Brett (2006) recommend a 'fusion' model of international teamworking, by which different cultural approaches should not be equalled out, but respected, coexist and be used where they are most useful. In contrast, the 'dominant coalition model' accepts power differentials, leading to the adjustment of one nationality to the dominant nationality, typically the nationality of headquarters, who also speak the common language most fluently. Such adjustment may however be beneficial when it leads to easier coordination and better work results (Zimmermann and Sparrow 2007).

Managers can also take a number of preventive actions to avoid process losses. Regular face-to-face meetings are again essential, particularly at the point of launching the teamwork, to build a personal basis for trust. Moreover, systematic teambuilding throughout the team's lifecycle is highly recommended. Setting shared goals, defining clear team roles and interaction rules, as well as an adequate communication structure can help to avoid differential conceptions from the beginning. This can also serve to increase the commitment of the team members to the team as a whole. Overall, international, virtual teams will have to be led in a more delegative manner, given that direct control is not possible over the distance. A clear team structure is therefore beneficial. This can include designated subgroup leaders and coordinating 'window' employees (those with the greatest language fluency and intercultural skills). Reviews at regular intervals are more necessary than in co-located teams to monitor the team's performance (DiStefano and Maznevski 2000). Careful knowledge management (e.g. through shared databases) should help shared (team) mental models to develop. Finally, although often neglected, many researchers (Canney-Davison and Ward 1999; Hertel et al. 2005) suggest that the disbanding of the team after task completion should be accompanied by celebrating successes and feeding the learning points back to the organization.

Skilled individuals working in geographically remote centres of excellence serving global operations

Multinationals have many strategies at their disposal to address skills shortages in any one national labour market. The development of centres of excellence – sometimes in geographically remote areas – is one option to disseminate organizational learning throughout operations and offshore outsourcing.

Ashton et al. (2008) draw attention to changing assumptions within the IHRM literature as a result of such developments. Briscoe and Schuler (2004) see IHRM as a unique set of activities confined to additional requisite activities, e.g. the management of international assignees and working alongside HR professionals from other countries and adapting HR practices to multicultural and cross-cultural environments. In contrast, they argue, the perspective of Sparrow et al. (2004) suggests that IHRM is confronted with new developments and problems that cannot be adequately handled by treating IHRM in this way. Experimentation through the development of extended talent pipelines, accompanied by market mapping activities, has enabled multinationals to gain control over the attraction and skill formation process. Associated developments in internal organization designs have then been used to derive greater value out of the deployment of such talent and the knowledge produced. These knowledge management structures include the use of centres of excellence. This last perspective acknowledges that while only a few multinationals have penetrated markets across the globe in that they have the capability to locate, source and manage resources anywhere in the world, nonetheless, they are combining novel skills supply mechanisms and organization designs to create modern forms of international working. In theory, networked organizations with dispersed centres of excellence help assist this mobility, but in practice the concept of centres of excellence and the pragmatic control and coordination needs have made such structures difficult to operate.

Ashton et al. (2008) question the functionality of this. They collected data on skill formation strategies through interviews with 180 senior managers and chief executive officers in 20 multinationals in China, Germany, India, Singapore, South Korea, the UK and USA in the financial services, automobiles and the electronic/communications sectors between 2004 and 2007. National institutional frameworks and cultures were considered to be primary forces shaping the process of skill formation and the competitive strategies of organizations. Now, the authors argue, it is the ability to manage and deploy skills globally. The process of skill formation is being transformed. Multinationals have developed a series of global strategies to exploit differences in the cost of educated labour, with consequent decline in its value. For Brown and Lauder (2006) the process of globalization has made the link between educated labour and subsequent rewards in the labour market more tenuous. To develop consistency in the management of relationships across the globe, firms are 'internalizing' the process of skill creation and the use of these skills. Different components of the supply chain are being modularized and sourced wherever there are cost and business advantages to the company (Berger 2005) – providing there is a basic infrastructure and education service – and this 'commoditization' has spread to knowledge work.

Analyses of the mobility of experts within multinationals show that within the IT sector at least (Salt and Millar 2006), employers have preferred to recruit IT staff from overseas even when skills were still available in the domestic labour market. Highly integrated global internal labour markets, capable of short-term circulation of expertise, have developed. The rise of business process outsourcing models and client pressure to reduce costs have encouraged multinationals to adopt novel skill supply strategies, for example, using their UK bases to host (and rotate) overseas and offshore nationals working at or near end-client sites for short periods of time on development work, backed up by bulk delivery 'campuses' sited in low-cost locations. Overseas rotation is used to build up repositories of client

230

and market-specific knowledge in offshore locations, undermining the requirement that overseas recruitment be used for genuine additional new posts.

Across all these developments, it might be argued that in one way or another, work moves to where expert staff are and not the other way round. As employers rely more on distributed networks of expertise that can be combined flexibly to create market opportunities, the use of global resourcing models that allow both the injection of critical knowledge into a receiving country and the mining of critical knowledge from domestic markets by overseas suppliers will increase.

Case study 11.1
Best practice of IHRM: Robert Bosch GmbH

The Robert Bosch Group, which presently employs over 240,000 members, was originally a purely German company. However, Bosch is now spread over 130 countries, with less than 50% of its workforce located in Germany and more than 70% of its turnover made outside Germany. This international distribution was developed strategically to achieve proximity with the large international automotive producers that are the company's main customers, to draw on local expertise and to reduce labour costs. A tight network and close coordination is required between the globally distributed sites. Bosch is therefore a typical example of a company whose employees work internationally at all levels, from top managers to factory workers. The company uses a rather traditional nomenclature of international employees, which, in practice, covers many of the following types:

1 Stays abroad that are shorter than 3 months are classified as business trips. These are common among employees with border-spanning functions, such as sales, purchasing or technological advisers for new sites. In practice, business trips range from occasional task-related travels to regular, frequent trips of international commuters.

2 International, virtual teams exist at all levels. These teams can be tasked with planning, development or production. Typically, not all team members have the same amount of contact with the members of other countries. Rather, one or more 'window' people manage the international interfaces. Business trips to the other site are necessary for transferring know-how, providing technical assistance and meeting the local customer. Most of the non-German members are assigned to German headquarters at some stage of the collaboration.

3 International transferees (or expatriates) are classified into (a) long-termers (1 to ca. 4 years) and (b) 'delegates' or short-termers (between 3 months and 1 year). The long-termers' contract can be based either on German or on local law, but they always receive their salary from the local site.

They are commonly employed with longer term tasks, such as building up substantial local skill bases. Delegates, in contrast, are paid by their home office and employed for shorter term projects. Since at least 1990 there is a trend of increasing the number of expatriates moving between subsidiaries and to Germany, as compared to the amount of German expatriates moving to other countries. This serves the strategic purpose of decentralizing the operations and strengthening the international network.

4   Internationally working personnel officers are identified as a separate group. They are tasked with selecting, supporting and coordinating international transferees, teams and business travellers.

Internationally working employees of all these categories can take part in **intercultural training** as part of their development plan. Such training thereby serves as a platform for exchanging intercultural know-how. In-house training is offered on general intercultural sensitivity, specific intercultural skills such as negotiation and presentation. Country-specific training is conducted for all relevant countries. International teams can request teambuilding workshops and follow-ups throughout their lifecycle. Training is also provided for leading international virtual teams. Intercultural coaching and post-merger integration support takes place on request. For all long-term transferees, places on intercultural pre-departure training and returnee workshops are guaranteed. On their return, expatriates are invited to be trained as country advisers and to join pre-departure trainings in that role. A cycle of intercultural knowledge transfer is thereby created.

At management level, international employees are developed through special programmes. In an **international development programme**, young leadership potential is selected internationally, sent to Germany for on-the-job training for 1 year and provided with various training measures. A special talent pool is selected for a **management development programme** that exists at different national locations. At an early stage of the programme, a 1-week intercultural training is conducted. At a later stage, trainees of different locations join a real-life international project over a period of 4 to 6 months. The task of the project is provided by any of the business areas. Feedback is given by an experienced coach, project sponsors and top management.

This amount of intercultural development, in particular for non-transferees, is above average when compared within Germany (Konradt et al. 2002: 201). It does not come as a surprise then that the Robert Bosch Group has been at the forefront of intercultural support since the beginning, in the early 1990s. Its training policy is also embedded in a corporate culture that explicitly names 'cultural diversity' as one of its core values and a vision stating that additional force shall be drawn from the multitude of national cultures within the company.

Questions

In today's global environment, many forms of international work – within the confines of a state or across national borders – exist. Choose one organization you are familiar with and examine:

1 What forms of international work this organization uses.
2 Why these approaches are used.
3 Weaknesses or risks associated with the current approach.
4 What ideas/steps may be developed to improve the situation.

Fragmentation of international resourcing or coherent integration?

As the examples throughout the text show, firms have recognized the management value of these modern forms of international working. However, the degree of their organizational integration is still open to debate. Two aspects seem crucial: integration into organizational routines and into strategic HRM.

First, integration into organizational routines requires signals acknowledging that practices belong to the standard repertoire of an organization (e.g. established practical routines, explicit organizational policies and procedures or specialized organizational units). Specifically, a clear understanding of the monetary and non-monetary costs involved is a crucial test in organizations operating under the dictum of scarce resources.

Given the great variety of forms of international working and the scarce empirical evidence, it is, of course, difficult to generalize. By and large, however, it seems fair to say that while established practical routines have emerged, the integration of these modern forms of working into explicit organizational policies and procedure lags behind. Most likely, this is truer for some of the forms discussed such as self-initiated movers and less the case for more established forms such as international commuters or virtual teams.

Especially telling is the awareness of and management of costs, i.e. the difficulty to gain meaningful management information, capability data and insights into discernible motives for the use of each form of working. One has to concede that firms are unlikely to have the data that enable tight cost control of many of these forms of working – certainly this will be true of frequent commuters where there are hidden travel and coordination costs. The use of international transferees, virtual teams and self-initiated movers are all tactics (the word is informative) often aimed at reducing costs of international coordination.

Yet even here, experience often shows firms that the initial setup costs are unexpectedly high. This is because integration requires three outcomes: the development of sufficient shared understanding of and alignment with the strategy

233

(sensemaking); trust to ensure effective operation of modern forms of international working; and the ability of the form to build understanding in the organization at large (sensegiving). To the extent that firms use these forms of working without dealing with these issues, the initiatives are not driven by strategy but by reaction. Yet, for other forms of international working, such as the use of immigration to address skills shortages and gaps in international capability or the use of centres of excellence to streamline and develop the provision of capability, it appears that there is a clearer economic and skills supply rationale.

Second, integration into strategic HRM is another important criterion for judging whether we are witnessing fragmentation of international working or not. This includes, most prominently, the link with existing HR core processes and to the strategic goals of the organization. There needs to be 'line of sight' to and from these individuals back into the core HR systems, such as talent management and performance management processes. Ensuring this was difficult even for small elites of centrally reporting expatriates, and likely will be shown to be even more challenging for some of the forms of working covered here. If any sense of coherence to international strategy and coordination is to be delivered, then two very practical questions can be asked of organizations looking across these forms of working:

1 Do firms know who the talent is and where it resides within their remote operational centres, cross-border teams and networks and self-initiated movers in third-country operations? Most talent management systems have only limited information about relatively small centrally overseen populations. International experience and expertise is now much more diffuse and distributed among these modern forms of working.
2 Even if firms do know where their talent is, do they have a high-quality and consistent management process that 'touches' these people or is their management left to the vagaries of overstretched line management? Do, for example, country HR business partners have any 'line of sight' to key individuals, or collective knowledge, that resides within and across these modern forms of international management?

We suspect not, but, to be fair, this assertion has yet to be tested. Regarding the link to the organization's strategic goals, this is arguably the most weakly developed aspect of the discussed forms of international working. While they grow out of concrete needs and opportunities when facing processes of internationalization of the organization and its various input and output markets, currently it is hard to see how these forms of international resourcing are coherently linked to the overall strategy.

234

NEW RESEARCH AGENDA

This chapter shows that one cannot separate out research into modern forms of international working from the broader psychological, social, organizational and societal contexts that such patterns of working create. Viewing many of the developments in modern forms of international working under a broader academic umbrella with research at different analytical levels would seem to be a fruitful way forward.

At a micro-level, a common issue that cuts across these modern forms of international working is the need to understand both the motivations for individuals to engage in this type of work and the required attitudes, skills and competencies. Clearly, most of our understanding about this has been based on the study of expatriate success and to a lesser extent the development of an international mindset. Rather than relying on knowledge about expatriates and global leaders, as a consequence of international resourcing policies, organizations face a new context of *intra-cultural diversity*. Some recent psychological work has focused specifically on some of the newer forms of international working drawing on social cognitive career theory to explain how career interests develop and how people successfully function within cultures. This type of research will have some clear practical benefits for selection, assessment and development of many forms of international employees, but especially for those HR functions relying on more culturally diverse workforces, even in domestic markets. They show the importance of personal agency, also called *self-efficacy* (Bandura 1997), collective agency skills, but also the stability of the attitude of receptivity to international careers and its early development. Broadening the perspective, the question of personal and professional identity emerges. Rapid changes between various work locations in different countries and cultures, belonging to a cadre of internationals with little or no attachment to a 'home country' leads to questions about how individuals cope with the lack of external structures supporting personal and social identity.

At the meso-level of the organization, several research issues can be identified. They include questions such as:

- How (fast) is the management of these modern forms of working internationally transformed into standardized HR activities?
- What effects do a greater diversity of the workforce and the existence of a variety of international work forms have on other employees and on organizational processes such as knowledge sharing, strategic alignment or speed of organizational change?
- How do organizations cope with an increasingly internationally mobile workforce that leaves universities and business schools, ready to take on international positions throughout their careers as 'born or socialized internationals'?

235

In addition, transcending the current focus on firms would seem beneficial. Much research is done in the business context, implicitly meaning large firms. However, modern forms of working internationally also frequently occur in organizations such as small and medium-sized enterprises (SMEs); non-profit and non-governmental organizations (NPOs, NGOs); international organizations belonging to supra-national bodies such as the UN or the EU; newly internationalizing companies working the market on a strictly regional basis as is the case in many EU border regions. Looking at these organizations can lead to a more refined understanding of varieties of working internationally.

At a macro-level there are some very important changes taking place within the field. From the research covered in this chapter it can be seen that as globalization progresses, the field of IHRM is both broadening and engaging in a dialogue with other disciplines. For example, Ashton et al. (2008) drew on both the national business system and IHRM literatures to contextualize the nature of skill supply strategies. This directs attention towards a pressing research need at the macro-level: to unravel the external and societal impact that the development of new internal skills webs has at a national and policy level and concern about the types of knowledge and skills that global HR strategies are delivering. Pointing towards more interdisciplinary research, the study on the use of high-skilled migrants as a source of international labour by Salt and Millar (2006) discussed earlier has brought perspectives from the field of economic geography into the IHRM literature. In addition, regional studies taking into account the cultural, institutional and natural specifics of world regions and their effects on different forms of working internationally in these regions are needed. The EU with its specific institutional environment or Africa with its high number of developing countries provide examples for this.

Hence, in the years to come, we should expect to see increasing synthesis and reliance on cross-disciplinary research into the phenomena that are thrown up by modern forms of international working.

KEY LEARNING POINTS

- In addition to expatriation, modern forms of working internationally emerge due to global change drivers, e.g. increase in cross-border business transactions and programmes sponsoring international mobility; organizational factors such as emerging global internal labour markets; and individual determinants (e.g. changing career and life concepts).
- Modern forms of working internationally include international commuters; employees utilized on long-term business trips; inpatriate managers and permanent cadres of global managers; self-initiated movers transferring abroad on their own initiative; immigrants actively and passively attracted to

a national labour market; virtual international employees active in cross-border project teams; skilled individuals working in geographically remote centres of excellence serving global operations.

- Organizational and HR expertise only partly covers modern forms of working internationally, thus underscoring the importance of individual competencies; while this supports personal development, it also comprises the risk of fragmentation and little coherence.

- Modern forms of working internationally are only partially integrated into organizational routines and strategic HRM; organizations still have a long way to go due to the recency of the phenomenon and the difficulties involved.

- Future research should be interdisciplinary and encompass macro-level issues, e.g. the role of various institutional contexts for different forms of working internationally and their management; meso-level issues such as the way and speed of integration of these work forms into HRM; and micro-level aspects (e.g. required competencies and identity issues).

REFERENCES

Arthur, M.B. and Rousseau, D.B. (eds) (1996) *The Boundaryless Career. A New Employment for a New Organizational Era,* New York, Oxford: Oxford University Press.

Ashton, D., Brown, P. and Lauder, H. (2008) 'Developing a theory of skills for global HR', in P.R. Sparrow (ed.) *Handbook of International HR Research: Integrating People, Process and Context,* Oxford: Blackwell.

Axtell, C.M., Fleck, S.J. and Turner, N. (2004) 'Virtual teams: collaborating across distance', in C.L. Cooper and I.T. Robertson (eds) *International Review of Industrial and Organizational Psychology* 19:205–248.

Bandura, A. (1997) *Self-efficacy: The Exercise of Control,* New York: W.H. Freeman.

Bandura, A. (2001) 'Social cognitive theory: an agentic perspective', *Annual Review of Psychology* 52:1–26.

Bandura, A. (2002) 'Social cognitive theory in cultural context', *Applied Psychology: An International Review* 51, 2:269–290.

Barrett, A., Bergin, A. and Duffy, D. (2006) 'The labour market characteristics and labour market impacts of immigrants in Ireland', *Economic and Social Review* 37, 1:1–26.

Berger, S. (2005) *How We Compete. What Companies Around the World are Doing to Make in Today's Global Economy,* New York: Doubleday.

Briscoe, D.R. and Schuler, R. (2004) *International Human Resource Management,* 2nd edn, London: Routledge.

Brousseau, K.R., Driver, M.J., Eneroth, K. and Larsson, R. (1996) 'Career pandemoniums: realigning organizations and individuals', *Academy of Management Executive* 10, 4:52–66.

Brown, P. and Lauder, H. (2006) 'Globalisation, knowledge and the myth of the magnet economy', *Globalisation, Societies and Education* 4, 1:25–51.

Canney-Davison, S. and Ward, K. (1999) *Leading International Teams*, Berkshire: McGraw-Hill.

CIPD (2005) *Recruitment, Retention and Turnover Annual Survey Report*, London: CIPD.

Clark, P.F., Steward, J.B. and Clark, D.A. (2006) 'The globalisation of the labour market for health-care professionals', *International Labour Review* 145, 1/2:37–64.

Czerny, A. (2004) 'UK's foreign trawl continues', *People Management* 10, 20:7.

DiStefano, J.J. and Maznevski, M. (2000) 'Creating value with diverse teams in global management', *Organizational Dynamics* 29, 1:45–63.

Dowling, P., Engle, A. and Festing, M. (2008) *International Dimensions of Human Resource Management: Managing People in a Multinational Context*, 5th edition, London: Thomson Publishing.

Frawley, M. (2006) 'Irish resistance', *People Management* 12, 10:44–45.

GMAC Global Relocation Services (2005) *Global Relocation Trends 2005 Survey Report*, Woodridge, IL: GMAC.

Guthrie, J.P., Ash, R.A. and Stevens, C.D. (2003) 'Are women "better" than men? Personality differences and expatriate selection', *Journal of Managerial Psychology* 18, 3:229–243.

Hall, D.T. and Mirvis, P. (1996) 'The new Protean career: psychological success and the path with a heart', in D.T. Hall (ed.) *The Career is Dead – Long Live the Career*, San Francisco: Jossey-Bass.

Harris, H. (2000) *New Forms of International Working*, Cranfield: Center for Research into the Management of Expatriation.

Harris, H., Brewster, C. and Erten, C. (2005) 'Auslandseinsatz, aber wie? Klassisch oder alternative Formen: neueste empirische Erkenntnisse aus Europa und den USA', in G. Stahl, W. Mayrhofer and T.M. Kühlmann (eds) *Internationales Personalmanagement. Neue Aufgaben, neue Lösungen*, Münich: Hampp.

Harvey, M.G., Price, M.F., Speier, C. and Novicevic, M.M. (1999a) 'The role of inpatriates in a globalization strategy and challenges associated with the inpatriation process', *Human Resource Planning* 12, 1:38–50.

Harvey, M., Speier, C. and Novicevic, M.M. (1999b) 'The role of inpatriation in global staffing', *International Journal of Human Resource Management* 10, 3:459–476.

Hertel, G., Geister, S. and Konradt, U. (2005) 'Managing virtual teams: a review of current empirical research', *Human Resource Management Review* 15: 69–95.

Inkson, K. and Myers, B.A. (2003) 'The big OE: self-directed travel and career development', *Career Development International* 8, 4:170–182.

Inkson, K., Arthur, M.B., Pringle, J. and Barry, S. (1997) 'Expatriate assignment versus overseas experience: contrasting models of international human resource development', *Journal of World Business* 32, 4:351–368.

Janssens, M. and Brett, J.M. (2006) 'Cultural intelligence in global teams: a fusion model of collaboration', *Group and Organization Management* 31, 1:124–153.

Konradt, U., Hertel, U. and Behr, B. (2002) 'Interkulturelle Management Trainings. Eine Bestandsaufnahme von Konzepten, Methoden und Modalitäten in Deutschland', *Zeitschrift für Sozialpsychologie* 33, 4:197–207.

Linehan, M. and Mayrhofer, W. (2005) 'International careers and repatriation', in H. Scullion and M. Linehan (eds) *International Human Resource Management*, Basingstoke and New York: Palgrave.

Mayerhofer, H., Hartmann, L.C. and Herbert, A. (2004a) 'Career management issues for flexpatriate international staff', *Thunderbird International Business Review* 46, 6:647–666.

Mayerhofer, H., Hartmann, L.C., Michelitsch-Riedl, G. and Kollinger, I. (2004b) 'Flexpatriate assignments: a neglected issue in global staffing', *International Journal of Human Resource Management* 15, 8:1371–1389.

Mayrhofer, W. and Scullion, H. (2002) 'Female expatriates in international business. Empirical evidence from the German clothing industry', *International Journal of Human Resource Management* 13, 4:815–836.

McDonough, E.F., Kahn, K.B. and Barczak, G. (2001) 'An investigation of the use of global, virtual and collocated new product development teams', *Journal of Product Innovation Management* 18:110–120.

Mendenhall, M.E., Kühlmann, T.M. and Stahl, G. (2000) *Developing Global Business Leaders: Policies, Processes, and Innovations,* New York: Quorum Books.

Peppas, S.C. (2004) 'Making the most of international assignments: a training model for non-resident expatriates', *Journal of American Academy of Business,* 5, 1/2: 41–46.

Salt, J. and Millar, J. (2006) 'International migration in interesting times: the case of the UK', *People and Place* 14, 2:14–25.

Schein, E.H. (1978) *Career Dynamics: Matching Individual and Organizational Needs,* Reading, MA: Addison-Wesley.

Sparrow, P.R. (2007) 'Globalisation of HR at function level: four UK-based case studies of the international recruitment and selection process', *International Journal of Human Resource Management* 18, 5:144–166.

Sparrow, P.R., Brewster, C. and Harris, H. (2004) *Globalizing Human Resource Management,* London: Routledge.

Stanek, M.B. (2000) 'The need for global managers: a business necessity', *Management Decision* 38, 4:232–244.

Suutari, V. (2003) 'Global managers: career orientation, career tracks, life-style implications and career commitment', *Journal of Managerial Psychology* 18, 3:185–207.

Suutari, V. and Brewster, C. (2000) 'Making their own way: international experience through self-initiated foreign assignments', *Journal of World Business* 35, 4:417–432.

Suutari, V. and Taka, M. (2004) 'Career anchors of managers with global careers', *Journal of Management Development* 23, 9:833–847.

Tharenou, P. (2003) 'The initial development of receptivity to working abroad: self-initiated international work opportunities in young graduate employees', *Journal of Occupational and Organizational Psychology* 76:489–515.

Ward, C. (1996) 'Acculturation', in D. Landis and R.S. Bhagat (eds) *Handbook of Intercultural Training,* 2nd edn, Thousand Oaks, CA: Sage.

Ward, K. (2004) 'Going global? Internationalization and diversification in the temporary staffing industry', *Journal of Economic Geography* 4:251–273.

Zimmermann, A. and Sparrow, P. (2007) 'Mutual adjustment processes in international teams: lessons for the study of expatriation', *International Studies in Management and Organization* 37, 3:65–88.

Chapter 12

Capitalizing on an international career

Career capital perspectives

Noeleen Doherty and Michael Dickmann

CHAPTER OBJECTIVES

By the end of this chapter, readers will have:

- an overview of current ideas on careers
- a review of the concept of intelligent careers
- an awareness and understanding of the impact of the global context on careers
- an appreciation of organizational and individual issues in career management
- an understanding of the different phases within international assignments and their career capital impact
- a critique of current organizational practice in developing global career capital

INTRODUCTION

Careers are one mechanism that provides a link between individuals and their social and work habitats. As such, careers become channels for an individual's contribution to the effectiveness and efficiency of a company and for facilitating individual growth and development. In today's volatile and progressively global work environment, career management is a crucial issue for organizations attempting to maintain the right resources for survival and to sustain competitive advantage. Career management is not only an organizational issue but there is increasing onus on the individual to take responsibility for career self-management as the paradigm of career undergoes fundamental shifts. This chapter focuses on the dual nature of career management in the global environment and draws attention to individual careering and organizational structures and policies. It explores the concept of the intelligent career in understanding the current issues in career management within, across and outside organizations. The chapter includes a discussion of organizational and individual career issues related to the periods before, during and after international work. It challenges received wisdom on the utility of international careers and rehearses some of the current dilemmas for both companies and their employees.

CURRENT VIEWPOINTS ON CAREERS

Careers have been defined either as a sequence of positions filled by a person throughout their life; or through an aspect of their life such as their involvement in work (Arthur et al. 1989). The determinants of career include both individual factors such as gender and learning behaviour and organizational factors including development practices and learning opportunities. Career consequences can be measured as objective outcomes such as salary and hierarchical development; and as subjective outcomes such as perceptions of personal success, health and work–life balance. Career management systems and processes have been employed by many organizations in an attempt to direct the work behaviours of employees. In addition, career management is used to promote the development of individuals.

The concept of career has attracted much interest since the organizational parameters that have traditionally defined individual development and progression have undergone an almost complete metamorphosis over the last two decades. Traditional normative views of careers have characterized them as structured, predictable, hierarchical, competitive and organizationally focused. However, shifts in organizational structures and the relationships between employers and employees have led to new perspectives and concepts describing careers.

Researchers are increasingly observing new patterns in contemporary careers and this is attracting a whole new vocabulary and lexicon to describe and help understand the unfolding of careers within the shifting world of work. Terms such as 'kaleidoscope', 'boundaryless', 'post-industrial' and 'Protean' careers are now common in current texts, academic papers and practitioner vocabulary. Inkson (2006) suggested that at present there is an upsurge in the use of such metaphors in the study of careers, contributing to a more effective analysis of how individuals perceive their career and providing a richer illustration of the concepts being used to describe career.

According to Arthur and Rousseau (1996) boundaryless careers are sequences of job opportunities that go beyond the boundaries of single employment settings. This definition involves six different meanings of boundaryless careers, namely careers that:

1 move across the boundaries of separate employers
2 draw validation and marketability from outside the present employer

241

3 are sustained by external networks or information
4 break traditional organizational assumptions about hierarchy and career advancement
5 involve an individual rejecting existing career opportunities for personal or family reasons
6 are based on the interpretation of the career actor, who may perceive a boundaryless future regardless of structural constraints.

Sullivan and Arthur (2006) further developed the concept of the boundaryless career to capture the degree of career mobility, psychological and physical, experienced by the individual. Physical mobility includes changing jobs, moving across occupational boundaries as well as traversing cultural and geographical boundaries. Psychological mobility, by the same token, concerns the individual's perceptions of their capability to change and make such physical transitions.

Emphasizing the dynamic nature of the current context within which careers are realized, Baruch (2006) suggested that the dichotomous views of careers as traditional and organizationally focused as opposed to non-traditional and individually focused (boundaryless, Protean) do not capture the current reality. Rather, in our more complex world, hierarchical mobility co-exists with boundaryless opportunities. There is still a key role for organizations to play in career management and development, albeit more synchronous with the input of the individual. Focusing on global careers, Baruch (2006) argued that this poses two major challenges:

1 maintaining the threads of a general strategy while meeting the need for variations in systems that can operate across diverse contexts
2 the management of expatriation and repatriation – both the physical processes of movement and the psychological resilience required by these processes.

The career capital concept, outlined later, has been used as a frame of reference to explore the challenge of managing global careers. By capturing individual awareness and perception of capabilities that underpin and sustain psychological mobility, the career capital concept provides a means of exploring the international work experience. Further, the career capital concept can be used to map company and individual competencies and help to explore the alignment (or misalignment) of organizational and individual goals.

Concept of career capital

Quinn (1992) discussed the notion of the intelligent enterprise, focusing on the development and deployment of intellectual resources as opposed to the then

242

existing focus on the management of physical assets. Hailed as a new paradigm, this view provoked a rethink of many of the traditional views on the employment relationship and careers. Core competencies were proposed as key to delineating the scope of a firm's activity and what differentiated Quinn's view was the fundamental change in the employment relationship which bestowed increased agency on the individual.

The intelligent company: the intelligent career

Arthur et al. (1995) proposed that a new career paradigm was emerging in which the rules of the employment relationship were shifting from loyalty to exchange, from loyalty to one employer to occupational excellence, from power centralized in HQ to a strategic impetus at the business unit level, from a fortress to a regional approach and from corporate allegiance to project allegiance. These changes meant that an individual's career could hold currency in a much more fluid, flexible and opportunistic way. To expose the impact of these changes Arthur ct al. (1995) suggested a complementary approach to individual competencies, embodied in the intelligent career concept. This was an attempt to map the organizational competencies of culture, know-how and networks against employee competencies. The authors suggested that intelligent careers are the fundamental units through which people's and employer firms' competencies evolve over time (p. 9) and that each area of firm competency is paralleled by a complementary form of knowledge at the individual level.

Building blocks of the intelligent career

The concept of career capital is one mechanism for capturing the career experience. According to Arthur et al. (1995) the development of personal career competencies occurs across three distinct areas that mirror firm competencies. These areas are 'knowing whom', 'knowing how' and 'knowing why'.

Knowing whom competencies describe the personal contacts and networks in which individuals engage. Knowing whom encompasses the range of interpersonal relationships the individual has access to and the networks and contacts that they can contribute to the organizational network. These include career-related networks, but also extend to personal contacts that can be a resource for learning, accessing expertise and developing reputation. The individual's networks can be a source of social connections both for the organization's benefit (e.g. customers) and also a potential source of alternative employment for the individual (e.g. competitors). These social connections provide opportunities for building reputation, a knowledge resource and an opportunity to learn from others, as well as offering prospects for new jobs. Within the international context, it has been suggested that expatriation can facilitate the development of the social and political skills

243

essential to the crafting of global leadership skills. Exploiting the opportunity of expatriation to develop social connections and networks requires a delicate balance between maintaining home connections while building new networks (Harvey and Novicevic 2004).

Knowing how career competencies are concerned with the skills, knowledge and abilities that the individual brings to the organization, which they can develop over time. These are developed, Arthur et al. (1995) argued, both through formal learning in the occupational context and also through other learning opportunities such as on-the-job experiential activities. The emphasis is on the acquisition of a broad and flexible skills base and occupational rather than specific job-related learning. The intelligent career approach emphasizes the need for individual commitment to acquiring and enhancing a relevant and transferable knowledge and skill portfolio. Some authors suggest that international knowledge and experience is a valuable, unique and hard to imitate resource that differentiates global competitors (Peng and York 2001) and is a strategic role fulfilled by expatriates (Welch 2003). Therefore, in the increasingly competitive environment of global business, individuals and organizations need to continually develop and deploy know-how in new and innovative ways to meet the challenge of maintaining a competitive edge. The technical know-how, but increasingly the softer skills such as an ability to tune into cultural cues as suggested by Earley and Ang (2003) are now considered key capabilities underpinning success in the global context.

The *knowing why* competency concerns the nature and degree of the employee's identification with the employing firm. This identification is grounded in the individual's general work motivation and their personal beliefs, values and identity. These can impact upon the individual's level of adaptability and commitment to the employment environment and influence the person's identification with the employing firm's culture. Arthur et al. (1995) suggested that knowing why often involves non-work issues such as family context and dual-career issues and often evokes alternative employment choices to the traditional permanent full-time employment option. Mendenhall (2006) suggested that the core dimensions required for global leadership include organizing ability, visioning, business expertise, ability in building and maintaining relationships and cognitive capabilities such as the capacity to deal with complexity and a global mindset. It was suggested that the underlying dispositions that facilitate global leadership include traits such as commitment, maturity and inquisitiveness. Eby et al. (2003) explored the components of the 'knowing why' competency that could predict career success. They proposed that career identity (comprising career insight, knowledge of strengths and weaknesses and specific career goals), proactive personality (defined as the dispositional tendency towards proactive behaviour, i.e. demonstrating initiative, perseverance, opportunistic) and openness (imaginative, curious, broadminded and active, seeking out new experiences and new ideas) were the key components of knowing why. Also, they suggested that knowing

244

whom comprises both internal and external network resources that can provide important avenues to pursue career progression. Knowing how encompasses continuous learning geared to facilitate the development of skills, knowledge and abilities which are transferable across organizations with the result of developing a broad base of skills that hold currency both within the employing organization and in other companies. Developing this broad portfolio bestows on the individual the ability to move across organizational boundaries more readily. Their analysis found that all three ways of knowing are important to predicting individual perceptions of career success and perceived internal and external marketability. They indicated that all three types of career competence are likely to add value to the individual's career; however, the influence of the three ways of knowing on perceptions of success showed different patterns. Knowing how was perceived as most important to external marketability while knowing why was predictive of perceived career success and internal marketability.

The debate on intelligent careers continued and Inkson and Arthur (2001) extolled the virtues of becoming a successful career capitalist. Further shifting the career lens back to the individual and away from the organization, their piece placed agency firmly with the person. In their view taking an individual perspective on the development of career capital would serve to provide new insights into personal motivations and economic life in general. Supporting an individual career capitalist stance would, they argued, prove beneficial not only to the person but included multiple positive outcomes for companies, industry and the economy.

Seibert et al. (2001) found that social capital, conceptualized as network structures and social resources, contributed to the career success (both objective and subjective) of individuals through providing access to information, resources and career sponsorship. The social capital of global leaders has been considered essential to their ability to bridge and buffer relations between the HQ and subsidiary offices, facilitating their role as boundary spanners (Harvey and Novicevic 2004). Thus, a capital perspective has provided useful illumination of the various talents required to make a successful global leader.

CAREERS IN A GLOBAL CONTEXT

Global career strategies are an enduring organizational and individual phenomenon and are considered by some to be the key to successfully competing in the global marketplace (Black et al. 1999). Many organizations and employees now follow global strategies as companies formally endorse the significance of international careers in their drive to operate across international boundaries. It is suggested that international assignments (IAs) increase the competitive position of organizations by increasing the capability to function successfully in a global

245

environment (Sparrow et al. 2004). Strategies, policies and practices based on the assumption that international experience is beneficial to both company and employee, actively endeavour to develop future global leaders, through the use of development programmes and IAs often populated by those identified as high potential.

Mutual dependency

Several authors have argued that there is a dependency of organizations on individuals, related to the scarcity and criticality of employees to success. For individuals, dependency on organizations is due to their needs for security, prestige and sensemaking (Larsen 2004; Cappellen and Janssens 2005). This mutual dependency is especially prominent within global careers where the investment of organizations and the risks that individuals take are especially high (Dickmann and Harris 2005).

For the purpose of this chapter, we want to explore the mutual dependency in global career terms, using a long-term perspective that extends across the IA experience and beyond, to consider the outcomes over time. Our work builds on the expatriation cycle (Sparrow et al. 2004) but focuses more on the career issues that arise and distinguishes between organizational and individual career management. The original expatriation cycle embraces organizational activities in areas such as the strategic planning of expatriation, selection, pre-departure preparation, performance management, remuneration and repatriation. These activities can be organized into three phases (Harzing and Christensen 2004):

- pre-departure phase
- assignment phase
- post-assignment phase.

This categorization can also be employed with respect to the career strategies and career management and behaviour of individuals. Figure 12.1 depicts international career management systems, processes and activities of organizations and individuals. It presents a simplified view of organizational and individual perspectives on international careers in order to create an overview that incorporates key career actors over time. The outer ring represents the temporal perspective that distinguishes the time before international work, the time span during which an individual is embedded in a foreign culture at work and the time after the expatriate or other overseas assignment has ended. The next ring (inwards) outlines key stages that an individual goes through in expatriation. In the pre-departure phase individuals evaluate the likely consequences of working abroad and make a decision as to whether they want to expatriate and on what terms, which often includes negotiation with their employer (Dickmann et al. forthcoming).

246

Figure 12.1 *International career management from organizational and individual perspectives.*

Then they are likely to start some form of preparation for their IA. Once individuals (and potentially their families) have relocated, they may experience culture shock, go through a phase of adaptation (see Chapter 7) and are likely to acquire career capital (Cappellen and Janssens 2005; Dickmann and Harris 2005; Jokinen et al. forthcoming). In the post-assignment phase they are prone to experience reverse culture shock and a change to their lifestyles and expectations. In their new role(s) within the organization they are likely to attempt to use and to continue to build on the career capital they have acquired while working abroad (Dickmann and Doherty 2007).

The dividers between the stages are not solid, as many behaviours and individual attitudes have spillover effects on other stages. For instance, pre-departure preparation (see Chapter 6) may be augmented by post-arrival preparations and learning. The negotiated 'contract' may have implications for formal organizational support mechanisms such as those that may affect the three ways of knowing and, therefore, career capital acquisition. Examples might be formal seminars, travel home budgets, executive coaching opportunities that may have been determined in the expatriation 'deal'. Moreover, the 'deal' may also have implications for the post-assignment time in terms of job security, career progression and monetary compensation. For instance, a guaranteed job, a promotion and/or tie-over pay may have been negotiated between the individual and the employing organization.

The inner ring around international careers depicts the organizational perspective of international careers. In the pre-departure stage organizations define the purpose of international work, plan the assignment, select the individual, administer the relocation programme and conduct (preparatory) training and development (Chapters 5 and 6). The strategic purpose of international work has manifold implications in relation to areas such as the focus on the payoff time span, development and retention activities (Dickmann and Doherty 2006). Given certain support practices (compensation, family support) some of the key organizational activities during the assignment centre around performance management and development, aimed at the individual, potential local successors or broader teams and the career management of individuals (Sparrow et al. 2004). In the post-assignment stage the organizational activities concentrate on the (re-)integration of individuals in the next location and on the retention of these individuals (see Chapter 9 for a discussion of repatriation as part of a career lifecycle).

Figure 12.1 also exposes that in each of the three key stages individuals interact with other actors representing the organization. These organizational representatives can be from the parent-country HR department, business sponsors or other key people in the sending unit; and executives and the immediate superior in the receiving unit. While individuals are the managers of their career capital, the organizational representatives, often working with the existing development and career system, exert an influence on the international careers of assignees.

While Figure 12.1 is useful to draw attention to processes and interactions that are ongoing during the three phases of international mobility, the reality is neither linear nor simple. For instance, an individual does not only use accumulated career capital after the IA but also during work abroad. One example may be the use of newly acquired networks to gain a new position in a different location before the official assignment period runs out. Equally, from an organizational perspective, the international development of individuals does not only take place during their overseas assignment but is likely to start before the assignment in the preparation phase. Overall, Figure 12.1 depicts the broad areas that have been discussed in the literature, matches them to their relevant phase and enables the development of greater sensitivity to the various interactions that take place between individuals and their employers. The remainder of this

248

chapter will concentrate on the three phases of before, during and after international working.

BEFORE INTERNATIONAL WORKING

Rationale for international careers

There are high financial costs associated with traditional expatriation, yet companies continue to invest heavily in this strategy, with growing demands for more international assignees. Research has shown that all forms of international working, including long-term expatriation, short-term assignments, frequent flying and cross-national commuting, are growing in popularity, with expatriate populations on the increase (Harris et al. 2003).

The organizational drivers for using IAs have been critiqued as lacking clarity (Thomas 1998). The purpose of the IA is multifarious. A variety of organizational drivers have been articulated including skills gap filling, launching new initiatives, transferring technology, transferring knowledge, establishing or consolidating managerial control, developing management and global expertise, performance-related or cultural transfer. In a classic analysis, Edström and Galbraith (1977) identified three major purposes: first, management development; second, to help control and coordination, often through the transfer of firm culture; and third, filling positions when qualified locals were not available. Recent research identified that one in five IAs had development and career reasons as a primary organizational purpose with several companies planning to increase the percentage of assignments with a developmental impetus (Dickmann et al. 2006).

For global organizations, the ability to achieve sustained competitive advantage relies on the capability to deal with an array of complex variables including diverse cultural contexts, a range of competitive environments, control, coordination and the capability to leverage innovation across geographical boundaries. Gregersen et al. (1998) from a survey of Fortune 500 firms suggested that global leaders need a set of context-specific abilities and must have a core of certain characteristics for successful leadership. In a further survey of 50 firms across Europe, North America and Asia, the authors found four strategies that are used to develop competent global leaders: foreign travel, establishment of teams comprising individuals with diverse backgrounds and perspectives, training and transfers. Executives reported that their IA experience was the single most influential leadership development experience. The drivers of international working as a conduit to developing individual career capital are particularly apparent in companies where global talent development is a key strand in the organizational strategy (as outlined in the case that follows).

249

Organizational career capital development: creating a global talent pipeline

Case study 12.1
Linking IAs into talent pipelines at Company P

A central tenet in the utilization of IAs is the development of global leaders who can manage the increasing complexity of running an international business in order to compete successfully in a global environment. All too often, recent industry surveys have indicated that although the demand for international assignees is on the rise, employees are becoming increasingly discerning about committing to an IA. Multinational companies need to achieve performance on the current and subsequent assignments and also need to retain such individuals as part of the organization's talent pool. Therefore, identifying talented individuals who are willing to take up an IA and retaining them following assignment become the key foundations of a successful global development strategy. Additionally, internal promotion and improved performance over time become the challenge of populating and maintaining a top talent flow within the company.

Within Company P, IAs are business driven, not developmental, and objectives are set for the role and not the individual or the assignment. This clearly articulated business rationale means that IAs are not considered a must for career progression per se. However, the company does generate a focus on how IAs fit within talent management. The succession planning process considers the experiences required by individuals to facilitate their progress and to maintain a talent flow within the company. Thus, IAs are positioned as one of the critical experiences valued within the general career structure of the organization as a whole.

Since assignments are business driven and role based, the push comes via the job evaluation system. Promotion during assignment is regularly attained and a number of expatriates come back to a promoted role. Data on internal promotion of expatriates show a consistent trend of around one-third being promoted on return. Although there is no guaranteed return home for expatriates (because positions are role-vacancy driven) the organization reports a consistently high retention rate over time. Combined with longer term (over 2 years returned) consistently improving performance among the repatriate populations, these data would indicate the potential for good longer term utilization of skills within the organization with benefits to both company and individual potentially accruing.

250

Individual motivations

In relation to motivational factors, the literature distinguishes developmental and career considerations, the financial impact of working abroad, individual drives and interests, family and partner considerations, as well as national factors such as security or treatment of foreigners as key individual motives to work abroad (Stahl et al. 2002). Of these, career and professional development considerations are identified as among the most important motives for seeking or accepting work abroad. For instance, career advancement is seen as a key motivator for managers to accept an international posting and expatriates appreciate their international experience as an opportunity for personal and professional development and career advancement. Moreover, internationally mobile employees value the opportunity to learn unusual skills and gather foreign experiences in order to progress their careers. Future job and the impact of foreign work on their own development and career opportunities are likely to be key considerations of internationally mobile individuals (Yan et al. 2002; Dickmann et al. 2005).

Dickmann et al. (2005) explored the importance of a range of 25 motives such as career progression, perception of career risk, willingness of spouse to move and host-country factors in the expatriate's decision-making process. A sample of 310 individuals and organizational representatives from these employees' companies were asked to rate the importance attributed to these motives. While individuals regarded developmental and job-related aspects as significantly more important to their decision to go on an assignment, corporate respondents underestimated the influence of these factors and overestimated issues such as location and the financial impact of taking an assignment. Overall, career capital considerations and the longer term impact of an assignment on skills, knowledge and abilities are highly relevant to individual motivations to seek and/or accept the challenge of a global assignment and strategically to the organizational purpose for international working. Therefore, understanding individual motivations and harnessing them will become an increasingly important aspect of successful IA management (Dickmann et al. 2007).

DURING INTERNATIONAL WORKING

The expatriation literature focuses on what qualities are needed for an IA, such as general global leadership characteristics, essential if companies want to capitalize on global markets. The characteristics of such a management cadre include a set of context-specific abilities and a core of global leadership characteristics. These include exhibiting character, embracing duality, managing uncertainty and demonstrating savvy, which are all underpinned by inquisitiveness. Other authors concentrate on the specific elements of the expatriation cycle and conditions for success

251

of an IA (Bhaskar-Shrinivas et al. 2005). However, the competencies, insights and other changes that are the *result* of work abroad are relatively neglected (Bonache et al. 2001).

From a career capital perspective, research in the European context has suggested that an IA is likely to change the social capital (*knowing whom*) of an individual. An expatriate's social networks may be split into global, parent and host contacts. An assignment may give the expatriate access to more senior hierarchical levels on a day-to-day basis and the assignee may create more contacts outside the organization in the new location. However, the foreign work may equally lead to the loss of parent company contacts. Depending on the importance of global, parent and host networks (and the way the expatriate approaches old and new relationships) the overall effect in terms of individual career capital may not be positive (Dickmann and Harris 2005).

An IA may enhance the *knowing how* of assignees through a work context that is different. In comparison, the work abroad may result in skills that are not transferable to the home context (Bonache et al. 2001) or the non-acquisition of new techniques that are being developed at head office. Again, the effect of an IA on knowing how can be positive or negative. Contextual factors that seem to aid the acquisition of knowing how include going to a location that is perceived to be a centre of excellence or inpatriation (a move into headquarters).

An assignment may result in more and diverse insights and the challenging of the existing modus operandi: for instance, when the assignee is confronted with a radically different cultural context and work patterns. While this may lead to a strengthening of purpose and higher motivation, it may result in radical changes to the individual's inner drives and work–life balance (*knowing why*). The effects of the new drives and persuasions on 'traditional' careers within an organizational setting are unclear (Suutari and Brewster 2004).

There are manifold organizational activities that have an impact on the career capital acquisition of individuals. For instance, the professional service firm PricewaterhouseCoopers (see Case study 12.2) used a formal international development approach that explicitly addressed all three career capital areas (Harris and Dickmann 2005).

Other companies concentrate on systems and processes that focus on career and performance management during international work.

While the context of each organization and the specific role of individuals will vary, we present a case where an organization focuses on all three areas of career capital. In HSBC, a global bank, there is an acute awareness of both individual and organizational needs (see Case study 12.3). IAs are based on a business case that also includes career considerations for individuals. In fact, during an individual's work abroad, shadow career planning will be carried out each year so that the person stays 'on the radar screen'. Formal management development is organized on an international basis so that people on assignment have permanent access to

Case study 12.2
Developing career capital at Genesis Park

PricewaterhouseCoopers (PwC), the accounting company, operates a training centre called Genesis Park in the USA. In it, PwC gathered international teams of high-potential individuals (with between 2 and 9 years' work experience) for 5 months of formal development. During this time, knowing why was addressed through intensive coaching sessions, individuals were helped to build their knowing whom through interaction with key internal and external individuals and knowing how was given specific focus through intensive work on business cases and strategic projects. Much of this intervention was carried on after participants returned to their workplaces in that there was a Genesis Park alumni organization for a variety of purposes, including continued networking. Moreover, the projects would be continued and experience exchange supported. From the inception of the programme in February 2001, PwC found that retention among its more than 100 participants in the following 5 years was, at 97%, exceptionally high.

activities designed to broaden their skills, knowledge and abilities. The bank employs various methods to encourage networking, including visits, trips home and regular contacts with a home business sponsor. Moreover, there are conversations planned to explore the assignees' inner drives and motivations, most prominent a career conversation near the end of the expatriation to 'manage expectations'. The case indicates that the role of business sponsor is crucial to the international career approach within IISDC.

The importance of context in steering the ways in which career capital is developed and used by individuals has been highlighted by Dickmann and Harris (2005). They suggested that there can be equivocal outcomes from expatriation experiences.

Other research from a European base has also indicated that the organizational context impacts upon individuals' interpretations and actions. Dickmann and Doherty (2007) suggested that the HR mechanisms employed within different firms impact upon the individual career behaviours of employees. The authors suggested that all three capital areas had the potential to benefit from an IA. However, the organizational context, policies and practices had a different impact on the career capital perceptions and behaviours of expatriates. For example, there were noticeable differences between organizational contexts with respect to knowing whom. In the more formally structured environment of a financial services organization many managers invested their personal time and effort in nurturing and extending their host and global networks to the detriment of maintaining their

253

Case study 12.3
The critical role of the home business sponsor in HSBC

All secondees should have a sponsor at the level of general manager, chief executive or business head, who will:

- sign off the secondment letter
- make sure that the proposed secondee is a member of a talent pool and/or subject expert who is valued by the business and warrants the investment of an international secondment
- ensure that talent pool secondees, in particular, are closely career managed
- ensure a suitable role, ideally utilizing the secondee's new international skills, is found when they return.

The sponsor, or designated senior manager, will also:

- review the annual performance of the secondee, to understand how they are performing and countersign the performance appraisal
- review and sign off the pay, bonus and share awards
- make contact with the secondee on a regular basis
- review the impact of any request to extend the assignment (or localize) on the secondee's career plan
- agree the severance terms if a return role is not identified.

Sponsorship of international secondees should be a key accountability in sponsors' job descriptions. If a sponsor moves to a new role while the secondee is abroad, responsibility should be transferred to the sponsor's successor as part of the handover process. Secondees should also initiate contact with their 'new' sponsor if a change takes place during the life of their secondment. Furthermore, a range of responsibilities and processes are outlined, including how sponsors and HR business partners interact.
Source: Harris and Dickmann (2005)

home contacts. Conversely, for employees in the relatively unstructured social environment of a fast moving consumer goods (FMCG) company, the informal context resulted in concentrated efforts on maintaining and retaining home base networks, with the express intention of securing a job on repatriation to the HQ.

For knowing why, the international experience generally resulted in the maturation of new insights and motivations that were perceived as positive by employees. Among these changes were perceived enhanced marketability and a keener sense of personal career and life goals. These changes could potentially challenge organizational retention goals. There was noticeable diversity in how different organizational cultural contexts and management processes mediated the outcomes. In the financial services company, again the formal systems of career management were geared up to manage expectations and in combination with a strong culture of rewarding loyalty, resulted in none of the repatriates considering or engaging in activities to find alternative employment. In contrast, within the FMCG organization there were no formal mechanisms to manage career aspirations or work–life issues either during or after assignments. Employees were expected to fend for themselves, which resulted in a higher level of readiness to consider leaving the company.

In general, the impact of IA on knowing how was to develop a broader range of capabilities including business acumen and perspective and greater cultural sensitivity. A subtle difference was apparent in that those from the financial services company predominantly acquired softer knowing how skills with few reporting an improvement in technical skills.

While the findings on knowing how improvements are in line with the views of CEOs or HR specialists (Gregersen et al. 1998; Sparrow et al. 2004) and match the perceived general goals of IAs (Caligiuri and Di Santo 2001) they add some nuances with respect to possible detrimental effects of IAs that go beyond current understanding. Expatriation can but does not necessarily improve the perceived skills, knowledge and abilities of individuals. Knowing how could suffer if individuals worked in jobs in which they could not use more highly developed capabilities or be diminished due to individuals not having the opportunity to practise more specialized skills. Knowing whom may benefit by extending the reach of the individual's network, both personal and organizational, and the impact on knowing why may challenge the organizational motives for using expatriation.

The insecure payoff of IAs in terms of career capital fits well with the changing reality of careers within organizations. The dynamic nature of organizations means that a vertical career move after an assignment can normally no longer be offered as a certainty (Stahl et al. 2002). There are still many gaps in our understanding of the outcomes of expatriation. Neither the immediate nor the long-term impact of IAs on the career capital of individuals has been sufficiently researched and more empirical research is needed on linking international work with career capital development.

Although we now have considerable data about both individual and organizational perspectives on expatriation and repatriation, these have largely been researched independently. Many organizations appear to apply a one-size-fits-all approach to managing IAs. However, with the advent of policies and practices which use many variations on the types of international working such as short-term assignments, international commuting and frequent flying, not only is the need to understand individual motivation vital but there is a compelling need to review the IA deal and how it is managed. Yan et al. (2002) highlighted the importance of

255

striving for individual and organizational alignment in the context of IAs and argued that the need for a dynamic perspective is paramount. Since the assignment cycle can vary considerably in duration any mutual expectations set at one point in time may well evolve or change. Such changes may extend across the perceived type of relationship between the individual and the organization and purpose of the assignment, which could have a fundamental impact on individual behaviour.

In contexts where there is a lack of harmony between individual career capital-related behaviour and organizational career and HR management geared to meet strategic business needs, the actions and behaviour and subsequent outcomes of an IA may result in the array of problems. Not only may the assignment be perceived as unsuccessful to the organization at best in terms of poorer job performance or at worst attrition and turnover of the talent pool but for the individual non-alignment may result in frustration and missed opportunities to make use of their acquired skills or in defection to a competitor.

AFTER INTERNATIONAL WORKING

A range of employee concerns about international working have surfaced. High-potential managers may refuse expatriate assignments as they often see them as a career detour or derailment, which causes a hiatus in career progression. Other key barriers were familial strain, financial stress and poor repatriation, where expatriates are given unimportant jobs at reduced salaries meaning they are worse off than before they left (Dickmann et al. 2005). Further concerns included the reluctance to travel to particular locations where there is regional turmoil, lack of communication, role ambiguity, compensation and healthcare benefits. For individuals international work may create higher demands on their capabilities including the challenges of cultural and work adaptation. There are the risks of missed opportunities for career progression while abroad; a lack of career clarity; and often a lack of suitable positions on repatriation (Doherty et al. 2006). A significant frustration appears to be the lack of challenging positions to facilitate use of the capabilities acquired, which can lead to greater intention to leave or exit to another firm.

Chapter 9 has covered the topic of repatriation. A central theme in many studies on international working is the pivotal nature of career issues to repatriation (Suutari and Brewster 2003). However, many writers have acknowledged that the repatriation element of international working lacks a coherent focus and often is not well planned. Therefore there are still gaps in understanding the career impact of an IA (Bonache et al. 2001; Stahl and Cerdin 2004).

What we do know is that, despite compelling reasons for retaining expatriates for their acquired skills and experience, a considerable number leave their company within 1 year of repatriation (Suutari and Brewster 2003). Dickmann et al. (2006) present figures based on 881 returnees in nine firms. During the reporting period of 2005 on average more than twice as many repatriates decided to leave their employer compared to their non-expatriated peers. If leavers were seen as future leaders of the organization and the IA as developmental, this outcome represents a loss to the corporation.

The case of HSBC describes one approach that was viewed as successful by the company. Current research on this topic would suggest that there is much room for improvement in helping repatriates to make use of their skills and to facilitate the integration of individual career capital into the development of organizational human capital.

Rather than repatriation being perceived as the end of an expatriation cycle (see Chapter 9) the potential detrimental effects of repatriation may be more temporary and less severe in terms of repatriate turnover. Individuals who cannot use their acquired skills on return or feel disoriented may suffer a 'career wobble' (Doherty et al. 2006). Such outcomes of expatriation challenge the benefits of the IA for individual career advancement and for company benefits (Dickmann and Harris 2005). Thus, the outcomes of an IA are far from a straightforward win–win scenario (see Case study 12.4).

Case study 12.4
Bob's 'career wobble'

Bob was concerned: it was only about 3 months before his return home from a 3-year IA and there was no defined role for him to return to as yet. In his conversations with HR, which were infrequent, he had been reassured that the company would 'look after him'. They certainly had done that when he went out – everything had gone like clockwork. Accommodation had been sorted out for his family and places at an excellent school secured for his two young daughters. His wife had been able to get involved with the local expatriate community and although she had left behind her job as a teacher in the UK, she had been able to put her experience to good use and was running a crèche and nursery for expatriate families. So, all in all, the experience had been amazing for the family. Bob himself was buoyant with his new appreciation of the global environment that the company had to tackle. He had been on a developmental assignment and was sure that his international exposure would be a real leg up in his career. But the notion of coming back to HQ with no job was very worrying. What would he do? He had been advised that a project role would be waiting for him but that was hardly what he expected after his transformation – surely the fact that he had set up and run the new branch abroad would count for something??

Three months back at home and Bob was still 'on a project' – he felt deflated. The family had been re-accommodated OK, but Bob had struggled to get back into the swing of things. Pushing paper was not on the top of his list on return. And there seemed to be nothing on the horizon. Should he stick with it and see what came up or should he take his very valuable skills, knowledge and experience somewhere else?

Fifteen months back home, Bob was relieved that he had persevered. He had just achieved a promotion to departmental head – a position he knew he was well equipped to fill. The last few months had been frustrating. He had drawn on the extensive network of contacts that he'd developed on assignment throughout the company and had more or less built a role for himself in the first year or so. That gave him the profile to be considered for a key position and at last now was his chance to show them what he could do!

Questions

1 What made Bob feel deflated and frustrated?
2 What are the organizational issues implicit in this case?
3 What could companies do to pre-empt a 'career wobble'? What are the key considerations for organizations in managing careers in a global context?
4 How can individuals like Bob develop and use their career capital?
5 What tensions exist between individuals and organizations in developing career capital?

If companies are to reap the benefits of IAs then short- and particularly longer term issues such as repatriate performance, retention over the longer term and promotion as a proxy for added value to the organization become important factors. Recent research indicates that where companies do not address issues of career progression, security of employment and provide jobs that are meaningful to repatriates (and where they can use their acquired career capital) these organizations may experience higher expatriate 'churn' and lower performance (Dickmann et al. 2005). More research is needed to explore the topic of career capital impact in the long term in more depth.

CONCLUSION

This chapter has considered the career capital implications of international careers. Using a dual-dependency approach, the organizational purpose and individual motivations for working abroad in the pre-departure phase were explored. Organizational systems and processes in terms of international development, performance and career management during international careering were reviewed. For both the individuals and the organizations these areas are highly interrelated, for instance, with performance being one important decision criterion for career progression. The career capital impact of global work for individual assignees was explored. In the post-assignment phase organizational repatriation (or next move) activities were considered relative to strategic intent and expatriate turnover. The phenomenon of the 'career wobble' described individual behaviours and experiences of repatriation and their attempts to make use of their international career capital. Overall, there is still much room for further insights, in particular to extend understanding of the interrelationships of individuals and organizations, the temporal elements of the stages of international career management and the individual behaviours and organizational activities that may help to overcome the 'career wobble'.

Due to a lack of data because of limited measurement systems, many organizations continue to make the often very expensive 'leap of faith' that IAs will result in payoffs in terms of business benefits and individual career impact. For example, a range of issues have been highlighted in the literature critiquing the received wisdom of the utility, particularly longer term, of expatriation (Bonache et al. 2001; Stahl and Cerdin 2004).

Although developed originally as a parallel to the competency-based view of the firm, the career capital concept has been used to explore a variety of individual-level skills development situations in international careers including expatriation and self-initiated foreign work experiences. This chapter has applied the concept to global careers and explored three phases of international working and the diverse interdependencies of individuals and their employers during these phases.

The career capital concept has aided our understanding of the way in which individuals can develop their personal portfolio of skills, knowledge and abilities, social capital and inner drives. While there are still gaps in knowledge about the relationships between individual-level career capital and organization-level human capital, it is clear that context and agency matter tremendously. Improving our understanding of international careers from multiple perspectives and exploring the links and dependencies between organizations, individuals and their wider contexts will be crucial for future research.

KEY LEARNING POINTS

- The map of the terrain in which individuals can realize an organizational career have changed dramatically over the last decade.
- Globalization has driven a variety of strategic responses by organizations to meet the demand for talent throughout the globe.
- Career paths and patterns have taken many new forms for individuals.
- Career capital is a popular contemporary concept providing a lens through which we can view the way in which individuals can develop their personal

259

portfolio of skills, knowledge and abilities, social networks and insights/ inner drives.

■ Tensions exist between the individual and organization drivers in career capital development.

■ It is possible that individuals may reap benefits for their career capital from working abroad, while the outcomes for the organization are less obvious. It could be that both employee and employer benefit or that neither gains positive outcomes.

■ Alternatively, the organization could experience positive results from an IA while the career capital of the individual suffers. Thus, the development of career capital from an IA is multifaceted and mediated by both individual and organizational factors.

REFERENCES

Arthur, M.B. and Rousseau, D.M. (1996) *The Boundaryless Career: A New Employment Principle for a New Organizational Era*, New York: Oxford University Press.

Arthur, M.B., Claman, P.H. and DeFillippi, J R. (1995) 'Intelligent enterprise, intelligent careers', *Academy of Management Executive* 9, 4:7–22.

Arthur, M.B., Hall, D.T. and Lawrence, B.S. (eds) (1989) *The Handbook of Career Theory*, Cambridge: Cambridge University Press.

Baruch, Y. (2006) 'Career development in organizations and beyond: balancing traditional and contemporary viewpoints', *Human Resource Management Review* 16:125–138.

Bhaskar-Shrinivas, P., Shaffer, M. and Luk, D. (2005) 'Input-based and time-based models of international adjustment: meta-analytic evidence and theoretical extensions', *Academy of Management Journal* 48, 2:257–281.

Black, J.S., Gregersen, H.B., Mendenhall, M.E. and Stroh, L.K. (1999) *Globalizing People through International Assignments*, Reading, MA: Addison-Wesley.

Bonache, J., Brewster, C. and Suutari, V. (2001) 'Expatriation: a developing research agenda', *Thunderbird International Business Review* 43, 1:3–20.

Caligiuri, P. and Di Santo, V. (2001) 'Global competence: what it is and can it be developed through global assignments?', *Human Resource Planning* 24, 3:27–35.

Cappellen, T. and Janssens, M. (2005) 'Career paths of global managers: towards future research', *Journal of World Business* 40, 4:348–360.

Dickmann, M. and Doherty, N. (2006) 'The meaning of success in expatriation', 22nd EGOS Conference, Bergen, Norway, 6–8 July.

Dickmann, M. and Doherty, N. (2007) 'Exploring the career capital impact of international assignments within distinct organizational contexts', *British Journal of Management*, downloadable internet version, 22 June 2007.

Dickmann, M. and Harris, H. (2005) 'Developing career capital for global careers: the role of international assignments', *Journal of World Business* 40, 4:399–408.

Dickmann, M., Doherty, N. and Johnson, A. (2006) 'Measuring the value of international assignments', report for Geodesy Member Firms, PricewaterhouseCoopers, London.

Dickmann, M., Doherty, N. and Mills, T. (2005) 'Understanding mobility – influence factors in the decision to accept an international assignment, repatriation issues and long-term career considerations', report compiled for PricewaterhouseCoopers, Cranfield: Cranfield University Press.

Dickmann, M., Doherty, N. Mills, T. and Brewster, C. (forthcoming) 'Why do they go? Individual and corporate perspectives on the factors influencing the decision to accept an international assignment', *International Journal of Human Resource Management*.

Doherty, N., Dickmann, M. and Brewster, C. (2006) 'Using the career capital of international assignments back home. The "career wobble"', British Academy of Management Conference, Belfast, 12–14 September.

Earley, P.C. and Ang, S. (2003) *Cultural Intelligence: Individual Interactions Across Cultures,* Stanford, CA: Stanford University Press.

Eby, L.T., Butts, M. and Lockwood, A. (2003) 'Predictors of success in the era of the boundaryless career', *Journal of Organizational Behaviour* 24, 6:689–708.

Edström, A. and Galbraith, J.R. (1977) 'Transfer of managers as a coordination and control strategy in multinational organizations', *Administrative Science Quarterly* 22, 2:248–263.

Gregersen, H.B., Morrison, A.J. and Black, J.S. (1998) 'Developing leaders for the global frontier', *Sloan Management Review* 40, 1:21–33.

Harris, H. and Dickmann, M. (2005) 'The CIPD guide on international management development', London: The Chartered Institute of Personnel and Development.

Harris, H., Brewster, C. and Sparrow, P. (2003) *International Human Resource Management,* London: CIPD.

Harvey, M.C. and Novicevic, M.M. (2004) 'The development of political skill and political capital by global leaders through global assignments', *International Journal of Human Resource Management* 15, 7:1173–1188.

Harzing, A-W. and Christensen, C. (2004) 'Expatriate failure: time to abandon the concept?', *Career Development International* 9, 7:616–626.

Inkson, K. (2006) 'Protean and boundaryless careers as metaphors', *Journal of Vocational Behaviour* 61, 1:48–63.

Inkson, K. and Arthur, M. (2001) 'How to be a successful career capitalist', *Organizational Dynamics* 30, 1:48–60.

Jokinen, T., Brewster, C. and Suutari, V. (forthcoming) 'Career capital during international work experiences: contrasting self initiated expatriate experiences and assigned expatriation', *International Journal of Human Resource Management*.

Larsen, H.H. (2004) 'Global career as dual dependency between organization and the individual', *Journal of Management Development* 23, 9:860–869.

Mendenhall, M.E. (2006) 'The elusive, yet critical challenge of developing global leaders', *European Management Journal* 24, 6:422–429.

Peng, M.W. and York, A. (2001) 'Behind intermediary performance in export trade: transactions, agents and resources', *Journal of International Business Studies* 32, 2:327–346.

Quinn, J.B. (1992) 'The intelligent enterprise: a new paradigm', in *Intelligent Enterprise: A Knowledge and Service Based Paradigm for Industry*, New York: Free Press.

Seibert, S.E., Kraimer, M.L. and Liden, R.C. (2001) 'A social capital theory of career success', *Academy of Management Journal* 4, 6:219–237.

Sparrow, P., Brewster, C. and Harris, H. (2004) *Globalizing Human Resource Management,* London: Routledge.

Stahl, G. and Cerdin, J.L. (2004) 'Global careers in French and German multinational corporations', *Journal of Management Development* 23, 9:885–902.

Stahl, G.K., Miller, E. and Tung, R. (2002) 'Towards the boundaryless career: a closer look at the expatriate career concept and the perceived implications of an international assignment', *Journal of World Business* 37:216–227.

Sullivan, S.E. and Arthur, M.B. (2006) 'The evolution of the boundaryless career concept: examining physical and psychological mobility', *Journal of Vocational Behaviour* 69:19–29.

Suutari, V. and Brewster, C. (2003) 'Repatriation: empirical evidence of a longitudinal study from careers and expectations among Finnish expatriates', *International Journal of Human Resource Management* 14, 7:1132–1151.

Suutari, V. and Brewster, C. (2004) 'Repatriation: empirical evidence from a longitudinal study on careers and expectations among Finnish expatriates', *International Journal of Human Resource Management* 17, 7:1132–1151.

Thomas, D.C. (1998) 'The expatriate experience: a critical review and synthesis', *Advances in Comparative Management,* 12:237–273.

Welch, D.E. (2003) 'Globalisation of staff movements: beyond cultural adjustment', *Management International Review* 43, 2:149–169.

Yan, A., Zhu, G. and Hall, D. (2002) 'International assignments for career building: a model of agency relationships and psychological contracts', *Academy of Management Review* 27, 3:373–391.

Chapter 13

Women on international assignments

Iris Kollinger and Margaret Linehan

CHAPTER OBJECTIVES

By the end of this chapter, readers will have:

- an understanding of why there is a dearth of literature relating to female international managers
- traced the development of literature in this field from the mid-1960s to the present day
- an appreciation of why women have been and still remain under-represented in international assignments
- identified how organizations can benefit from having women international managers
- explored international human resource management policies and practices with regard to areas such as selection, networking and mentoring that have the potential to improve the female international assignment rate

INTRODUCTION

Over the years the rapid pace of global activity and global competition has resulted in international work assignments gaining in importance and an increasing number of employees spending some of their working lives abroad. Given the strategic importance of foreign assignments in establishing world-wide cooperation and maintaining the quality of human resources, their effective management and development have become crucial factors for the success of global business. But, as the willingness of employees to go abroad appears to be declining in some western countries and the possible future lack of an adequate and sufficient qualified recruitment pool for global assignments, identifying, attracting, developing and retaining international talent becomes a key challenge for multinational corporations (MNCs) (Atlas Van Lines 2001;

Greene 2001). A look at the rate of women's participation in international management shows that the percentage of female managers varies by country but, overall, is less than 17% of total expatriate staff (Taylor et al. 2002; GMAC Global Relocation Services 2003). Women, therefore, seem to be an under-utilized resource, a fact companies cannot afford as they come under increasing pressure from global competition. This under-representation is significant as more women are now entering lower level managerial positions. Interestingly, the increased participation of women in the workforce has been one of the major changes in recent years, and it is anticipated that this trend will continue (Davidson and Burke 2004).

The structure of the chapter is as follows. First, the participation rate of women in international management is briefly introduced. Second, research on female international managers from the 1960s to the early 21st century is summarized. Third, the reasons for the under-representation of women in international management are explored and the implications for organizations of excluding women from international assignments are discussed. The chapter ends by reflecting on the role of women managers – including a call to be more proactive – and by developing conclusions.

FEMALE PARTICIPATION RATES IN INTERNATIONAL MANAGEMENT

According to Alimo-Metcalfe and Wedderburn-Tate (1993), in terms of the managerial population, it is difficult to establish accurate figures for the proportions of women in management since definitions of management used by different studies vary. According to the ISCO-88 classification (adopted in 1987) managers are defined as 'legislators, senior officials and managers'. The International Labour Organization (ILO) provides comprehensive country comparisons on the number of women in management in various European countries. In 1995, for example, the numbers varied between 16% and 31%. By 2003 these figures had risen to between 25% and 34% (ILO 2003). It has been established that, while organizations may be prepared to promote women through their domestic managerial hierarchy, few women are given opportunities to expand their career horizons through access to international careers. Despite growing numbers of women in employment, the rate of progression of women to international managerial positions remains low in all countries. The 2–3% of international managers represented by women in the early 1980s has now increased to around 17% (GMAC Global Relocation Services 2003). The number of female international managers, however, is still proportionally low in relation to the overall size of the qualified female labour pool.

The presence of women in international managerial positions is of interest for four reasons:

1 It may indicate a change in the power distribution between men and women in organizations that would result in a change of corporate culture and would thereby provide different/new opportunities for female managers (Burke and Davidson 1994; Napier and Taylor 1995).

2 It may show an increased recognition of the importance of having a diverse workforce as companies benefit financially and economically from diversity. Creativity, innovation and problem-solving capabilities are also increased with a diverse workforce (Wilson 1996; Woodhall 1996).

3 International experience is often considered as a requisite for promotion to the top of the organizational hierarchy (Buschermöhle 2000). This situation leads to a vicious circle for women: on one hand, women do not have the senior managerial experience that some organizations deem necessary for a foreign assignment and, on the other hand, a foreign assignment frequently represents a central condition for further career promotion (Bittner 2000). Despite the positive career impact of a foreign assignment for individuals, however, career theorists critically argue that sending somebody abroad does not necessarily lead to an attractive career move for the organization. Suutari and Brewster (2005) suggest that a foreign assignment frequently leads the international manager to resign his or her job on return as they are often faced with an unchallenging job, have unexpectedly low levels of authority and few possibilities of utilizing their additional competences that they achieved abroad (see Chapter 12).

4 Given that shortages of international managers are an increasing concern for many MNCs, and that this may constrain the implementation of their international strategies, the failure to develop female managers for international managerial positions increasingly becomes a strategic human resource issue for many organizations (Smith and Still 1996).

FEMALE INTERNATIONAL MANAGERS: GETTING BACK TO THE ROOTS

Research on international human resource management began only in the late 1960s (Borrmann 1968; Perlmutter 1969), thus research on foreign assignments and especially research on female international managers is still a relatively new discipline. One of the reasons for this is that the international human resource management literature has paid very little attention to women as expatriates, as several empirical studies indicate that the typical expatriate is male, married and between 30 and 45 years (cf. Gross 1994). Besides, up to the early 1980s, research on women in international management was mostly restricted to the role of the 'expatriate wife'. However, this emphasis on male expatriates has not led to increased attention of the under-representation of female expatriates, although disadvantaged groups and aspects of potential discrimination tend to be of high interest to the 'scientific community'. No objective reason can be given to explain why female international managers are an under-researched field.

Female international managers were not considered in the early literature on foreign assignments in contrast to other aspects – such as the selection, training and rewarding of expatriates. Similarly, the scope of gender studies that deal intensively with the under-representation of women in national management did not transfer to an international level.

In the mid-1980s, however, Adler was one of the first researchers who concentrated on female expatriates and focused her pioneering work on women's under-representation in international management and investigated the main reasons for this phenomenon. From the 1980s onwards, there has been an increasing interest in the subject of female expatriates and in the reasons for their minority representation. This may partly be explained by the lack of highly qualified employees, the requirement of new strategies for staffing and retention and an increased consideration of women for certain positions. Furthermore, until recent years research on female expatriates has mainly been conducted by North American researchers and innovative concepts have their origin in North America or the UK, while studies dealing with female expatriates from a continental European point of view are still quite rare. Table 13.1 gives an overview of the authors who have contributed strongly to the findings in this field.

FEMALE INTERNATIONAL HUMAN RESOURCE MANAGEMENT LITERATURE THROUGH THE YEARS

To a large extent the literature on female expatriates deals with aspects of under-representation and concentrates on three main fields:

1 Studies dealing with the *reasons for under-representation of female expatriates* and research into potentially problematic aspects for women abroad (Adler 1984a, 1984b, 1984c; Mendenhall et al. 1995).

2 *Individual experiences* of female expatriates, especially intercultural adaptation in the host country (Taylor and Napier 1996; Caligiuri et al. 1999).

3 *Gender-specific differences* between expatriates concerning relevant aspects of assignments such as motivation and willingness to relocate (Domsch and Lichtenberger 1991), as well as selection and preparation for assignments (Stone 1991; Harris 1995).

266

Table 13.1 Key papers on female international managers

Author	Title
Adler	Women in international management: where are they? (1984a)
	Expecting international success: female managers overseas (1984b)
	Women do not want international careers and other myths about international management (1984c)
	Pacific Basin managers/a gaijin, not a woman (1987)
Caligiuri et al.	Factors influencing the adjustment of women on global assignments (1999)
	A model for the influence of social interaction and social support on female expatriates' cross-cultural adjustment (2002)
Fischlmayr	Female expatriates in international management (1999)
	Female self-perception as barriers to international careers? (2002)
Harris	Researching discrimination in selection for international management assignments: the role of repertory grid technique (2001)
	Think international manager, think male – why are women not selected for international management assignments? (2002)
	Global careers: work–life issues and the adjustment of women international managers (2004)
Kollinger	Women and expatriate work opportunities in Austrian organizations (2005a)
Linehan	Senior female international managers: why so few (2000)
Linehan/Scullion	European female expatriate careers: critical success factors (2001)
	Repatriation of female executives: empirical evidence from Europe (2002)
Napier/Taylor	Western women working in Japan: breaking corporate barriers (1995)
Selmer/Leung	Experiences of women professionals abroad: comparisons across Japan, China and Turkey (2002)
	Who are the female expatriates? (2001a)
	Female business expatriates/availability of corporate career development support (2001b)
	Provision and adequacy of corporate support to male expatriate spouses: an exploratory study (2003)
Tung	Female expatriates – the model global manager? (2004)
Varma et al.	Women and international assignments: the impact of supervisor–subordinate relationships (2001)
	A new perspective on the female expatriate experience: the role of host-country national categorization (2006)

Within these different fields, a strict differentiation is not possible since they all address the aspect of under-representation: for instance, both studies of gender-specific differences and empirical reports of female expatriates discuss possible differences between female and male managers as well as impediments that explain or define the small share of female expatriates, respectively. Having a look at shifts in the research emphases over time, three main research phases may be distinguished:

1 The 1980s: as indicated already, research on female expatriates started mainly with Adler's pioneering studies investigating the reasons for their under-representation.
2 The 1990s: most research during this period refers to Adler's studies and was primarily conducted in North America. Studies which considered different samples, countries or other contextual changes seemed to be very rare.
3 The new millennium: starting with the beginning of the new millennium, the range of different aspects has increased; mainstream paths are frequently left and new research fields are explored.

The 1980s: the seminal work of Adler

In the 1980s Adler undertook comprehensive research to determine the reasons for the under-representation of female expatriates in North American companies. Adler's (1984a) results indicated that women's participation rates did not exceed 3%. In her studies she tested whether three widely held 'myths' on women in international management were true or not. These assumptions were called 'myths' by Adler, since they do not reflect reality but companies nonetheless tend to rely on them. Since Adler used this term, it is widely used when discussing the under-representation of female expatriates.

Myth 1: women do not want to be international managers

In her survey with MBA students Adler (1984c) found that male and female students were both highly interested in working abroad. Gender-specific differences could be found neither in their interest nor in the reasons why they would reject an offer to go abroad. Adler, therefore, concluded this was a myth.

Myth 2: companies refuse to send women abroad

Adler (1984b) found out that although only one-third of respondents ever had any experience with female expatriates, about half of them were sceptical regarding the selection of women. Quite obviously, this myth could be confirmed: home-country management is a major barrier for sending female managers on a foreign assignment.

 268

Myth 3: foreigners' prejudices against women render them ineffective when women are interested in international assignments and are sent on an assignment

Having interviewed female expatriates in Southeast Asia, Adler found that almost all respondents (97%) rated their foreign assignment as successful and nearly half of the female managers said that they benefited from being women when working together with clients and business partners. This myth, therefore, could also be disproved in Southeast Asia.

The 1990s: not many novelties?

In the 1990s research on female expatriates was characterized by little innovation and, if examined closely, it seems to be repetitive, as much of the research deals with the under-representation of female expatriates and refers to Adler's studies of the 1980s, which underpins the importance and sustainability of her work, but does not take the debate much further. Research conducted during this period was primarily in North America (cf. Chusmir and Frontczak 1990; Coyle and Shortland 1992; Antal and Izraeli 1993; Mendenhall et al. 1995; Grove and Hallowell 1997; Weber et al. 1998; Stroh et al. 1999).

In general, during this period, comparative studies which consider different samples, different countries or other possible contextual changes – factors that may influence the current levels of female participation in expatriate assignments – seem to be rare. Generally, the same problems and the same solutions for those problems are dealt with, creating little new knowledge.

Another research area that emerged during this period was the phenomenon of the dual-career couple in international assignments, and in particular when the male partner is the accompanying partner. Research conducted in North America by Punnett et al. (1992) examined issues associated with female expatriates and their partners and concluded that this issue will pose a dramatic challenge for international organizations in the coming decades. In almost all countries, it is not yet the accepted social norm for the male partner to be the accompanying partner. Australian research conduced by Smith and Still (1996) suggested that international relocation can have detrimental and lasting effects on the expatriate's partner. They also suggested that dual-career and family conflicts, rather than personal competence or commitment, are frequently responsible for employees refusing overseas opportunities. Similarly, Dowling et al. (1999) noted that there was widespread expatriate failure and this was attributed to the growing number of dual-career couples.

Research emerging from Britain at this time focused on the organizational influences on women's career opportunities in international management (Harris 1995). Harris investigated the complex dynamics between formal policies and

269

informal organizational practices and their impact on women's perceptions of probable success in obtaining international management positions. Harris suggested that home-country selection procedures may play a critical role in determining the low level of female participation in international assignments. Simultaneously, in North America, Davison and Punnett (1995) questioned whether there is a role for gender and race in international assignments. They concluded that stereotypes of and biases against minorities and women still continued.

Despite these limitations, however, research began to concentrate on female international managers and their experiences abroad. This new research outlined the success stories of women and proved that female managers are as successful as their male colleagues in international business. This is significant since the majority of those studies were conducted in Asian countries such as Hong Kong, China and Japan, i.e. countries where prejudices towards female expatriates could make them fail easily and return prematurely from their foreign assignments. In-depth research conducted by Napier and Taylor (1995) examined how foreign women can succeed in Japan and found that the factors that affect the adjustment of women expatriates are similar to those that affect male expatriates. The women in their study perceived that they were almost as well accepted professionally by clients in Japan as they would be in their home countries. Westwood and Leung (1994) also came to similar conclusions, noting that their sample of female expatriates in Hong Kong had very positive experiences. Gender had no impact on their effective managerial performance.

The new millennium: new approaches, changed perspectives

During the late 1990s and at the beginning of the new millennium studies emerged that examined gender-specific differences between expatriates regarding different aspects of their assignment, such as selection and preparation for the assignment. Research by Caligiuri and Cascio (1998) examined factors affecting the performance of western women on global assignments. The authors offered 15 strategies for MNCs to maximize the likelihood of success of their female international managers. Results of a study by Caligiuri and Tung (1999) which compared the success of male and female expatriates in a US-based multinational suggested that overall male and female expatriates can perform equally well in international assignments regardless of the country's predisposition to women in management.

Harris (2001, 2002) examined the selection methods used by UK companies in relation to female international managers and concluded that informal management practices worked against espoused official equal opportunity policies. Mayrhofer and Scullion (1998) analysed potential differences between male and female expatriates in the German clothing industry in terms of selection, preparation and support during the assignment. They found that gender differences were rather small but, significantly, age was an important influencing factor. The only

270

point where there were clear differences between male and female expatriates in the selection process was where the partners of female expatriates were less frequently included in comparison to their male counterparts.

A further research area that was investigated during this period related to whether female and male managers are willing and motivated to relocate abroad to the same extent as their male colleagues. Domsch and Lieberum (1998) found that in Germany there were no gender differences in the willingness to work abroad or in the reasons for rejecting a foreign assignment. In contrast, research conducted by Lowe et al. (1999) with business students in two universities in the United States found that males and females differ in their willingness to relocate depending on (i) the cultural differences between the culture of the respondent's home country and that of the referent location and (ii) the levels of development in the host country. The results show that no gender differences were found in the willingness to work in Britain, Canada, France, Italy or Venezuela. The largest differences were found in the responses from female participants regarding their unwillingness to work in Indonesia, Saudi Arabia and Vietnam. European research conducted by Linehan (2000) suggested that female managers do want international careers, but one of the main barriers to achieving this is the attitudes and perceptions of home-country senior management. Home-country management mistakenly assumes that because of balancing work and home life, in particular among married women, they would not be interested in an international career. Linehan concluded that female international managers are as motivated and as mobile as their male counterparts, but have frequently to ask to be sent abroad.

Further research investigated the manner in which females adapt to foreign cultures and their overall perceptions of their experiences abroad. Mathur-Helm (2002), for example, conducted research with female international managers in South African MNCs. Her research revealed that these women were not only successful as expatriates but achieved high performance, career growth, and promotion. Caligiuri and Lazarova (2002) developed a model in order to determine the impact of social relationships and support on cross-cultural adjustment. Their research concluded that because of the strong influence which social networks have on the success of foreign assignments organizations should encourage opportunities to support such interactions. These supports and networks would be particularly advantageous to female international managers as very many of them are in a pioneering role. Similarly, research conducted by Tzeng (2006) with 21 female international managers in Taiwan revealed that women who are married and raising children have to utilize other kinds of support in order to balance family and job responsibilities. Recent research conducted by Varma et al. (2006) investigated host-country acceptance and preference of US female expatriates in India and found that they were preferred by Indian host-country nationals as co-workers significantly more than their male counterparts.

Other areas of research which continue to be investigated include the impact of work–family conflict on the international career move and the relevance of gender (Harris 2004). Harcar and Harcar (2003) and Selmer and Leung (2003) also examined the effect of family issues for female international managers. Their research focused on partners and children of international female managers, and in particular, how human resource management policies could support work–life balance. Some of these research areas will now be discussed.

SOME DEFICITS IN THE FEMALE INTERNATIONAL MANAGEMENT LITERATURE

Three main deficits may be identified from the existing female international management literature:

1 Theoretical deficits: there is a lack of strategic questions as most studies focus on operational issues (Festing 1996). Besides, the female expatriate literature lacks a well-founded theoretical basis. There are no theoretical approaches and no theoretical frameworks which could explain correlations or context (Clermont and Schmeisser 1997).
2 Empirical deficits: there is a lack of empirical research, particularly in a European context. This applies not only to the general foreign assignment literature (Dowling and Schuler 1990) but also to female expatriate literature. There are general descriptive studies that focus on narrow research questions and thus their value is relatively limited (Scherm 1999).
3 Content deficits: the variety of topics is limited and, in comparison to other research fields, there is a deficit of new research areas. As in the case of general foreign assignment literature, researchers frequently rely on standard works – such as Adler, Linehan or Tung – and rarely make diversions from mainstream paths. Moreover, the typical characteristics of foreign assignment literature are continued in this field: the research is almost exclusively confined to Anglo-Saxon countries, is descriptive and seldom supported by theory.

UNDER-REPRESENTATION OF WOMEN IN INTERNATIONAL MANAGEMENT

The under-representation of women in positions of power emerged as a 'problem' on the agenda of many industrialized countries in the 1980s. Having a look on country-specific differences, research by Rosener (1995) and Caligiuri and Tung (1999) established that the number of female managers may vary due to the country of origin. The proportion of female expatriates in Japan, for example, is much smaller than in Australia, Canada and the USA while there are many more female expatriates in Finland. This situation may be attributed to the different values each society places on masculinity and femininity, which, in turn, impacts on women's access to senior management in their home country. Hofstede (1995) suggests that women in management will have the greater difficulties in 'masculine' countries like Austria and Japan and fewer problems in 'feminine' countries like Finland.

Cultural prejudices of the host country are still a central argument against sending female managers abroad, particularly in relation to Arab, African and Asian countries, even though Adler proved that those prejudices relate more to the home-country decision makers than to the host country itself. Due to such prejudices, female managers are thought to lack acceptance of their authority and credibility abroad, which hinders their efficient performance (Adler 1984b). Some organizations, therefore, perceive that sending women managers on international assignments could pose a high risk and could increase the probability of an early and costly return. This attitude remains quite stable and unchanged; although several counterarguments indicate that female managers can be successful in international management: because female expatriates differ in their appearance, their actions and by their professional status from local women, therefore, they will experience different treatment and acceptance (Grove and Hallowell 1997). Interestingly, female expatriates may be viewed first as 'foreigners' and representatives of the company and second as women (Forster 1999). So the respect that is shown to a manager abroad depends more on formal status and not so much on gender (Mendenhall et al. 1995). This means that companies may possibly project their own prejudices against female managers on to host-country nationals or use this argument consciously as a justification for the under-representation of female expatriates.

Another central argument for the under-representation of women in international management is a lack of female candidates in the recruitment pool for foreign assignments. Women may be under-represented in international management because of work areas and industries that involve foreign assignments, thereby limiting the number of women available for selection for international assignments (Nye 1988; Kollinger 2005b). Studies show that female international managers tend to work more frequently in the service sector than in the industrial sector and they appear to be concentrated in areas such as banking and finance, publishing and retailing (Adler 1987; Forster 1999). The fact that many jobs are still seen as 'men's' or 'women's' jobs influences the initial intake of a particular gender to organizations (Lang 1991; Kreimer 1999). If the initial intakes for particular career routes are unbalanced, it is unlikely that the pattern will improve later, particularly in organizations that have a policy of 'promotion from within' where possible. Women, therefore, may not be included in the recruitment pool for international assignments, because they are not represented in the relevant positions and functions (Domsch and Lieberum 1997; Forster 1999). As international assign-ments are primarily conducted at top and middle management level, this is a dis-advantage for women who, although increasingly represented in lower and middle management, are still exceptions in upper or top management and therefore under-represented compared with their male colleagues (Antal and Izraeli 1993). As noted previously, this is a dilemma for women managers if, on the one hand, senior management in their home organizations deems that they do not reach the minimum selection criteria for international assignments and, on the other hand, experience in foreign assignments is considered central for their career advance-ment (Brandenburger 1995). This situation, however, should change as more women now not only have the educational and technical skills and the required professional experience but are willing to develop their careers to meet the requirements for an international position (Linehan 2000; Collins-O'Sullivan 2005; Kollinger 2005a). Given the shortage of female international managers, companies may need to consider offering foreign assignments to younger women who have not yet reached senior managerial positions in their home organizations (Collins-O'Sullivan 2005). This would be in line with a trend to expatriate people earlier in their careers (GMAC 2003).

The issue of dual-career couples and work–family conflict are still perceived by home-country managers to be more problematic for women because women are still taken to be primarily responsible for care of the children and household (see Chapter 10). Work–family conflict is experienced when pressures from the work and family roles are mutually incompatible, such that participation in one role makes it more difficult to participate in the other. Despite women's increased involvement in the workforce research over time and across cultures continues to document the persistence of inequality in the allocation of household work and family responsibilities, even among couples with 'modern ideologies' and in coun-tries with commitment to gender equality at home and at work. Women's extra domestic responsibilities can create role conflict and overload and can reduce the potential for achievement in their careers (Davidson and Cooper 1992; Lewis 1994; Linehan 2000).

Closely linked to dual-career and work–family conflict is the partner of the international manager. It is evident that one of the most important factors in deter-mining the success of an international assignment for both males and females is the willingness of a partner to leave home – and possibly a career – to live abroad (Monka 1992; Buschermöhle 2000). The refusal of the partner to go abroad and/or children of school age are of high relevance for both genders and are one of the leading reasons for turning down the offer of a foreign assignment (Napier and Taylor 2002; Valcour and Tolbert 2003). Currently, most issues concerning dual-career couples are left to the individual couple to resolve with no help from the company. Managing career moves for both partners simultaneously is usually a difficult process and the conflicts associated with career transitions can be either eased or increased by organizational policies (see Chapters 10 and 12). As the majority of international managers is still male, the non-working expatriate partner is most often female and the non-working husband or partner may find himself the lone man in a group composed otherwise of wives or female partners (Coyle and Shortland 1992). Additionally, sex role stereotypes suggest that male accompanying partners will be less willing to relocate internationally than female partners. It may be construed that a male following his wife or partner on an international assignment is a significant departure from social norms associated with the male role as primary provider for the family. The male accompanying partner is, therefore, considered atypical and may have been conditioned to feel less worthy if not contributing financially (Mendenhall et al. 1995). It is clear, therefore, that additional emotional stress is experienced when the accompanying partner is male and this can lead to some dual-career couples preferring to avoid international transfers, thereby potentially sacrificing the female partner's career advancement (Adler 1984c). In order to avoid the additional stresses associated with dual-career couples, it has been established that female international managers may choose to remain single in order to advance their careers. Research by Forster (1999) found that 89% of female international managers are single, whereas only 27% of male international managers are unmarried.

IMPACT OF INFORMAL ORGANIZATIONAL INFLUENCES

Recruiting international managers is still influenced by informal practices (Harris and Brewster 1999; see also Chapter 5). This is seen to be particularly problematic for women, given the large proportion of international managers that is currently male. Within a selection context where the nature of the vacancies reflects a male-type bias, there appears to be even more need for selection systems to ensure that potential 'prejudice' on the part of selectors is constrained by a process which forces them continually to question their assumptions about women's suitability and, critically, their acceptability in international management positions. Selection is also seen as a social process used by those in power in organizations as a means of recruiting and promoting only those employees who most closely conform to organizational norms (Antal and Izraeli 1993). Employees are likely therefore to be judged more on the basis of their acceptability rather than their suitability. Perry et al. (1994) argued that occupations where there is a predominance of one gender over the other can lead to gender-typed jobholder schema in the minds of selectors. Research into selection systems for international assignments points to a preponderance of systems where primarily subjective knowledge of an individual determines who is seen to 'fit in' best with existing organizational norms (Brewster 1991; Scullion 1994). In summary, gender is still a main barrier to selection for international managerial assignments because the stereotypical image that

275

an international manager is male still exists in organizations and society (Friedel-Howe 1999).

Two additional informal organizational processes that contribute to the under-representation of female international managers are mentoring and networking. Informal networking and informal mentoring provide training in managerial career norms and help individual managers to gain membership of their career group (Barham and Oates 1991; Harris 1995). A number of significant advantages are afforded to an individual through networking. These include exchanging information, collaboration, developing alliances, acquisition of tacit knowledge, visibility and support (Adler 1987; Harris 1995). Networking forms an essential dimension of organizational life and individuals who excel at networking generally excel within the organizations in which they operate. Networks usually involve contacts with a variety of colleagues for the purpose of mutual work benefits. Networking skills, in particular, are important for the international manager because he or she will need to be able to exploit information, expertise and other resources wherever they might be found in the organization worldwide (Burke and McKeen 1994; Powell 1999). Female international managers, however, may be disadvantaged in accessing informal career networks – as an important aspect of the informal socialization process is sharing with members of a group who are similar to themselves and who have similar backgrounds (Davidson and Cooper 1992; Linehan 2000). In this regard, women are sometimes seen as 'non-typical, and therefore risky' by men who comprise the majority of informal networks.

In many organizations, the concept of networks is understood to mean a male club or an 'old boy network' model; therefore, women have been largely excluded from 'old boy' networks' traditionally composed of individuals who hold power in the organization. The exclusion of females from these male managerial groups often perpetuates the more exclusively male customs, traditions and negative attitudes towards female managers (Scase and Goffee 1989; Burke and McKeen 1994). The negative effects of these covert barriers include: blocked promotion and blocked career development, discrimination, occupational stress and lower salaries. Networking and the old boy system is dependent on informal interactions involving favours, persuasion and connections to people who already have influence.

Overall, it is apparent that the informal networking facilities that are available to male international managers are not equally available to female managers – despite instances of women-only networks in companies such as PricewaterhouseCoopers or among lawyers. If women are excluded from informal networks they may lack information, advice, influence and power, all of which are important for international career success. Although the impact of informal networking processes remains an under-researched area, it is clear that managerial women are still less integrated in organizational networks and it is these networks which can influence promotion and acceptance.

276

Networking and mentoring suggest some similarities. Both mentors and peer relationships (networking) can facilitate career and personal development. Networking can be useful at all stages in career development, while mentors are particularly useful at the early stages in career development. Although mentoring relationships may be particularly important for the advancement of women in international management, there is a smaller supply of mentors available to women than to men. There are many possible explanations for the infrequency of mentoring relationships among women in organizations. Generally, these explanations are that (i) women may not seek mentors; and (ii) mentors may not select female protégées. A difficulty for women in approaching male mentors may be compounded by the female's fear that her attempts to initiate a relationship may be misconstrued as a sexual approach by either the mentor or others in the organization. Women, therefore, may have trouble finding mentors because there may be potential discomfort in cross-gender relationships.

The second explanation relating to mentors being unwilling to select female protégées suggests that even if women are considered as suitable candidates for the protégée role, male mentors may choose male protégés because they may be more comfortable developing a professional and personal relationship with another male. The mentor may also identify with the male protégé and perceive the protégé to be a younger version of himself. It can be suggested, therefore, that female protégées may be perceived as being a greater professional risk than their male counterparts and failure of a protégé could be a reflection on the competency and judgement of the mentor. Women, therefore, may seek to avoid the difficulties associated with obtaining a male mentor by seeking a female mentor. Another difficulty may arise, however, in attempts at finding a female mentor, as there are still very few senior female international managers in comparison to males. The few women in mentoring positions, therefore, may receive an overload of requests from the relatively larger block of women in lower levels of the organization, which may result in a reduction of access to mentors.

In summary, then, in an international management context, a mentoring relationship is even more important than in domestic management (Linehan 2000). Mentors provide the contact and support from the home organization, which in turn facilitates re-entry – in addition to improving the self-confidence of protégées, increasing their visibility in organizations and increasing their promotional prospects. Additionally, in the absence of family and friends, mentors also provide many support benefits and help keep the international manager in touch with their home organization which in turn reduces the 'out of sight, out of mind' disadvantage (Linehan and Scullion 2002).

Case study 13.1
Austrian female managers breaking the glass border

This case illustrates the current situation for Austrian female international managers. One of the aims of the case is to investigate whether obtaining an international assignment represents a further barrier for Austrian women or whether they are able to break the glass border. Mandelker's (1994) term the 'glass border' describes stereotypical assumptions by home-country senior management about women as managers and about their availability, suitability and preferences for international appointments. A questionnaire was distributed to the human resource managers of the TOP 500 companies and the 25 largest banks, insurance companies and management consultants in Austria, regardless of the nationality of the parent company.

The results indicate that, for this sample, the number of Austrian female international managers is 12% and therefore only slightly smaller than the number of local female Austrian managers, which is 13%. Interestingly, this result is quite similar to the findings of other international, e.g. US, studies where female international managers make up to 17% of the global expatriate population (GMAC Global Relocation Services 2003; Taylor et al. 2002). There are wide variations among organizations; as almost half of these companies send no females abroad, in 10% of the organizations surveyed women make up more than 40% of international managers. Surprisingly, these organizations are mainly industrial enterprises with fewer than 500 employees and not service companies as one may have expected since women are usually more highly represented in the service industry according to the horizontal segregation of the labour market. The results indicate that an international foreign assignment does not have to be a further barrier in a woman's career, although women are still under-represented in international management in comparison to their male colleagues in this sample. In one-quarter of the cases, women who have already succeeded in breaking through the glass ceiling in their home organizations will be sent more frequently on a foreign assignment. So, there are strong indications that a foreign assignment does not necessarily mean a further barrier in a woman's career and that not all Austrian women are discriminated against when it comes to filling an international position.

When comparing these results with mainly Anglo-Saxon studies, the relative importance of the arguments for the under-representation of female expatriates is different. Fifty per cent of Austrian companies in the sample, however, regard the lack of female managers in (i) senior managerial positions in their home organizations and (ii) in the relevant industry sectors where most opportunities for foreign assignments occur as the main reasons for the under-representation of women in international management. In contrast to this the Anglo-Saxon studies highlight the cultural prejudices of host-country nationals regarding women together with family obligations as major barriers to women in international management. The explanation for these findings could be twofold: either Anglo-Saxon studies neglect these two factors (representation of women in senior managerial positions and in relevant industry sectors) in their research settings or there are country-specific differences for explaining the minor representation of female expatriates.

Source: Kollinger (2005a)

Questions

1 Why do you think the number of female Austrian international managers is almost equal to (i) the number of home-country female Austrian managers and (ii) female global international managers?

2 Could the reasons cited for the under-representation of Austrian female international managers' help to explain the under-representation of female international managers worldwide?

3 Given that Austrian organizations are perceived to have a 'male' culture, how do you think Austrian female managers have managed to break through (i) the glass ceiling and (ii) the glass border?

IMPLICATIONS FOR INTERNATIONAL HUMAN RESOURCE MANAGEMENT POLICY AND PRACTICE

The development of women in international management deserves special attention despite the current human resources policy initiatives directing attention away from equal opportunity policy towards diversity management. Women will remain a small minority in international management until organizations re-examine and reassess their human resource management policies and practices. Many of these practices, however, are not neutral assessments but rest on a set of gender-based assumptions about what managerial competence looks like and how it should be rewarded (Sinclair and Ewing 1993). These practices are often embedded in organizational cultures and entrenched in organizational power structures. Human resource management practices primarily reflect the interests of the dominant group in the organization, and organizations generally have not succeeded in introducing training and development strategies that effectively meet the needs of women. Despite the rhetoric of strategic human resource management few organizations have introduced a fundamentally new approach to the management of human resources and sophisticated and progressive approaches to human resource management remain the exception rather than the rule (Torbiörn 2005).

As identified, the lack of mentoring and networking relationships are significant barriers facing women managers in their pursuit of careers in international management. Organizations, therefore, should introduce formal and informal mentoring strategies specifically designed to promote the participation of women managers in international management. Female managers may have different

279

mentoring needs than men; therefore, women are likely to be assisted in their career development in different ways from their male colleagues. To encourage commitment to mentoring programmes it may be necessary to introduce incentives such as making mentoring part of the formal duties of managers and to include it in the performance assessment of senior managers. Additionally, given the severe shortage of female mentors, organizations urgently need to address the question of how to encourage female managers to take on the role of mentors. Organizations need to develop a pool of senior female mentors who can advise, support and sponsor and, very importantly, act as role models for the new generation of female managers seeking to break into careers in international management.

Another aspect of human resource policy should be to encourage women to join and develop a variety of networks. As discussed earlier, a range of benefits can be provided by networks, but this still does not address the problem of females gaining access to male networks. This suggests that the significant problems facing women seeking international careers can be found within the organizational culture. Organizational interventions such as raising men's gender awareness need to be promoted together with a public relations campaign where the benefits and successes of equal opportunities are stressed.

Organizations should also proactively seek information about the individual requirements and career aspirations of women managers who may be interested in a career in international management. Human resource practices need to be customized to meet the very different needs of various groups of women managers based on listening to views of different groups of women and developing human resource strategies which are geared to an understanding of what motivates women and drives their career paths. This approach suggests the application of basic marketing principles in segmenting employees, understanding their requirements and customizing human resource policies accordingly. This segmentation and customization could usefully be extended to women seeking to progress their careers in international management.

It would also be useful if organizations developed a formalized but voluntary pool of candidates who are interested in pursuing international careers. By doing so, companies could easily gain an overview of potential candidates and prove whether their qualifications and competencies correspond with the required job profile. Additionally, given that registration in those recruitment pools is voluntary, companies could thereby reduce their hesitations that female candidates are not really interested in foreign assignments (Kollinger 2005b). It is important that there are formal, written recruitment policies as well as well-defined selection criteria and job profiles. The more comprehensible and the more formal the selection process, the more probable it is that female managers will be included in the potential candidate pool for foreign assignments since they have only limited access to informal policies such as networks and mentors (Wiegand 1995). International assignments could also be integrated as part of a career plan. This would indicate

280

when an employee is ready to be considered for expatriation, for example, by having sufficient organizational experience thereby offering transparency in the selection process. Organizations could benefit from such a process since career planning would ensure an adequate number of candidates to choose from thereby reducing the uncertainty of availability. As discussed earlier, it is uncertainty that makes organizations choose candidates who are most similar to the selecting decision makers, who are, in general, men (Veith 1987; Antal and Izraeli 1993). By formally integrating foreign assignments into the managerial career path, a basis for the promotion of female expatriates would then be created.

Additionally, organizations need to develop policies in relation to dual-career couples, which may include realistic pre-assignment briefings, individually tailored corporate assistance in order to work or study in the host country or considering alternative solutions like 'short-term assignments' or 'commuting-assignments' (Reynolds and Bennett 1991; Solomon 1996; see also Chapter 11). Regardless of the respective solution depending on the individual circumstances, questions arise in general regarding the financial, personal and emotional costs experienced by the partner in an international move. The failure of organizations to respond to dual-career issues results in costs, not only to the couple, but also to their organizations. The willingness of organizations to address dual-career issues may be important for achieving competitive advantage in the future. The failure to develop effective strategies to promote increased participation of women in international management will become increasingly costly to organizations and will limit the potential supply of international managers.

CONCLUSION

In the international arena, the quality of management seems to be even more critical than in domestic operations. The effective management of human resources, therefore, has increasingly been recognized as a major determinant of success or failure in international business (Black and Gregersen 1999; Dowling et al. 1999; Forster 2000; Scullion and Collings 2006; see also Chapter 5). As discussed, during the past 20 years, the promotion of females to international managerial positions has grown at a very slow rate. In most countries still the perception is to 'think manager, think male'. Recent research by Schein (2007) reveals the strength and inflexibility of the 'think manager, think male' attitude held by males across time and national borders. Schein suggests that since the 1970s corporate males in the USA continue to see women as less qualified than men for managerial positions. Internationally, the view of women as less likely than men to possess requisite management characteristics is also a commonly held belief among male management students in China, Germany, Japan, the UK and the USA. Despite the difficulties outlined above, however, female managers are capable of becoming successful

international managers. There is now growing evidence that female international managers are successful once they have been sent abroad. Interestingly, being a woman could be an advantage, for example, in countries like Asia where male leadership characteristics correspond to western female characteristics (Westwood and Leung 1994; Wah 1998). Home-country male managers, however, often perceive women as being different and not like themselves, so they tend not to select women for international positions. If female managers want to be selected for international assignments, therefore, they will have to be prepared to ask for such positions, as up to now, they are rarely offered such opportunities. They may also need to convince their home-country managers of their availability to partake in international management. Female managers may have to strive harder and show that they are more ambitious and more mobile than their male colleagues to prove their worth in the male-dominated environment of organizational management. Female managers, however, who know what they want, and demonstrate their capabilities in this regard may be very successful.

Similarly, for organizations it is important to consider female managers as potential candidates to go abroad since the willingness of employees to move abroad appears to be declining (Greene 2001). As global competition intensifies, competition for global leaders to manage international operations will steadily intensify and organizations must develop new ways to identify, attract and retain new pools of international executive talent. Moreover, it would not make sense to limit the pool of candidates to exclude female managers because this would mean abandoning highly qualified and motivated human resources. Given the rapid process of global activity and the fight between companies for the most talented people, such a behaviour would not be appropriate, because as Adler states, 'in a ferociously competitive global economy, no company can afford to waste valuable brainpower simply because it is wearing a skirt' (Adler 1997: 310).

KEY LEARNING POINTS

- This chapter has provided an understanding of why there is a dearth of literature relating to female international managers.
- We have traced the development of literature in this field from the mid-1960s to the present day.
- There has been an examination and explanation of why women have been and still remain under-represented in international assignments.
- Organizations can clearly benefit from having women international managers.
- International human resource management policies and practices with regard to areas such as selection, networking and mentoring that have the potential to improve the female international assignment rate need to be explored and, in many cases, adapted.

282

REFERENCES

Adler, N. (1984a) 'Woman in international management: where are they?', *California Management Review* 26, 4:78–89.

Adler, N. (1984b) 'Expecting international success: female managers overseas', *Columbia Journal of World Business* 19: 79–85.

Adler, N. (1984c) 'Women do not want international careers and other myths about international management', *Organizational Dynamics* 13, 3:66–79.

Adler, N. (1987) 'Pacific Basin managers: a gaijin, not a woman', *Human Resource Management* 26, 2:169–191.

Adler, N. (1997) *International Dimensions of Organizational Behaviour*, 3rd edn, Cincinnati, OH: South Western College Publications.

Alimo-Metcalfe, B. and Wedderburn-Tate, C. (1993) 'Women in business and management: the United Kingdom', in M.J. Davidson and C.L. Cooper (eds) *European Women in Business and Management*, London: Paul Chapman.

Antal, A. and Izraeli, D. (1993) 'A global comparison of women in management: women managers in their homelands and as expatriates', in E. Fagenson (ed.) *Women in Management: Trends, Issues, and Challenges in Managerial Diversity*, Newbury Park, CA: Sage.

Atlas Van Lines (2001) *Annual Survey of Corporate Relocation Policies: 2001 Results,* online, http://www.atlasvanlines.com/survey/survey.html (accessed 8 November 2001).

Barham, K. and Oates, D. (1991) *The International Manager*, London: Economist Books.

Bittner, A. (2000) 'Reintegration von Europa Enstandten', in E. Regent and L. Hofmann (eds) *Personalmanagement in Europa*, Göttingen: Hogrefe, Verlag für angewandte Psychologie.

Black, J.S. and Gregersen, H.B. (1999) 'The right way to manage expatriates', *Harvard Business Review* March-April: 52–62.

Borrmann, W. (1968) *Personalwirtschaftliche Sonderprobleme internationaler Unternehmungen*, thesis, University of Munich.

Brandenburger, M. (1995) *Interkulturelles Management: Ein Konzept zur Entsendung von Führungskräften unter besonderer Berücksichtigung von Auswahl und Vorbereitung*, Cologne: Bottermann und Bottermann.

Brewster, C. (1991) *The Management of Expatriates,* London: Kogan Page.

Burke, R.J. and Davidson, M.J. (1994) 'Women in management: current research issues', in M.J. Davidson and R.J. Burke (eds) *Women in Management: Current Research Issues,* London: Paul Chapman.

Burke, R.J. and McKeen, C.A. (1994) 'Career development among managerial and professional women', in M.J. Davidson and R.J. Burke (eds) *Women in Management: Current Research Issues,* London: Paul Chapman.

Buschermöhle, U. (2000) 'Ein neuer Expatriate-Typus entsteht', *Personalwirtschaft* 27, 5:30–34.

Caligiuri, P.M. and Cascio, W.F. (1998) 'Can we send her there? Maximizing the success of western women on global assignments', *Journal of World Business* 33, 4:394–416.

Caligiuri, P. and Lazarova, M. (2002) 'A model for the influence of social interaction and social support on female expatriates' cross-cultural adjustment', *International Journal of Human Resource Management* 13, 5:761–772.

Caligiuri, P.M. and Tung, R.L. (1999) 'Comparing the success of male and female expatriates from a US-based multinational company', *International Journal of Human Resource Management* 10, 5:763–782.

Caligiuri, P.M., Joshi, A. and Lazarova, M. (1999) 'Factors influencing the adjustment of women on global assignments', *International Journal of Human Resource Management* 10, 2:163–179.

Chusmir, L. and Frontczak, N. (1990) 'International management opportunities for women: women and men paint different pictures', *International Journal of Management* 7, 3:295–301.

Clermont, A. and Schmeisser, W. (eds) (1997) *Internationales Personalmanagement*, Munich: Vahlen.

Collins-O'Sullivan, C. (2005) 'Key issues in the repatriation of senior international female executives: a qualitative study in a European context', *Irish Business Journal* 1, 1:62–69.

Coyle, W. and Shortland, S. (1992) *International Relocation: A Global Perspective*, Oxford: Butterworth-Heinemann.

Davidson, M.J. and Burke, R.J. (2004) *Women in Management Worldwide: Facts, Figures and Analysis*, Aldershot: Ashgate.

Davidson, M.J. and Cooper, C.L. (1992) *Shattering the Glass Ceiling: The Woman Manager*, London: Paul Chapman.

Davison, E.D. and Punnett, B.J. (1995) 'International assignments: is there a role for gender and race in decisions?', *International Journal of Human Resource Management* 6, 2:411–440.

Domsch, M. and Lichtenberger, B. (1991) 'Konsequenzen der Internationalisierung für das Personalmanagement: Vertrauensgrundlage ist Voraussetzung', *Gablers Magazin: Personalführung im Wandel - Die Zeitschrift für innovative Führungskräfte* 2: 21–25.

Domsch, M.E. and Lieberum, U.B. (1997) 'Weibliche Führungskräfte im Ausland', *Personalwirtschaft: Erfolgreiches Personalmanagement* 9: 18–21.

Domsch, M.E. and Lieberum, U.B. (1998) 'Auslandseinsatz weiblicher Führungskräfte', in: G. Krell (ed.) *Chancengleichheit durch Personalpolitik: Gleichstellung von Frauen und Männern in Unternehmen und Verwaltungen – Rechtliche Regelungen – Problemanalysen - Lösungen*, 3rd edn, Wiesbaden: Gabler.

Dowling, P.J. and Schuler, R.S. (1990) *International Dimensions of Human Resource Management*, Boston, MA: PWS-Kent.

Dowling, P.J., Welch, D.E. and Schuler, R.S. (1999) *International Human Resource Management: Managing People in a Multinational Context*, 3rd edn, Cincinnati, OH: South Western College Publishing.

Festing, M. (1996) *Strategisches internationales Personalmanagement: Eine transaktionstheoretisch fundierte Analyse*, Munich: Hampp.

Fischlmayr, I.C. (1999) 'Female expatriates in international management', in A. Freisler-Traub and C. Innreiter-Moser (eds) *Zerreissproben – Linzer Schriften zur Frauenforschung*, Linz: Rudolf Trauner.

Fischlmayr, I.C. (2002) 'Female self perception as barrier to international careers', *International Journal of Human Resource Management* 13, 5:773–783.

Forster, N. (1999) 'Another "glass ceiling?": the experiences of women professionals and managers on international assignments', *Gender, Work and Organization* 6, 2:79–90.

Forster, N. (2000) 'The myth of the international manager', *International Journal of Human Resource Management* 11, 1:126–142.

284

Friedel-Howe, H. (1999) 'Frauen und Führung: Mythen und Fakten', in L.V. Rosenstiel, E. Regnet and M. Domsch (eds) *Führung von Mitarbeitern: Handbuch für erfolgreiches Personalmanagement*, 4th edn, Stuttgart: Schaeffer-Poeschl.

GMAC Global Relocation Services (2003) *Global Relocation Trends Survey*, Warren, NJ: GMAC Global Relocation Services.

Greene, A. (2001) 'A virtual reality?', *Chartered Accountants Magazine* 134, 1:10.

Gross, P. (1994) *Die Integration der Familie beim Auslandseinsatz von Führungskräften Möglichkeiten und Grenzen international tätiger Unternehmen*, St Gallen: Hochsch für Wirtschafts -, Rechts – u. Sozialwiss., Diss.

Grove, C. and Hallowell, W. (1997) *Guidelines for Women Expatriates*, online, available http://www.grovewell.com/pub-expat-women.hmtl (accessed 18 November 2001).

Harcar, T. and Harcar, T. (2003) 'Expatriate women's success in international assignments: exploring the relationship between family issues and human resource policies', *Journal of International Management Development* 8, 4:19–36.

Harris, H. (1995) 'Organizational influences on women's career opportunities in international management', *Women in Management Review* 10, 3:26–31.

Harris, H. (2001) 'Researching discrimination in selection for international management assignments: the role of repertory grid technique', *Women in Management Review* 16, 3:118–126.

Harris, H. (2002) 'Think international manager, think male: why are women not selected for international management assignments?', *Thunderbird International Business Review* 44, 2:175–203.

Harris, H. (2004) 'Global careers: work–life issues and the adjustment of women international managers', *Journal of Management Development*, 23, 9:818–832.

Harris, H. and Brewster, C. (1999) 'The coffee-machine system: how international selection really works', *International Journal of Human Resource Management* 10, 3:229–251.

Hofstede, G. (1995) 'Gender stereotypes and partner preferences of Asian women in masculine and feminine cultures', *Journal of Cross-cultural Psychology* 27, 5: 533–546.

International Labour Organization (2003) www.laboursta.llo.org.

Kollinger, I. (2005a) 'Women and expatriate work opportunities in Austrian organizations', *International Journal of Human Resource Management* 16, 7:1243–1260.

Kollinger, I. (2005b) *Der Auslandseinsatz von weiblichen Führungskräften*, Munich and Mering: Rainer Hampp Verlag.

Kreimer, M. (1999) *Arbeitsteilung als Diskriminierungsmechanismus: Theorie und Empirie geschlechtsspezifischer Arbeitsmarktsegregation*, Frankfurt-am-Main: Lang.

Lang, M. (1991) 'Die Situation der weiblichen Führungskraft im öffentlichen Dienst', in E.M. Raml (ed.) *Die Frau als Führungskraft: Dokumentation zur gleichnamigen Tagung am 17. Oktober 1990 an der Johannes-Kepler-Universität Linz*, Linz: Rudolf Trauner.

Lewis, S. (1994) 'Role tensions and dual-career couples', in M.J. Davidson and R.J. Burke (eds) *Women in Management: Current Research Issues*. London: Paul Chapman.

Linehan, M. (2000) *Senior Female International Managers: Why so Few?*, Aldershot: Ashgate.

Linehan, M. and Scullion, H. (2001) 'European female expatriate careers: critical success factors', *Journal of European Industrial Training* 25, 8:392–418.

285

Linehan, M. and Scullion, H. (2002) 'Repatriation of female executives: empirical evidence from Europe', *Women in Management Review* 17, 2:80–88.

Lowe, K., Downes, M. and Kroeck, G. (1999) 'The impact of gender and location on the willingness to accept overseas assignments', *International Journal of Human Resource Management* 10, 2:223–224.

Mandelker, J. (1994) 'Breaking the glass border', *Working Woman* 19, 1:16.

Mathur-Helm, B. (2002) 'Expatriate women managers: at the crossroads of success, challenges and career goals', *Women in Management Review* 17, 1:18–28.

Mayrhofer, W. and Scullion, H. (1998) 'Female expatriates in international business: empirical evidence from the German clothing industry', paper for the 1998 EIBA conference, Jerusalem.

Mendenhall, M., Punnett, B.J. and Ricks, D. (1995) *Global Management*, Cambridge, MA: Blackwell.

Monka, D. (1992) 'Auslandseinsatz als Instrument der Personalentwicklung', in H. Strutz and K. Wiedemann (eds) *Internationales Personalmarketing: Konzepte, Erfahrungen, Perspektiven*, Wiesbaden: Gabler.

Napier, N. and Taylor, S. (1995) *Western Women Working in Japan: Breaking Corporate Barriers*, London: Quorum Books.

Napier, N. and Taylor, S. (2002) 'Experiences of women professionals abroad: comparisons across Japan, China, and Turkey', *International Journal of Human Resource Management* 13, 5:837–851.

Nye, D. (1988) 'The female expat's promise', *Across the Board* 25, 2:38–43.

Perlmutter, H. (1969) 'The tortuous evolution of the multinational corporation', *Columbia Journal of World Business* 4: 9–18.

Perry, E.L., Davis-Blake, A. and Kulik, C. (1994) 'Explaining gender-based selection decisions: a synthesis of contextual and cognitive approaches', *Academy of Management Review* 19, 4:786–820.

Powell, G. (ed.) (1999) *Handbook of Gender in Organizations*. Thousand Oaks, CA: Sage.

Punnett, B.J., Crocker, O.I. and Stevens, M.A. (1992) 'The challenge for women expatriates and spouses: some empirical evidence', *International Journal of Human Resource Management* 3, 3:585–592.

Reynolds, C. and Bennett, R. (1991) 'The career couple challenge', *Personnel Journal* 70, 3:46–48.

Rosener, J. (1995) *America's Competitive Secret: Utilizing Women as a Management Strategy*, London: Oxford University Press.

Scase, R. and Goffee, R. (1989) *Reluctant Managers: Their Work and Lifestyles*, London: Unwin Hyman.

Schein, V.E. (2007) 'Women in management: reflections and projections', *Women in Management Review* 22, 1:6–18.

Scherm, E. (1999) *Internationales Personalmanagement*, 2nd edn, Munich and Vienna: Oldenbourg.

Scullion, H. (1994) 'Staffing policies and strategic control in British multinationals', *International Studies of Management and Organization* 24, 3:86–104.

Scullion, H. and Collings, D. (eds) (2006) *Global Staffing*, London: Routledge.

Selmer, J. and Leung, A. (2001a) 'Who are the female business expatriates?', BRC Papers on Cross-cultural Management, Hong Kong Baptist University: 1–39.

Selmer, J. and Leung, A. (2001b) 'Female business expatriates: availability of corporative career development support', BRC Papers on Cross-cultural Management. Hong Kong Baptist University: 1–25.

Selmer, J. and Leung, A. (2003) 'Provision and adequacy of corporate support to male expatriate spouses: an exploratory study', *Personnel Review* 32, 1:9–21.

Sinclair, A. and Ewing, J. (1993) 'What women managers want: customising human resource management practices', *Human Resource Management Journal* 3, 2:14–28.

Smith, C.R. and Still, L. (1996) *Breaking the Glass Border: Barriers to Global Careers for Women Managers in Australia*, paper presented at 5th International Human Resource Management Conference, San Diego, CA, 24–28 June.

Solomon, C.M. 1996 'Expats say: help make us mobile', *Personnel Journal* 75, 7: 47–52.

Stone, R. (1991) 'Expatriate selection and failure', *Human Resource Planning* 14, 1: 9–18.

Stroh, L., Varma, A. and Valy-Durbin, S.J. (1999) *International Gender Gap – Why Woman are Encountering Barriers to Being Sent Abroad*, online, available http://www.crc.org/mobility/articles/1099stroh.html (accessed 15 November 2000).

Suutari, V. and Brewster, C. (2005) 'Guest editorial: global HRM – aspects of a research agenda', *Personnel Review* 34, 1:5–21.

Taylor, S. and Napier, N. (1996) 'Working in Japan: lessons from women expatriates', *Sloan Management Review* 37, 3:76–84.

Taylor, S., Napier, N.K. and Mayrhofer, W. (2002) 'Women in global business: an introduction', *International Journal of Human Resource Management* 13, 5:739–742.

Torbiörn, I. (2005) 'Staffing policies and practices in European MNCs: strategic sophistication, culture-bound policies or *ad hoc* reactivity?', in H. Scullion and M. Linehan (eds) *International Human Resource Management: A Critical Text*, London: Palgrave Macmillan.

Tung, R.L. (2004) 'Female expatriates – the model global manager?', *Organizational Dynamics* 33, 3:243 253.

Tzeng, R. (2006) 'Gender issues and family concerns for women with international careers: female expatriates in western multinational corporations in Taiwan', *Women in Management Review* 21, 5:376–392.

Valcour, P.M. and Tolbert, P. (2003) 'Gender, family and career in the era of boundarylessness: determinants and effects of intra-and organizational mobility', *International Journal of Human Resource Management* 14, 5:768–787.

Varma, A., Stroh, L.K. and Schmitt, L.B. (2001) 'Women and international assignments: the impact of supervisor–subordinate relationships', *Journal of World Business* 36, 4:380–388.

Varma, A., Toh, S.M. and Budhwar, P. (2006) 'A new perspective on the female expatriate experience: the role of host country national categorization', *Journal of World Business* 41: 112–120.

Veith, M. (1987) *Frauenkarriere im Management, Einstiegsbarrieren und Diskriminierungsmechanismen*, Frankfurt-am-Main and New York: Campus.

Wah, L. (1998) 'Surfing the rough sea', *Management Review* 25–29.

Weber, W., Festing, M., Dowling, P. and Schuler, R. (1998) *Internationales Personalmanagement*, Wiesbaden: Gabler.

Westwood, R. and Leung, A. (1994) 'The female expatriate manager experience: coping with gender and culture', *International Studies of Management & Organization* 24, 3:64–85.

Wiegand, H. (1995) *Berufstätigkeit und Aufstiegschancen von Frauen: Eine (nicht nur) ökonomische Analyse*, Berlin: Duncker & Humblot.

Wilson, E. (1996) 'Managing diversity and HRD', in J. Stewart and J. McGoddrick (eds) *Human Resource Development: Perspectives, Strategies and Practice,* London: Pitman.

Woodhall, J. (1996) 'Human resource management and women: the vision of the gender blind?', in B.Towers (ed.) *The Handbook of Human Resource Management,* 2nd edn, Oxford: Blackwell.

Chapter 14

HRM and international organizations

Estelle Toomey and Chris Brewster

CHAPTER OBJECTIVES

By the end of this chapter, readers will have:

- an appreciation of the features of international organizations (IOs) that make them a unique type of international employer, including the United Nations as perhaps the most visible example
- an understanding of what international human resource management (IHRM) issues IOs are challenged by and how these may be similar or different to those of multinational corporations (MNCs)
- knowledge of some of the differences between the employees of IOs and the employees of MNCs
- an idea of how some of the research about MNC expatriates may be considered in terms of IO employees

INTRODUCTION

This chapter explores international HRM (IHRM) in a group of important but previously largely unresearched organizations – intergovernmental civil services. Using the United Nations as its exemplar, this chapter outlines some of the characteristics of these organizations that make them unusual and some of the features of their work and their staff that mean that expatriation in these contexts is quite different from that found elsewhere. In particular, the chapter argues that these most international of organizations, where typically people are managed by, and in turn manage, people of a different nationality from themselves, have a series of unique circumstances to deal with in their IHRM policies and practices. The chapter gives examples of the practices of these organizations and outlines some of the problems that they face in the effective management of IHRM.

Anecdotal evidence and the majority of empirical studies regarding IHRM, particularly involving expatriation, relate to multinational corporations (MNCs). This knowledge forms an important basis for our understanding of the issues and the stakeholders engaged in international assignments. Generally speaking, there has been little research examining the ways in which the concepts used and the issues identified are applicable to other types of organization, including the international organizations (IOs) like those found within the public sector, including national civil services, North Atlantic Treaty Organization (NATO), European Union (EU) and the United Nations (UN). In many ways, these organizations are the most international of all, yet their IHRM practices are not widely understood.

This chapter serves to fill this gap in the IHRM literature by considering knowledge from the fields of human resources and organizational behaviour with regard to international organizations. Just as traditional IHRM literature on MNCs tends to generalize about organizational type, structure and size, etc., the diversity of IOs necessitates a chapter of this scope to do so as well. Thus, we consider this topic broadly in terms of IHRM issues relevant to IOs overall, and defer comparative analysis of IOs to organizations such as non-governmental organizations (NGOs) to other sources (Brewster and Lee 2006). In the same vein, recognizing that there is a wide range of MNCs with different approaches to IHRM, we have chosen to highlight research that relates generally to large multinational companies since, as a group, they have a richer history of employing expatriates overall. We adopt this approach as a basis for considering application of existing knowledge to IOs, as well as proposing new ideas that may warrant further consideration.

More specifically, based on extensive consultancy work within IOs, on research conducted for a professional association of HRM in these organizations, and on an international study[1] focused on expatriate employees, we address this topic in two sections. In the first part of the chapter, we provide an overview of IOs, with a profile of the UN as perhaps one of the most well-known IOs. Related IHRM challenges impacting upon the UN and other IOs are then highlighted. In the second part, we consider how existing knowledge related to MNC expatriates may be applicable to IO employees. To facilitate learning, within each section we also offer a key question related to the subtopic. We challenge the reader to engage in an activity for situational analysis. Lastly, we suggest a point for debate among readers that will help raise awareness of different points of view and the complexities of these issues.

AN OVERVIEW OF IOs

IOs are generally organizations established by treaty, funded or supported by governments (see Table 14.1). A number of IOs have a specialist focus and are less visible except to those involved in specific fields (e.g. the European Patent

290

Table 14.1 *An overview of IOs in comparison to large MNCs*

Structural features
- MNCs are usually large international operations, responsive to stakeholders and investors. Administrative components of their structure are likely to be smaller. IOs are often perceived as large bureaucracies with complex structures, administrative and managerial processes

Political features
- MNCs generally operate independent of the external influences that IOs must deal with. The latter operates in a highly political environment, subject to external influences from member states, donors and, through the media, even the general public. This influences political relations, organizational mandate, operational priorities, as well as day-to-day administration and management

Employee features
- MNC expatriates tend to do fewer long assignments yet more 'frequent flyer' travel, often linked to promotion. IO employees are more commonly 'transnationals' in terms of doing frequent long-term assignments as a condition of employment. These may include dangerous locations, unaccompanied by family members. MNCs offer highly competitive compensation/benefits that IOs cannot afford. A particularly strong motivation for many IO employees is doing public service

Office, EPO), whereas others are high profile and must cope with shifting agendas (e.g. the United Nations High Commission for Refugees, UNHCR). Some IOs are less funded while others are multi-million dollar-funded organizations (e.g. European Union). Some struggle for money, whereas others (e.g. the World Intellectual Property Organization) generate a substantial income and receive a small level of government funding, although this still gives the latter some influence over the organization. Inevitably, some IOs appear to be well managed while others seem to struggle (Davies 2002).

Although some IOs have competitive entry, others fill positions through staff secondment from member governments' civil services. Generally speaking, however, unlike MNCs where expatriates are often offered an assignment later in their careers, employees of many IOs are employed knowing that international mobility is a condition of service. Most of the employees of IOs are the kind called self-initiated expatriates (SEs) by Suutari and Brewster (2000). Whereas some IOs offer long-term careers, others utilize more term-limited contracts. Most IOs have either a formal or an informal distinction between their general staff (responsible for such matters as security, logistics, administration, etc.) and professional staff (responsible for carrying out the mission of the organization). The former are often recruited and employed locally; the latter are most often recruited and employed from the outset as international personnel. Collectively, they are likely to represent a broad range of countries and thus usually work with colleagues from cultures other than their own.

Professional category staff members are usually required to move internationally on one or more occasions in their careers, often becoming either *frequent flyers* (spending large amounts of their working year travelling between locations) or *transnational* expats (continually moving from assignment to assignment, with or without stops at HQ or their home country). Assignment locations can vary significantly. In UN terminology, 'A' or 'B' locations are likely to include large sophisticated cities characterized by comfortable living conditions and a high standard of available amenities, as well as a greater level of access to senior officials and other important policymakers. Brussels, Geneva, London, New York and Paris are usually thought of in this fashion and are often where staff members try to remain if possible.

At the other extreme, assignments may include hardship ('D' or 'E' category) locations such as those associated with peacekeeping, refugee work or poverty alleviation. In these settings especially, employees may experience particularly highly stressful conditions and security risks (although the latter has, of course, affected personnel in a broader range of locations in recent years). Significant numbers of IO employees have been killed in the pursuit of achieving their mission. It is not uncommon for such assignments to have 'unaccompanied status', meaning families must either remain at home or possibly live in a country near the employee's location. Over extended periods of time, this may place considerable strain on employees and their families.

These difficulties notwithstanding, many IO employees express a high degree of commitment to the 'public service' nature of their work (Toomey 2007). They also speak favourably of having the opportunity to travel and to learn about other cultures; essentially becoming *internationalists*. They may speak a number of languages, have lived in a number of countries and readily identify with being a 'citizen of the globe'. When asked 'where [he] was from?' one such person replied:

> My mother is English, my father is an Arab who grew up in Germany. I was born in Rome and I have lived in four different countries before moving to Geneva. I speak four languages fluently and three or four others reasonably well. Since I work for one of the UN agencies, I pay no tax to any country and I travel on a UN pass. So 'where are you from?' is not a question I find easy to answer.
>
> (Brewster and Lee 2006)

Profile of an IO: the United Nations

What kind of organizations are IOs? We take the example of perhaps the best-known IO in the world: the United Nations (UN). The UN can be characterized as:

- a highly political family of agencies under continual pressure by member states to raise organizational capacity and improve programme delivery

- an organization that operates in a framework of complex relationships, policies, programmes and processes, often with shifting priorities and available resources
- an organization that needs to further develop attitudes, competencies and skills suited to improve recruitment, retention and staff mobility.

The UN and its affiliated organizations exemplify many facets of IOs. It is, for example, a highly complex structure, often referred to as a family of agencies. Some agencies only have restricted membership (e.g. the IAEA only includes states that have a declared nuclear capability), whereas others have representatives of many countries attending to a wide range of issues. Some programmes (e.g. the World Meteorological Organization) are very small, whereas others are very large (e.g. UNDP). Some agencies are focused on very specific tasks (e.g. the World Food Programme, WFP), whereas others respond to complex international problems with ever changing needs and available resources (e.g. United Nations High Commission for Refugees, UNHCR; and the Department of Peacekeeping, DPKO). There are also those that could possibly exist without the governmental support they receive (e.g. the World Intellectual Property Organization, WIPO, gets a large income from the fees it charges for registering copyrights and patents).

The headquarters of the UN may be in New York but it stands on 'international territory'. Employees while there are not subject to the laws of the USA. Only a small proportion of the professional staff there will be citizens of the USA, they will not be covered by US employment law and they do not pay taxes to the US government. For many of the staff, being employed at headquarters is already an international assignment.

At the core of the UN structure is the Secretariat, servicing the General Assembly, the Security Council and other bodies. There are also a number of independent agencies linked to the system through special agreements, each with its own secretariat, budget and stakeholder relationships. The International Civil Service Commission (ICSC) is the independent expert body established by the United Nations General Assembly to regulate and coordinate the conditions of service of staff and promote high standards in the international civil service.

The UN's guiding principles (see Slater 1992; Udom 2003) have a strong influence in this area. *Internationalism* and *universality* are expressed in personnel policies of geographical distribution (the staff should reflect the makeup of the members of the organization), for example, as well as in the notion that employees become servants of the UN rather than the country of which they are citizens. The principles of *competence* and *integrity* are intended to prevent employing individuals based on criteria other than merit, despite the challenges of comparing national differences in education and professional experience. These principles have implications for a wide range of HR policies from recruitment and training, particularly related to language and cross-cultural skills. *Allegiance* and *loyalty*,

293

along with *independence* and *impartiality,* are important in limiting any official from seeking or receiving instructions from an authority other than the UN. This enables employees to act without fear or intimidation, and thus also has implications for the equal treatment across staff. Lastly, *continuity* and *permanence* support the notion that there is value in institutional memory.

Through the UN Common System (UNCS), these and other guidelines under-lie ICSC policies impacting upon over 56,000 staff members in headquarter (HQ) locations and other established offices, working in six official languages (Arabic, Chinese, English, French, Russian and Spanish). The latest available data (UN 2005) show that UN employees are generally highly qualified. Although there is a near gender balance in the total number of UN personnel, women are under-represented in professional and managerial positions.

A majority of professional staff are over the age of 50, many of them in the most senior grades. The retirement age is 60 for those hired before 1990; 62 for those hired after that date – so a considerable employee group will retire within the next 10 years. It is interesting to note though that in recent years two-thirds of resigna-tions have been in the junior professional group (Sunoo 2000).

Within this context, key IHRM issues related to turnover, engagement and per-formance and international mobility are among the major challenges facing IOs such as the UN. Moreover, these issues are related to concerns identified by the UN and its critics, in terms of its organizational capacity in years to come (GAO 2006; UN 2006).

In terms of turnover, two types may be of particular concern to HR managers in IOs (see Table 14.2). First, there is the turnover of retiring 'baby boomer' gener-ation employees. Many HR managers express this as a looming 'talent crisis', rep-resenting anticipated difficulties in recruiting a large group of new employees, loss of institutional memory, facilitating knowledge transfer, training and development to increase leadership capability and a host of administrative challenges such as pension scheme management, among other matters. Second, there is turnover related to employees generally, who may move within an HQ location (often to accept a position in a different agency or company in order to remain in the same city for a longer period of time), from the field to an HQ of an alternate organi-zation or, less typically, between sectors. Staff members with under 5 years' serv-ice are the most likely to leave the UN, which is a problem that the organization is just beginning to face up to. The costs of turnover in any sector are important but, given their more limited general and HR budgets, IOs may be hit hardest by this development.

IOs are also likely to be disproportionately affected by employees who would like to quit but choose to remain. IO employees in particular may do so when they perceive poor availability of comparable alternative employment within the sector. They may fear a 'political black eye' that would jeopardize their career within a small sector (relative to MNCs) where 'everyone knows everyone', particularly

294

Table 14.2 *Some key IHRM challenges in IOs and MNCs compared*

Concern	IOs	MNCs
Turnover and engagement	A considerable concern; IOs are viewed by some as being less prepared for transition planning of retiring baby boomer employees. IOs are also impacted by turnover of younger employees. Recruitment, leadership, training and development are related areas of concern. IOs have also been criticized for poor employee engagement and performance, although efforts have been undertaken to address both internal and external calls for reform	Although they share many of the same concerns regarding turnover, MNCs are generally thought to have greater ability to attract top talent and have a longer history of engaging HR professionals at strategic and functional levels to prepare for current labour market developments. Greater HR budgets support their competitiveness. They are generally considered as being more oriented to productivity and efficiency; longer history of systems for personal evaluation, performance monitoring and training/development
Mobility	Have a long history of international mobility, although differentially applied to HQ and field personnel. Many are implementing stricter and more encompassing mobility policies now. 'Transnational' family traits may facilitate mobility success	Increasingly express difficulty in motivating employees to accept an assignment, especially those with employed partners. Large MNCS have a long history of offering family support to increase assignment acceptance and success, among other considerable incentives

within niche functional or leadership areas. They may also have concerns about losing valuable benefits, such as education grants for children where applicable and, in particular, pensions. So some IO employees feel as if they are 'in a golden cage' (Toomey 2007). In such circumstances, employees may try to manage their feelings by withholding effort. Withdrawal cognitions may also be represented by absenteeism, lateness, inattention or neglect of basic duties, poor performance, and by a reduction of organizational citizenship and extra-role behaviours. Again, while such developments occur in MNCs (see Van Dyne and LePine 1998; Kidwell and Robie 2003), given the resource strain influencing IOs, potential loss of performance may further hinder their ability to meet stakeholder and public expectations especially.

In terms of international mobility, both MNCs and IOs share some frustrations over how to motivate employees to accept international assignments – for MNCs, typically from HQ to a foreign office; for the UN, in terms of within an organization (from one location to another) and between agencies through interagency mobility agreements (ICSC 2003). Among other factors, employees express concerns related to the potential impact of the assignment on their career, through a fear of not having the visibility they perceive is necessary to maximize career advancement – 'out of sight, out of mind' (Toomey 2007).

Another major deterrent to accepting international assignments is either a lack of 'accompanied status' posts, or posts where family members are permitted to join the employee but they are prevented from working. Limitations to employment may be due to reasons ranging from a lack of suitability to the local market (e.g. language skills, qualifications, etc.) to official restrictions by host governments. Once in the field, family members may experience a range of emotional and practical challenges (see Harvey 1995; Shaffer et al. 2001; see also Chapters 6 and 9). Under such circumstances, it is understandable that partners may desire to repatriate or become reluctant to do further international assignments. This would be a particularly difficult situation for employees of IOs, for whom mobility is often a requirement of employment.

With this in mind, it is argued that there are advantages to organizations offering support including practices such as continuous language and cultural training for assignees and their families, pre-departure programmes (see Chapter 6), family mentoring programmes with host-country assignees, psychological counselling for those experiencing stress and anxiety, spousal education, career development, organization-encouraged activity in international social clubs, the development of hobbies and active exploration of the local setting and support required on repatriation (see Chapters 6, 7 and 9).

The degree to which such initiatives can be provided by IOs, however, is likely to be less, since any 'diversion' of funds away from delivery of the mission is a politically sensitive matter. Furthermore the very 'international' nature of these

296

Text box 14.1
Structural and political features of international organizations

Question
What are the structural and political features of IOs that influence their HRM issues?

Activity
Imagine you are meeting with representatives of member states to communicate a need for additional resources for the development and operation of the HRM functions within your IO. Anticipating their concerns, what will you say?

Debate
Should nations contributing the highest amount of funds to an IO have preferential influence on that organization's human resource management? Should they be entitled to withhold funds? Why and why not?

---

organizations and their staff means that the promotion of such support may be seen as some sort of failure in the system or on the part of the employee and/or their families for not being well suited to the IO international life. It seems likely that the lower amounts of such support in the IOs in comparison to the MNCs also reflect the notion that the nature of IO employees means that they 'should' be able to adapt without such support.

Overall therefore, further research may be needed to determine the extent of adaptation problems experienced by IO staff and their families in different settings, so as to consider all possibilities within mobility policy development. Increased frequent flying rather than transfers to unattractive locations may be a case of 'out of the frying pan into the fire', for example, since families may find this more disruptive of daily life. Moreover, this would probably be unfeasible for long-distance IO employees.

The final concern expressed by some IO employees with regard to mobility is associated with equity. That is, despite steps to increase transparency and opportunity for employees in all locations and to apply such policies to HQ posts among others, field personnel often feel 'stuck' in those locations (Toomey 2007), while they see others spending all their working lives in pleasant locations like Geneva, New York, Rome or Vienna. Such sentiments are likely to be exacerbated if staff members have, or have been socialized towards, a 'promotion to HQ' orientation. In turn, this could facilitate a polarization of the organization, creating a 'them versus us' mentality, with field staff expressing resentment towards HQ employees who have not worked in the field and yet are involved in formulating and administering policies without 'really knowing what it's like' there (Toomey 2007). As many IOs are making mobility an explicit condition of employment (whereas with MNCs it is more often tied to promotion), it will also be important to consider to what extent individuals are actively engaged in the assignment and not merely 'doing their time' until they 'can rotate out' – in which case it is likely that some element of withdrawal behaviour would be expressed as just examined, thus diminishing performance.

INTERNATIONAL PERSONNEL ATTITUDES: LESSONS LEARNED AND OPPORTUNITIES FOR FURTHER RESEARCH

When it comes to employee-level factors, a great deal of knowledge has been developed through studies of the adjustment processes of MNC expatriates (see Chapter 7). With this in mind, a closer look at some personal and employment factors may be helpful to considering how research in these areas may assist our understanding of IO employees (see Table 14.3).

Personal factors

Assignment adjustment has become a common feature of research related to MNC expatriates (see Chapter 7). Relationships have been found between expatriate adjustment and outcomes of job strain, job satisfaction, organizational citizenship, organizational commitment, job performance and intent to leave the organization (Shaffer et al. 2001; Hechanova et al. 2003). However, antecedents to, and outcomes of, adjustment for employees of IOs have not been established and, given the foregoing, may well generate different relationships. With sometimes decades of 'transnational' life experience, IO employees and their families may develop considerable skills and attitudes suited to assignment adjustment.

It may also be informative to understand how the 'Big 5' personality traits (extroversion, agreeableness, conscientiousness, emotional stability, and openness or intellect) among others, apply to employees of IOs and the outcomes just discussed. Compared to MNC employees (Caligiuri 2000), it may be that the organizational mandate (more oriented to a global 'good') is correlated with conscientiousness and agreeability may be correlated with factors related to working with a more diverse group of colleagues. It would also be interesting to learn more about the relationship between emotional stability and experiences of overcoming extremely demanding environments such as those experienced by some field staff in particular. Employee differences may also help to understand phases and types of adjustment, establishing realistic norms and expectations of IO staff.

298

Table 14.3 *Personal, employment and family factors impacting upon HRM issues in IOs and MNCs*

MNCs: lessons learned	IOs: further research
Personal factors and international mobility	
■ Assignment adjustment is a multidimensional concept; it has been linked to a range of international employee outcomes	■ Assignment adjustment may be enhanced by 'internationalist' skills
	■ Differential personality factor strengths may be associated with IO employee outcomes
■ Family factors also influence assignment acceptance, especially for dual-career couples. Support programmes have been reported as helpful, although organizations would like to find ways to reduce associated costs	■ Family factors are likely to influence IO employees; this may be moderated by family members being 'internationalists'; support programmes may be unpopular to donors though some alternatives may exist
Employment factors related to mobility and other outcomes	
■ Factors related to job satisfaction are important in terms of assignment completion and performance	■ Similar job factors are likely to be important, although features of IOs may make these difficult to respond to
■ High compensation packages (salary, benefits and perks) are traditional incentives among large MNCs	■ Job meaningfulness and affective commitment may help the 'branding' of IOs to support IHRM strategy

Finally in terms of personal factors, understanding how research related to the employees' family may be even more important for IOs than MNCs. That is, other issues may arise over the course of their transnational life; especially when families are separated and when the employee may be in danger, over a prolonged period of time. For individual family members, these may include greater effects of the more frequent loss of friends and support networks, potential inconsistency in education for children over a longer period of time and long-term impact on career potential for the employee's partner. It may be, conversely, that transnational families become resilient to these experiences, facilitating a greater orientation to international life (Toomey 2007). More subtle but meaningful effects may also include those based in family relationships and functioning. Repeated and/or long-term separations may place great strain on family relationships. This may result in lower marital satisfaction and lower family communication among other indicators. Alternatively, overcoming many difficult challenges experienced in a diverse range of settings may result in stronger cohesion within IO families, supported by intra-family spillover and crossover effects associated to adjustment and support among other factors (Toomey 2007).

From an organizational perspective, therefore, while family effects have been considered to a limited extent with MNC employees (Caligiuri 1998), they may be particularly important for IOs in terms of recruitment, retention, engagement and international mobility. In terms of existing employees, for example, such issues may be significantly associated with employee withdrawal behaviours among other outcomes. For prospective IO employees, contrariwise, considerations may even go beyond influencing increasingly important perceptions of work–life balance to wondering if being an employee realistically precludes having a family at all (Toomey 2007).

IOs may need, therefore, to continue assessing these issues and approaches that are viable within their budgetary and operational constraints. For example, continued provision of education grants for children of IO employees (who may need to have their children in boarding schools) is likely to be positively perceived. In terms of less instrumental initiatives though, IOs might take a more proactive approach of highlighting to both prospective and onboard families the stories of employees and their families' positive experiences of overcoming adversities. This might encourage the further development of a 'transnational life' family orientation that could contribute to a favourable branding of the organization (see Hardaker and Fill 2005) where families are recognized as important members of the organization; part of the 'UN Family *of Families*', for example. Encouraging positive experiences in transnational life may even have a knock-on effect in terms of expatriate children who, with many skills suited to transnational life and an inability or lack of desire to settle, may become a natural next generation of IO employees.

300

Employment factors

Employment factors are likely to be important to IO staff as they are to MNCs' expatriates. These include satisfaction with one's pay, job security, supervisory experience and opportunities for growth (Warr et al. 1979; Naumann 1992, 1993; Feldman and Thompson 1993), low role ambiguity and role overload (Rizzo et al. 1970) and sufficient role discretion (Dawis and Lofquist 1984; Nicholson 1984). Career-related factors are also likely to be important, including feeling underemployed or under-utilized (Bolino and Feldman 2000), being able to build expertise over a career path and having the chance to build on successful past behaviours (Karasek 1979). Unfortunately, the changing mandate and budgets of many IOs can make even the most efficient MNC struggle to optimize motivation in these areas.

Nevertheless, for political reasons, IOs are unlikely to be able to compete with MNCS in these areas by offering tangible incentives such as higher salary and benefits (e.g. signing bonuses, additional travel support, assistance with the financing of house purchases, etc.). Also, compared to MNCs, IOs may find it difficult to utilize training and development initiatives that could positively impact upon many of the motivators just examined. Specifically, within IOs, programmes are likely to be more difficult to administer (facilitating training for an extremely diverse range of employees) and/or unpopular with donors and governments (sending personnel to their HQ location or an alternate country leaves the organization wide open to criticism for spending limited funds on staff 'holidays'). In addition, structural HRM innovations that the IOs may wish to implement could have negative effects on employee motivation. Seeking to manage changing needs for personnel through the use of short-term contracts, for example, may mean that employees may spend time and energy influencing contract renewal through behaviours that are not congruent with that organization's guiding principles (Udom 2003).

While IOs may have more problems in providing tangible rewards and support to their international staff they may be better positioned to draw on a greater range of less tangible and more normative incentives. These might include a culture of cooperative leadership, flatter hierarchies and greater opportunities for educational/professional development (OECD 2002). Recognition at an organizational level may also be evidence that you have reached the pinnacle of your career (e.g. a 5-year spell in the International Atomic Energy Agency, the IAEA, is seen by nuclear physicists as being recognition of their eminence). For employees such as those in peacekeeping operations or humanitarian agencies, where working conditions in the field are literally life threatening, it seems clear that a set of moral values is a key motivator.

Thus, IOs also have the opportunity to develop an understanding as to how these factors may positively influence an employees' sense of 'meaningfulness of work' (Kanungo 1982) and organizational commitment (Meyer and Allen 1991).

301

Recent research has shown evidence for the direct effects of both affective (expressed through feelings like loyalty, affection, warmth and belongingness) and normative (reflecting an employee's internalization of the organization's goals, values and mission) commitment on withdrawal cognitions (Shaffer and Harrison 1998; Shaffer et al. 2001). IOs may find, therefore, that the value-oriented normative motivations for public service will be a key element of their HRM strategies. By building this into the organizations' brand too, organizational commitment may be increased and willingness to consider alternative types of employer like an MNC diminished. The potentially significant correlations between commitment, job meaningfulness and/or perceived brand value may only be positive, however, to the point at which employees feel other motivation factors are worth more.

Finally, in terms of employee factors, just as it may encourage the development and support of transnational families, as described earlier, the idea of an employer brand may also be associated with employees being encouraged to adopt a 'commitment to expatriate life' (adapted from the previously mentioned research on affective commitment; Toomey 2007). That is, there may be a subgroup of employees who can become 'emotionally attached' to a transnational life that spans their career. Cultivating this orientation, and positive associations with the motivators, may be especially helpful in terms of mobility and succession planning.

Of course, all of these factors may be differentially experienced and expressed by various staff groups. Some evidence regarding MNCs, for example, suggests that individuals who are more committed to the parent organization are expected to perform better and be less likely to leave the assignment prematurely (Hechanova et al. 2003). Factors that may moderate IO employee attitudes in this regard may include their personal values, the extent to which they are socialized in the field, how connected they feel to HQ through organizational sponsors and mentors in the home office and the amount and quality of training and family support they receive. Employee attitudes may also differ in terms of those rotating between the field and HQ locations, those who remain in the field for considerable periods of time and those who have spent most of their time in HQ locations and have little or no field experience. Differences are also likely to exist between the different types of international organization (technical specialist groups, normative organizations, relief organizations and peacekeeping organizations).

IOs may also need to adapt their policies and practices to motivate in particular their Generation X employees. It is argued that, increasingly, employees will become more likely to take an instrumental view to employment, considering working with either public or private sector depending on a wider range of factors such as potential for greater work–life balance, increased autonomy, superior leadership, and possible training and promotion (Doverspike et al. 2000). In terms of flexible work schedules, work–life balance initiatives and a greater range of training and development programmes, while some IOs demonstrate a growing

302

Text box 14.2
Differences of motivations and experiences during international work

Question
How might the motivations and experience of the IO employee be similar or different from an MNC employee regarding an international assignment?

Activity
Imagine you are an international employee who has worked for the past 10 years in Geneva. You have been asked to accept a hardship assignment for 2 years. What are the issues that would be of concern to you?

Debate
To what extent should employees be able to reject assignments when they are recruited to work as an international representative of an IO? What are the pros and contras for addressing individual situations?

---

awareness of such issues, at present MNCs appear to present a greater range of tangible employee benefits in these areas with the best receiving industry awards such as 'Employer of Choice'. In many cases, of course, the work of the IOs in such areas as famine relief or peacekeeping hardly lends itself to work–life balance issues. For many others, however, the IOs have been slow to adopt the kinds of practice they could. Again, this may reflect a higher level of budget that the MNCs can allocate to such initiatives, so it remains to be seen how IOs may offset this point with innovative practices of their own.

CONCLUSION

IOs are an important segment of the labour market, with considerable numbers of employees working in HQ and field settings. We have focused on the United Nations as perhaps the most visible IO, but there are many others ranging in size, role, experience and geographic scope – and, particularly, in terms of mission. All IOs, though, will share at least some of the characteristics noted here. Moreover, while some of these are also found in many MNCs, other features of IO employees may be distinct. There is a need, therefore, for further study of this area, which has been the focus of little research to date. Lastly, to the extent that this may be achieved through collaboration between researchers, IOs and MNCs, ideas generated may be adapted to each sector as appropriate to provide a basis for the development of practical and effective HRM policies and programmes.

> **Text box 14.3**
> **International mobility changes in ABC organization**
>
> ABC (not the organization's real initials) is a small IO mainly headquartered in Geneva, aiming to expand world trade. It employs around 600 staff of whom 500 work in Geneva, the rest in offices around the world. Nearly all of these, including the professional staff, are recruited in those countries and tend to stay there. Of the 450 professional staff, most are involved in a great deal of frequent flying: the governing body is concerned to keep costs under control and has questioned the amount spent that way. Following the recent retirement of almost the whole of the management team in the last 12 months, a new team has been put in place (including only two of six from within the organization) and has pledged to reduce the number of employees in Geneva, as part of giving the regional offices more autonomy and reducing costs.
>
> Although some of the senior staff have been very supportive of the new policy, for most this has not been a popular step. These staff point out that there will still be a lot of travelling – staff will have to come back to HQ rather than go the other way; that many of their families are settled in Geneva; that the organization has no possibility of paying extra money to encourage them to move; and that organizing local offices will be expensive.
>
> If you were a member of the senior management team, how would you deal with these members of staff? What changes would you make to the policy? What arguments could you advance to persuade people to move?

KEY LEARNING POINTS

- IOs are typically complex entities existing in highly political environments whereby their mandate and resources may often change. A comprehensive system of policies and processes is often in place to prevent undue influence of a range of external stakeholders; however, donor relations continue to impact upon mandate and available resources.
- The UN is a high-profile example of an IO currently under considerable pressure to reform in order to meet increasing expectations of managerial and operational performance.
- In the context of labour market trends, IHRM issues that have the potential to impact upon IOs in particular include turnover, recruitment, retention, training and development and international mobility.
- Researchers have identified personal, employment and family domain factors that influence IHRM. Some of these may be adapted by IOs to support their endeavours in these areas, although new innovative ideas may also be helpful.

304

NOTE

1 Toomey 2007. This is a quantitative study of expatriate staff employed within the UN Common System, other international organizations and MNCs.

REFERENCES

Bolino, M. and Feldman, D. (2000) 'Increasing the skill utilization of expatriates', *Human Resource Management* Winter, 39, 4:367–379.

Brewster, C. and Lee, S. (2006) 'HRM in not-for-profit international organizations: different, but also alike', in H.H. Larsen and W. Mayrhofer (eds) *European Human Resource Management*, London: Routledge.

Caligiuri, P. (1998) 'Testing a theoretical model for examining the relationship between family adjustment and expatriates' work adjustment', *Journal of Applied Psychology* 83, 4:598–614.

Caligiuri, P. (2000) 'The big five personality characteristics as predictors of expatriate's desire to terminate the assignment and supervisor rated performance', *Personnel Psychology* 53:67–88.

Davies, M.D.V. (2002) *The Administration of International Organizations: Top Down and Bottom Up*, Aldershot: Ashgate.

Dawis, R.V. and Lofquist, L.H. (1984) *A Psychological Theory of Adjustment*, Minneapolis, MN: University of Minneapolis Press.

Doverspike, D., Taylor, M., Shultz, K. and McKay, P. (2000) 'Responding to the challenge of a changing workforce: recruiting nontraditional demographic groups', *Public Personnel Management* Winter: 1–16.

Feldman, D. and Thompson, H. (1993) 'Expatriation, repatriation, and domestic relocation: an empirical investigation of adjustment to new job assignments', *Journal of International Business Studies* Third Quarter: 507–529.

GAO (2006) 'Management reforms progressing slowly with many awaiting general assembly review', *United States Government Accountability Office*, GAO-07–14.

Hardaker, S. and Fill, C. (2005) 'Corporate services brands: the intellectual and emotional engagement of employees', *Corporate Reputation Review*, 7, 4:365–376.

Harvey, M.G. (1995) 'The impact of dual-career families on international relocations', *Human Resource Management Review* 5, 2:223–244.

Hechanova, R., Beehr, T. and Christiansen, N. (2003) 'Antecedents and consequences of employees' adjustment to overseas assignment: a meta-analytic review', *Applied Psychology: An International Review* 52, 2:213–236.

ICSC (2003) *Framework for Human Resources Management: Mobility*, New York: ICSC/57/R.4.

Kanungo, R. (1982) 'Measurement of job and work involvement', *Journal of Applied Psychology* 67, 3:341–349.

Karasek, R.A. (1979) 'Job demands, job decision latitude and mental strain: implications for job redesign', *Administrative Science Quarterly* 24:285–308.

Kidwell, R. and Robie, C. (2003) 'Withholding effort in organizations: toward development and validation of a measure', *Journal of Business and Psychology* Summer, 17, 4:538–561.

Meyer, J. and Allen, N. (1991) 'A three-component conceptualization of organizational commitment', *Human Resource Management Review* 1:61–89.

Naumann, E. (1992) 'A conceptual model of expatriate turnover', *Journal of International Business Studies* 23, 2:499–531.

Naumann, E. (1993) 'Antecedents and consequences of satisfaction and commitment among expatriate managers', *Group and Organization Management* 18, 2:153–187.

Nicholson, N. (1984) 'A theory of work role transitions', *Administrative Science Quarterly* 29:172–191.

OECD (2002) 'Public service as an employer of choice', policy brief, Paris Organization for Economic Cooperation and Development.

Rizzo, J., House, R. and Lirtzman, S. (1970) 'Role conflict and ambiguity in complex organizations', *Administrative Science Quarterly* 150–163.

Shaffer, M. and Harrison, D.A. (1998) 'Expatriate's psychological withdrawal from international assignments: work, nonwork, and family influences', *Personnel Psychology* 51:87–118.

Shaffer, M., Harrison, D., Gilley, K., Matthew, L. and Dora, M. (2001) 'Struggling for balance amid turbulence on international assignments: work–family conflict, support and commitment', *Journal of Management* 27, 1:99–121.

Slater, T. (1992) 'UN personnel policies support world body's unique organizational values', *Public Personnel Management* Fall, 21, 3:383–399.

Sunoo, B.P. (2000) 'Around the world in HR ways', *Workforce* March, www.workforce.com.

Suutari, V. and Brewster, C. (2000) 'Making their own way: international experience through self-initiated foreign assignments' *Journal of World Business* 35, 4: 417–436.

Toomey, E. (2007) 'Expatriates in TRANSITion[(c)]', Doctoral dissertation (in progress), SAID Business School, University of Oxford.

Udom, U.E. (2003) 'The international civil service: historical development and potential for the 21st century', *Public Personnel Management* Spring, 32, 1:99–124.

United Nations (UN) (2005) CEB/2005/HLCM/29 – Personnel Statistics, 31 December 2004.

United Nations (UN) (2006) A/RES/60/283 – 'Investing in the United Nations for a Stronger Organization Worldwide: Detailed Report'.

Van Dyne, L. and LePine, J. (1998) 'Helping and voice extra-role behaviors: evidence of construct and predictive validity', *Academy of Management Journal* February, 41, 1:108–119.

Warr, P., Cook, J. and Wall T. (1979) 'Scales for the measurement of some work attitudes and aspects of psychological wellbeing', *Journal of Occupational Psychology* 52: 129–148.

Author Index

Note: *italic* page numbers denote references to Figures/Tables.

307 ▇

Subject Index

317